# Mutiny: 1857

# Mutiny: 1857

Authentic Voices from the
Indian Mutiny—First Hand
Accounts of Battles, Sieges
and Personal Hardships

edited by

James Humphries

LEONAUR

*Mutiny: 1857—Authentic Voices from the Indian Mutiny—*
*First Hand Accounts of Battles, Sieges and Personal Hardships*
edited by James Humphries

This is an original publication of Leonaur Ltd

Published by Leonaur Ltd

Copyright © 2007 Leonaur Ltd

FIRST EDITION

ISBN: 978-1-84677-279-5 (hardcover)
ISBN: 978-1-84677-280-1 (softcover)

**http://www.leonaur.com**

This Book is Respectfully Dedicated to

# VIJAY SINGH CHAUHAN

Friend and Guide to the Leonaur Editors

Vijay and his family have lived in Gwalior Fort for several generations as custodians and guides, and Vijay has been an essential and entertaining travelling companion as, in his company, we visited many of the historic locations mentioned in this book.

# Contents

# Introduction

In the time of war, the first casualty is truth

*Johnson*

It takes two to tell the truth—one to speak
and another to hear

*Thoreau*

Since the invention of chess—in its original form, some
millennia in the past—the 'game of war' has been analysed
by successive players until today it is dominated by 'masters'
whose understanding of its potential combined with their
own intellectual talents is demonstrated in tournaments the
complexities of which are often beyond the capacities of the
uninitiated to comprehend.

Yet, the game itself is—and always has been—fundamen-
tally simple. Two 'commanders' face each other across a field
of conflict. Each initially occupies his own 'lines' in which his
'troops' are clearly identified by the colour of their 'uniform'
and each faces an 'enemy' force in its allotted place. The vic-
tor will be he who occupies the enemy territory ,destroys the
opposing army and denies the enemy commander the ability
to manoeuvre strategically or tactically.

No chess master has been required to commence his game
with opposing pieces already strongly positioned inside his
own forces nor have they had to contend with the transforma-
tion of the colour—and so status—of pieces instantaneously

or by increments. The reaction and subsequent performance of players, in the unlikely event this ever becomes a new rule would be interesting to witness for spectators Perhaps such a departure from convention would be thought too unrealistic and unworkable by all concerned to be considered seriously.

In fact, over the centuries of human conflict most wars have been fought broadly under circumstances similar to the game of chess in its conventional form,

The one year of hostilities commonly known as 'the Indian Mutiny' can also be described in these terms.

In 1857, a century after Robert Clive made his mark in a pivotal role in the conquest of the Sub-Continent at the Battle of Plassey, an insurrection against occupying British rule broke out in north-eastern India.

On one side fought the British with their outnumbered 'Queen's', European and loyal Indian regiments of the Honourable East India Company's Presidential armies—supported by civilians and civil servants, including Eurasians and natives united by extreme adversity. On the opposing side fought large numbers of native troops formerly under the command the Bengal Presidency Army, supported by civilians from the Indian population—both Mohammedan and Hindu—and politically motivated by Indian aristocrats and landowners.

Throughout the first six months of the year 1857 mutinies broke out in the Bengal Army at various military garrisons. By the end of May of that year there had been a major escalation of hostilities including the slaughter of European officers and their families at Meerut, the massacre of Europeans in Delhi and its occupation by the insurrectionists and the mutiny of regiments of the native army around Lucknow. By early June, Cawnpore was under siege and risings and massacres of Europeans spread throughout the region. At the end the month Cawnpore had surrendered and its defenders were almost entirely annihilated. The Lucknow Residency was surrounded and placed under siege.

In open battle the British suffered reverses and instability spread westwards to engulf Agra, Gwalior and the countryside around those towns.

The month of July saw the British turn upon the offensive with concerted advances on Cawnpore and Delhi. Fighting was costly in lives, but the tide turned in favour of the British and by early September Cawnpore had been entered and after an assault, Delhi fell on the 20th of that month. The first relief of Lucknow had taken place on July 25th but difficulties there continued. During November 1857, Lucknow was relieved for the second time and its women and children evacuated. A series of battles resulted in the main—but not entirely—in British victories culminating in the decisive defeat of the insurrectionists in Lucknow in March,1858.

By the middle of June 1858, most of the serious organised opposition to British rule had been eradicated and 'the Indian Mutiny', with the exception of some minor 'mopping up' operations, was over.

The areas governed by the Bombay or Madras Presidencies were unaffected by the mutiny and there had been no been uprisings in their armies. To the north-west of Delhi lay the Punjab, which had been subjugated by the British eight years previously. Its people, the Sikhs, were mostly staunch supporters of the British in both empathy and arms. The Gurkhas of the north-east, whose own empire had fallen under British control some 40 years previously, also supported the cause of their European rulers.

Such is the 'history' of the event!

In fact, very little which concerns the Indian Mutiny is straightforward. There are many, indeed who would begin any debate on the subject, by contesting its very name. Therefore the term 'mutiny' has been used in the title of this book principally because it is by this appellation that most readers will understand its subject matter, it is not used as an endorsement of its accuracy or appropriateness in describing those terrible months of 1857 and 58. I leave that for others to decide.

This was not a conflict of the usual kind where each side stood clearly in its camp from the outset. This was no game of chess! In this conflict the subservient became aggressors, the friend became a foe, the loyal rose in bitter rebellion, the uniform of one army became that of the enemy and the land that was safe became one of threat and danger. Essentially, this was a conflict based on a sense of the betrayal of established trusts by both sides. With this came outrage—and with that, revenge and brutality.

The central issue of the Indian Mutiny has ever been: *what was its true nature and what was the cause of it?*

The book you are now holding is intended as neither a work of analysis or a sequential recounting of all the events of the mutiny in a historical context—there are any number of excellent and balanced works that achieve this. Equally, it has not been my intention to avoid the essential elements of this conflict. Indeed, I *could not* avoid them because these pages speak with the voices of people who experienced mutiny personally. Much of what you are about to read was written as the events described actually unfolded; history was literally being made—what could be more immediate? Through these narratives, arranged as closely as possible in chronological order, one can experience what those who were there experienced and create in the mind a *living history*.

This is a book about strife, hardships and the horrors seen and experienced by ordinary men and women caught up in extraordinary events; soldiers and civilians, the literate and the uneducated, those beleaguered, those in flight and those who fought for survival, principal, patriotism, retribution and, indeed, those who fought to earn a living. Within these pages you will feel palpable tension, fear, panic, uncertainty, anger, sorrow and all the other thoughts and emotions that occur when human beings undergo great trials.

In almost every account included here, the writer feels compelled to ask the question—Why? They, of course, have their own ideas about the causes of the mutiny and you are invited to consider them 'in the raw', rather than by way of an academic wisdom and interpretation formulated many years after the fact.

Were some of the bullets offered to the sepoys covered in polluting animal fat? One writer included here claims that this was absolutely not the case, and yet another claims that this was so! Were the British insensitive to the religions of the native population and set on a course of conversion to Christianity through missionaries? Where one writer claims that this was not so, another—a clergyman—claims that the British were over lenient when it came to the 'idolatry' of the Hindu religion.

History, it is said, is ultimately written by the victorious. Mutiny:1857 is not that history.

In 2007, the year of first publication of this book, one hundred and fifty years have elapsed since the 'red year'—the year of blood. It is proper that it is commemorated—as all wars should be—in the hope that the lessons it taught us are learnt to the degree that the experience need never be repeated.

While it may seem inappropriate to wish that you might enjoy this book, the fact remains that all of its contributors have gripping stories to tell and have displayed no mean penmanship in their telling. Some have even revealed exceptional talent when it comes to making their experiences real for others.

The first account begins on an ordinary Sunday in the garrison of Meerut in May,1857. A young British officer of the Native Light Cavalry is taking his ease in his bungalow while the more pious of his friends and acquaintances are attending church services. The world he has for so long known is about—quite uncomprehendingly to him and those around him—to be torn apart forever.

*James Humphries*
May, 2007

# Chronology

| | |
|---|---|
| July 1st | Native troops mutiny at Indore |
| July 16th | British vistory at first battle of Cawnpore |
| July 27th | Siege at Arrah begins |
| August 5th | Mutineers defeated at Bashirat-ganj |
| August 13th | British troops on Delhi Ridge |
| August 16th | Mutineers defeated at Bithur |
| September 14th | Assault on Delhi |
| September 19th | British begin march on Lucknow |
| September 20th | Delhi falls |
| September 25th | First relief of Lucknow |
| October 10th | Mutineers defeated at Agra |
| November 17th | Second Relief of Lucknow |
| November 22nd | British troops begin withdrawal from Lucknow after evacuating women and children |
| November 28th | British defeated at second battle of Cawnpore |
| December 6th | British success at third battle of Cawnpore |

| | |
|---|---|
| January 6th | British reoccupy Fatehgarh |
| March 2nd | Operations commence to retake Lucknow |
| March 21st | Lucknow finally taken |
| April 3rd | British take Jhansi |
| June 19th | Battle of Gwalior |

# Map of Northern India at
# the Time of the Mutiny

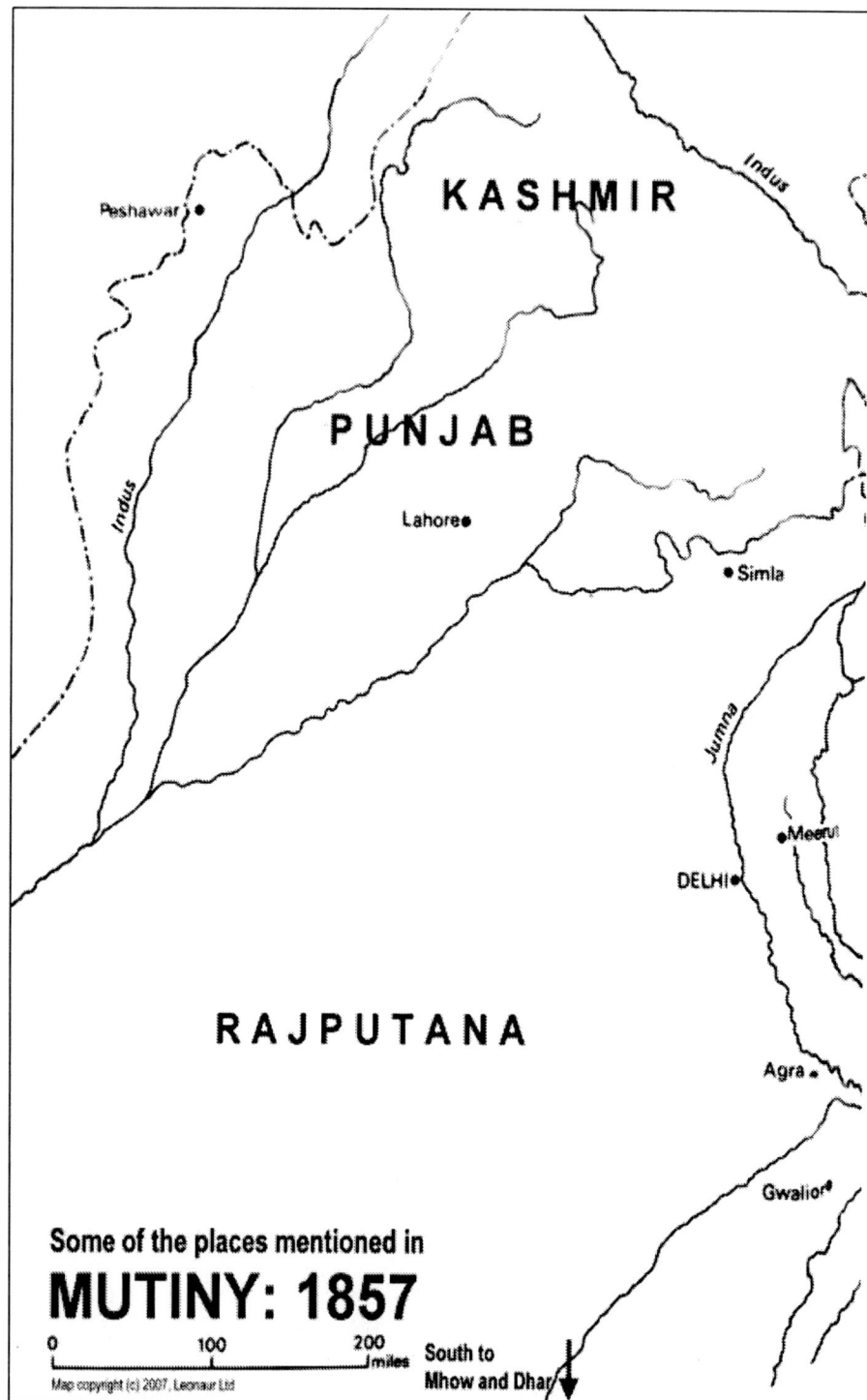

Peshawar •

KASHMIR

Indus

PUNJAB

Indus

Lahore•

• Simla

Jumna

•Meerut

DELHI•

RAJPUTANA

Agra •

Gwalior•

Some of the places mentioned in

# MUTINY: 1857

0        100        200
                     miles
Map copyright (c) 2007, Leonaur Ltd

South to
Mhow and Dhar

NEPAL

OUDH

Meerut

Ganges

Sitapur

Bani

LUCKNOW

Bithur

Cawnpore

Gumti

Arra

Patna

Jumna

Ganges

# The Mutiny Begins

A. R. D. Mackenzie
3rd Bengal Light Cavalry

# The Mutiny Begins

It is not my intention to inflict on the reader my own views as to the origin of the Mutiny. Whether the *fons et ortgo malt* was deep-seated and of slow growth—whether it was due to political discontent at the overthrow of the great Mogul Empire, the annexation of Oudh, and the reduction of the King of Delhi to the position of a puppet of John Company Bahadur—or whether it arose simply from the excessive and pampered growth of the sepoy army, which, like the ass Jeshuron, waxed fat and kicked, is a question which has been often dealt with by abler pens than mine. It is, however, a significant fact that many clear-sighted men had, from time to time, issued notes of warning as to the likelihood of such a catastrophe.

When at length the threatened storm burst, my regiment, the late 3rd Bengal Light Cavalry, was one of those which broke into revolt at Meerut. In its ranks were ninety men armed with muzzle-loading carbines; and it was these carabineers who first set authority at defiance by refusing to use the cartridges supplied to them, on the ground that they suspected the grease used in lubricating them to have been composed of hog's lard. This pretext was, on the face of it, absurd; since, as a matter of fact, the cartridges had been made regimentally; and all the men perfectly well knew that so innocent a compound as bees' wax and clarified butter had been applied as a lubricant. The word had, however, been passed throughout the Bengal native army to make the cartridge question the test as to which was stronger—the native soldier or the Government. Every one remembers the mysterious *chuppatties* or flat wheaten cakes which, shortly before the Mutiny, were circulated from regiment to regiment. The message conveyed by them has never been fathomed by Englishmen; but there can be no doubt that they were in some way a signal, understood by the sepoys, of warning to be in readiness for coming events.

Colonel Carmichael Smith, Commanding the 3rd Light Cavalry, with a view to test the willingness or otherwise of the carabineers of his regiment to use the cartridges, held a special parade for the purpose on the 24th of April 1857; and, after an explanatory speech, pointing out to the men the groundlessness of their fears, ordered them to use the cartridges. Eighty-five of them refused to do so. A court of inquiry was subsequently held on their conduct, followed, by the inevitable court-martial. Only one finding was possible; and the sentence pronounced on all the culprits was one of ten years' imprisonment. This, in the case of some of the younger soldiers, was reduced to five years by the confirming officer, General Hewett, Commanding the Meerut Division. On the morning of the 9th of May the whole garrison of Meerut paraded to hear the sentences read out; after which each convict was fitted with a pair of leg-irons, fitted there and then, on to his ankles by blacksmiths.

In sullen silence the two native infantry corps, the 11th and 20th, and my own regiment, which was dismounted on that occasion, witnessed the degrading punishment. It would have been madness for them then to have attempted a rescue; for they would have been swept off the face of the earth by the guns of the artillery and the rifles of Her Majesty's 60th Foot, not to speak of the swords of the 6th Dragoon Guards, the Carabineers, all of whom were provided with service ammunition, and were so placed as to have the native regiments at their mercy.

For more than an hour the troops stood motionless, their nerves at the highest tension, while the felon shackles were being methodically and of necessity slowly hammered on the ankles of the wretched criminals, each in turn loudly calling on his comrades for help, and abusing, in fierce language, now their Colonel, now the officers who composed the court-martial, now the Government. No response came from the ranks. The impressive ceremony was duly finished.

The prisoners were taken charge of by the authorities of the jail and a guard of native infantry; and the troops marched back to quarters. For a few hours all was quiet. The snake of insubordination was, to all appearance, scotched, if not killed. Every one hoped that the stern lesson had been effectual; but a rough disillusion was in store for us. On the evening of the next day, the memorable Sunday, 10th of May 1857, at the hour when better folk were on their way to church, I was quietly reading a book in my own bungalow when my bearer Sheodeen suddenly rushed into the room, exclaiming that a *hulla-goolla* (in our vernacular, a riot) was going on in the lines, that the sepoys had risen, and were murdering the Sahib Logue.

Not for an instant did I believe the latter part of his story, even though the rapid and frequent reports of fire-arms, which now broke the quiet of the Sabbath evening, made only too clear the truth of the first. The thought that flashed through my mind was that our men of the cavalry were attacking the native infantry in revenge for the sneers with which we all knew these others had freely, since the punishment parade, lashed their submissive apathy in witnessing, without an attempt at rescue, the degradation of their comrades. Sooth to say—so strong is the tie of camaraderie—my sympathies were all in the wrong direction; and I would secretly have rejoiced to have seen the insult avenged.

Hurriedly putting on my uniform and sword, I jumped on a horse, and galloped towards the regimental lines; but, I had scarcely got out of the gate of my compound when I met the English Quartermaster-Sergeant of my regiment flying for his life on foot from his house in the lines.

"Oh God! Sir," he exclaimed, "the troopers are coming to cut us up. "

"Let us then stick together," I answered; "two are better than one. " For a moment he hesitated. Then, looking back, the sight of a small cloud of dust rapidly approaching from the distance overcame his resolution, and he rushed through the gate into the grounds of my bungalow, and scaled the wall between them and those of the next house.

Instantly a small mob of *budmashes,* prominent among whom I recognised my own night watchman, attacked him. The *chowkidar* thrust at him with his spear as he was crossing the wall, and cut open his lips. To my joy he fired one barrel of a gun which he carried with him, and shot the brute dead. He then dropped on to the ground on the other side, and disappeared from view.

At this moment an infantry sepoy, armed with a sword, made a sudden swoop with it at my head. I had not drawn my sword, and had only time to dig a spur into my horse's flank and force him almost on to my enemy. This spoilt his stroke, and his *tulwar* fortunately missed its aim, and only cut my right shoulder cord. By this time I had pulled my weapon out of its scabbard, but the sepoy declined any further sword-play, and promptly climbed over a wall out of my reach. As I turned from him and looked down the road to the lines, I saw that it was full of cavalry troopers galloping towards me. Even then it did not occur to me that they could have any hostile intent towards myself. I shouted to them to halt. This they did, and surrounded me; and, before I knew what was happening, I found myself warding off, as well as I could, a fierce onslaught from many blades.

A few moments would have sealed my fate, when, providentially, the late Lieutenant Craigie emerged from his gate a little further down the road and came straight to my help. This diversion saved me.

The troopers scattered past us and made off towards the European lines. It was only too clear now that a mutiny, and that of the most serious kind, was in full swing. Our duty was plain, though very hard to perform, for at this moment Lieutenant Craigie's Wife and my Sister were on their way together in his carriage to the church, situated in the European lines, and our first natural impulse was to gallop after them. But they had started some little time previously, and we hoped that they had already reached their destination, and were in safety among the British troops.

Military discipline sometimes tries a soldier to the utmost; and now we felt that Wife and Sister must be left in the hands of God, and that our place was among the mutineers on the parade ground. Thither we went as fast as our horses could carry us, and found ourselves in a scene of the utmost uproar. Most of the men were already mounted, and were careering wildly about, shouting and brandishing their swords, firing carbines and pistols into the air, or forming themselves into excited groups. Others were hurriedly saddling their horses and joining their comrades in hot haste.

Nearly every British officer of the Regiment came to the ground, and used every effort of entreaty, and even menace, to restore order, but utterly without effect. To their credit be it said the men did not attack us, but warned us to be off, shouting that the Company's *raj* was over forever! Some even seemed to hesitate about joining the noisiest mutineers; and Craigie, observing this, was led to hope that they might be won over to our side. He was an excellent linguist and had great influence among them, and he eventually managed to get some forty or fifty troopers to listen to him and keep apart in a group.

Suddenly a rumour reached us that the jail was being attacked and the prisoners released. Calling to Lieutenant Melville Clarke and myself to come with him, Craigie persuaded the group which he had assembled to follow him, and away we went towards the jail. The roads were full of excited natives who actually roared approbation as we rode through them, for they evidently did not distinguish in the dusk the

British officers, and took the whole party for a band of mutineers. We three officers led, and as we neared the jail our pace increased, till from a smart trot we broke into a gallop. Already the sepoys and the mob had begun their destructive work.

Clouds of smoke on all sides marked where houses had been set on fire. The telegraph lines were cut, and a slack wire, which I did not see as it swung across the road, caught me full on the chest, and bowled me over into the dust. Over my prostrate body poured the whole column of our followers, and I well remember my feelings as I looked up at the shining hoofs.

Fortunately I was not hurt, and regaining my horse I remounted, and soon nearly overtook Craigie and Clarke, when I was horror-struck to see a *palanquin gharry*—a sort of box-shaped Venetian-sided carriage—being dragged slowly onwards by its driverless horse, while beside it rode a trooper of the 3rd Cavalry, plunging his sword repeatedly through the open window into the body of its already dead occupant—an unfortunate European woman. But Nemesis was upon the murderer. In a moment Craigie had dealt him a swinging cut across the back of the neck, and Clarke had run him through the body. The wretch fell dead—the first sepoy victim at Meerut—to the sword of the avenger of blood.

All this passed in a second, and it was out of the power of our men to prevent it; but the fate of their comrade evidently greatly excited and angered them. Shouts of *"Maro! Maro!"*—"Kill! Kill!"—began to be heard among them, and we all thought the end was approaching. However, none of the men attacked us, and in a few minutes we reached the jail, only to find that we were too late.

The prisoners were already swarming out of it; their shackles were being knocked off by blacksmiths before our eyes; and the jail-guard of native infantry on our riding up to it answered our questions by firing at us, fortunately without hitting any of us. There was nothing to be done but to ride back to the cantonment.

No sooner had we turned our horses' heads than the full horror of what was taking place burst upon us. The whole cantonments seemed one mass of flames. If before we rode fast, now we flew; for the most urgent fears for the safety of those dear to us tortured us almost to madness. As we tore along Craigie allowed me to leave him and go in search of his Wife and my Sister, and to take any of the men who would go with me. I lifted my sword and shouted for volunteers to come to save my Sister, and some dozen of them galloped after me. As hard as our horses could gallop we tore along.

Every house we passed was in flames, my own included, and my heart sank within me. Craigie's house alone was not burning when we reached it—a large double-storeyed building, in very extensive grounds, surrounded, as was then usual, by a mud wall. Here I found Mrs. Craigie and my Sister. They had never reached the church. Their coachman had turned back in terror of the mob. As they passed the bazaar a soldier of the 6th Dragoon Guards rushed out of a bye-lane, pursued by a yelling crowd. The brave ladies, at the imminent risk of their own lives, stopped the carriage, took him in and drove off at full speed, followed for some distance by the bloodthirsty wretches who, being on foot, were soon left behind, not, however, till they had slashed with their *tulwars* in several places the hood of the carriage, in vain efforts to reach the inmates.

It is impossible to realise what terrors these ladies must have suffered till the moment of my arrival. Every minute they despaired of surviving to the next. All round them flames of burning houses and mobs of yelling demons! Not knowing whether the Husband and Brother were alive or dead—deserted apparently by God and man—hopeless of help,—they yet never despaired, nor lost their courage or presence of mind. Their first thought had been to find Craigie's weapons and place them where they would be ready to hand if he or I did ever come.

Nothing had they overlooked. Three double-barrelled guns stood against the wall, with powder-flask and bullets and caps. They were not loaded, for the ladies did not know how to load them; and the unfortunate Carabineer was in a state of nervous collapse. Overjoyed, and thankful to Providence as I was to find them still alive and unhurt, I could not conceal from them that extreme danger was by no means over, and that they would yet have need of all their courage.

The greatest risk I instinctively felt was from the uncertain temper of my men; and I determined on a desperate stroke. I therefore brought the ladies down to the door of the house, and calling to me the troopers commended their lives to their charge. It is impossible to understand the swift torrents of feeling that flood the hearts of Orientals in periods of intense excitement. Like madmen they threw themselves off their horses and prostrated themselves before the ladies, seizing their feet and placing them on their heads, as they vowed with tears and sobs to protect their lives with their own.

Greatly reassured by this burst of evidently genuine emotion, I now ordered the men to mount and patrol the grounds, while I took the ladies upstairs, and then loaded all the guns with ball. One of them I placed by itself against the wall. Long afterwards, in quiet England, my Sister, told me that both she and Mrs. Craigie well understood the sacred use to which that gun was, in the last resort, devoted, and that the knowledge comforted and strengthened them.

Through the windows flashed brilliant light from the flaming houses on all sides. The hiss and crackle of the burning timbers—the yells of the mob—the frequent sharp reports of firearms—all formed a confused roar of sound, the horror of which might well have overpowered the nerves of the ladies; but I learned during that awful night the quiet heroism of which our gentle countrywomen are capable in the hour of need. As I stepped out on to the upper veranda I was seen by some of the mob who were wrecking the opposite house.

"There is a feringi," they cried; "let us burn this big *kothi*" (house), and several of them ran forward with lighted brands to the boundary wall; but on seeing my gun levelled at them they thought better of it and recoiled. More than once this happened. It seemed only a matter of time before our house should be set on fire at one point or another.

Fortunately I remembered the existence in the grounds of a small Hindu shrine, strongly built of masonry, on a high plinth, and with only one entrance, approached by a flight of stone or brick steps. If I could only get my charges and the guns and ammunition safely across the open space between us and that building, I felt sure of being able to hold out till help should come: for surely help would soon come! Were not the 6th Dragoon Guards, the 60th Rifles, and the Horse Artillery Batteries within a couple of miles?

At this juncture we were cheered by the arrival of Lieutenant Craigie, who, after I left him, had gone back to the parade-ground where the uproar was still at its height, the heroic efforts of the British officers to bring the men to reason being quite futile. At length, seeing the hopelessness of further endeavour, and finding the men getting more and more uncontrollable, they were compelled to retire and make for the European lines, carrying away with them the now forever disgraced standards of the regiment. One of them, Major Fairlie, also carried with him a bullet which was lodged in his saddle-tree.

Craigie then made his way back to us at great risk of his life, accompanied by a few men who had never left him. He warmly approved of my plan; and, having explained it to the ladies, they quickly gathered together a few necessary articles of apparel, &c. ; and each carrying her bundle, and concealed as far as possible under a covering of dark blanket, while Craigie and the Carabineer and I carried the guns and ammunition, we seized a favourable moment and ran rapidly across to our new stronghold.

Once there, we were safe from being burnt out, and indeed from successful attack of any kind by the cowardly crew with which we had to deal. The interior space was very small, probably about ten feet square. In front was the narrow doorway; and in the massive walls were slits like loopholes through which we could observe if any attempts were made to approach the place.

Every now and then our troopers brought us news of what was going on. The night had not long closed in when they told us that apparently the whole body of mutineers, horse and foot, had marched away to Delhi. Their attack on the European lines, if they had made one, had clearly failed; and the only marauders remaining in Meerut were the butchers and other scum of the city and bazaars.

Presently one of our men went over to the opposite house, which by this time was burnt nearly to the ground. He returned with awful news. He had found the dead body of its occupant, a lady, whose husband at the outbreak of the mutiny was absent in the European quarter. She had been most cruelly and brutally murdered, her unborn infant sharing her pitiable fate. He showed us, in confirmation of his story, a portion of her dress reeking with blood. Not far from us, another lady, while attempting to escape, disguised as an *ayah*, was recognised as a European, and murdered.

Two veterinary surgeons, attached to the regiment, had been killed—one of them with his wife—under circumstances of ghastly horror. They were both sick in bed with smallpox when the uproar of the mob startled them; and they came, in their night clothes, into the veranda, he carrying a gun loaded with shot, which he discharged at the crowd, only further enraging it. He was instantly shot dead. His wife met with a worse fate. The cowardly demons, afraid to touch her because of the danger of infection, threw lighted brands at her. Her dress caught fire; and she perished thus miserably.

My own house-comrade, a fine young officer, had been mobbed on his way to church, and so hacked to pieces that but for his length—he was very tall—and the rags of his uniform which still clung to him, his remains would have been unrecognisable when they were subsequently recovered. A poor little girl, daughter of one of the British Non-Commissioned Officers of the regiment, had been slaughtered by a blow of a sword which cut her skull in two. Scenes like the above had been enacted all over Meerut; but I will spare the reader further details. If he is sickened by what I have already written, I can only say that mere generalities, however graphic, are insufficient to place before him a true picture of what English men, women, and children suffered at the hands of the mutineers, not only in Meerut, but almost everywhere through the North-West of India.

Anxiously did we now listen for the rattle of horses' hoofs, the rumble of guns, or the tramp of feet coming to our help—but none came! Hour after hour passed—and still the mob were left undisturbed in their work of destruction and murder. We heard afterwards that a strong mounted party had been sent to clear the cantonments and rescue any survivors of the massacre; but—incredible to relate—it had been misled by the Staff Officer who was detailed to guide it, and never reached its intended destination.

Among the troopers with us were one or two traitors, whose sole object in remaining was to undermine the loyalty of the rest. A young recruit who had, not long previously, passed through riding school in the same squad with myself, presently came to me as I was standing among a group of the men outside our stronghold (for Craigie and I now took it in turns to try and reassure them by mixing with them), and warned me to be beware of the Havildar-Major, who had, he said, at that moment, been urging the others to kill me. It may be well imagined that I took very good care afterwards to keep a watchful eye on that Non-Commissioned Officer, and to let him see by a touch of my hand on the hilt of my sword that I was quite ready for any suspicious movement on his part. Soon afterwards he and a few others rode out of the gate, and we saw them no more.

They had not long gone when a servant of Craigie's, a Hindu bearer, came up to us in great excitement with the news that a crowd of *budmashes* was coming in at the gate.

He implored us to give him one of the guns, and let him go and fire at them. Whether wisely or not, we did so; and almost immediately afterwards we heard a report, followed by yells and groans. In a few moments the bearer returned, and gave us back the gun, saying that he had fired into "the brown" of the advancing mob, and brought one of them down, and the rest had fled.

It was now about midnight. The uproar was quieting down; and we determined on making our escape, if possible. So, with our own hands—the *syces* (grooms) having bolted—we harnessed Craigie's horses to his carriage; placed the ladies and the Carabineer inside with the three guns; made a native boy who usually rode postillion, and who fortunately had not gone off with the *syces*, mount one of the horses and set off, Craigie and I riding with drawn swords beside the carriage. This was a critical moment.

A knot of the troopers, evidently wavering in their intentions, occupied the avenue before us, loudly talking and gesticulating. The postillion hesitated; but, on our threatening to run him through the body if he did not at once gallop on, he took heart of grace, lashed his horses, and in a moment we had charged through and scattered the impeding group, and were racing along the avenue at full speed over the body of the man who had been killed by the faithful bearer, and who was afterwards identified as a Musalman butcher, a class of men who were among the most blood-thirsty actors on that night.

Turning out of the gate to our left we made along the road to the regimental parade-ground, from which a nearly unbroken plain stretched to the European lines.

We found the plain deserted; and rapidly made our way till we reached a short length of straight road which ran to the stables of the Carabineers. At the far end of it we saw a light, which we rightly took to be a port-fire.

Making the postillion slacken speed, Craigie and I galloped forward, shouting "Friend! Friend!" at the utmost stretch of our lungs; and well was it we did so; for we found at a point where a bridge crossed a *nullah* a piquet with a gun trailed up the road; and the subaltern in command told us he was on the point of firing at our rapidly approaching group when our voices reached him.

At last—with deep gratitude—we felt that our dear ones were once more safe among our own countrymen. The wife of a Sergeant of the Carabineers very kindly gave the ladies shelter for the rest of the night; and Craigie and I shifted for ourselves, *al fresco.*

To revert to the adventures of the regimental Quartermaster-Sergeant after he left me. Covered with blood from the wound in his lip and carrying his gun in one hand and his sword in the other, he presented a sufficiently startling spectacle as he burst into a room of a neighbouring bungalow occupied by two young officers, and warned them—still unconscious—of what was taking place. Not a moment did they lose in buckling on their swords and rushing to the stables. As they did so they saw one of their own *syces* running away with a saddle on his head. They could only find two other saddles; but fortunately bridles for three horses were hanging on their usual pegs. Rapidly slipping them on, they mounted, giving the Sergeant a bare-backed animal, and they made for a gate. It was blocked by mutineers.

They turned to the other: that also was blocked. Their lives seemed lost, when one of their servants, a sweeper, the lowest and most despised caste of Indian domestics, heedless of the certainty that his own life would be sacrificed to the fury of the mob disappointed of its prey, implored them to follow him. Running before them he led them to the back of the outhouses, and showed them a gap in the compound wall which the servants had made for their own convenience. Through this gap they filed, and galloped off, escaping the hurried shots which were fired after them, and eventually reaching in safety the barracks of the 60th Rifles. The sweeper fell a victim to the rage of the pursuers. He was hacked to pieces. No more beautiful deed ever brightened the dark days of 1857 than the self-sacrifice of this obscure and nameless hero.

Before continuing my narrative, I wish to draw particular attention to a circumstance which, so far as I know, has been overlooked by every historian of the Mutiny. This is the fact that as I was at the time informed, the military authorities, in view of the lengthening days and the increasing heat of the season, had caused, on May 10th, 1857, the evening church parade to take place half an hour later than formerly. In my firm belief, this change saved us from an awful catastrophe. In those days British troops attended divine service practically unarmed, for they did not take with them their rifles or carbines and ammunition. Their only weapons were their side-arms.

The mutineers were, of course, unaware of this change.

They broke into revolt half an hour too soon. Had they waited till the 60th Rifles were securely gathered into the church, what could have prevented them from overpowering the small guards over the rifles and the guns, and utterly destroying the defenceless crowd of soldiers penned, like sheep, within four walls. Providence befriended us.

When the first scouts of the cavalry came galloping down to the European lines, they found the white soldiers falling into their places on parade. Once the alarm was given, all attempt at surprise was out of the question, and the hope of achieving an easy massacre was changed into fear of the awful retribution which they thought the European troops, now on the alert, would not fail speedily to exact. This fear altered all their plans, and hastened their flight to Delhi, but, alas, no swift retribution followed. The European troops, 1,500 strong, were paralysed by the irresolution of their chief.

Had the gallant Hearsey or Sidney Cotton occupied Hewett's place at Meerut, it is safe to say that, in spite of the wings which fear lent to the mutineers on their flight to Delhi, few of them would ever have reached that haven of their hopes. The shrapnel of the artillery and the swords of the Carabineers would have annihilated them. It is true that Generals Hewett and Archdale Wilson, late in the evening, moved the troops over the open plain of the infantry parade-ground and that they caused a few rounds to be fired, in the dark, at some belated stragglers of the cavalry, which said rounds, by the way, nearly killed an officer, Lieutenant Galloway, of my regiment, who had taken refuge in an outhouse in the line of fire; but General Hewett, instead of even then detaching the Carabineers and a battery of horse artillery in pursuit of the flying mutineers, acted on the ill-starred advice of his Brigadier to withdraw the whole force to the European lines. No greater mistake from any point of view was ever committed.

There can be no doubt that the offer of Captain Rosser, of the 6th Dragoon Guards, to take a squadron and a couple of guns in pursuit, was really made and declined; for it was well known and much discussed at the time. It is true that intimation of this offer never reached the Colonel Commanding the Regiment; but it is equally certain that somebody blundered in not taking immediate steps to bring it to the notice of Colonel Custance. The prompt punishment which even such a small body could have inflicted would have been of the utmost value as a lesson both to the rebels and to the faint-hearted among ourselves; but the opportunity was wilfully thrown away; and the magnificent brigade of British troops of all arms, which afterwards covered itself with glory at the Hindun Nuddee, at Delhi, at Lucknow, and wherever its members met the enemy, was marched back to Meerut, and condemned for a period to the humiliating role of passive inaction.

Difficult as it is to understand, and impossible to excuse the motives which paralysed the nerves of General Hewett, it can only be hoped that all our officers have laid to heart the lesson so frequently learned in the great school of the Sepoy Mutiny that, in dealing with an Oriental enemy, *l'audace! et toujours l'audace* is not only the most soldier-like but the surest road to success. "Strike promptly and strike hard" should be their motto.

Over and over again have small bodies of Englishmen, under the most desperate circumstances, and against the most fearful odds, by acting on this maxim, "plucked the flower safely from the nettle of danger." When the day comes, as come it will, that we Englishmen will once more have to fight for the preservation of our Indian Empire, the issue will only be doubtful if timid and irresolute counsels prevent us from putting forth the whole of our strength at the first serious symptoms of internal disaffection or external menace.

During the next few days the Meerut garrison lay inert. Far from undertaking any distant reconnaisances or making any active efforts to restore to quiet the surrounding districts, not even was punishment inflicted on the city or the bazaars, which had poured forth their swarms of murderers and robbers on the night of the 10th. A few individual marauders were, it is true, caught and hanged; but there retributive measures ceased. Native houses, choked with plunder, were left unsearched, and their occupants were allowed unmolested to swagger about in the sight of all men, and to boast among themselves of the shame and havoc they had wrought on the "Feringhi."

Our women and children and unarmed civilian refugees were given shelter in the Dumdama, a walled enclosure. The Generals and their staffs and many other officers took refuge in a barrack, over which a guard was duly mounted. Piquets, in-lying and outlying, were told off; and every precaution was taken to prevent the cantonments being rushed by the *budmashes* of the Burra Bazaar or the Goojars of the neighbouring villages!

As a comic element is never absent from the most tragic events, I may interpolate here a little story about Colonel Blank. That gallant officer rejoiced in a long and scanty moustache, which up to the moment of the Mutiny had retained the glossy black of youth. A few days afterwards, an officer who met me asked me if I had observed the terrible effect which late events had evidently wrought on the Colonel.

"Poor fellow!" said he, "his hair has turned perfectly white!"

My irreverent laughter amazed and shocked him. He little knew that the blanching of the old gentleman's moustache was due to his not having had the time or the presence of mind to bring with him in his hurried flight from the mutineers his trusty bottle of hair-dye.

A very few nights after the Generals and other officers had taken up their quarters in the barrack already mentioned, they suffered from a scare which, if it did not whiten their hair, might easily have proved a very serious matter to its innocent cause. This was how it happened.

It must be premised that a row of beds lined each wall of the long barrack-room, each bed containing a General, a staff, or at the least a field officer, every one of whom reposed his head on a pillow under which lay a revolver, while his sword was either resting on a chair beside him or hanging on the wall. Outside was a guard of British soldiers, and in the immediate vicinity were some fifteen or sixteen hundred more. Altogether as secure and well guarded a dormitory as it is possible to conceive, and one in which the most timid and nerve-shaken creature might placidly entrust himself to the arms of Morpheus.

Not so, thought one of its warrior occupants. Were there not three Hindu *punkah*-coolies in the veranda, and were not all their lives at the mercy of these miscreants? It behoved one at least to remain on the alert, and, with a watchful eye on the coolie toiling at the *punkah* rope at one end of the room, to safeguard the lives of all the careless sleepers. He should be that one! So, ostentatiously snoring, and pretending to be wrapped in slumber, he devoted himself to his task. A couple of hours passed without incident; but at last his vigilance was justified and rewarded.

The ruffian at the rope who, while there remained a chance that any of his proposed victims might be still awake, had pulled with steady cadence the heavy *punkahs*, now began to simulate slumber, and at intervals to cease pulling. Evidently this was a deep and artful ruse to discover if the cessation of the fanning breeze might, peradventure, rouse any of the sleepers; but none of them stirred. The moment for action had clearly arrived. So the blood-thirsty coolie coughed a smothered cough once or twice as a signal to his two confederates in the veranda; but as no response came, he prepared to go and personally warn them. As a precautionary measure, however, he noiselessly laid down the rope, and, approaching the nearest sleepers, bent over them to satisfy himself that they were really unconscious. As he repeated this performance over our watchful friend, whose hair was now standing on end with horror, he found himself suddenly clutched in the embrace of a pair of arms nerved with the strength of panic fear, while loud shouts of "I've got him! I've got him!" echoed through the room.

Breathless with excitement, the bold captor told his thrilling tale, and demanded that the three villains should be led to instant execution. He laughed to scorn the plausible story of his captive, to the effect that he had been left at the *punkah* rope longer than his rightful turn, that he had coughed to attract the attention of his *budlee* or relieving coolie, that on this signal failing he had then determined to go and fetch him; but *dur ki maree*—the fear of being beaten—had induced him to make sure, before doing so, that none of the sahibs was likely to jump up, and, *more Anglo-Indico*, chastise him.

Fortunately for the wretched coolie his explanation was accepted, not without much laughter, and he escaped the gallows; but nothing could ever convince his gallant captor that he had not by his courage and presence of mind averted a dreadful massacre.

It is really difficult to exaggerate the demoralisation which at that period seemed to overcome the nerves of certain of the more weak-kneed among us. Every native was to their excited imagination a *pandy*. My own faithful bearer, Sheodeen, owed to the natty twist of his turban and the martial way in which he habitually curled up his moustaches, a very close interview with the hangman. He was, during my absence, arrested, and would undoubtedly have been given a short shrift if an officer who knew him had not sent for me in hot haste.

My earnest advice to him after that grim experience was to roll his *puggrie* anyhow, to take the curl out of his moustaches, to drop his jaunty swaggering gait, and generally to look as mean and dirty as possible.

On the night of the 11th an adventure happened to myself, which at the time I was rather shy of mentioning, but which I may now relate. I had taken it on myself to do a little patrolling on my own account; and as I was starting from near the main gate of the Dumdama, I came across a Eurasian Trumpeter named Murray, of my own regiment. As he was mounted I asked him to accompany me. This he did. We had not gone far before we saw, indistinctly, through the dusk, what appeared to be a small group of the rebels, cautiously creeping towards where a, tree, growing close to the wall, gave them a fair chance of successfully scaling it.

"Will you stick by me, Murray, and charge them?" I whispered.

"That I will, sir," replied he: "I will stand by you to the last drop of my blood."

So, drawing our swords, and moving quietly forward for a few yards, we suddenly clapped spurs to our horses and charged—to the bewilderment and complete demoralisation of a speckled cow, over whose body we narrowly escaped "coming to grief," and who, as soon as she could recover her senses, dashed off into the darkness.

"Never mind, Murray," said I. "It might have been the *pandies*, you know. We'll just say nothing about this—yet a while."

Poor fellow! He was killed not many days afterwards, bravely fighting, at the Hindun Nuddee.

On the evening of the 15th May the native Sappers and Miners from Roorkee marched into Meerut. Next afternoon it so happened that a small party of the faithful remnant of the 3rd Light Cavalry, which was about to proceed under my command to the support of the civil authorities in a neighbouring station, was paraded, mounted, for the General's inspection, close to the barrack where he had taken up his quarters, when I heard the report of a single shot, rapidly followed by two or three more, from the direction of the Sapper Camp; and presently saw that a scene of confusion and uproar was going on there. A rumour reached me—how I do not remember—that the Sappers had mutinied, had killed Alfred Light, the artillery officer who afterwards became so distinguished, and were about to fly into the jungle.

Naturally I lost no time in dismounting and running in to the barrack to inform General Hewett, whom I found in the dishabille of shirt and pyjamas. While I was making my report to the bewildered General, Brigadier Archdale Wilson pushed up to us, buckling on his sword-belt, and ordered me to mount at once and follow the Sappers and keep them in sight till he could come up with some of the Carabineers and guns. By this time the Sappers, who, I firmly believe, had at first no intention whatever of mutinying, but had been seized by sudden panic through groundless fear of an attack by the European troops, were swarming in flight over the plain, some in uniform, some in native clothes, but all armed with their muskets.

The shot which I had heard had been fired, as I subsequently learnt, by an Afghan, and had killed the Commanding-Officer, Major Fraser. The action of this one man compromised all his comrades. However loyally disposed they might have been, they must have felt that now appearances were so fatally against them that no quarter could be hoped for from the enraged European troops who surrounded them; and that instant flight offered the only slender chance of escape from destruction.

As my little party galloped after them I was stopped by an artillery officer, evidently senior in rank to myself, who ordered me to halt and asked me where I was going. I told him that the Brigadier-General had ordered me to follow the Sappers who had mutinied and killed Alfred Light.

"That is hardly possible," he said, "seeing that I am Alfred Light. These Sappers are not mutinying at all, but are going with permission to destroy a neighbouring village of *budmashes*. You stop where you are. I will take the responsibility."

Taken quite aback by all this, I was still remonstrating with him when the Brigadier-General rode up, furious with me for having halted, and ordered me on again. I was glad to leave Alfred Light to settle the question of my delay with him, and dashed on in pursuit. Soon we overtook about fifty men, who took refuge in a grove of trees surrounded by a wall; and there I kept guard over them till the arrival of the Brigadier-General with a squadron of Carabineers and some guns, A few rounds were fired into the grove, but without much effect, and then dismounted Carabineers and a number of officers skirmished into it, and pursued the Sappers from tree to tree.

The poor fellows fought with the energy of despair. No quarter was given, and all were destroyed, except two who were made prisoners by myself, and who, I believe, were afterwards retained in the service, and proved perfectly loyal.

At the close of this affair I noticed a man who had retreated through the grove and had taken refuge behind a low wall on its further side, from which shelter he betrayed himself by firing at us.

As I rode round the outside of the enclosure on its left and got in line with him, a Trooper of the Carabineers appeared at the opposite end of the wall, and we both came down on him at full gallop. The Sapper jumped to his feet and fixed his bayonet. We reached him almost at the same moment. As the Trooper lifted his sword to deliver a swinging cut the Sapper charged him with his bayonet and transfixed him through the breast, with a sickening ripping sound which still haunts my ears, while my straining sword arm failed by an inch to reach and lift the bayonet. Before he could withdraw the bayonet I

had run him through the body. The uplifted arm of the Carabineer dropped, the sword slipped from his grasp, he reeled for
a moment on his saddle, and then fell to the ground dead.

A correspondent wrote to the Pioneer:

The Carabineer who was killed just outside Meerut
in the Sapper Affair was a Trooper, named Frederick
Kingsford, who rode an untrained horse, which became
unsteady at the time of charging the rebel. He was the
first man killed in action in the Mutiny, although many
Europeans had fallen before that day.

It was late in the evening when we returned to cantonments. The destination of my small party, which was to have
started next morning into the district, was unexpectedly
changed. A message had been received by General Hewett
from a party of fugitives from Delhi, who were wandering
about in the jungles near that place, and who implored that
help should be sent to them.

When I heard of this I felt that women and children could
not possibly be left to their fate among the rebels without at
least an effort being made to save them; so I went to General
Hewett and offered to attempt the rescue with twenty-five
men of the remnant of my regiment. He asked if I was in
earnest, and told me that the fugitives had not got far from
Delhi, and that he had considered it hopeless to send a suc-
couring party. The letter, which was written in the French
language, had been thrown under a table, whence I saw it
picked up.

The General then gave me permission, and on the forenoon of the 17th my party started.

On our way out of Meerut we met Lieutenant Hugh Gough
of our regiment. He told me that he had just heard of my having volunteered for this duty, and that he could not let me go
alone. So he galloped back to get his arms, and thus, in this
most gallant and self-sacrificing manner, came with me on an
errand which both of us felt pretty sure was to be our last.

We rode all day, expecting every moment our men to turn on us and bolt to Delhi. The temptation must have been very sore to them; for they had witnessed the extreme demoralisation which the Mutiny had caused in Meerut; but providentially they remained staunch.

Only once did we meet with a show of opposition at a large village, but most fortunately we thought it probable that the inhabitants were alarmed at our French-grey uniforms, and took us for a party of mutineers on the prowl. So Gough and I halted the men and rode on alone. The sight of our white faces reassured the villagers, and our explanations calmed them.

Late in the evening we arrived at the village of Hirchinpore, where we had ascertained from people in the fields that the fugitives were to be found. Again our light-grey uniforms caused alarm and confusion. The gate of a walled enclosure was shut in our faces, and it was with great difficulty that we got those inside to believe that we were friends. At last, on our promising to leave the men outside, Gough and I were admitted; and we rode in, not without suspicion that we might ourselves have fallen into a trap.

We found a very dark old gentleman called Cohen, the *zemindar* of the village, an Orientalised Jew I think, seated in the doorway with a gun in his hand, evidently determined in case of treachery to sell his life dearly.

The fugitives of whom we were in search had in despair stowed themselves away in various hiding places, and when they appeared presented a pitiable spectacle from the effects of the hardships they, had undergone. All that night we had to remain there while Cohen's people collected carts to convey the women and children. If one of our men or one of the villagers had bolted and carried to Delhi the news of what a haul could be made at Hirchinpore, two or three hours would have sealed our fate. But again, Providence befriended us, and early next morning our little caravan started for Meerut, where we safely arrived that night, and I had the joy of once more seeing my Sister, of whom I could not bear to take leave when I started, and who had been in ignorance of my having gone till I was miles on my way.

Very glad was I to turn in that night with the prospect of a good rest, but I had not been asleep very long before Lieutenant Sanford of my regiment came and woke me up and told me that he had volunteered to carry despatches from General Hewett to the Commander-in-Chief at Umballa via Kurnal, and that he wanted me to escort him with my little faithful party. Of course I agreed, and went off to our lines, where the already tired men willingly consented to undertake the fresh and still more fatiguing and possibly more dangerous journey. Their horses were, however, quite knocked up, so I asked and obtained permission to select for them twenty-five of the partially broken remounts of the Carabineers.

Early in the morning we paraded in the lightest of light marching order, the young horses vigorously resenting being so unceremoniously pressed into the ranks before passing through Riding School. For the first few miles there was not much order in our little column.

The half-broken troopers rearing, buck-jumping and plunging about, had it pretty much their own way; but before night they were quiet enough. All day we marched, and all night, and all next day, halting for an hour or so at a time, when a wayside well enabled us to water the horses. We requisitioned feeds of grain for them and of *chuppatis* for ourselves as we went along, duly giving receipts for them.

En route we made a long detour off the road to a district where we had been ordered to go in search of baggage camels, which we were to have seized if we had found them; but they had departed.

On the second day we met Lieutenant Hodson who, escorted by a party of the Jhind Horse, had started on his ride to Meerut with despatches from General Anson to General Hewett, and who was to return with despatches from the latter to Army Headquarters. So unexpected was this meeting that at first each party took the other for *moofsids,* as we used in those days to designate the rebels; but we soon discovered our mistake.

Hodson was naturally much relieved to find that the road in front of him was open, though doubtless disappointed that his errand was forestalled.

In the evening we arrived at Kurnal, having traversed in less than thirty-six hours more than ninety miles: for the straight road between Meerut and Kurnal is seventy-six, and our fruitless detour after the camels took us many more miles. Sanford at once went on by *dâk* to Umballa and delivered his despatches to General Anson.

My small party was not then sent back to Meerut, but moved down towards Delhi with the advanced body of troops, making itself useful in collecting supplies and scouting. On the road we succeeded in capturing several miscreants who had committed murderous outrages on our unfortunate countrymen and women while trying to effect their escape from Delhi. They were given the benefit of a fair trial; and those who were found guilty were duly hanged. One of these wretches who had been tried and sentenced one afternoon was subsequently confined till sunset—the usual hour for executions—in the guard tent of the 1st Bengal Fusiliers, which happened on that occasion to contain another tenant, an Irish soldier who had been drinking, "not wisely but too well. " When the Provost Marshal's party came in the evening for the condemned criminal they found him in a sorry plight. The half-sober Irishman begged that they would not take him away.

"Bedad," said he, "he has been the most divarting companion I iver had." The "divarsion" had been perhaps a little one-sided.

One evening, shortly before the force reached Alipore, I was suddenly ordered to take my party back to Meerut *via* Bagput, for the General expected an engagement, and evidently felt uncertain as to whether my men were to be trusted under such trying circumstances as an actual fight against their old comrades. Previously to this poor General Anson had died, worn out by anxiety and fatigue, and General Barnard was in command.

Accompanied by the Adjutant-General, Colonel Chester, and by his Interpreter, Captain Howell, he inspected my little party on parade, and after praising its conduct in the highest terms, informed us that he would give each native member of it a step of substantive rank for each of the two expeditions in which they had shared. He then told them that in a short time he expected to engage the rebels, and that, though he had no doubt of their loyalty, he was unwilling to take them into action against men who so lately had been their comrades, of their own race and religions, and that therefore he had decided to send them back to Meerut. The whole of them implored to be allowed to remain and to prove their loyalty in the field; but the General was not to be turned from his decision.

He was evidently much moved, and for a moment I hoped that he was wavering; but presently he turned away; and with deep disappointment I felt that there was nothing for it but to turn our horses' heads to the east and make for the ferry at Bagput. Before General Barnard could carry out his promise he fell a victim to cholera.

Colonel Chester was killed in action, and Captain Howell also died—I think from that scourge of the camp—cholera. Thus was left on my shoulders the whole onus of securing to my men the fulfilment of the General's promise—a task in which, after much trouble and delay, I was—happily—eventually successful.

To march off the ground and out of camp no preparations were needed, for we were without camp equipage of any kind whatever. It must be remembered that all this took place in the middle of the hot weather, before the rains; so that it was no hardship to sleep in the open air on the ground beside our horses, who also required no blankets. Except our horses, their saddles and bridles and our arms, and the clothes on our backs, we possessed literally nothing in the world. It was not long, therefore, before we had put a good distance between ourselves and our late comrades.

When dawn broke we found ourselves debouching from a grove of trees onto a plain, at the further side of which was the river and the bridge-of-boats with the village of Bagput on the opposite bank; but to our horror the bridge was occupied by a strong body of apparently rebel troops, whom our appearance threw into sudden commotion. We could see infantry rapidly falling in, troopers mounting in hot haste, and camels and elephants rushing to the bridge, flying from our expected onslaught.

Scant time was there to decide on a course of action.

With our tired horses escape from so strong a body of cavalry was hopeless. Nothing was left but to charge the bridge and trust to luck and the rapidity of our attack to disconcert the enemy, and enable some at least of us to get through with whole skins. These were the days of drilling by "threes;" but as I judged that there would be room for four men abreast on the bridge, I formed my party as quickly as possible into a column of sections of fours, and moved down the slope on to the plain at a gallop, increasing our pace as we approached the bridge.

To my delight and surprise the enemy seemed quite demoralised and in confusion, and I was beginning to feel sure of a successful rush through them, when I was startled by the apparition of a white face peering at: me from behind a mass of stones, and the shout of an English voice yelling at me to halt.

Never was man more relieved and pleased to be out of a frightful scrape. In another second I had halted my party and had ridden across the bridge and was talking to ——, an officer who informed me that he had been sent with a strong body of the Raja of Jhind's troops to occupy the bridge and hold it till further orders; but he said that he was not going to stay any longer.

The place was a great deal too near Delhi and too liable to sudden attack to please him, and the fright he had got from the sudden appearance of my small party had put the finishing touch to his resolution. He said that our French-grey uniforms and the swiftness of our attack had convinced him that we were the advanced party of a large body of the enemy, and he had given himself up for lost. At any rate he had had enough of Bagput and meant to be off at once.

In vain I implored him to defer his departure till the evening, pointing out that my horses were quite done up, and that we would be obliged to stop there for some hours to rest and feed. Nothing would move him, and there and then he marched off, bag and baggage, and left us to our own devices. We could plainly hear the guns of a fight, which must have been that at the Hindun Nuddee; and, tired as we were, rest was impossible.

In the afternoon we moved on, and next morning marched into Meerut without further misadventure.

# The Wind of Madness

## Sita Ram
### A Soldier of the Bengal Native Infantry

# The Wind of Madness

After the fall of Multan and the total defeat of the Sikhs at Gujerat, the English took possession of all the land of the Punjab, or Five Rivers. The mighty power of the Sikh nation became as dust and the mantle of rule descended upon the *Sirkar*, the great Company *Bahadur*. The *sirdars* were all taken prisoner and their troops, deprived of their weapons, were disbanded and sent to their homes. English regiments were stationed all over the Punjab—at Lahore, Wazirabad, Jhelum, Rawal Pindi, Attock, Peshawar, and many other places—without any further opposition. Truly, the English are a remarkable people; within six months barracks rose out of the ground as if by magic. The *sahibs* built houses, police were organized, and the country appeared as if it had belonged to the *Sirkar* for many years.

My regiment was now sent to Jullundur. Two regiments of old Sikh soldiers were enlisted for the *Sirkar* and young Sikhs were taken into the native regiments. This annoyed the *sepoys* exceedingly, for the Sikhs were disliked by the Hindustanis who considered them to be unclean and were not permitted to associate with them. Their position was very uncomfortable for a long time but after a while this dislike to some extent disappeared. However, these men always kept to themselves and were regarded as interlopers by the older *sepoys*. They were never as smart as we were on parade and their practice of using curds to clean their long hair gave them an extremely disagreeable odour, but many of them became like Hindus after they had been away from their own country for a long time.

No wars took place for several years in Hindustan and nothing particular occurred apart from several innovations which were introduced into the Army, and into the Civil Courts, which caused great offence among the people.

In 1855 a small war broke out in Bengal with some jungle people called Santhals, and my regiment formed part of the force and was stationed near Raniganj, not far from Calcutta. It was there that I first saw the iron road and the steam monster and this was more wonderful than anything I had ever seen before. When I asked the people about it they said they believed that the English put some powerful demon into each iron box, and it was his efforts to escape which made the wheels turn round. However I saw the water put in, and the coals lighted under it, but I am so ignorant of how it works that if an officer had not told me that it was all the force of steam, I might easily have believed that this demon fed on wood, coal, or stones, and drank gallons of water.

The Santhals used bows, arrows, and large sharp axes, but they always dispersed when we fired on them. At first it was reported that they used poisoned arrows, and for this reason they were much feared, but we soon discovered that this was not the case. After a good deal of marching through thick jungle, and after guarding the main road by the Sone river throughout one hot weather, the rebellion was put down and my regiment was sent to ———. I was told by some of the Santhals that they rebelled because they could obtain no justice from the Civil Courts. They had no money with which to bribe the native officials and their complaints were all against the rich landlords and moneylenders, who had managed to get these simple folk into their clutches. I cannot vouch for the truth of this but it was certainly a curious war. In one part of the jungle we were firing at them, while in another the *Sirkar* was providing them with cart-loads of rice.

There was now a rumour that the *Sirkar* was going to take Oudh from the Nawab. This led to great excitement within the army, which was largely composed of men from Oudh.

Many of them did not much care whether the *Sirkar* took Oudh or not but these were men who owned no property there. Nevertheless an undefined dislike and disquiet took possession of all of us.

During 1856 the *Sirkar* removed the Nawab to Calcutta and took over the government of the Kingdom of Oudh. Regiments of local infantry and cavalry were formed, officered by English officers, and a number of Assistant Commissioner *sahibs* were brought in. Many of these officers came from the Bombay and Madras Armies and were totally ignorant of the language, manners, and customs of the people, and the same was true of all the *sahibs* who came from Bengal from the college. The occupation of the country was effected without any open resistance at the time. It took place so quickly that the people did not have time to combine against it but the minds of all the *Taluqdars* and headmen were excited against the *Sirkar*, which in their view had acted dishonourably, and had been unfair to the Nawab.

There were plenty of interested people to keep this feeling alive. They assured everyone that the estates of the rich would soon be confiscated by the *Sirkar*, which could easily manipulate the law courts to show that the present owners had no right to these estates. The truth was that so many people in Oudh had acquired property by methods which the Government would never recognize that they began to fear an inquiry. Since all these people had large numbers of relations, retainers, and servants living with them, who were all interested parties, it explains the great excitement prevailing in Oudh at the time, and consequently throughout the *Sirkars* army.

It is my humble opinion that this seizing of Oudh filled the minds of the *sepoys* with distrust and led them to plot against the Government. Agents of the Nawab of Oudh and also of the King of Delhi were sent all over India to discover the temper of the army. They worked upon the feelings of the *sepoys*, telling them how treacherously the foreigners had behaved towards their king. They invented ten thousand lies and promises to persuade the soldiers to mutiny and turn against their masters, the English, with the object of restoring the Emperor of Delhi to the throne. They maintained that this was wholly within the army's powers if the soldiers would only act together and do as they were advised.

It chanced that about this time the *Sirkar* sent parties of men from each regiment to different garrisons for instruction in the use of the new rifle. These men performed the new drill for some time until a report got about, by some means or other, that the cartridges used for these new rifles were greased with the fat of cows and pigs. The men from our regiment wrote to others in the regiment telling them of this, and there was soon excitement in every regiment. Some men pointed out that in forty years' service nothing had ever been done by the *Sirkar* to insult their religion, but as I have already mentioned the *sepoys'* minds had been inflamed by the seizure of Oudh. Interested parties were quick to point out that the great aim of the English was to turn us all into Christians, and they had therefore introduced the cartridge in order to bring this about, since both Mohammedans and Hindus would be defiled by using it.

I reported this curious story to my officer but no notice was taken. He only told me not to talk about it. Some time later an order was read out to the regiment from the Commander-in-Chief, or Governor-General *sahib,* saying that the *Sirkar* had not used any objectionable fat but that in future the men could make up their own cartridges and use their own grease. They could then be satisfied that the *Sirkar* had no intention whatsoever of hurting their feelings or breaking their caste.

However the very reading out of this order was seized upon by many as proof that the *Sirkar* had broken our caste, since otherwise the order would never have been issued. What was the use of a denial if it had not been the Government's intention originally to break our caste?

It was the time of year for furlough—that is the month of

April—and it was my turn to go on leave. Before I went I told my Commanding Officer what I had heard, and I warned him that great madness had possessed the minds of all men. I could not say what shape the discontent would take, but I never thought the entire army would mutiny—only those men who might have suffered as a result of annexation of Oudh—and at present only a few of the really bad characters were disaffected. The Colonel *sahib* was of the opinion that the excitement, which even he could not fail to see, would pass off, as it had often done before, and he recommended me to go to my home.

I arrived at my own village without hearing anything out of the ordinary on the road, but shortly afterwards we heard that the troops of Meerut and Delhi had risen and killed their officers, and had proclaimed the King of Delhi as Emperor. They were excited to revolt because a complete regiment had been cast into jail, having been loaded with irons which destroyed their honour.

This was such an extraordinary story that I refused to believe it, considering it a story invented to inflame the minds of the populace, but the rumour gathered strength daily, so I went to the Deputy Commissioner to enquire whether it was true. I could not do this openly without arousing suspicion, for at this time all the office staff were on the watch for all who came to the office. I went to the Deputy Commissioner's house with a petition, but the *chaprassi* refused to take it in to the *sahib*, saying the orders stated that no-one would be received except during office hours. However I managed to see the *sahib*, and I told him the tale I had heard and asked if there was any truth in it. The *sahib* said neither one thing nor the other but asked me a number of questions to discover how much I knew and what effect it was having on the minds of the people in my district. Finally the *sahib* admitted that he had heard the rumour—as I had known from the beginning by the questions he asked me—but said that the reports were very vague.

Had I asked some important Indian official, he would probably have denied any knowledge of the facts, and the more vehemently he denied any knowledge, the more I would have been certain that he knew all about it. Had I persisted, he would have attempted to discover my own feelings on the subject, and then, if I had committed myself by wishing the mutineers well, he would have informed against me, even though he himself might have been heart and soul in their favour.

By the time I returned to my village the whole place was talking about the news, in a short time the entire country was in a ferment and every regiment was reported to be ripe for mutiny. Reports came in every day that the regiments at the different stations had risen and killed their officers. I went again to see the Deputy Commissioner and offered to collect the furlough men of my own regiment, as well as any pensioners who could use arms. He thanked me and promised to let me know if I would be required to do this.

Shortly afterwards the regiments at Lucknow, Sitapore, and other stations in Oudh broke out into open mutiny, and the country was overrun with *sepoys* from these regiments. Many of these men returned to their homes and had nothing further to do with the mutiny, other than having been in a regiment which had mutinied.

I now discovered that I was being watched. I was suspected of giving information to the civilian officials. One day a large party of *sepoys* from one of the mutinied regiments came through my village, and I tried to persuade them to go quietly to their houses. I explained to them the folly of going against the English Government, but these men were so intoxicated with the plunder they had taken, and by their hope of reward from the Emperor of Delhi, that they turned on me and were about to shoot me on the spot for having dared to speak out in favour of the English Government. They called me a traitor, and ended by taking me prisoner.

They put heavy irons on me and a chain round my neck, declaring they would take me to Lucknow where they would receive a large reward for having captured me, and where my punishment would be to have molten lead poured down my throat for having dared uphold the English rule under which I had served and eaten salt for so many years. I was treated with every possible indignity. My captors boasted of the deeds they had done—how the *sahibs* had been so easily killed, or terrified into running away into the jungles like hares—and they were convinced that the English rule had ended throughout India. I never saw men behave in such a shameless fashion—not even during *Holi*. They all believed they would be made princes for what they had done, and debated among themselves about the offices they would be given by the King of Delhi. I could not discover what they had done, other than that they had shot down their officers on the parade ground, looted the station without any resistance, and set it on fire.

While we were on the march some people informed them that there was a European regiment not far behind, and their boasting was redoubled. They would immediately annihilate it! This was what they said in public but inwardly they were terrified of coming up against the English. The European regiment never materialized, nor indeed was there the slightest truth in the report. I was relieved to hear this since they had told me that I should be shot at once if any Europeans appeared on the scene.

The leader of this party was a *sepoy*, although there were two *subedars* with it. He came one day and showed me a proclamation from the King of Delhi. It called upon all the *sepoys* to rise and destroy the English, promising great rewards and promotion if the men of any regiment would mutiny and kill their officers. It stated that the English *Sirkar* intended to make all Brahmins into Christians, which had in fact been proved correct, and in proof of it one hundred Padres were about to be stationed in Oudh. Caste was going to be broken by forcing everyone to eat beef and pork. The *sepoys* were exhorted not to allow this to happen, but to fight for their religion and drive the detested foreigners out of the country.

It also stated that the king had received information from the Sultan of Turkey that all the English soldiers had been destroyed by the Russians; there were only left the few regiments remaining in India; and these were all separated by great distances and could easily be surrounded and destroyed. This proclamation was printed on yellow paper and was said to have been issued by order of the king. Every man who heard it believed every word of it.

Even I was impressed by it. I had never known the *Sirkar* to interfere with our religion or our caste in all the years since I had been a soldier, but I was nevertheless filled with doubt. I remembered the treatment of many regiments with regard to field allowance—how it had first been promised and then withheld. I could not forget that the *Sirkar* had seized Oudh without due cause.

I had also remarked the increase of Padre *sahibs* during recent years, who stood up in the streets of our cities and told the people that their cherished religion was all false, and who exhorted them to become Christians. They always maintained that they were not employed by the *Sirkar,* but how could they have acted like this without the Government's sanction? Everyone believed that they were secretly employed by the Government; why else should they take such trouble?

Then I remembered how the *Sirkar* had been my protector, and that I had eaten its salt for over forty years, and I was determined never to betray it so long as it continued to rule but to do all that I could to support it.

As each day passed and I heard that city after city, garrison after garrison, had fallen into the hands of the local population, I must confess that the thought passed through my mind that the mighty Company's rule was passing away. All its guns had been captured, and also all its arsenals—how could I help thinking otherwise? However I still had faith in the incredible good fortune of the *Sirkar*, which had always been so wonderful and marvellous. I also believe that those who had broken their word and committed such crimes could not expect to have good fortune for long.

When the party of *sepoys* with whom I was drew near to Lucknow, from some orders they pretended to have received direct from the Nana of Bithur the route was changed and they marched towards Cawnpore and crossed over the river. While on the march, however, our party was surprised by a troop of mounted *sahibs*. It was early morning, just before the dawn, and we were attacked so suddenly that these brave warriors, so far from attempting to fight and annihilate the Europeans, fled into the jungle. Luckily for me, they forgot to carry out their threat to shoot me. I was pulled out of the pony trap in which I was travelling and narrowly escaped being shot by one of these trooper *sahibs* who thought I was a wounded or sick *sepoy*. He had not noticed my chains and could not understand Hindustani. Luckily there was an officer nearby who came up, heard my story, and saw my chains, which were very convincing proof of my story.

He gave orders for my chains to be knocked off and took me to the officer commanding who wrote down my statement, my name, and my regiment. He was also very anxious to learn of the conditions in Oudh, and whether I had seen or heard of any *sahibs* or ladies in the jungles. The last English officer I had seen was the Deputy Commissioner of ——, who was, when I left, carrying on his work as usual but this was a month ago.

As I was not a very good horseman, the Captain *sahib* could not turn me into a trooper but when he found out that I could read and write Persian, he made me interpreter for the Troop. He also gave me a certificate of the account of my recapture etc. I went about with this *rissalah* for about six weeks, during which time it destroyed several bands of mutineers and one day had a hand-to-hand fight with a party of regular cavalry. They fired off their pistols and made off as hard as they could although they were three times the size of our party. Nineteen *sowars* were killed and twenty-one of the best of the Government's horses were taken. We lost five men killed and seven wounded.

Through the kindness of my Captain—may the shadow of greatness always surround him—he took me to the officer commanding a Punjab regiment, and I was taken on the strength of this corps as a supernumerary *Jemadar* and attached to it.

# Flight to Agra

E. W Churcher
Indian Civil Service

# Flight to Agra

In the month of March, 1857, I was encamped in some forest near the foot of the hills, when a very decided change in the behaviour of the natives was noticeable, which I could not account for. They were wanting in respect, a trait I had never noticed in them before.

I spoke to my gamekeeper, and asked him if he had any news from the station (Fatehgarh). He said he had heard nothing of any consequence: he however said that some *Sadhoos* (Hindu devotees) had spread a report that the end of the British Raj was at hand, as the Kings of Delhi and Oudh were compassing our overthrow, with the assistance of the Sepoys of the British Army. This news was very unexpected: I was then arranging for the capture of some elephants.

Throughout the length and breadth of the country there are resting-places, distant about ten miles from each other, to which the Sadhoos resort. They go about besmeared with ashes, and with little clothing on their persons. They stay the night, and then move on to make room for others. They are attended to by women of their own caste, who reside at the rest-houses. During the night the principal people in the villages close by visit these men. They impart to them information regarding the state of the country, and spread reports which have no foundation. The people make offerings to them. The Sadhoos travel on foot from one end of India to the other.

In 1857 they had spread some reports which disturbed the minds of the people, and made them impertinent in their behaviour. Through their medium word had been passed on to the *chowkidars* (watchmen) of villages, the meaning of which only a few of them at first understood; they were told to prepare small wheaten cakes, called chuppaties, similar to those given to them, and to distribute them to the Chowkidars of the neighbouring villages.

Two of these watchmen brought these cakes for me to see. They inquired of me what it all meant. I of course could not tell them, but said that coming from Sadhoos, a most detestable class of people, they were to take no notice of the matter. The *chuppaties* were about the size of a five-shilling piece, and a quarter of an inch in thickness.

Soon after this I was suddenly awakened to a danger, which, in spite of the premonitory symptoms noticed, I did not anticipate, by receiving a letter from my brother Thomas, who resided at Fatehgarh, distant eighty miles from Cawnpore, in which he told me that rumours were being circulated that a serious rebellion in the native army was then hatching throughout the country. He added that the 9th Native Infantry, stationed at Fatehgarh, was implicated, and he strongly advised me to come home at once, which I did.

The rumours were soon confirmed by news of an outbreak at Barrackpur, near Calcutta, and of an attempt at rebellion by the Sepoy Regiments stationed there.

So insensible were the Government all through the month of March of actual danger, and so certain was everyone of the loyalty of the native army, that the daily routine of work all over the country went on as usual. If officers commanding native regiments were asked what the rumours meant, they were ready to swear to the loyalty of every man in their regiments, and scouted the idea of a rebellion.

It was only after the outbreak, and when some officers of these regiments had been shot by their men, that they woke up to the fact that a rebellion had actually broken out. It was most painful for them to believe that they were about to lose soldiers whose equal in physique could not be found in other parts of the world, and we all know that their gallant behaviour, when led by British officers, in times of war, was beyond all praise.

The troops, both native and English, were armed with the old Brown Bess, a single barrel muzzle-loader. Breech-loaders had not, to my knowledge, been then invented. The Brown Bess caused all the mischief, which culminated in the mutiny. The natives had never made any objection to the weapon so long as they were supplied with cartridges containing no lubricating substance. It was only when they found out that the cartridges contained pigs' and bullocks' fat, that they objected to them.

There is no disguising the fact that the military authorities were entirely responsible for the rebellion, for they could not have been ignorant of the caste prejudices of both Mahomedan and Hindu soldiers. The utter abhorrence of these men of the bare idea of touching anything containing pigs' or bullocks' fat was commonly known, and yet in the face of this knowledge the troops were supplied with cartridges containing both descriptions of fat, and they were not only expected to receive them, but were made to bite off the ends with their teeth before inserting them into their guns. In doing so they would of course lose caste amongst their brethren, who would no longer eat, drink, or smoke with them, so long as they were not again reinstated in caste.

This did not matter much in the case of the Mahomedans, for all they would have to do would be to distribute a few *pice* worth of *batasas* (native sweetmeats) amongst those of their brethren then present, to recover their position. But with the Hindus it was a much more difficult matter, for it necessitated their going to some sacred place—Ajodhia or Benares—to bathe and to propitiate the Brahmins, and only after they had done so would they be reinstated in caste. The soldiers felt convinced that the whole thing was an attempt to Christianize them all.

The Mahomedans, with the annexation of Oudh fresh in

their minds, were only too eager to fan the flame, for they had received their instructions from the Courts of the Kings of Delhi and Oudh. They did their utmost to poison the minds of the Hindus, and to induce them to join in the revolt. The Hindus had no king or emperor under whose flag to rally, whilst the Mahomedans had, and they made cats-paws of their comrades. The Mahomedans, of all the different castes and classes in India, were then most to be distrusted. In case of a revolt they had everything to gain, and it was not for want of trying that their cause was lost.

A little time before the outbreak little Mahomedan children would be seen in the streets, swaggering about with wooden swords in their hands, a thing they had never before been seen to do. The Hindus soon began to see that they had been made dupes of, and were righting to reinstate the Mahomedans in power, but the revelation came too late.

It was about the middle of April that I returned to Fatehgarh to my brothers, Thomas and David. Reports of bloodshed and lawlessness were beginning to come in. We three brothers got together the silver coin and valuables we possessed, locked all up in an iron safe, and at night threw the safe into a well close by. Our parents were then residing at Omerghur, distant twenty-five miles from Agra. We determined that one of us should go to protect them.

The roads were quite unsafe for any other means of conveyance but horseback. We sent for our upper servant and gave him a Bible, and told him to go into the garden, and place three straws, of different lengths, between the leaves, with the ends projecting, and then to bring the book to us. We had decided that the one who drew the longest straw was to start for Omerghur, distant a little over 100 miles.

It fell to my lot to draw the longest straw, and then we all prepared for my departure. I had a Waler cob, a splendid animal for endurance. A quantity of *chuppatie* cakes for my horse and self were tied in a cloth, and strapped round my waist. The servant also tied to my waist a small tin pail and pan, with a long string attached to it, with which to water the horse and myself from the numerous wells we should pass.

I started about eight o'clock at night, having had, as it turned out, my last dinner with my brother Thomas, whom I saw no more. It was a dark night; I made first for Thana Durriogunge, situated in the Etah district, and distant forty miles, and reached it about 2 a.m. There was an indigo factory there belonging to Mr. M———. His servants fed my horse and myself. They also made a fresh lot of *chuppaties*, while I had a short rest. There had been no appearance of actual danger so far. I went on my way again at 4 a.m., and arrived at the *dak* bungalow—a government travellers' resting place—at Etah, distant about twenty miles from the last place, about 7 a.m. There my horse and I had more refreshments, and a short rest. I started again about 9 a.m. for Omerghur. This proved to be the most dangerous part of the journey, for I was occasionally fired at, and at times chased by horsemen from villages near the road, but my dear cob used to outdistance them all.

I reached Omerghur, 55 miles from Etah, none too soon, and fagged out. On arrival at my father's house I saw gangs of armed men about the premises. The servants told me that they belonged to the Rajah of Omerghur, who had arrived in great state, followed by retainers, and that the Rajah himself, and some of his armed bodyguard, were seated in the drawing room. I went in, and to my astonishment found that to be the case.

The Rajah, a horrid black pockmarked individual, was seated at a table, and his men on chairs and sofas round about the room. I asked the Rajah what he meant by taking so great a liberty, when he said that my father and mother were arranging to start for Agra, but that unless my father paid him Rs. 5,000 he would not let them go. Owing to my fatigue I was not in a fit state to remonstrate with him.

Just before my arrival the Rajah had sent word to my father that those were his terms. My father was an old man, with a very bad temper. I found him in a great state of excitement, with my mother holding him, to prevent his leaving the room, to confront the Rajah. Had it not been for my most opportune arrival he would have gone into the room and shot the Rajah. With much difficulty I quieted him, and persuaded him to give me a cheque for Rs. 5,000 on the Agra bank, assuring him that we should get back the money when peace was established. He at last gave me the cheque, which I took to the Rajah. He then left, promising to help us as soon as the cheque had been cashed.

In the course of three or four days he sent word that we were at liberty to go. I reported the circumstances to Mr. Drummond, the magistrate at Agra. The difficulty in arranging for *palanquins* and bearers, for my father and mother, was very great. We left the servants at the house, with the exception of a Mahomedan cook and my groom.

The journey was a very perilous one, and the wonder is we ever reached the fort alive. We had to pass through the town of Etmadpur. On the roadside a rebel sepoy sat, with a musket in his hand. I made the bearers, who carried the *palanquins*, make as much noise as they could in passing through the town, to give the people an idea that we were a large party. We were forty men in all. The rebel sepoy did not move, but every moment after I passed him I expected a bullet through my back; nothing however occurred until we entered some deep ravines through which the road passed on the way to the fort.

There we came across gangs of disbanded sepoys, about a thousand men, belonging to two regiments which had been disarmed at Agra, and told to return to their homes. They were in a very excited state; they stopped us as soon as we met, and made the bearers put down the *palanquins*. My father, in his impetuous way, insisted upon knowing why they had been put down, and shouted to the bearers to go on. This added to the danger, and to my anxiety. I tried to explain our situation, but every moment was of importance. In my perplexity I did not know what to do.

A fine stalwart Brahmin sepoy, evidently a non-commissioned officer, was standing near my horse. He had strings of beads round his neck. It suddenly struck me that he might be of use to us. I whispered into his ear that I would give him all the money I had with me, if he would help us to get to the fort. He promised to do so, and called to his comrades, telling them that we were his friends, that he lived near our estate, and that if they molested us they would have to pass over his dead body to do so. The man was a high caste Brahmin, and they dared not hurt him, for any man killing a Brahmin was forever debarred from entering heaven.

The bearers had kept the sepoys from robbing my father and mother. My father, who was very fearless, did not understand the common dialect of the country, and increased the danger which surrounded us by his impatience. Our friend the Brahmin started with us for the bridge of boats, over the river Jamna, which was close to the fort. We were stopped by many gangs of sepoys, but our friend saw us through them. On arrival at the bridge I gave him all the money I had, which was about Rs. 60. We parted with many protestations of loyalty from him, he made a low obeisance to my father, who shouted to him in an angry voice, *"Jow"* (go). Needless to say we never again met the Brahmin.

We entered the fort at sunset. Then I was confronted with further difficulties, for how to obtain decent quarters for my parents in such a crowd was very perplexing. The *palanquins* were put down in a corner, and my father got out to stretch his legs, as he said.

After explaining to my parents what I was going to seek for, I left them, and in about half an hour I succeeded in finding a room, in a large marble square, a corner of which was occupied by the Lieutenant-Governor, Mr. Colvin. I took my parents to the room, and both before, and after, had many a squabble with people trying to secure rooms for themselves. Once my father was in possession nothing would have induced him to quit the place. I was sure of that, and never hesitated to leave him to see to our requirements.

71

The room was in three small divisions, with a screen, made of reeds, between them. My first thought was for my mother, to make her comfortable. I arranged the blankets and rugs we had brought with us on the straw, for a bed for her. I then went outside the fort, and purchased two stools. Nothing more could be done that night. The cook, who followed us, prepared hot water in some marvellous way, as only Indian cooks on a pinch know how to do, and we had tea and biscuits that night.

Next morning I managed to put together a small table, and to pick up a few oddments, and, with the food the cook purchased outside the fort, we soon got on comfortably. After seeing to my parents I attended to my dear cob, and had him tethered outside the fort, with numerous other horses. I saw him fed, and properly cared for.

The cook took a great burden off my mind. He was an old servant, and knew how to set about getting things ready. Outside the fort gates, fowls, mutton, and vegetables were procurable, and there was a room below us where he cooked them.

With the money my father had I paid up the *palanquin* bearers. These men, who are Hindus by caste, form the most useful class of servants we have in India. In times of war they are enlisted by hundreds. They follow the army and carry, on *doolies*—a bed strung on a pole—all the dead and wounded to the hospitals in the rear. In the house they do all the dusting, after the sweeper has swept out the rooms; they also wait on their masters, and look after their clothes.

Agra was the capital of the North West Provinces, now called the United Provinces. The Hon. John Russell Colvin was the Lieutenant-Governor of the Province. Agra was his headquarters. At the time of the outbreak the 3rd European Regiment, and the 67th and 44th Regiments of native infantry, were stationed there, under the command of Brigadier Polwheel.

At the Brigadier's suggestion the two native infantry regiments were disbanded on May 31, and the men were told to go to their homes. All combatants in the fort, capable of bearing arms, were enrolled. I felt proud of my father, then a very old man, when he stood beside me, and insisted on being enrolled, although, owing to his age, he certainly would have been excused had he wished it. A fortnight afterwards the Gwalior contingent, stationed at Sindhias capital, mutinied, and it was then that detachments of that force, serving in the Agra division, also did so.

Soon after a strong body of mutineers from Nemach appeared. They were on their way to Delhi, and we were told that they were coming to Agra for the purpose of taking the heads of the Agra garrison, and of all other Christians they could get hold of, as an offering to the King of Delhi. In spite of this grandiloquent talk they met with disaster.

On approaching Shahgunge, also called Sacheta, distant about four miles from the fort of Agra, a body of 500 men of the 3rd Europeans, about thirty mounted volunteers, and six guns, marched out to meet them. The rebels were found to be about 3,000 strong in horse and foot.

I was late in joining the volunteer horse, and fell in with the Europeans. To all present at the action which ensued it was apparent that our men were badly handled. The enemy entered the village in great strength before we approached it. Our guns did much havoc. Soon the enemy appeared to have had enough of it, and were seen to be moving off.

All this time the Europeans were lying down, and many of them lost their lives owing to the long period of inaction. The Brigadier was informed that the ammunition for the guns was expended, and that Captain D'Oyley, who had charge of the guns, had been killed. He then ordered the Europeans to storm the village, which they promptly did in gallant style. I believe they had never before that day been in action.

The enemy could now be seen retreating fast, but with our guns useless, it was considered unadvisable to follow them, and soon the order was given that we were to return to the fort.

After getting to within half the distance to the fort, the

enemy's cavalry, finding that we were retiring, came round to intercept us. The volunteers, commanded by Major Prendergast, were told to check the advance of the rebel cavalry. They faced about for that purpose, and charged. The odds were very much against them, and they lost twelve men. The rebel cavalry then fancied that they had the volunteers in a hole, but our men were beating time to give the Europeans, who were then on the double, time to get to the fort. The volunteers, seeing our men had made good progress, cut their way through the rebel cavalry, and rejoined us, leaving more of their number behind. We lost in all 130 men and two officers. This was a serious matter, and need not have been so bad if the whole affair had been better managed.

The enemy reoccupied the village. Early that night their cavalry visited the station, and with the assistance of the Agra *budmashes*—bad characters—they looted and burnt down almost all the houses in it, after which they went on their way to Delhi. We might have given them a taste of our guns, mounted on the ramparts, but the sun had long set, and, as on other memorable occasions, we were too late.

During the whole period of the mutiny only one round shot was fired from the ramparts of the fort, and that at an imaginary enemy. The fort is faced with red sandstone, and has never had a shot fired against it, nor was there the slightest semblance of a siege during the mutiny. There were upwards of 5,000 people in the fort, of which number only about 1,000 men, I believe, were actual combatants. I never witnessed any disorder in the fort, nor did I see dead or wounded cattle in it, as some people have asserted. Cholera broke out at one time, but I had left the fort to carry out a commission entrusted to me by the Government.

On the morning following the departure of the Namuch mutineers, I was outside the fort, armed and mounted on my cob. Other men were also there. Colonel Cotton rode up, and asked if any of us would accompany him for a ride round the station, to see what damage the enemy had done. I offered to go with him, and six other men, who wanted to see how their houses had fared, rode away in another direction.

The Colonel and I came across house after house burnt to the ground. We saw a lot of men assembled near the church. They fired at us, and unfortunately killed the Colonel's horse. To enable us to obtain assistance from the fort I tried to persuade him to get up behind me. He scouted the idea, drew his sword, and said "Come on." The fear of losing my cob made me hesitate, but it would never have done to leave the Colonel.

Just then we saw the six men who had ridden away coming in our direction. We all assembled in a mango copse, and the Colonel then sent one of the men for assistance to the fort. It was a two mile ride, and somewhat unsafe. The Brigadier would not send assistance, saying it was too late. The Colonel was very wroth, but we were obliged to ride home.

Next morning the Colonel obtained a gun and some men from the Brigadier. We blew the principal part of the buildings, where the horse had been killed, about the ears of the people . In looking into one of the houses we saw much furniture and parts of tents stacked in it. We saw an old hag, with an infant in her arms, crouching in a corner. The Colonel asked her for some fire, and as she did not understand him, he snatched the infant from her arms and handed the child to me. I spoke to the old woman. She hobbled away and returned with a light, with which we set fire to a great many of the houses. I was thankful to return the infant, who was squalling, to the old woman, and soon after we all returned to the fort satisfied with the work we had done.

After the battle of Shahgunge the behaviour of the town people was somewhat reassuring. No steps had been taken for the suppression of lawlessness in the district. The policy of Mr. Drummond, the magistrate and collector of Agra, met with disapproval, and things became worse, when a lot of men were seen, armed with *lathies*—long clubs—painted to represent muskets, patrolling the streets. They were the laughing stock of the place. Mr. Drummond was removed from his appointment, and was made Sessions Judge of Banda, a district in the south, pertaining to the North West Provinces.

Whenever there was any semblance of authority the people rose against it. The Mawaties, a Mahomedan sect, at Fatehpur Sikri, one of the palaces of the late Mogul emperors, a short distance from Agra, had to be driven out by a small force, which was commanded by Captain Patton. Here unfortunately I lost my cob; he was wounded severely in the chest, and died soon after. I had him buried in the grounds of the palace.

It was about the end of June that it occurred to the Lieutenant-Governor to depute an officer to Etah, distant seventy miles from Agra, for the purpose of re-establishing British authority. There were upwards of twenty members of the Indian Civil Service, including Messrs. Phillips and Hall, the magistrate and joint magistrate of Etah itself, besides some numbers of the uncovenanted Civil Service, who were refugees in the fort of Agra. These men had their lucrative appointments to return to when peace was established; they therefore saw no reason why they should risk their lives upon, as they said, so foolhardy an expedition; nevertheless it was imperative that the wishes of the Lieutenant-Governor should be obeyed. It was during a consultation amongst them, that it was decided to ask me to go out.

The Governor was informed that with my knowledge of the language, and of the district, and also of the neighbouring districts, I was best fitted to carry out his commission. The Lieutenant-Governor sent Mr. H. B. Harrington to me with a message that he wished to see me. In company with Mr. Harrington. I waited upon the Governor. After some preliminary conversation he asked me if I would go out to Etah to re-establish British authority there. I naturally inquired what assistance in money and men I should have. He answered that they could not spare a man from the fort, but that he would give me an order for Rs. 5,000 on the Agra treasury, then located in the fort, to enable me to raise a body of horse and foot. He gave me the order, and also authority in writing, arming me with powers of life and death, and granting me permission to raise a force of irregular troops.

Being young and strong I agreed to his honour's proposal on condition that my parents were looked after. He said that my parents should lack for nothing, and that he would make my interest his own. I must here mention that Miss H., a beautiful girl, was engaged to be married to Mr. P., the magistrate and collector of Etah, and one of the refugees in the fort. She was waiting in my mother's room anxiously expecting my return, for she believed that if I refused to go to Etah, nothing would dissuade the Governor from insisting that Mr. P. should return there. The poor girl wept for joy when I told her that I had accepted the Governor's commission, whilst my good mother wept for my folly, and prayed me not to go.

In spite of my mother's tears I could not withdraw from the promise I had made to the Governor. My father was very dejected over the whole thing, but he was the last person to persuade me to break my word, for a more true and upright, and honest man never breathed, although I, his son, say so. Miss H. begged me to see her before I started. In a little time I had enlisted 40 horse and 100 footmen. I also wrote to two well-to-do landlords in the Etah district whom I knew, sending the letter by my groom, telling them that I had been appointed to Etah with powers of a commissioner, and asking them to send twenty-five horsemen to escort me. They lost no time in doing so.

On arrival at the banks of the river, under the fort, they were mistaken for rebels. They held out a white cloth, and sent word that they wished to see me. It caused much amusement in the fort, as people said that the rebels wanted me in particular. I had a pleasant interview with the men, gave them money, and told them to make themselves comfortable in a neighbouring village, and that I should be with them at noon next day. These men were Googurs by caste. The head man amongst them was called Bahadoor Sing. These people are great marauders. They keep camels, and when a *dacoity* (robbery attended by hurt or murder) was determined upon, at a distance of 30 or 40 miles from their villages, they always rode out, leaving their camels in charge of some of their own people on arrival, and committed the *dacoity* during the night. Early next day they were back in their homes with their booty. They are of fine physique, and regular daredevils, but I had a daredevil undertaking in hand, so they were just the men for me.

Next morning I had a most painful parting with my mother. Of her five sons I seemed to be the only one who had been spared to her, and nothing would pacify her. I was obliged to tear myself away from her. My father, a most austere man, took my hand when I went up to him and said, "Go, my boy, and may God bless you." The parting with my parents was all the more painful as I was acting against my mother's wishes.

What shall I say of the parting with Miss H.? That also was very distressing. I knelt on one knee before her—we were chivalrous in those days—and took her hand. She wept, and put her other hand on my head, and blessed me, calling upon God most fervently to protect me. I can never forget her giving me a small box of chocolates, which she put into my coat pocket, saying she had prayed over them, and made me promise most faithfully to put one of them into my mouth on the approach of danger, which I took care to do, and considering the many miraculous escapes I had in carrying out the Governor's commission, who can doubt but that her prayers were heard? At last I left her, feeling happy that I had been able to do the dear girl a good turn. I never saw her again.

My first march was to Omerghur, where my parents had lived. The Rajah, of whose conduct the reader has already been informed, had had his turn, it was for me now to have mine. On arrival at his place, I ordered his men to produce him, which they reluctantly did. On his appearing I made my men seize him, and told him to disgorge the Rs. 5,000 he had taken from my father.

The man had the impudence to laugh in my face. I made my men strip him and tie him to a tree by his hands and feet, and whip him with their *corahs* (horsewhips) until he paid up the money. After a few strokes of the whip he shouted for mercy, and then the money was produced, and was weighed out to my Jamadar of Horse. The man was then released. It was a sight never to be forgotten to see that huge, black, almost shapeless mass of flesh, dress and waddle away to his door.

Before my arrival he had looted the country all round, but the summary treatment he had received made the men he had robbed come to my camp from all directions, making complaints of robbery against him. I took all these people to his place and told him that he would be tied to the tree again, and horsewhipped, unless he returned the property he had taken from them. It was astonishing to see the bales upon bales of cloth, and the large number of brass and iron utensils, and the coin and jewellery which was produced. All this was made over to the men who claimed them, and then I went on my way, hoping that I had seen the last of the scoundrel.

Some time afterwards I heard that the man had turned over a new leaf, that he had been protecting native officials, and had sent daily reports of the state of the district to the magistrate of Agra. When peace was established he made his obeisance most humbly to all in authority who approached his place. At last he was put down for a downright good subject of the Company Bahadoor, and to make the farce complete he was rewarded.

On leaving the Rajah after my first visit, I assembled my men in a copse of trees, had a white *chudder* (sheet) spread, and all the money poured on it. I then had the whole of it divided between the men I had enlisted, and the twenty-five horsemen from Etah. They received, I believe, Rs. 35 each. This liberal *douceur* was such an unexpected windfall, that there was nothing the men would not do for me after it.

The Agra men were the scum of the city. It required a very strong hand to keep them straight. I felt sure that if I did not divide the money between them, some of them would go off with the whole of it.

I put up in my father's house. The place had a most forsaken appearance. The property the Rajah had taken out of it was all put back that night. I was glad of the shelter the house afforded, and the servants made me comfortable They told me that a body of rebel cavalry had been to the house soon after we had left, and that they had tried to burn it down, but had not succeeded in doing so, as they were in a hurry to depart.

The next morning I marched to Awah, halfway to Etah. The Rajah was profuse in his offers of hospitality, and made me welcome. He informed me of the state of affairs at Etah, saying that the Rajah, Dumber Sing, had quite gone over to the King of Delhi, and had planted a green flag on the Grand Trunk Road, to denote that he had done so. Awah also told me that Dumber Sing would most certainly oppose me.

To prepare for this turn of affairs I got him to lend me a gun, with ammunition, and bullocks harnessed to it. As I approached Etah, I made the man in charge of the gun fire it occasionally, to make my approach known, and to give *eclat* to my arrival.

We reached Etah about 4 p.m., after a very hot march. I did not like the prospect of living in a tent in such weather, and therefore sent a horseman with a polite letter to the Rajah, telling him of my arrival, and intimating to him that I had been posted to Etah, with powers of a Commissioner, by the Government and that as it would be impossible for me to carry on my work in a tent, all the houses in the station having been burnt, I should be obliged if he would give me shelter in his fort. This was done to see if there was truth in what Awah had told me. The Rajah sent word by my messenger that he had heard that the ramparts of the fort at Agra had been destroyed by the rebels from Namuch, and the garrison killed, and that having escaped, I had come to

Etah, and was trying to deceive him by making out I was a Commissioner, also that I had better betake myself elsewhere, as otherwise he would soon make it too hot for me. I was not prepared for so much bluff.

To make matters worse one of my men ran up and said that some rebels had arrived, and were preparing to encamp in the parade ground. I felt that I was in an awkward position. On questioning my man he said that the rebels were Sikhs, and that they were about twenty in number. It struck me that I might be able to utilize their services, for the Sikhs are fine soldiers, and had done great things for us, and besides, with their assistance I would be better able to take a little of the Rajah's bluff out of him.

The Jamadar (head of my horse) was at once summoned. I told him to make all inquiries, and to try and persuade the principal man amongst the Sikhs to come to me. In half an hour's time the Jamadar returned with one of the men, a fine soldierly looking fellow. I explained to him my situation, and offered him and his men Rs. 100 each, for a night's work, if they would help me to take the fort, and make the Rajah a prisoner. He returned to his comrades. Soon after they all marched up, and grounded arms at my tent door.

I was greatly elated at the success of my manoeuvre. I took them all aside, and explained what I wished them to do. They were willing to help me in any way in their power. They received a sumptuous supply of food.

At midnight they set to work, in a most businesslike manner, by cutting branches off the mango trees under which we were encamped. With horse's heel ropes they made three ladders. At 3 o'clock the ladders were carried, and put up against the walls of the fort.

The Sikhs led the attack. My men and I followed, for a spy was with me, who knew all the interior of the fort. With him to guide me, and one of the Sikhs, we ran to the Rajah's apartments. The entrance into them was by a glass door, which we found closed. The room was lighted up. We could see the Rajah, a fat man, seated on a platform, propped up with pillows, and on either side of him sat two powerful-looking fellows. Owing to the lights in the room they could not see us in the dark. My men had been told to spike the guns on the ramparts first, as noiselessly as they could, and after that to secure the fort.

As firing had begun I told the Sikh to burst open the door, which he promptly did, with the butt end of his musket. We rushed in, and I told the Rajah if he attempted to rise that I would shoot him. The two men sprang to their feet as soon as the door was burst open. They drew their swords. I ordered them to go, as otherwise myself and the Sikh would shoot them. One of these men was Nihal Sing, and the other Rungbahadoor, both related to the Rajah. I shall have occasion to refer to the former of these men later on. They left us, saying that they would return better armed. I took the Rajah with us to see what was going on in the fort.

There was incessant firing from the ramparts, and the spy, who had accompanied us, ran up to say that our men were shooting at the entrance into the fort, where there was a large wooden gateway, with the usual wicket for one person to go in and out at a time. The wicket alone was open. As soon as the Rajah's retainers found that it was useless to oppose us, they rushed for the wicket, but as they could only get out one at a time, there was sad havoc amongst them. After the fort had been cleared, between thirty and thirty-five dead and wounded were found at the wicket. They were put out of the fort, and their friends were told to take them away, which they did. The wicket was then closed.

By this time the sun had risen, and a great crowd had assembled, outside the fort. I made the Rajah accompany me to the top of his gate, and tell the people to disperse, as otherwise the sahib—meaning me—would bring the guns on the ramparts to bear upon the town, and destroy it. After a time the men disappeared. I allowed the Rajah to return to his quarters.

The next day a great many people appeared, with petitions in their hands; they begged that the Rajah be made to return their property which he had taken from them. The fort contained great quantities of merchandise of all kinds. I let the petitioners into the fort, and allowed them to cart away all that belonged to them. This went on for another day. At last the fort was cleared, and made to look ship-shape.

Before many days the Rajah took poison, and killed himself, as he felt sure that he would be hanged, for a great deal of evidence was daily coming in against him, as many of the owners, whose property had been plundered, had been killed by his people. The women of his household were left undisturbed for a few days; their relations were then allowed to take them away to their own homes. A sharp lookout was kept for Nihal Sing and Rungbahadoor. It was said that they had gone away to distant relations. The former of the two men returned after a short absence to avenge the death of his uncle Dumber Sing.

I had returned, much fatigued after a skirmish with a small body of rebels, and was asleep at night under some trees, with my guard around me, when I heard one of the guard challenge a man. The stranger rushed in and aimed a blow at my head, which was then on the pillow, with a hatchet. He missed me, but cut a nasty gash on the side of the bed. He then ran, thinking evidently that he had killed me, but was followed by some of my men. One of my horses was always ready saddled near my bed, and I invariably slept with my pistols strapped to my waist. I jumped on the horse just as I was, and gave chase to the man. Fortunately it was not a very dark night. In some unaccountable way the man disappeared.

On returning we passed a small temple under a tree. One of my men had the curiosity to peep into it, and saw a cloth lying inside. Then another man shouted saying that he saw a man crouching behind a branch of the tree which overshadowed the temple. I called to him to come down. After a little hesitation he commenced to do so, but when about ten feet from the ground he threw an open sheet on the three men who were standing below, ready to receive him, and jumped down and ran. I chased him, and fortunately, with a pistol shot, broke his sword arm. The weapon dropped from his hand, and I rode him down. My men secured him: he was considerably hurt. He was placed on a *charpoy*, and carried to camp, where to my great relief he was recognized. He was found to be my great enemy, Nihal Sing, who had sworn to kill me.

He was very insolent, and asked my men to shoot him, or to kill him with a sword, saying that all his people had lost their lives in that way. I said that death, in the way he desired to die, was awarded to brave men, that he had tried to kill me in a defenceless position, and was a coward, and would certainly be hanged. Rather than that he should be longer in suspense he was hanged on a tree on the side of the Grand Trunk Road. I fancy that all this was a little too much for his brother Rungbahadoor, for no more was seen or heard of him. He was a most lawless freebooter.

********

I established police stations in different parts of the district, but on more than one occasion the staff were put to flight. I received daily reports from the stations I set up, and issued such orders as were practicable through the officers in charge. The ordinary judicial and administrative procedure of a district was quite in abeyance, and we were practically under martial law.

As the district quieted down, the native revenue sub-collectors came back, and were reinstated in their old offices. Dawur Ali and Najaf Khun, were the first to return. Agricultural operations began to be taken vigorously in hand, as the monsoon was a good one.

# A Lady's Escape from Gwalior

Mrs R. M. Coopland
Wife of a British Clergyman

# A Lady's Escape from Gwalior

It seems surpassingly strange that so little notice was taken of the impending danger by those whose duty it was to care for the safety of a mighty empire. We had, at the beginning of the year 1857, three regiments *less* than before the annexation of Oude. There were no European regiments at many of the largest stations: Allahabad, Cawnpore, Benares, and Delhi, were all left to the protection of disaffected regiments. The Government at Calcutta, in serene complacency, was coolly issuing orders for the disbanding of regiments: as though that could in any way stop the evil.

We now heard of the hanging of Mungul Pandy and of incendiarisms at Umballa. Many reasons were assigned for these disturbances: first, the trumpery one of the greased cartridges; and, secondly, the annexation of Oude. But neither of these were the *real* reason.

The heat now began to be overpowering: I was awakened one morning by the most stifling sensation in the air, and felt quite ill. The *ayah* and bearer said the hot winds had commenced. Really, I did think it was very *arg ke mâfick* (like fire): it made your brain feel on fire, and all the blood in your body throb and burn like liquid fire. We drove out for a short time, and I was struck with the grey, lurid look of the sky: the trees looked dry and withered. We could no longer drive round the "course;" the only bearable place was the well-watered road between the houses. Gwalior cantonments are situated in a hollow, therefore the hot winds sweep over them unimpeded.

We felt languid and weary, and every precaution was taken to mitigate the intense heat We bathed many times in the day, and drank cooling drinks—particularly soda-water. Indeed, so much of this do the Europeans drink, the natives think it is the only water we have at home, and call it *belathee arnee* (foreign water).

Mr. and Mrs. Pierson arrived during the hot weather. It seems strange that in the mutiny, though Mr. Pierson was not so well known or so much liked by his men as Major Blake, Captain Stuart, and Dr. Kirke, yet they not only spared him and his wife, but assisted them to escape. A little before this, a man from Calcutta arrived to take photographs, and stayed some time. Some of these photographs were actually recovered after the mutinies, and sent into Agra. The Stuarts were taken in groups, and made very pretty pictures, which were sent home, and, I believe, arrived there safely. What a comfort they must have been! I saw several groups of sepoys taken also. Many photographs were found in the room of horrors at Cawnpore!

The tempest had been brewing at Meerut for some time: bungalows and houses were burnt, and no one knew who had perpetrated these flagrant acts of revolt. At last eighty-five troopers, having refused to fire with the cartridges supplied them, were sentenced to six and ten years' imprisonment. In spite of the sullen, defiant looks of the sepoys, they were carried to a prison two miles off, in the native city, instead of being under an English guard. But for this, the terrible plot would have remained concealed till the day fixed for a simultaneous rising; when, doubtless, the consequences would have been much more terrible than they were. All went on as usual till Sunday (the fatal day), the 10th of May.

The news, by means of the telegraph, was all over India by the 13th; but we then hoped it was not known to the natives, precautions having been taken to prevent them corresponding. It burst on us at Gwalior like a thunderclap, and paralysed us with horror. We could not help wondering how a plot, known to so many thousands, could so long remain secret, and all things go on quietly as ever. We did not see the terrible details till a day or two afterwards, when we were dining with the Stuarts: I remember our gloomy forebodings, and how we talked of what had happened. Little more than a month after, out of the nine people assembled together that night, there were only three survivors, Captain Stuart sent to the *dâk* office, at the Lushkur, for the papers, that we might see the list of killed and escaped, as many of us were in anxious suspense about friends at Meerut. Oh! what a number of people have been cut off in the full pride and vigour of youth in these fearful mutinies. What happy homes have been desolated and hearts broken! The particulars of the Delhi and Meerut mutinies are now too well known: I will not dwell on them; but *think* how we must have heard of them at Gwalior!

Martial law was now proclaimed in the Meerut district, and Sir Henry Lawrence sent the following telegraphic message to the Governor-General:

All is quiet here; but affairs are critical Get every European you can from China, Ceylon, and elsewhere; also all the Goorkas from the Hills: time is everything.

On the 17th, the whole Contingent was paraded to hear the Government proclamation, which was read by Brigadier Ramsey, who also addressed them. This he could do very well, as he knew the language perfectly. Captain Pearson and Lieutenant Cockbourn left Gwalior with half the cavalry and artillery regiments. Captain Campbell left also for Agra in command of the Rajah's bodyguard.

Major Macpherson now took up his abode in the cantonments. We went one day to dine with him, and I was introduced to the Maharajah Scindiah, who happened to be there. I have a distinct recollection, when he shook hands with me, of his limp cold hand—just like all natives.

From that time the Rajah used frequently to come to the cantonments to see Major Macpherson.

I can never forget the fearful gloom of that month; but as our feelings are better described in my own and my husband's letters home, I will here insert some of them.

*Gwalior, Saturday, May 16th, 1857*

I write to you today, although the mail does not leave Bombay until the 28th, because there is no knowing now how long the road between this and Bombay will be open for the passage of the mails. The country, north of Agra, is in a dreadful state. You will probably have heard of mutiny and disaffection having shown itself in some native regiments near Calcutta, in consequence of which some men were hung, and one whole native regiment and part of another were disbanded: apparently the severest punishment the Government dared to inflict. Well, it appears now that there has been an attempt at conspiracy for a general rising throughout the country.

It is known that it was intended to rise upon all the Europeans and murder them. And now the insurrection has broken out at Lucknow, Meerut, and Delhi, and other places, where there are no European regiments, the English are of course entirely at the mercy of the brutal, treacherous native soldiers; and, as you see, it has been only the presence of two English regiments at Meerut that has saved any of the Europeans. Of course we are alarmed here. There are only about twenty English officers, with their wives and children, in the station, and about 5,000 native troops, so that we are entirely at their mercy. Already, half of our native cavalry and half of the artillery have been sent to Agra, and these were far more to be trusted than the infantry who remain. Even the Rajah's bodyguard has gone to Agra. There is an English regiment at Agra, but there are many native regiments, 3,000 cutthroats in the gaol, and a hostile population; so that they would have little chance against so many enemies. And, positively, the Governor has called up all the native regiments, and told them that if they do not like the service, they are at liberty to leave it without molestation. Fancy such a course as this when a rising is feared throughout the country!

I do not think that our lives are safe for a moment. Oh, how gladly would I send off my wife to England, or even to Agra, this moment if I could. The insurgents, of course, will be increasing every day, and if they come here, the native soldiers have as good as told their officers that they will not resist them—they will not fight against their brethren; and it would not be simply death to fall into their hands.

This is God's punishment upon all the weak tampering with idolatry and flattering vile superstitions. The sepoys have been allowed to have their own way as to this and that thing which they pretended was part of their religion, and so have been spoiled and allowed to see that we were frightened of them. And now no-one can tell what will be the end of it. There is no great general to put things right by a bold stroke. We shall all be cut up piecemeal. Instead of remaining to have our throats cut, we ought to have gone to Agra long ago, or towards Bombay; and all the European regiments should have been drawn together, and every native regiment that showed the least sign of disaffection at once destroyed, or at least driven away: for, as a leading article in the Agra paper of this morning observes, what native regiment can now be trusted?

I would leave for Bombay at once, but it would be death to be exposed even for an hour to the sun. What to do I know not. The officers of course dare not stir one step, but I wonder they do not contrive some plan for sending the ladies and children up to Agra, or to some place where there are English troops.

There is gloom on the few English faces, and a scowl upon the face of every native already. This letter will certainly make you very anxious about us. Sarah happily is all safe, being near Calcutta; but I hope you will get a more favourable account from me enclosed with this, or, at least, hear that we are in some place of safety. I would send my wife off at once if I had the chance. The possibility even of our falling into the hands of these demons is horrible.....

G. W. Coopland

P. S. It is dreadfully hot here: everything is like fire.

*Gwalior, May 19th, 1857*

I shall write to you sometime before the mail will leave Bombay, but in the very unsettled state of the country, and the *dak* being stopped, it is better not to lose any time. You will know what dreadful times we live in, when we cannot be sure of our lives for a day, and live in a state of constant anxiety and dread. You will perhaps have seen in the papers that there have been riots in India. The insurgents are now spreading themselves all over. Nothing has yet been heard of the officers, their wives, and families, at Delhi. The rebels have set up a king and a judge there. They seem to have chosen the best time for rebelling, when the hot weather is commencing, and it would be dangerous for the European troops to be exposed to it. All the regiments from the Hills are being ordered down to reinforce Delhi, Meerut, and other important stations; but it will be long before anything can be done, as no reliance can be placed on the native troops.

Here the troops say they won't fight against their brethren. The artillery and cavalry have left here for Agra, together with the Maharajah's bodyguard, which Captain Campbell has the temporary command of. There are only about thirty Englishmen in this station, and the native troops are not the least to be depended upon. They would most likely take part with the insurgents, of whom there must now be a great number; and they will soon be joined by all who hate the English.

The insubordination in our own servants is most remarkable. They look as if they would like to cut our throats.

The life we lead is quite miserable; the heat before was bad enough to bear, but now it is dreadful, when you live in fear of your life. Here we are in the midst of a lot of savages (for most of them are nothing better), seventy miles from any European regiment, and the insurgents are not far from us. They attacked a small station between here and Agra, and nearly murdered an officer. They murder people in the most cold-blooded way. At Agra there are 3,000 cutthroats in the gaol, very badly guarded, and if they were let out, what would be the consequences?

I wish we were safe at home. George has his rifle in readiness. All night long we are only separated by a thin piece of wood from our coolies who pull the *punkahs*, and who would not hesitate to cut our throats if they had the chance.

We do not know from day to day what will happen. Captain Campbell gave his wife a brace of loaded pistols before he left her, so you may fancy the state we live in. I hope we shall soon hear better news when the English troops meet the rebels; but they will never be able to stand the heat, as they are only invalided troops from the Hills. Poor Sarah Money (formerly Menteath) had to part from her husband not a month after their marriage, as his regiment was ordered against the rebels.

R. M. Coopland

*Gwalior, May 22nd, 1857*

I have already sent off a letter for you, for the mail which is to leave Bombay on May 28th, giving you an account of the dreadful rebellion that has broken out in India. I am very sorry that I have no better news to give you now; we are still in great uncertainty and danger.

Nothing of course is heard from Delhi, which is still in the hands of the rebels; and it is to be feared that many of the Europeans who were there when the rebellion broke out have been massacred. I gave you before the names of some that had been murdered there, and nothing further has been heard.

It is a dreadful time for Europeans to have to move down into the plains; but of course it was necessary to strike a blow at once.

We hear that the Commander-in-Chief is already on his way to Delhi with three European regiments, cavalry and artillery, and two or three native regiments that are supposed to be yet faithful; and it is said that native troops will be found sufficiently trustworthy from stations near Delhi to help in surrounding and investing it. It will be long even before they reach it, so we shall have to wait to know our fate, and the fate, apparently, of the English empire in India.

It seems that the massacre at Meerut was frightful; that though there were two English regiments in the station, the natives succeeded in murdering a large number of their officers, and many women and children. But we have heard nothing certain. The mutineers from Meerut and other places have already spread themselves over the country, and just now something terrible has happened at Etawah, a small station only about forty miles to the east of this place, for a whole regiment has been hurried away thither from here this morning. It is to be hoped that they will be faithful. They are all natives, and have only three English officers.

We get no newspapers, and as I, of course, am not admitted to military consultations here, the only news we get is by chance conversation, or by my writing to the Brigade Major, or some other officer, and asking what is going on. You know that we are not in English dominions, but in those of the Rajah of Gwalior. Happily he remains faithful to the English, at least so far, and in appearance, though now no one can tell what native is to be trusted. The weather is now dreadfully close and hot, though they say that the extreme heat has not yet set in.

The change in the behaviour of all servants and natives is wonderful, since the disturbances broke out. All are insolent, no longer like submissive slaves, but as if they were very forbearing in not at once murdering you; and the people eye us, when we drive out, in the most sinister and malicious way.

*G. W. Coopland*

*Gwalior, May 23rd, 1857*
I write again, as I think you may be anxious to know how things go on.

We are all in a very anxious and dreadful position; for what must be a decisive blow to this dreadful conspiracy, is now going on at Delhi. A large force of English troops have reached Delhi and are to commence operations today.

The last mail from Agra, which came in today, brought word that the rebels had taken Allyghur, where there is a treasury, and so had got possession of a large amount of money, and had stopped the communication with the Punjab; so that now we can know nothing certain of the state of things there, and. can only hope that the sepoys will remain faithful there; for if they join the rebels, all is lost The fate of India will be decided in two or three days—perhaps is deciding now.

There are supposed to be 7,000 sepoys, all trained by the English, in possession of Delhi; and it is now believed they have a large number of English officers prisoners, whom they have not yet murdered. Our fate depends upon the result at Delhi; the slightest failure will be the signal for revolt and massacre among all the native troops throughout the country.

Of course here, as everywhere else, there is the most

anxious expectation. There are now only ten English officers in the station, with many ladies and children, and in the midst of native troops ready to break out at a moment's notice, and are only waiting to see what happens at Delhi. We hope that Agra is safe, as our own lot depends, in a great measure, upon it. There is great fear, if Delhi is not taken, of the insurgents coming here, as Gwalior is on their way, and the atrocities they commit are fearful to think of. The insurgents have burnt down a railway station house not very far from Calcutta, so it will be very difficult to get there now; they have also burnt down a large hospital at Agra.

The rebels intend to make terms, by means of the prisoners, with the English who are now besieging Delhi. One young officer did a very brave thing—he blew up a place containing firearms of all sorts. It is supposed he blew himself up with it, as nothing has been since heard of him.

You have no idea of the gloom here; people seldom go out of their houses, and all look as if they expected some dreadful calamity. We dined last night with the Stuarts. Several officers were there, and they all spoke most doubtfully of things, and said, if a decisive blow was not struck at Delhi, it would be all over with the English.

It will be dreadful work for the regiments to have forced marches in these scorching winds. We have no news from the Punjab, as the *dak* is stopped. Things have been in a very unsettled state at Peshawar for some time; they killed an officer who was out of cantonments lately. This is worse than the Santal rebellion, as it is amongst the Company's own troops. Some of the native regiments that left here are now at Delhi. Some of the officers I met last night said they had observed the insolent manner of the sepoys here for some time.

*R. M. Coopland*

P.S.—Before I write again, I hope to have better news for you; if not, there is no knowing if we shall be alive.

I am very sorry to say that the aspect of things is not at all more favourable now, and we ourselves have been during the last few days in the midst of the greatest alarm and trouble.

The rebellion continues to spread all around us, and has broken out, it is to be feared, even in the Punjab; but we do not hear much, and that very irregularly, since, in many places, the post roads and telegraphs are in the possession of the rebels, and where it is open the Government keep it to themselves, and seem to hide the real state of things as much as possible from the people. But we know that at Etawah (perhaps sixty or seventy miles from us) the houses of the officers have been pillaged and burnt down, and the treasury carried off; the same has been done at Mynpoorie, a considerable station between Agra and Cawnpore. The insurgents are all over the country, plundering and murdering as they please.

Nothing has yet been heard from Delhi, everything being in the hands of many thousands of rebels, who have got possession of treasure, it is said, to the amount of between half a million and a million of rupees, besides the property that they have got in Delhi, which was a very wealthy city. It was expected that the Commander-in-Chief would have made an attack upon Delhi a week ago, and now that nothing is heard of him, we are almost in despair; either he is panic-struck, or the native troops we trusted have turned traitors, or he has been defeated, or cholera has broken out among his troops. And everything depends upon his success; if he is defeated, we shall all go at once.

It is terrible to watch how fear has gradually come over the Government. First, there was a proclamation promising speedy extermination to all rebels, saying that English troops were gathering from all quarters, and that vengeance would soon overtake their enemies. Now, to our shame and humiliation, a proclamation has appeared, declaring that every sepoy who has taken part in this rebellion will be allowed to go to his home in peace on giving up his arms at the nearest station, *i.e.* offering entire impunity to the wretches that have murdered and treated with every outrage our women and children, and devastated everything with fire and sword.

But now to come to ourselves. Two regiments and the cavalry having been lately sent off to other places, there are now here two regiments of infantry, two companies of artillery, and perhaps a hundred cavalry. The English community consists now of eleven officers, mostly with wives and children, three surgeons, the wives and families of four officers that have been sent off with their regiments, and four sergeants with wives and children.

Well, it seems that on Wednesday last, and during Thursday, the most dreadful reports kept coming in to the brigadier, the political agent, and some other officers secretly, that the whole of the troops here were to rise simultaneously on Thursday evening, at eleven o'clock, and burn down all our houses and murder us; of course none of these reports ever reached us, and about half-past five on Thursday evening Captain Murray came rushing into our house, and asked to see me alone.

He told me that he had been sent by the brigade-major to inform me that the troops were going to rise at eleven o'clock that night, and make wholesale burning and slaughtering; that every woman and child either had fled, or must at once make off to the Residency—a large house between seven and eight miles off, where the political agent at the Court of Gwalior lives; and that I must drive my wife over there in our buggy, since arrangements had been made for the occupation of all carriages in the station. It was of the utmost importance that our flight should be made unobserved; we must wait till the usual time of our evening drive, and pretending that we were going out as usual, must slip off on the road to the Residency; we must not take anything with us, for fear of exciting suspicion.

This was all said in a few moments, and the officer hurried away. You may imagine our feelings, not knowing how many had escaped, nor whether we should succeed in doing so, or should be stopped on the road. We hastily dressed, and ordered our buggy to be ready, not without many fears that perhaps the groom had run away, or the horse would be found lame; we took each a night-dress, gave a last look at our nice drawing-room, favourite books, &c, and my wife played on her piano, probably for the last time, and then about half-past six we got into our buggy and drove off, leaving our money and everything we had, just as if we were going out for our customary evening drive.

I first drove down the station, thinking to avoid suspicion, and then drove into Mrs. Campbell's compound, to ask if she had gone. We found that she had gone early that morning, and so, thinking there was no time to lose, turned down the road towards our place of refuge. We had at once to pass a long bridge guarded by soldiers, and there feared we should be stopped; but happily they let us pass, and we got clear out upon the road. The road was frightfully bad, in some places covered by gullies, and I had never been that way before, so that as darkness came on, and we were obliged to depend on the directions of any passing natives, and we were frequently passed by armed cavalry, we were not a little uncomfortable, and began at last to think (such was the wild, desolate look of the surrounding country) that we were being entrapped. At last we reached a large encampment of Mahratta horse and infantry surrounding a large stone house, which we were glad to find was to be our place of refuge.

I have not time to give you a minute description of all

that occurred here. You must imagine thirteen ladies, almost all with one or two children, and four sergeants' wives with their children, crowded together, having just left their husbands, as they supposed, in the greatest danger, and expecting that their houses, and all that they had, would in a few hours be in flames, and a birth and death both expected to happen any time; no beds, no change of dress, and suffocatingly hot; and then an order that everyone should be ready to start at a moment's notice, for perhaps we might have to hurry off towards Agra. The political agent, a son of one of our officers, and an invalid soldier, were the only white men present You must imagine what a night we passed, entirely in the hands of the Rajah's troops, and expecting to hear the officers that might have survived come galloping in with news that all was over.

But news came at last that the officers had gone among their men, and that the dreadful hour was passed, and no outbreak had been made; and then that the officers were sleeping among the lines, and the artillery officers and the Brigadier before the guns, so that it was supposed that the storm had passed for the present—to burst out on another opportunity.

Early in the morning we were told that the Rajah had intimated that he could not afford troops to guard us at that distance; we must come down to one of his palaces. Of course we were obliged to submit; and before long the natives of Gwalior crowded to a sight such as never had been seen in their streets before. Fifteen or sixteen carriages dashing through, surrounded by hundreds of wild Mahratta horsemen, and filled with English ladies and children. A gallop of four or five miles, through heat and dust, brought us to the Rajah's palace.

After waiting some time in the courtyard, we were conducted up a long flight of steps to the top of one part of the palace, which we were afterwards informed was near the Rajah's harem. Such misery I have seldom seen—poor little children crying, ladies half dead with heat and fatigue, some in tears; nothing to defend us from the heat; one mother weeping over a child supposed to be dying, without medical aid or necessaries of any kind. The Rajah, however, did what he could—sent in some old English chairs and a table which he happened to possess, and two or three native beds; and even had frames, filled with thorns, put in where there were no windows, in order that water might be thrown upon them to keep us cooler. The heat, however, was terrific, and we began to think how many such days it would be possible to survive. As night came on, a few native beds were brought in, and, as far as they went, assigned to the different ladies.

The excitement in the native city below us was immense—the people crowding round the palace and gathering on the tops of the neighbouring houses to get a glimpse of the English prisoners. An immense number of troops was brought up to guard us, and large cannon without end.

After another miserable night—I never got water to wash my face, or changed my linen; my wife, happily for her, shared a bed with another lady this night. We were told a messenger had arrived from the Brigadier, to the effect that we were to return at once to the station.

It appeared that the men had determined to remain faithful for the present, and that the native officers had gone to the Brigadier, and explained that they were offended at the departure of the ladies and at their being placed under the care of the Rajah; that their men would remain faithful, and we had nothing to fear.

About six a.m. we bade farewell to the Rajah's palace, and reached our houses again about seven, finding all just as we had left it This was Saturday morning, and here we are still, Tuesday morning; but our condition is very pitiable. We are here only on sufferance; our masters are always around us: we have to be obliged to them for not burning down our houses and massacring us. How can we trust one of them, when we know that regiments just like them have been guilty of every enormity? How gladly should I find myself with my wife on board an English steamer! But we cannot escape now, the roads are unsafe, even if the climate spared us. If a great blow is not struck soon at Delhi, all will go.

The Governor of Agra is most anxious that the news of our alarm here should not reach Agra, fearing the effects of it there, though they have one English regiment. Where this will end no one can tell.

The country is no longer ours, but in the hands of sepoys; and our lives, and all we have, too. I hope you will all have compassion for us, and think about us; and if it is not *too late,* I hope England will not leave us to be massacred with impunity, but send troops to save us: though, perhaps, all will be over before they reach us.

*G. W. Coopland*

P. S. Wednesday morning, June 3rd—Worse news still. We depended upon Agra, and now we hear that the European regiment there has had to set upon the two native regiments, and disarm them. What the 1,600 villains let loose will do, we cannot tell. No news from Delhi; everyone asks what the Commander-in-Chief can be about? There are also fears about the native troops at Allahabad; and if they took the fort there, they would get, it is said, 30,000 or 40,000 stand of arms. Enough to arm the whole country against us.

*Gwalior, June 11th, 1857*

You will be anxious to hear how things are going on. Well, first of all, I must tell you that the good news of the fall of Delhi has just now come to us by telegraph from Agra. We have heard no particulars, and only know that Delhi was taken on the 8th, and that arrangements were being made for levelling the whole place to the ground.

When I wrote to you last, I said that we were all wondering what had become of the Commander-in-Chief and his army, and hoping soon to hear of his arrival before Delhi. Well, next morning news came that he had died of cholera at Kurnaul. Since then, up to this morning, each day has brought us intelligence of some additional disaster.

First, we heard that at Lucknow, where encomiums had been delivered by the authorities on the loyalty of the troops, everything was in disorder, the city burnt down, the troops in open mutiny. Next, that the same was occurring throughout the Punjab, at Mean Meer, Ferozepore, and other places; that even in Peshawar, it had become necessary to disarm the native troops; that at Umballa all the native troops had mutinied, and been cut up by the Europeans coming down from the hills.

Next came news of an alarm from Simla, where invalids, ladies, and children are assembled in multitudes, having gone up to escape the heat of the plains. The native troops had proposed terms to these poor creatures, on which they were to be spared. Hundreds had been crowded for safety into some magazine, or building of the kind, without beds or any other comfort Several ladies had lost their intellects through terror; some had escaped on foot into the jungles; many had fled to Dugshai and Kussowlie, and there cholera had broken out among them.

Another day informed us that all the native troops at Bareilly had mutinied, and that the whole district of Rohilcund was up in arms. Then came word that in our own neighbourhood, at Ajmere and Nusseerabad, the whole of the native troops had risen and carried off the artillery towards Delhi, though there was a European regiment present, and that several officers of this regiment had fallen in a fight with them.

Then we heard worse news, that at Neemuch the same tragedy had been enacted, and that all the troops there had mutinied, including even one regiment of this Gwalior contingent.

This last news has been carefully kept secret, since it was feared that the troops here might be shaken when they heard of the defection of one of their own regiments. This contingent having, up to this time, remained sound.

On Sunday night last, we were alarmed by loud shouting, and on going out I found the roads full of artillery and native troops making off towards Jhansi: a neighbouring station, where the troops had risen and carried off the treasury, the officers and their families having fled into the fort They went out some distance, but were recalled the same evening, it being feared that they would not face the rebels at Jhansi.

Since then we have been in great doubt and uncertainty, not knowing that the next hour might not bring a like calamity on ourselves. As yet the men here remain quiet, but we are altogether at their mercy. They do almost what they like: lie down while on guard; laugh at us, and seem to enjoy the consternation and looks of constraint and uneasiness that are plainly visible among us. The least hope of success at Delhi would have set all into a flame. You may imagine our peace of mind has not been very great, receiving, as we have done, every day fresh details of horrible outrages and massacres.

Some time ago we heard very bad news from Calcutta. The fort there, Fort William, the bulwark of India, with all its stores, arsenals, and magazines, was within a hair's breadth of falling into the hands of the traitors. If it had not been for the loyalty of one native officer, who divulged the plot, the Fort would have been seized by mutineers, and the whole capital of India would have fallen into their hands.

We afterwards heard that there had been a panic in Calcutta. Multitudes had fled on board the shipping in the river, arms had been served out to all Europeans, volunteers were being enrolled, and even the French were preparing to assist against the enemy. But now we cannot hear what may be the fate of Calcutta, or even of Allahabad and Cawnpore; all the country towards Calcutta and the trunk road being in the possession of the traitors, and every *dak* and telegraph being destroyed, even as far as Mynpoorie, near Agra.

I hope you will have good news from Benares. I think they are as safe there as anywhere. English troops have been sent up there, and as this is completely a Mahomedan rising, there is not much to be feared from the Hindus of Benares; who are, moreover, cowardly, unwarlike Bengalees.

However, I believe we are all in the greatest danger. The European troops in India are very few, and almost incapable of acting in weather like this, and the worst season is coming. If cholera becomes general at Delhi, no one can tell what will befall them, and it will be six months before an army can be sent out from England. There are, I think, 71 native Bengal regiments, forming an army of between 50,000 and 60,000 men. Between twenty and thirty regiments have already mutinied, and everywhere the natives are ready to rise against us. In fact, it is the villagers that in many places have committed the worst outrages.

The English officers and their families are scattered all over the country at innumerable little stations. In this weather it is almost impossible to move, and if they could move they must abandon all their houses and property. Probably, too, they are afraid to move, because on the least appearance of their abandoning the country, the whole population would rise behind them. They cannot move, either, without the orders of their superiors. Even

105

though Delhi is taken, I do not see how the small European force that we have, will be able to stand against the daily increasing hordes of rebels. Even at Seepree, the next station to this, the regiment is insubordinate or disaffected. This, with Jhansi and Neemuch, which I spoke of before, are out-stations which I have to visit

The detailed accounts of the massacres at Meerut and Delhi are most horrible. At Delhi a large number of gentlemen (including some civilians and the chaplain) and ladies had taken refuge in the palace of the old native King. The rebels, raving like demons, tore them out one after another and murdered them deliberately, and then dragged their bodies about the streets. The escapes of some, after wandering in the jungles and hiding there for days, are most wonderful. One family escaped in a carriage, having shot down, several times, the rebels who tried to stop them. In many places the regiments have first murdered their officers, in some cases not one has survived. In one instance, the commanding officer committed suicide.

I hope now Delhi is taken things will take a turn for the better. The mail does not leave Bombay, I believe, until the 27th, so that I shall be able, all well, to send you another letter about the 20th.

*G. W. Coopland*

The day after my husband wrote this letter—the last he ever wrote—the news came that *Delhi had not been taken:* it was a mistake in the telegram.

What it cost us to bear this dreadful reverse and give up this last hope, I cannot tell. We were again plunged into uncertainty as to our fate; for we felt that the sepoys would no longer keep quiet when they heard of failure. Our last hope of escape was now cut off, as a telegram arrived from Mr. Colvin, the Lieut.-Governor at Agra, to say that the ladies and children were *not* to be sent into Agra till the mutiny really broke out at Gwalior. Before this, my husband had often wished to send me to Agra; but he would not desert his post, and I would not leave him. I have often thought since that had I done so he might have escaped, by riding off unimpeded by me; many unmarried officers having escaped in this way.

When the mutinies first began, if all the ladies and children at the numerous small stations had been instantly sent away to Calcutta or some place of safety before the roads were obstructed, their husbands and fathers would probably have had a better chance of escape. Instead of which, the lives of men, women, and children were sacrificed, through the efforts to avoid arousing the suspicions of the troops.

Gwalior was one of the worst places in India to effect an escape from. The houses were in rows on each side of a long road, a mile in length; behind them, on one side, were the lines of the cavalry and artillery, and branching off from them were the lines of the infantry regiments.

On the other side, behind the houses, was the *nullah*. The only people who escaped on the night of the 14th, lived on this side. On the first alarm, they instantly rushed across the *nullah*. Had the guards of their houses resisted their escape, nothing could have saved them: had soldiers been placed there to stop them, it would have been useless to attempt it; but for the first ten minutes the *nullah* was left unguarded.

Our house was some distance from the nullah, and we had not been long enough in Gwalior to know the locality exactly. Besides, almost immediately after the alarm, the banks of the *nullah* were lined with sepoys, hunting for those who had already crossed. I believe the Brigadier lay hidden under the bridge whilst they were passing over it and searching for him.

At one end of the long street was a small bazaar, the natives of which were instantly up in arms. Our house was near this end of the street, and at the opposite end was a cemetery, a parade ground and gaol At the back of the houses and lines were the cavalry stacks, the course, the magazine, and a small place where elephants were kept.

I got a letter from one of my cousins, saying that they had all been obliged to escape by riding from Simla to Kussowlie; it was a long distance; and my uncle, who. had been very ill, was greatly exhausted by riding so far in the sun. They were also very much alarmed about their brother at Peshawar, the Punjab being in such an unsettled state.

I was much struck with the conduct of our servants—they grew so impertinent My *ayah* evidently looked on all my property as her share of the plunder. When I opened my dressing-case, she would ask me questions about the ornaments, and inquire if the tops of the scent-bottles were real silver; and she always watched where I put my things. One evening, on returning from our drive, we heard a tremendous quarrelling going on between the sepoys of our guard and the *ayah* and *kitmutghar*. They were evidently disputing about the spoil; and it afterwards turned out that the sepoys got quite masters, and would not let the servants share any of the plunder, but kept them prisoners, and starved and ill-treated them.

They had much better have remained faithful to us, and have helped us to escape; instead of which, at the first shot, they vanished, and began to plunder what they could. My husband overheard the *punkah* coolies outside talking about us, and saying that these Feringhis would soon have a different home, and *they* would then be masters; and that the Feringhis were quite different in the cool weather, but were now such poor creatures as to require to be *punkahed* and kept cool. I could not help fancying they might have made us *punkah* and fan *them,* so completely were we in their power.

During this week the *bunian*, who supplied us with grain for the cattle and other things, the church-bearer and the schoolmaster, all came to be paid at once; they said they were going to take all their property to the Lushkur. This looked at if mischief was brewing.

Letters came from home full of news about the Manchester Exhibition, tours in Scotland, and all sorts of pleasures. Of course, our friends knew nothing then of the state of misery we were in.

Our last consolation was now taken away, for the telegraph between us and Agra was destroyed, and we were dependent upon rumour for intelligence. We heard dreadful reports from Jhansi, but could not ascertain the extent of the calamity there. An order appeared for a regiment to hold itself in readiness for marching, and the guard returned from the Residency, for the Rajah gave Major Macpherson a guard.

Major Blake was constantly consulting with the Brigadier as to what was to be done. We went to call on the Blakes, and heard from Mrs. Raikes, who was staying there (her husband being at Agra), that their house had been burnt down, at one of the out-stations; though it was thought not by the sepoys.

On Friday and Saturday we heard nothing; and we lived in a state of dread uncertainty. My husband seldom undressed at night, and I had a dress always ready to escape in. My husband's rifle was kept loaded (I learnt to load and fire it), as we were determined not to die without a struggle. Oh! the misery of those days! None but the condemned criminal can know what it is to wait death passively; and even he is not kept in suspense, and knows he will be put to a merciful end.

I well remember one Saturday night (the last night we spent in our own house) we were kept awake by the ominous sound of the *maistree* making a coffin for a poor little child that was to be buried early the following morning. My husband rose at half-past four, as the funeral was at five. The *ayah* was particularly attentive in her manner to me, and began pitying the poor *mem sahib*, saying, "How she will grieve now her baby is dead." She stood at the window watching, and telling me all that was going on.

When the buggy returned for me, I drove to church, and found service had begun. I passed many sepoys idling about the road—as is usual on Sunday. They all saluted me; but I thought I observed a treacherous look on their races. I wondered they did not attack us when we were in church, and heard afterwards that they were very sorry they did not The church was well attended, and we afterwards received the Holy Communion. Singular that we should all meet for the last time at such a solemn service!

Whilst walking in the garden, before going to church, when my husband was at the funeral of Captain Murray's little baby, I saw about a hundred *sowars* ride past the back of our house; they rode quietly in, all wrapped in long cloaks. I cannot help thinking they were the mutinous *sowars* of Captain Alexander's party, returned to join in the outbreak.

After breakfast we bathed and dressed, and whilst my husband was resting, and I playing one of Mozart's *Masses*, we heard a tremendous noise in our garden. After waiting a little time to see if it would cease, my husband went out, and found one or two sepoys again disputing with our servants. He ordered them to be quiet; but it was of no use, they did not now care even to keep up appearances. At last they settled the dispute among themselves; and for two hours we had perfect silence—not a sound was heard; it was a dread, foreboding stillness. I read the lines, "While drooping sadness enfolds us here like mist," in *The Christian Year*, and felt comforted. I afterwards recovered that very book.

My husband laid down, and tried to get a little sleep, he was so worn out. He had just before been telling me the particulars of the Jhansi massacre, too frightful to be repeated; and we did not know how soon we might meet the same fate ourselves.

I hope few will know how awful it is to wait quietly for death. There was now *no* escape; and we waited for our death-stroke. The dread calm of apprehension was awful. We indeed drank the cup of bitterness to the dregs. The words "O death in life, the days that are no more," kept recurring to my memory like a dirge. But God helps us in all our woes; otherwise we could not have borne the horrible suspense.

Silence still reigned, and I was again reading home letters—one from my sister on her wedding tour—when in rushed some of the servants, calling out that the little bungalow where we had formerly lived was on fire, and that the wind was blowing the flames in our direction. Something must be done, as the sparks were being blown all about: the 1st N. I. were very active in either putting out—or increasing—the flames. All the residents began to take the furniture out of their houses and pour water on the roofs; and my husband, at the head of our servants, instantly took similar precautions with our house. The heat was dreadful, the wind high, and the mess-house was soon also a mass of flames.

Everyone who has seen a great fire in a village may imagine what a sight it was. The road was crowded, the air filled with smoke, and I heard the crackling and roaring of the flames: it was a great contrast to the dead calm that had reigned before; but scarcely more awful.

While my husband was busily assisting the men, who were running about with water, and using the fire-engine; to my astonishment I found the *ayah* making bundles of my clothes, which she had taken out of the wardrobes and spread over the floor: she came to me for my keys, saying I had better have my things packed up and she would take care of them. I ordered her to replace them in the drawers and come and *punkah* me, as it was fearfully hot; I wished to keep her quiet, but she was constantly running off.

At last the wind fell, and the fire was extinguished; but not till the mess-house, the large bath-house adjoining, and little bungalow were burnt to the ground: my husband came in, greatly exhausted with his exertions.

After dinner the poor clerk, Collins, came in to know about service: he was dreadfully agitated, and my husband had to wait some time before he was sufficiently composed to speak. He said he was quite sure the sepoys intended to rise that night and murder us all. Poor man! I shall never forget his look of distress: he was the first to be shot that night.

My husband advised me to put on a plain dark dress and

jacket, and not to wear any ornaments or hide anything about me, that the sepoys might not kill me for the sake of my dress or trinkets; we then selected one or two trifles that we prized and some valuable papers, which we made into small packets, and again sat down in silent suspense.

Meanwhile my husband wrote to Captain Meade (the brigade-major) to ask if we were to have service in the church that evening, as the mess-house was destroyed; and also to inquire what he thought of things. Captain Meade replied that under present circumstances no one would be prepared to go to church, and we must expect "such things" to happen in these times. I then finished a letter for home; which never went, as it was burnt in our house.

After coffee we received a note from Major Sherriff, saying he wished to see my husband; at 5 o'clock he came, and they had a long talk together. He said it was a hard thing that we should stay to be butchered like sheep; for now there was no doubt but that such would be our fate. He also told us Mrs. Hawkins had come in from Sepree, to join her husband, and that she had been confined on Saturday. "It is dreadful," he added, " that women and children should be exposed to such horrors: they will receive no mercy I fear."

We wished him to dine with us, but he was engaged to the Brigadier; and after walking some time in the garden he went away, having first left some money which he had forgotten to give at the holy communion that morning.

A few hours after he was shot, when at the lines of his regiment.

My husband now sent for all the servants and gave them each handsome presents in money: to his bearer and my *ayah* he gave double; he also rewarded the guard of six sepoys, who had come to guard our house when the fire broke out. We then drove out. We saw scarcely anyone about, everything looked as it had done for days past; but as we were returning we passed several parties of sepoys, none of whom saluted us. We met the Brigadier and Major Blake, who were just going to pass a party of sepoys, and I remember saying to my husband, "If the sepoys don't salute the Brigadier the storm is nigh at hand." *They did not.*

The Brigadier and Major Blake turned and looked at them. We found our guard still at our house, but they also took no notice of us. We then had tea, and sat reading till gun-fire; and at 9 we retired to rest, as my husband was much exhausted.

I hope no one will think me unfeeling in writing what follows: it *must* be obvious to all that I cannot do so without great pain; but I think that Englishmen ought to know what their own countrywomen hare endured at the hands of the sepoys; and what we went through that night and the following week, hundreds of ladies suffered all over India. Only a few survived to tell the tale; which can only be *faithfully* told by one who has experienced the misery.

Some men may think that women are weak and only fitted to do trivial things, and endure petty troubles; and there are women who deserve no higher opinion: such as faint at the sight of blood, are terrified at a harmless cow, or make themselves miserable by imagining terrors, and unreal sorrows; but there are many who can endure with fortitude and patience what even soldiers shrink from. Men are fitted by education and constitution to dare and to do; yet they have been surpassed, in presence of mind and in the power of endurance, by weak women.

My husband went into his dressing room, and I, after undressing and dismissing my *ayah*, arranged my dress for flight, and lay down. A single lamp shed a ghostly glimmer in the room. Soon afterwards the gun fired—instantly the alarm bugle rang out its shrill warning on the still night. Our guard loaded their muskets, and I felt that our death knell had sounded when the butts went down with a muffled sound. My husband opened his door and said, "All is over with us! Dress immediately."

The *ayah* and bearer rushed in, calling out, "Fly! the sepoys have risen, and will kill you."

The *ayah* then quickly helped me to dress. I put on a morning wrapper, cloth jacket, and bonnet, and snatched up a bottle of aromatic vinegar and another of opium from the dressing table, but left my watch and rings. My husband then came in, and we opened my bathroom door, which led into the garden, and rushed out. Fortunately it was very dark. I said, "Let us go to the Stuarts, and see what they are doing."

We soon reached their house, and found Mrs. Stuart in great distress, as her husband had just ridden off to the lines. Poor Mrs. Hawkins lay in the next room, with a Sergeant's wife attending to the little baby (only a few hours old). Mrs. Hawkins' children and the little Stuarts were crying, and the servants sobbing, thus adding to the confusion.

Whilst my husband tried to soothe Mrs. Stuart, I went in to talk to Mrs. Hawkins, whose husband had also gone to the lines. Suddenly a horse dashed into the compound, and Mrs. Stuart cried out, "Oh! They have killed my husband!"

I returned to her, as my husband went out to speak to the *syce*. I held her hand, and never can I forget her agonised clasp! The *syce* told my husband that the sepoys had shot Captain Stuart; that he thought the captain was not dead, but had been taken to the artillery lines: he also brought a message from Major Hawkins, directing his wife and children to go to the lines. So Mrs. Hawkins was carried out on a bed, followed by the nurse with the infant, and a large party of servants carrying the other four children. They all went to the artillery lines, as the artillery had promised to remain faithful. Mrs. Stuart also set off in her carriage with her children; my husband helped her in, and tried to comfort her. Mrs. Stuart had before told me that when she returned from her former flight to the Residency, a sepoy had said to her, "Why did you leave your husband, *mem-sahib*? That was not brave; but you women, are so weak and faint-hearted, you take flight at nothing. See! the Sahib trusted us; we will always be faithful, whatever happens."

Our *syce* now appeared with the buggy, accompanied by our *kitmutghar,* the latter appeared very much excited, and had a *tulwah* in each hand. He advised us to cross the bridge leading to the Lushkur; but the *syce* said it was guarded with guns and sentries. At first we thought we would follow Mrs. Stuart and Mrs. Hawkins to the artillery lines, as the artillery were thought to be better inclined towards us; it was the 4th we dreaded, for they had often let fall suspicious and mutinous words. It is believed that they committed, that night and the following morning, most of the murders at the station.

Just as we were going to turn towards the artillery lines, a young sepoy came running from them towards us, weeping and sobbing. He called out, "They have shot the *sahib*," and though my husband spoke to him, he ran past without answering.

All this time we heard volleys of musketry, bugles, shots, and terrible shrieks, and saw some of the houses burning. We drove to the Blakes' bungalow, where we found Mrs. Blake, Mrs. Raikes, and Dr. and Mrs. Kirke; none of them knowing what to do. Major Blake had ridden off to the lines the instant the alarm bugle had sounded; and things were rather quieter here.

It was now 10 o'clock. Dr. Kirke said the guard had promised to stay by us, and that now it was utterly impossible to escape, as every road was guarded and planted with guns, and cavalry were riding about. After a short time, passed in terrible suspense, the guard of the house suggested that we had better hide in the garden, as the sepoys would soon be coming to *loot* the house, and would kill us. It was only postponing our deaths, as we knew that escape was now hopeless; but as life is dear to all, we did what we could to save it.

I shall not attempt to describe my feelings; but leave readers to imagine them—*if they can*. I will only relate the simple facts.

We followed the advice of the guard, and went into the garden, where we remained for some time. Mrs. Raikes with her baby was taken by her servant to hide elsewhere, and the Kirkes, with their little boy, went back to their own house. My husband had his rifle, which was afterwards lost. I was told afterwards by several natives that he killed two sepoys with it: I know not if he did.

115

Mrs. Blake's *kitmutghar*, Muza, who remained faithful, now took us to a shady place in the garden, where we lay concealed behind a bank, well covered with trees. He told us to lie down and not to move, and then brought a large dark shawl for my husband, who was in a white suit. It was now about 11. The guard (composed of men of the 1st) still remained faithful; though they took no active part in helping us. They kept coming to us with reports that Mrs. Campbell was lying dead in her compound; that the Brigadier was shot on the bridge, and Dr. Mackeller near one of the hospitals, and (worst of all) that poor Major Blake was killed. This last report was only too true.

At last about a hundred sepoys came to attack Mrs. Campbell's house, which was close to our hiding place. We heard them tearing down the doors and windows, and smashing the glass and furniture; they even brought carts into the garden to carry off the plunder; then they set fire to it, and the flames shot up into the clear night air. They seemed to take pleasure in their mad work, for their wild shouts of laughter mingled with the crackling of the flames. The moon looked calmly down on our misery, and lighted the heavens, which were flecked with myriads of stars, only occasionally obscured by the smoke of the burning houses. Oh, the sight of that moon! How I longed that she would hide her brightness behind some cloud, and not seem to look so serenely down upon our misery.

At last, when the mutineers had wreaked their vengeance on Mrs. Campbell's house, and only a heap of smouldering and blackened ruins remained, they commenced their attack on the Blakes' house.

We heard them looking for us; but not finding their victims there, they came into the garden and made a diligent search for us. I saw the moonlight glancing on their bayonets, as they thrust aside the bushes, and they passed so close by us that we might have touched them. But God baffled their malice for a time; though they sought us with a deadly hatred, they were unsuccessful, and we were again left to wait a little longer in bitter suspense. When they were burning the Blakes' house, the flames and smoke swept over us. Gradually the fury of the sepoys died away, and they seemed to be gone in search of fresh plunder, or other victims; for we heard them shouting and firing in the distance.

Our faithful Muza now crept to us, and said we were no longer safe where we were, but that he might hide us in his house, and perhaps get us some native dresses to disguise ourselves in; and gratefully we hurried after him during a lull in the storm.

His house was a low, small hut, close to the garden, where the other houses of the Blakes' servants were; and we rushed past so quickly that, though we saw a number of sepoys, yet they, in the excitement, did not see us. Mrs. Blake, in her hurry, fell, and hurt her head and shoulder. We crouched down in the hut, not daring to move, and scarcely to breathe. I remember asking Mrs. Blake to take off her silk cape, as it rustled, which she did. In the dark I fell backward over a small bed and hurt myself. Muza then barred the door, and fastened it with a chain. After half an hour the sepoys returned, more furious than before; they evidently knew we were somewhere about We heard them disputing, and the clang of their guns sounded as though they were loading them.

They entered the kitchen of the house, which was only separated from the room we were in by a thin wooden partition. Muza then went out; we did not know what for. Had he deserted us?

The sepoys talked and argued with him; we heard them count over the cooking vessels and dishes, and distinctly say, *"do, tien, char, awr eck nai hai?"* "two, three, four, is there not another." After dividing the spoil, we heard them again ask Muza if we were in his house, and say they must search; but he replied that his mother was ill, and that they might frighten her.

They asked him, "Have you no Feringhis concealed?"

And he swore the most sacred oath on the Koran, that there were none in his house: but this did not appear to satisfy them, and we heard them coming in; they forced open the door with the butts of their muskets, the chain fell with a clang, and as the door burst open, we saw the moon glistening on their fixed bayonets. We thought they were going to charge in upon us: but no; the hut was so dark that they could not see us. They called for a light; but Muza stopped them, and said, "You see they are not here: come, and I will show you where they are." He then shut and fastened the door, and they again went away.

There was again a dead silence, followed by the dying shrieks of a horse, as it rushed past our hiding place; so we supposed they had gone to the stables. After a time Muza returned and said: "They will be here again soon, and will kill me for concealing you, when I swore you were not here; so I will take you to the bearer's hut: he will not betray you."

He then opened the door and we went out. Day was beginning to dawn, and the air felt cool, after the close atmosphere of the house we had been in for so many hours; it was the bearer's hut we were taken to; one of a cluster of huts built of mud, and very low and small. I again fell and hurt myself, as it was not yet light, and we again lay on the ground, quite worn out with watching, and terror; our lips were parched, and we listened intently to hear the least sound: but a brooding silence prevailed.

We were soon joined by Mrs. Raikes, with her baby and *ayah*; the poor baby crying and fretting.

It was now nearly six o'clock, and grew gradually lighter, when the sepoys again returned howling and raging like wild beasts. They came round the hut, the baby cried, and we heard them ask, "Whose child is that?" One of the women replied they did not know; they called "Bring it out."

Then Mrs. Raikes exclaimed in an agony of fear, "Oh! They will kill my child."

When the woman carried it out, the sepoys yelled, *"Feringhi, hi*: kill them!" and I saw through the doorway a great number of them loading their muskets.

They then ordered the woman to bring out a large quantity of plunder that lay on the floor of the hut, pictures, plate, &c; she took them out slowly, *one by one,* and gave them to the sepoys.

We all stood up close together in a corner of the hut; each of us took up one of the logs of wood that lay on the ground, as some means of defence. I did not know if my husband had his gun, as it was too dark in the hut to see even our faces.

The sepoys then began to pull off the roof: the cowardly wretches dared not come in, as they thought we had weapons. When they had unroofed the hut, they fired in upon us. At the first shot we dropped our pieces of wood, and my husband said, "We will not die here, let us go outside." We all rushed out, and Mrs. Blake, Mrs. Raikes, and I, clasped our hands and cried, *"Mut maro, mut maro"* (do not kill us).

The sepoys said, "We will not kill the *mem-sahibs,* only the *sahib.*"

We were surrounded by a crowd of them, and as soon as they distinguished my husband, they fired at him. Instantly they dragged Mrs. Blake, Mrs. Raikes, and me back; but not into the bearer's hut; the *mehter's* was good enough for us, they said.

I saw no more; but volley after volley soon told me that all was over.

Here we again lay crouched on the ground; and the stillness was such, that a little mouse crept out and looked at us with its bright eyes, and was not afraid. Mrs. Campbell came rushing in with her hair hanging about; she wore a native's dress, her own having been torn off her: she had been left alone the whole night. Then poor Mrs. Kirke, with her little boy, joined us: she had that instant seen her husband shot before her eyes; and on her crying "Kill me too!" they answered, "No, we have killed you in killing him." Her arms were bruised and swollen; they had torn off her bracelets so roughly: even her wedding ring was gone. They spared her little boy; saying; "Don't kill the *bûtcha*; it is a *missie buba.*" Poor child! His long curls and girlish face saved his life! He was only four years of age.

I was very thankful to see Mrs. Campbell, after the frightful report we had heard; for till then we had thought her to be safe under Major Macpherson's protection.

The sepoys soon returned, and crowded in to stare at us. They made the most insulting remarks, and then said, "Let us carry them to our lines;" whereupon they seized our hands, and dragged us along very fast. It was a beautiful morning, and the birds were singing. Oh! How could the bright sun and clear blue sky look on such a scene of cruelty! It seemed as if God had forgotten us, and that hell reigned on earth. No words can describe the hellish looks of these human fiends, or picture their horrid appearance: they had rifled all the stores, and drank brandy and beer to excess, besides being intoxicated with *bhang*.

They were all armed, and dressed in their fatigue uniform. I noticed the number on them; it was the 4th—that dreaded regiment Some were evidently the prisoners who had been let out from the gaol the night before; and they were, if possible, more furious than the rest. Several mounted *sowars* (the same, I believe, whom I had seen ride in the day before) were riding about the roads and keeping guard, and wished to fire at us, but the infantry would not let them. The road was crowded with sepoys laden with plunder, some of which I recognised as our own.

After they had dragged us to their lines, they took us from house to house, and at last placed us on a *charpoy* under some trees. Mrs. Gilbert and her child now arrived, and poor Mrs. Procter; the latter in a dreadful state, having just seen her husband killed. All our horses and carriages were drawn up in a line under some trees, and I saw a beautiful Arab of Mrs. Raikes' lying shot.

Hundreds of sepoys now came to stare at us, and thronged round us so densely we could scarcely breathe. They mocked and laughed at us, and reviled us with the most bitter language, saying: "Why don't you go home to your houses? Don't you think it is very hot here? Would you like to see your *sahibs* now?"

We said we wished to go to Agra.

They replied, "Oh! Agra is burnt to the ground, and all the Feringhis are killed." They then struck the native gong. I think it was about eight o'clock.

After keeping us for some time, as a spectacle on which to wreak their contempt, when they had tired themselves with using insulting language, they said we might go where we liked; but when we asked *how?* they demurred at giving us one of the carriages, till some, more merciful than the rest, at last said we might have one. They gave us Mrs. Blake's—a large landau. The horses were very spirited and plunged a good deal: the morning before, they had broken the traces. How we all got in I can't say: there were Mrs. Blake, Mrs. Raikes, her baby and *ayah*, Mrs. Kirke and her little boy, Mrs. Campbell and myself; and some sergeants' wives clung to the carriage: how they hung on I don't know. The sepoys threw into the carriage one or two bottles of beer, and a bottle of camphor-water.

The first thing the horses did, was to run down a bank and across a small *nullah*. Muza drove; and a *syce* went with us a little way, but soon grew tired, and fell back. When we got a little way from the station, we came up with some more sergeants' wives and children; some of them nearly naked, and in great distress, having seen their husbands shot, and dragged about, and others not knowing the fate of their husbands. Poor things, their distress was very pitiable; their feelings being less under control than ours.

I never can remember how it was we were separated from Mrs. Proctor and Mrs. Gilbert, with her nurse and child; but think the Grenadiers carried them off to their lines, as they afterwards rejoined us.

The horses now grew very restless and tried to run away, and Muza did not know how to manage them. We came up to a *chowki* and were afraid the mutineers would stop us: they did not; but they. told us that Mrs. Hennessy and Captain Murray had been killed in escaping. We here debated where we should go, and at last agreed to go to the Rajah and entreat him for protection.

The Lushkur was five or six miles from the Mora and we reached it about noon. We passed crowds of natives, whom we expected to stop us every instant. When we reached the palace, we asked to see the Rajah.

The palace was surrounded by a crowd of horsemen, soldiers and natives, all most insolent in their manner to us, calling out "your *raj* is over now." The Maharajah refused to see us: though we entreated some of the Rajah's servants to be allowed to speak to him, we were roughly refused. Some say he was looking at us from a balcony all the time. Why were we so heartlessly treated by him, when he had been so kind to Major Macpherson and his party, even lending them carriages and a guard, and facilitating their escape in every way? Did be shelter Major Macpherson in his political capacity, and the brigadier as a man of importance? Perhaps he thought that helpless women could never be of any use to him. This is a mystery that no-one can explain to the Rajah's credit. We felt it keenly, to be thus driven from his palace gate with contempt.

We proceeded on our way, the people yelling and shouting after us, and we expecting every instant to be stopped and torn out of our carriage and given up to be killed by them; for nothing could exceed their savage looks and language. At the outskirts of the Lushkur we were obliged to stop, as the horses kept breaking the traces as fast as we tied them together again; moreover they were much exhausted, having been in harness the whole night before, for Mrs. Blake's escape.

A *chuprassi* of the Rajah's took the carriage from us, and made us get out and wait by the roadside till he sent us two or three native carts; they were miserable things without springs, had no covers to protect us from the sun, and were drawn by wretchedly weak bullocks. We got in and were taken to a large *pucka* house in a garden, where some great bullocks were munching grain in a room; and there we stayed.

It was now about one o'clock, I think. We here found a European belonging to the telegraph, and his wife with her little baby: she was a half-caste, and they were disguised in native dresses. The weak childish conduct of this man was sickening; he almost cried, and kept saying, "O we shall all be killed;" instead of trying to help, he only proved a burden to us.

We had now almost lost the power of thinking and acting, for we had been from nine the preceding evening without food, water, or rest; and our minds were on the rack, tortured by grief and suspense. Here we were, about eight miserable women, alone and unprotected, without food or proper clothing, exhausted by fatigue, and not knowing what to do; some had no shoes or covering for their heads. At last Muza said we had better get into our carts and push on; for the natives of the Lushkur, hearing we were here, would follow and kill us. The bullocks went very slowly, and we could not make them move faster. The sensation of horror and helplessness oppressed us like a nightmare: for all this time we were only a few miles from Gwalior, and could even hear the shouting and crying there.

Mrs. Campbell having broken one of the bottles of beer, we had each drank a little, which greatly refreshed us.

We toiled slowly onwards the whole of that long, hot afternoon; the dust rising in clouds, and the hot wind parching us. The men who drove the bullocks could hardly make them move. We mixed a few drops of the camphor-water with the water Muza occasionally brought us from the wells we passed, and found it supported us a little.

The shades of evening were drawing on, and we were as yet only a few miles on our weary way, when Muza said we were pursued by some *sowars*, who were coming to kill us, and he feared he could not save us, as we were on a flat sandy plain with no shelter. We reached, at last, a small *chowki* by the roadside, where the horses for the mail and the *dak gharries* were kept, and the *syces* who attended to them.

There were some wild, savage-looking men cooking food round a fire. Muza spoke to them, and then told us to get out of our carts and hide here. We all sat on the ground, and Muza said, "Only pretend to go to sleep: but I fear I cannot save you, as they are bent on killing you."

We waited, with our carts drawn up. It was nearly dark, and we heard the horsemen coming quickly on. At last five *sowars* appeared, armed with matchlocks and *tulwahs*, and as soon as they saw the carts they stopped and dismounted. Muza went towards them and began talking to them. We heard him say, "See how tired they are; they have had no rest. Let them sleep to-night; you can kill them tomorrow: only let them sleep now."

This they consented to do, and went a little way from us; but when it grew darker they crept near us, and began loading their matchlocks and unsheathing their *tulwahs*. Muza came to us, and said he feared they would not spare us. He then asked us for all the ornaments we had.

Mrs. Blake was the only one who had any, Mrs. Campbell and Mrs. Kirke having been stripped of theirs, and I had left mine behind. I instantly took off my wedding ring and tied it round my waist, as I was determined to save it if possible. Mrs. Blake had several valuable rings, other ornaments, and money about her; these she gave to Muza, who handed them to the *sowars*. We heard them quarrelling together, and I believe they held a loaded pistol to his breast and made him swear that we had no more. Muza then said we must speak to them, as they would not believe him. So Mrs. Blake and Mrs. Campbell, who spoke Hindustani fluently, spoke to them, and offered them 40*l*. if they would take a note to Captain Campbell at Agra, asking for a guard. At first they said they would, and went to one of the *syces* to ask for paper; but presently returned and said we meant to betray them; and again they threatened to kill us.

Just then we heard in the distance the tramp of a large body of horse and the clang of arms: this rather startled the *sowars*, and gave us some hope. When the cavalry came nearer, we saw that they were part of the Rajah's bodyguard, returning from escorting Major Macpherson and his party. They stopped, and we all ran towards them; and Mrs. Campbell. whose husband had had the temporary command of them, entreated their native officer (who was dressed in an English officer's uniform) to guard us, and let some of his men go with us. She offered them a large sum of money if they would. The Maharajah owed Captain Campbell long arrears of pay, and this also I believe she offered them; but to no purpose.

She then entreated for the protection of only one or two of his men. As they had escorted Major Macpherson, why could they not escort us? The Rajah might have given orders for them to protect any helpless refugees from Gwalior. They refused, saying they had not the Maharajah's *hukum*. So we had the bitter disappointment of watching them ride off. Whether the *sowars* were frightened, I know not; but, so far as I remember, they did not again molest us. We then lay down, and some of us went to sleep: the poor children did, at least.

Very early next morning we again set out Muza got us some *gram* for food, like vetch, which the animals live on; it was very dry, and this, with a little water mixed with the camphor-water, was all we had to eat About noon on Tuesday we reached the second *dâk* bungalow on the way to Agra (when we had before come to Gwalior, we had come by another bye road, this not being then finished). Here we halted for an hour or two, as we heard frightful reports about Major Macpherson and his party; we were told that as soon as they had reached the Chumbul, the Rajah's bodyguard had left them, and that they had been attacked by the villagers, who had killed them. They even told us the names of those who had been killed, and so circumstantially that we could not doubt.

The Rajah of Dhalpore, they said, had taken possession of the ford and would not allow anyone to cross. We did not know what to do, whether to go on, not crediting what they said, or, believing them, stay where we were. The servants at the bungalow pressed us to stay, saying, we should all be killed if we went on; but we thought they wanted to entrap us, and would only wait till they were joined by others, and then kill us.

We sent for the *dâk*-book, in which travellers write their names, but only saw "Major Macpherson and party;" there was no list of names. This we much regretted, as we were anxious to see who had escaped; and I most earnestly wished to know if Mrs. Stuart, Mrs. Hawkins, Mrs. Hennessy, and several others, had escaped, as we had heard such frightful reports. Mrs. Campbell wrote all our names in the book, that others who might escape should see them. We then partook of a little *dhâl* and rice, the first food we had tasted since Sunday night, excepting the gram. The poor children were very glad of it, but we could eat little, being so weak with exposure to the sun: afterwards, however, the doctors told us, it was well we had eaten so little, as our weak state alone saved us from sun-strokes.

On looking at my foot, which was very painful, and inflamed, I found that I had cut it, as my boots were very thin; so I tied my pocket handkerchief round it. We were all covered with *prickly heat*, a very painful and irritable eruption; and we could not rest, as crowds of natives would continue thronging in to stare at us; even looking through the windows of all the rooms. They all had firearms, which they brandished, and they looked so ferocious that we did not feel at all safe.

Here we were joined by Mrs. Gilbert, poor Mrs. Proctor, and Mrs. Quick, a sergeant's wife; they had been very ill-treated at the Lushkur: Mrs. Proctor had even had a *tulwah* held to her throat.

In the evening we proceeded on our journey in the carts. Our faithful Muza had procured us some *chuddas* in which we wrapped our heads, and disguised ourselves as well as we could, so as to appear like a party of natives travelling. The oxen slowly dragged their weary limbs along, hanging their heads and stopping every instant. When we started we were surrounded by natives; but strange to say, they let us depart, thinking probably that we should never reach Agra, and that we should only die a lingering death on the way; or that if we did reach Agra we should only find it in ruins.

We met five or six large carriages returning from conveying Major Macpherson and his party to Agra. We stopped them and vainly entreated the drivers to take us only as far as the Chumbul; but this they scornfully refused to do, saying they had not the Rajah's *hukum*. Oh, how our hearts swelled with indignation at this second refusal! It was very hard to see them drive past our miserable carts. Mrs. Quick was a very large woman—for corpulency becomes a disease in India, and her weight was such she had already broken down one cart, a small frail one, and now, toiling slowly along on foot, she implored us to take her in or she should die: her expressions and language were violent and dreadful, but we felt for her, and she was at last taken into one of the carts.

At night we reached a large village, but met with no sympathy: when we asked the natives for some water, they said we might get it for ourselves. Muza got us some, at last. We were then obliged to get out of the carts, and lie on the ground, in the middle of a dusty road, huddled together, whilst the villagers collected to stare at us: they even brought torches to aid their scrutiny, as it was now getting dark. The drivers of the carts made a fire and cooked some food they had got *for themselves.*

The natives were very insolent; they looked at us all in succession, and said, "Well, they are not worth a *pice* each;" but to Mrs. Campbell they said, "You are worth an *anna:*" they said she was *burra kuhsoorut*—very handsome. She was a very beautiful woman, and had formerly been called the "Rose of Gibraltar," when she was there with her father. They pulled aside her *chudda*, with which she tried to conceal her face, and said, "We will look at you."

At last, worn out with fatigue, we slept, and the next morning (Wednesday) continued our journey.

We passed through the town of Dholepore, which is built on each side of the Chumbul. The natives are a rude, fierce set, and when we reached the ford they would not let us cross, and said they would kill us. A large party of men well armed assembled together on a bank, and seemed to watch us. Muza advised us not to stir out of the carts, as they belonged to the Rajah of Gwalior, and as long as they thought we were under his protection they dared not touch us.

He then left us, in order to try if he could get a boat for us to cross in; and crowds of natives collected to gaze at us. It will be evident to all, from the behaviour of the villagers to us, that the disaffection was not confined to sepoys, as is sometimes asserted: indeed, the villagers always flocked into the stations after the mutinies to murder and *loot*. Of course there are some exceptions like Muza; and some of the sepoys even remained faithful, and helped their officers to escape.

It was the afternoon, and oppressively hot, when Muza returned, saying he had got a boat for us. We left our carts and descended the hill to the ford, where we saw a sort of raft, or rough native boat, at some distance from the shore; we had to wade the stream before we reached it, and then we scrambled into it wet as we were. Just as the boat began to move, Muza piloting, some natives dashed into the water, and, as if vexed that they had let us depart, tore a piece of wood out of the side, so that the water rushed in.

The sergeants' wives and children began shrieking out, "They are going to drown us: they are pulling the boat to pieces." I don't know whether this stopped them: but they then gave over; though some of them continued swimming after the boat.

The river was very broad, and the boat began to fill with water; so as soon as we neared the opposite shore, we jumped out, and again waded a short distance. The Chumbul, like all Indian rivers during the rains, swells, and floods a large space beyond its banks, sweeping all before it; but during the dry season it shrinks up, leaving a large margin of sand and debris: through this we had now to drag ourselves, the sand sticking to our wet dresses.

Having left our carts on the other side, we entered a small *chowki* near the river bank, into which we were followed by at least twenty horrid, savage-looking men, armed with rusty old matchlocks and *tulwahs*. I shall never forget the expression of their faces; we could see well now, as it was light, and we were neither agitated nor excited, many of us having almost lost all longing for life. We sat here for more than an hour, surrounded by these men, who every now and then drew out their *tulwahs*, and slowly polished them with their fingers, seeming to whet and sharpen them. They watched us closely: one man especially, with only one eye, and that had a horrid basilisk expression in it, watched me the whole time. They appeared to consult how they should kill us, and I kept thinking what a dreadful death they would put us to with their rusty weapons: a bullet would have been a merciful death in comparison. They would occasionally leave us, and then return, as if purposely keeping us in suspense.

At last a camel *sowar* rode up, and gave Mrs. Campbell a note. It was one written by Captain Campbell to the Maharajah, requesting him to have all the bodies of the killed at Gwalior buried, and particularly his own wife. *This she herself read.* The *sowar* said he would take her to Captain Campbell, who had come a few miles out of Agra, and was at the *dâk* bungalow at Munnia, not daring to come further, fearing an ambush; but Mrs. Campbell was unwilling to leave us, and moreover, she did not like to trust herself alone with the *sowar*, who agreed, instead, to take a note to Captain Campbell.

Mrs. Campbell (I think) pricked with a pin on the back of the note, "We are here, more than a dozen women and children: send us help."

The *sowar* departed, and Captain Campbell actually received the note.

Muza now said we had better walk on a little way, till he could procure us some more carts; so we walked on under the burning sun, our wet clothes clinging to us. Some of the women had no shoes or stockings; and one tore off pieces of her dress to wrap round her bleeding feet. Mrs. Kirke and Mrs. Campbell, who had no bonnets, put part of their dresses over their beads, to protect them from the burning rays of the sun. Mrs. Gilbert could hardly walk; but some of the women helped her along, and others carried the children. At last Mrs. Quick fell down in an apoplectic fit, and became black in the face; some of the ladies kindly stayed with her, but in a quarter of an hour she died. The natives crowded round, laughing at her immense size, and mocked her. We asked them to bury her; but I don't know whether they did; as we left her body lying on the road.

We sat for a long time waiting for carts, in a lane with high banks on each side, which sheltered us a little from the sun; at last, to our great delight, a native mounted policeman, riding Captain Campbell's own Blacky, came up and told us that Captain Campbell was at the first *dâk* bungalow from Agra; not daring to come any further, and uncertain if we had escaped, as Major Macpherson and all who had escaped knew nothing about us. Captain Campbell had sent him with instructions to us to rest at the next *dak* bungalow, where he would provide us with food. The man then rode off to ask the Rajah of Dholepore for some carts for us. It seemed strange to see this man, and hear him speak so kindly to us. He alone remained faithful when all the other mounted policemen afterwards mutinied at Agra.

The horse too was an old friend which we had often driven, and Mrs. Campbell was delighted to see it again. The man soon returned; and when the carts and an elephant, which the Rajah allowed us to have, came, we went to the bungalow. It was the same at which I had rested on our way to Gwalior nearly six months before; and I shall never forget the feeling with which I now entered that house under such different circumstances.

It was quite dark when we reached the bungalow, and our kind messenger gave us some biscuits, bread and beer, which Captain Campbell had sent. Then we lay down, some on the floor—and slept.

In the morning (Thursday) at about 4 a. m. we set out in our carts, which were very uncomfortable, though drawn by fine large bullocks. Some of the sergeants' wives had tried the night before to sit on the elephant; but as it had no *howdah*, and they were too exhausted to hold on, we took them into our carts. About noon we came in sight of the bungalow at Munnia where Captain Campbell was: he had sent on his buggy for his wife, so she and Mrs. Gilbert preceded us in it.

We soon arrived, and never shall I forget Captain Campbell's kindness: he was truly a good Samaritan; he bathed our heads, fanned us, and procured us fowls and rice; for we were by this time utterly worn out with fatigue and exhaustion. Here Mrs. Gilbert's baby was born, and we halted till evening.

Captain Campbell had a small *charpoy* covered with some carpet belonging to the bungalow, for Mrs. Gilbert and the infant to be carried on. He had twenty horsemen with him, but could not trust them. We started about 4 p.m., and travelled all night, through bye lanes; and thus, it being dark, we avoided an ambush, as the rebels were collecting to attack us.

Poor Sergeant Quick now joined us, and was told of the death of his wife.

At 6 a.m. the next morning we reached Agra.

# The March to Arungabad and Mhow

Thomas Lowe
Medical Officer Madras Corps
of Sappers and Miners

# The March to Arungabad
# and Mhow

On the 31st of May 1857, the transport ship Hibernia sailed
into the harbour of Bombay with a detachment of troops
from the seat of war on the shores of the Persian Gulf. This
detachment was the B company of the Madras sappers, who
had orders to return to their own Presidency now that peace
with Persia was declared. In the same vessel were several other
officers returning to Bombay and Bengal.

The whole of the time occupied in the passage from Mo-
hurmah to Bombay had passed very pleasantly. The men were
in high spirits, and delighted to think that they were so soon
to be restored to their families; but when the pilot came on
board and related the news, astonishment, anxiety and uncertainty took the place of the bright visions of home. The cities
that had fallen from our power in the Bengal mutiny were
named, the mutinous regiments numbered, the atrocities detailed, the movement of troops canvassed, and the untimely
death of General Anson reported; and, worst of all, that the
rebellion was spreading with mercurial speed from city to city
throughout the whole land.

The word Delhi was in everybody's mouth. What will
be the result of such an unexpected catastrophe? And will
it spread to the armies of the sister Presidencies? Such, with
a hundred similar ones, were our questions one to another.
No-one doubted the ultimate result, but in the meantime,
long before relief could come from England—what might
not occur? What fearful tragedies might be committed?

The newspapers teemed with portentous articles; extras and telegraphic messages flew about with wonderful publicity and speed.

The mercantile community were in a high state of trepidation; the homeward bound ships soon filled with passengers; the military, aroused to the high sense of the vital importance of the daily events in Bengal, were as energetic and determined to do their best as though the honour of the British realm depended upon individual talent, industry, perseverance, and courage.

While military preparations were being made, and assistance in the field, already occupied by contending troops, accorded, the Government of Bombay, in its promptitude and wisdom, stretched out another mighty arm to the struggle. She despatched ships of her navy to the nearest British possessions for succour, and obtained it; she transported troops, elsewhere destined, to the seat of war, and by her timely foresight stayed such as were far on the high seas for the conservation of these our long held possessions.

All this time our position looked anything but favourable. Cloud upon cloud gathered darker and darker, day after day told fresh tales of mutiny, murder, and crime, and already the land was red with the blood of our brethren, and mourning sat in many a house.

Delhi was the goal—troops were reported to be gathering around its walls daily, and its fall into our hands was almost hourly expected. Indeed, one or two reports about the middle of June stated that it had already succumbed to our forces. These false statements, I need not say, had their corresponding effects upon the native minds, already too eager to hear of our overthrow. Delhi had not fallen, nor was this event destined to be the harbinger of the glorious past for many months afterwards.

In the meantime, the troops at Neemuch and Nusserabad had fallen from their allegiance, and foul murder had marked their perfidious conduct in this as in almost every other instance.

Central India tottered from Gwalior to the Nerbudda; the Deccan had symptoms of smouldering, and a fearful tempest seemed to be gathering over our devoted heads from every possible quarter.

In this season of excitement, when the balance of power in Northern India seemed so much against us, it will, of course, occur to every mind that the services of every available man to be trusted were not only sought but eagerly accepted, when offered. It was under such circumstances that the Bombay Government were induced to accept the services of a single company of Madras sappers. This was done in a most graceful and flattering manner, and after the necessary preliminaries had been arranged, the company received orders to march to Arungabad, and there to join the moveable column of the Deccan, then under the command of Major-General Woodburn.

On the 16th June, the company marched into the railway station at Bombay for the train that was to convey them to Wassind, some 60 miles on the road. All being as it was desired, the "fire-carriage" screamed, then groaned, and at length got into its usual rapid Herculean pant The train passed out of Bombay like a shot, as though it had been commissioned to transport us as quick as possible from everything humanizing to the scene of war.

The company cheered on the road up over and over again, joked the people in Tamil, and the people stared at them as though they had been shot out from his Satanic Majesty's magazines.

This pleased the fellows. They admired the bridges over which we passed, they shook their heads knowingly at a cutting here or a tunnelling there, and laughed and joked till we at length felt the train drawing in. its speed; a shrill scream again, as at starting, only more prolonged, informed us that its period of exhaustion had arrived; slower and slower, and at length we were politely told to walk out. This we did, and found ourselves in a very pretty spot, with good encamping ground, plenty of bullock *gharries* awaiting us near the station, and an excellent well-supplied Railway Hotel. What more could we want? There was the finger-post pointing to *the hotel*, and, some 100 yards off the station only, stood that most glorious of establishments, in all its purity and aerial beauty, and well stocked with all that could contribute to gladden the heart of man, improve his general state, and fit him for the march on the road which was indeed to come on the morrow.

Before the all-important hour of seven p.m. should arrive, we had all been attracted by a peculiarly beautiful peak in one of the neighbouring hills hard by. It was a most tempting afternoon, and as all had been done to make the men comfortable in the camp, two of us determined to have a walk as far as the curious peak on the hill, so we lighted our cheroots and started. By-and-bye we arrived at the margin of the wood, or, as in India, they call it, the jungle, and struck off into a path leading direct to the peak. On we wandered and talked, admiring the glorious foliage around us for some two hours, about which time the sun, that had been pencilling in rosy and golden tints every object around us, suddenly dipped behind the hills we were nearing. The wood dove cooed in silver sweetness, the birds sang richly in the balmy air, the hare skipped before us, and everything seemed in peace.

The hills grew deeply blue, and the smoke of the cottages curled upward from the distant thickets as softly as though tempest never visited that spot. On and on we went till at length we came to an open, and found that the hill which seemed at first so near was still so far off that we must return without having accomplished our object.

We turned back, but long before we could gain the open it was dark. The lightning flashed, the thunder roared, and large drops of rain told us what was in store. We hurried along and arrived at the hotel scarcely in time to avoid the storm.

As we entered we heard the sound and rattle of dinner; we were not too late. A good board was spread, and just as we were entering feelingly into the merits of the same, Lieut. Gordon entered, rather the worse for the rain, with a stranger, who was introduced to us by him as Mr. —ham. Now the stranger was a quiet, bland, smiling, gentlemanly man; never said a word about his existence, but enjoyed the dinner and the table-talk. As the sweet restorer of tired nature was evidently diffusing his balm around we parted for the night. Now it appears that Lieut. Gordon, while looking after his horse at the station house, met this stranger, who had just alighted from a train, upon which the gentleman said to him, "Where am I? I ought to be in Poona, or some such place." It was pitch dark.

His position was forlorn for the time, but the hotel and the table comforted him. Indeed, these were sad times to be taken so far into a country one might naturally wish to avoid, and he accordingly made as rapid a retreat the following morning as steam would enable him.

You will naturally wonder what kind of an establishment a railway hotel up country in India is. When I tell you what this was in 1857, you will be able to appreciate others. The magniloquent cognomen at once suggests to the mind comfort, luxury, brilliance, cool marble-topped tables, soft inviting couches, bitter beer, sandwiches, and comely waiters! Do they get this kind of thing up country in India? Wait a while! For the East it ought necessarily to. be something light, aerial, and cool. If you can conjure up the elegance of a Sydenham Palace design, wrought into the all-accommodating structure of an hotel, with cool and zephyry verandas, easy chairs, and servants mute in snowy investment; if you can fancy this, and imagine yourself thus canopied and comforted doing a Turner with a Ruskin's egotism for your guide, or anything alike Epicurean in the declining rays of a gorgeous sun, then you will fall far short in your realization of what an up-country hotel really is.

Yes, it *is* beautifully light and airy, much as Robinson Crusoe's house must have been, with bamboos for the walls, straw for the roof, straw for the windows at night, and plenty of man-eating tigers in the vicinity! But we must say thanks to the enterprising Parsee, for through him we get in almost every Hindu town something that reminds one of home, and in this miserable apology for an hotel we fared as well as any traveller could wish, enjoyed our bitter beer, and a good night's sleep. What more could one desire in such times?

Originally it was intended that we should march from Wassind to Malligaum, there to join other forces, but on the march our route was changed for Arungabad, from whence news came to us that mutiny had broken out among the troops of the Hyderabad Contingent.

In marching through this part of Western India from stage to stage we generally halted at the bungalows, so that our journey from Wassind as far as the famous old town of Nasik, was one of no great hardship, for in all of these wayside houses we, found everything that could conduce to the comfort of a traveller, and to be obtained at a very reasonable rate. In this respect the system of bungalow management in the Bombay Presidency is far superior to that of Madras, as are also the bungalows themselves. In fact, the Government seem in every way to consider the comfort of travellers, not only in the arrangement of the houses, but in their management. In each there is a mess-man ever ready to supply the sojourners with excellent food, beer, and spirits, if needed, and who has every necessary article at hand for the comfort of the meals, so that a traveller in these parts need not encumber himself with food, or the necessary paraphernalia of the table.

Each person pays one rupee *per diem* for the use of the bungalow, and a very moderate charge for his *viands*. This was a great comfort to us, for no sooner had we ended our day's march, and seen to the well-being of the men, than we were agreeably greeted on our return to the bungalow by a savoury meal None, save those who have travelled in both Presidencies, can fully appreciate this superior system of the Bombay bungalows. Madras would confer a boon were she to adopt the same plan.

Thus we fared on our march to the Arungabad force as far as Nasik. Little or nothing occurred of interest upon the road to excite one, save an occasional arrival of the mail-cart flying on its way burdened with news of fresh disasters. The mail's arrival was always an exciting moment, and as the sound of the post-horn echoed from hill to hill every one seemed moved by anxious expectation. The horses of the mail-carts or mounted carriers always came rattling along that splendid macadamized road at a gallop, the man simply blowing the post-horn to apprise us of his arrival, and throwing down the welcome letter-bag as he dashed past on his important duty. The mail thus carried thoroughly reminded one of the old coach and mail days of England just antecedent to the times of steam and the electric telegraph.

The scenery all along this road as far as Nasik is most varied and beautiful The beauty of the verdure and extent of the tropical forests, spreading here and there for miles on either side of the road, give a most gorgeous feature to the whole landscape. Vast plateaus, broken here and there by large boulders of granite or trap, and intersected by winding streams, are covered with acres of green vegetation, or undergoing renovation by the plough. Everywhere there are neat villages, small towns, carefully cultivated fields, and well-stocked gardens, yielding the plantain, the melon, the cucumber, and other succulents.

I cannot help noticing in this place the superior piece of engineering on this road, called the Thul-Ghaut, not only as a work of art, but as a specimen of tropical scenery of the most superb kind. In all India I have seen nothing so rich in verdure as the hills and valleys through which this pass is cut. For some twelve miles before arriving at the foot of the *ghaut*, the roadside scenery gradually increases in richness and beauty. Higher and higher as the road ascends the vegetable world multiplies in variety, fantastic forms, and mellow tints. One feels that another climate is soon to be enjoyed, for everything looks cool, and nature everywhere seems rich and inviting.

The pass commences at the foot of a high range of hills, and runs winding around the sides of the different peaks higher and higher till the table land beyond the summit of the highest points is gained, and the clouds are left under one's feet. This *ghaut*—some seven miles long—was engineered by Lieut. Chapman, who was afterwards drowned in the Indus. The hillside of the pass is nearly always perpendicular, that of the open guarded by a low wall, over which the valley scenery is seen. We entered the foot of the *ghaut*, about 3 a.m. As we ascended morning broke overhead.

Once over the Thul-Ghaut, we found ourselves on a fine open country everywhere bearing evidences of good cultivation and plenty. The houses on the road-side were well built and clean, and the larger houses of the landowners in the distance bore strong resemblance to well-stocked farmhouses in England. There were large stacks of golden-coloured grass, numerous herds of well-fed cattle, excellent wells and tanks, fine timber trees giving ample shade from the mid-day sun, and the houses and out-buildings well built and tiled. The wheelwrights' shops of the villages showed signs of industry and work in every way, and stores of grain and fruit and other necessaries lay exposed for sale in the many little houses, giving a very pleasing feature to the scenes.

The further we journeyed towards the seat of mutiny and war, the richer the country appeared, and the happier and more peaceful the inhabitants. At length, after passing six days upon the march up, we found ourselves within sight of the famous old Hindu town, Nasik—famous for its proximity to the source of the holy river Godavery, on whose banks it is built. We halted for a while on the road between the holy hill of Sanika and the town which lay before us, surrounded by dense clusters of trees.

We marched into the bungalow compound at Nasik at 7.30 a.m. on the 22nd June. Bad news was in everybody's mouth, and although at that time nothing had occurred to endanger the peace of the place, there was a haughty bear-

ing and an insolence of manners very apparent in the people, which plainly showed us that they cared not to evince
their hatred and disgust of our supremacy. Whatever Nasik
might have been in the days of the Peishwah, it exhibits
little of interest or importance now. Its streets are narrow,
dirty, and winding; its bazaars are large and well-stocked, and
here, as in most other towns of the Bombay Presidency, we
found the all-obliging, speculative Parsee with a shop full of
English goods.

On the evening of the second day we marched out of
Nasik for Arungabad, and here we left the made road for a
cross country, one little better in most respects than a mere
bullock-track As we wended our way on over miles and miles
of cotton soil, with scarcely a tree or shrub to break the monotony of the landscape, we found that we had at length arrived at a period of trial.

The villages we passed appeared only poor mud-built heaps
of hovels, the bullocks half-starved, and the people as amazed
at our presence as savages. There were no more bungalows,
so we pitched tents after each day's journey. As we marched
along we were frequently met by armed *sowars*, looking as
fierce as tigers; we were also constantly overtaken by these
same vigilant gentlemen bearing letters or useful information for us. These fine, courteous, soldierly men were "Tap's
horse," and exercising a careful watch on the boundary of the
Nizam's territory, nearer which we were approaching daily.

Of course we were all on the *qui vive*, and looking out for
runaway mutineers. The further we went the less inclined
people seemed to render us any assistance; but as the time
had come for action, we never waited twice for an acquiescence to any reasonable demand. I remember in one of our
marches towards Toka we saw something very like a *bear* on
the side of a hill, then it moved like a man, and it was voted
a *sepoy,* and then a *bear,* and if a bear, why not have a shot?
This however was stopped by the object rising erect in the
shape of a villager.

From Nasik to Toka there was little to see. Toka is the poverty-stricken, ruined remains of what was once a fine town situated at the confluence of the Godavery and Pera, on the high road from Ahmednugger to Arungabad.

Extensive works of stone masonry of a very elaborate kind still remain untouched by time along the bank of the holy river on the side of the town. They were evidently erected to protect Toka from inundation at the great freshets, and also to serve as bathing and washing places for its inhabitants. For miles around Toka there is scarcely a blade of vegetation save a long avenue of fine old mango trees in which we pitched our camp. A little below the town on the other side of a large tributary stream, the Pera, is the *dâk* bungalow, and the *flying-bridge* across the Godavery.

This flying-bridge is one of the simplest and most efficient means of crossing Indian rivers I have ever seen. From a strong pier on either bank runs an iron chain across the river, and from this chain a second hangs vertically from a ring, and is fastened to a large raft-like boat below. As soon as the raft is laden and loosed from either bank, off it runs to the other in some three minutes, guided by a helm, and kept to the line of road by the vertical chain which runs along the one suspended from pier to pier. This kind of bridge is eminently useful, easily repaired if necessary, and necessitates but little outlay.

All the kit and engineering implements were passed over the river above Toka by pontoons. To get the bullocks and horses across was the most laughable and tiresome business. Six or eight *biles* would go into the river, swim half way across, or even further than that, then turn round just as their owners had consoled themselves that that was all right—and swim back, to their mortification and disgust. The horses plunged and kicked and screamed, lay down in the water and rolled, then swam out twenty or thirty yards, evidently enjoying the bath, and then back to the side again, where they lay down in the water like immoveable hippopotami. This game could not be endured longer; swimmers were sent up from the town to swim the beasts across.

Some dozen men came up as nearly naked as possible, with huge necklaces of dried gourds to act as buoys while they stemmed the current and conducted their unwilling charges across. No sooner were horses and bullocks driven into the water than in they plunged and buffeted and capered about the snorting brutes like river gods until they urged them to the opposite shore. The fellows could have done their work on *terra firma* no better; and their reward was a few *pice*!

All being ready on the north side of the river for the on-ward move, we resolved to march from Toka on the evening of 3rd July, and after having received kindness at the hands of two officers of the 24th Bombay N. I., who lived at the *dâk* bungalow for the time being, we bade farewell, crossed the rivers, and started on our way for Deysgaum about 9 30 p.m. It was a delicious night, cool, and almost as bright as day. We were again upon the high road, and only two marches from Arungabad. We were in good spirits, the men walked at a fine rate, and sang their songs and joked all the way.

One of our party dashed ahead of us at a sharp canter, and we concluded that he would be at Deysgaum bungalow in no time. Some three-quarters of an hour after this we thought we saw something in the gutter on the road-side. We went towards it, lo! it was human! The moon has great influences at these times of the year. Off he went again, if possible, faster. This time he is for the bungalow doubtless. On we went, and halted to drink at a stream. As we ascended the bank on the other side of the river, we saw something huge and white in the middle of the road. It was a crowd of natives huddled together, and a little ahead of this ghostly gathering was our friend, this time snoring away on a cot.

This night's air was too soporific, *nolens volens* he must sleep, and so seized upon the cot, while the shivering natives said, "Sahib take to sleep, what can I do?" A bed on the high road was too good a thing to resign; the next couch might be a stone, so we left him to draw upon Morpheus *ad libitum*.

In about half an hour a horseman passed us like a shot,

'twas our friend of the cot, who had awoke to a sense of his loneliness in the wide-wide-world, and was now intent upon the bungalow bed: we saw him no more that night. We arrived at Deysgaum about 2 a.m., and once again rejoiced in bungalow comforts.

Here it was we first saw anything of the mutineers. A number of them were prisoners under a guard of the 24th Bombay N. I., and on their way towards Ahmednugger. A mild form of cholera now appeared among the men in our little camp. They had undergone great fatigue, and the water here was very bad, in fact, too foul for use. No death occurred.

The next day, July 5th, we marched into the standing camp at Arungabad, and at length formed a part of the Deccan field force, then under the command of Major-General Woodburn.

The *coup d'œil* of the camp at Arungabad, although a small one, with the cantonment and town, and the surrounding hills, and the strong fortress of Dowlatabad in the distance, was one of the most picturesque sights I ever witnessed. Although the column was small, the tents of the force covered a large area, and gave quite an imposing feature to the landscape.

We marched into the camp at an early hour on Sunday morning. We found them all in a state of quiet excitement. The mutiny, partial as it was, of the 1st Cavalry of the Hyderabad Contingent, on June 13th, had given a very serious air to the affairs of Central India. The musselman population was evidently strongly influenced against the British Raj. The fearful convulsions that had affected the North-Western Provinces, Oude, Bengal, and the lower states, began to manifest themselves among the people of the central territories.

The same day that witnessed mutiny at Arungabad saw also the discovery of a plot for the murder of all Europeans in Nagpore. This originated in the irregular cavalry of that station. Prompt measures and the fidelity of the Madras sepoys prevented bloodshed and pillage in Nagpore. The treacherous troops were disarmed, and three of the leaders hanged.

News had arrived in the camp of the horrid massacre of our people in Jhansi, second only in magnitude to that of Cawnpore, and the mutiny of the right wing of the 12th B. N. I., the Irregular Cavalry and Artillery, at Nowgong on 14th June, while two companies of the 56th N. I., with followers of the Nawab of Banda, seized our treasury there.

About this same time revolt and bloodshed seem to have been well nigh universal. We were, indeed, literally surrounded by villains thirsting for our blood. Almost the whole of that once splendid and powerful contingent, the Gwalior, had broken from their allegiance and stained their hands with the blood of the Feringhees, while they carried away with them unopposed treasure amounting to several *lacs*, thousands of rounds of ammunition, a park of artillery, and other munitions of war, that made their revolt sound like a mighty tocsin to our ears.

On 14th June fires broke out in the officers' quarters in Gwalior, and mutiny declared itself. Those who could escape, fled—some to the protection of the Maharajah, others to Agra. Many died of *coup de soleil,* and many were killed; and the rebels were reported to have taken up a strong position at Calpee, on the banks of the Jumna, and but a few miles from Cawnpore. Scindiah all this time behaved with marked loyalty and wisdom. The mania spread further south, and the blasting contagion at length broke forth among the troops of the Maharajah Holkar, in the city of Indore. On July 1st a couple of Holkar's regiments commenced an attack upon the Residency at Indore, then occupied by the Governor-General's acting agent, Colonel Durand. Guns were planted by the rebels in the Residency grounds, and they fired upon the house and commenced the work of murder in the various bungalows. Col. Durand despatched orders for Hungerford's battery, at Mhow, twelve miles off. Before the guns could arrive, all who had escaped falling into the hands of the rebels fled as best they could, and the battery, then on the road, returned to Mhow. The ladies, Col. Durand, and officers escaped to Sehore, thence to Hoosingabad, where the presence and fidelity of the Madras sepoys *again* ensured security to the unhappy refugees who had only escaped with their lives. Thirty-four men, women, and children had perished; their houses were plundered, and then burned.

A Parsee tradesman was blown away from a gun, for his knowledge and intercourse with Europeans, I presume. On the evening of the same day troopers rode from Indore into Mhow, frantic with having tasted blood, and at once incited the men of the 1st Cavalry (right wing, the left having already mutinied at Neemuch), and the 23rd Regt. N. I. to rise against their officers and murder them. They did so *en masse,* and in their coolest blood they slew their commanding officers, Col. Platt, of the 23rd N. I., and Major Harris, commandant of the 1st Light Cavalry, and Adjutant Fagan, of the 23rd. The other officers, ladies, and children, and European soldiers, their wives and children, and Parsee merchants and families escaped to the fort, there to defy the cowardly villains, and to await a timely succour.

Still further south was the famous old stronghold Asseerghur, and this, it was feared, would also fall into the hands of the rebels, as it was garrisoned by a wing of the 6th Gwalior Contingent. This fort was saved to us by a clever stroke of policy of the commandant, Col. Le Messurier. He had felt that there was a spirit of disaffection among the troops forming the garrison, who were indeed openly boastful in the bazaar of the Pettah of what they intended to do ere long, and therefore wished to get them out of the fort before they could know of the Indore and Mhow disasters. He embodied a few faithful men from the town and district, and then ordered the sepoys to encamp outside the fort, that they might join the field force then coming up from Arungabad.

The same night the detachment of this regiment stationed at the large town of Boorampore openly mutinied and started off for Asseerghur, a distance of only 12 miles. A loyal havildar with two sepoys were sent off by the commandant from the fort to meet these rebels, and endeavour to persuade them to return. He was successful. The next morn the remaining sepoys marched out of the fort, and the new levies marched in without their knowledge. The company at Boorampore was disarmed by a corps of the Bheels, and those who had marched out of the fort were, to their amazement, surrounded by a body of the 3rd Cavalry, Hyderabad Contingent, commanded by Lieut. Clark, and forthwith disarmed also; thus was Asseerghur, one of the strongest fortresses in India, saved.

But disaffection was spreading fast. The Bheel corps at Bhopawar, under the command of Col. Stockley and Capt. Waterman, rose and joined in the rebellion. In this station plunder and fire did their devastating work, while the officers, ladies, and children had to fly, as best they could, and endure privations and trials of no ordinary kind.

This, then, was the general state of the country through which our force was about to march on its way north. The relief of Mhow was the first and great object, and to get there before the rains set in was a matter of the highest import.

Every day of our sojourn in the camp at this station there was some little excitement afoot. Courts-martial were daily sitting in the mess-house upon such prisoners as were known to have been concerned in the mutiny of the 13th June. Major-Gen. Woodburn had now reported sick, and was about to leave the force for safer and quieter quarters. The command of the force devolved, *pro tempore,* upon Major Follett, then commanding the 25th Bombay N. I.

On the memorable day of the 13th of June, the 1st Cavalry, Hyderabad Contingent, refused to march or fight against men of their own religious persuasion. Capt. Abbott remonstrated with them, and as the terrible events of the northern stations were not to be unheeded, the ladies of the cantonment were at once sent away, and the mess-house barricaded. Here the officers took up their quarters. The force under Gen. Woodburn marched into Arungabad on 23rd June. The general, at the suggestion of Captain Abbott, proceeded to the cavalry lines to disarm the men. His force then consisted of two squadrons H. M. 14th Dragoons, Woolcomb's battery, the 25th Bombay N. I., and a detachment of Bombay sappers. The cavalry bugles sounded the assembly, and the men fell in from their lines on foot. The native officers only were mounted. Captain Abbott then rode past, ordering the faithful men to fall out, thus the mutineers remained alone in their front.

Woolcomb's battery was only some thirty yards off, each gun loaded with canister. The general and his staff, with Capt. Abbott, then rode up to the men, the latter officer addressing them on their allegiance and religion. At this instant, a *jemadar*, who was one of the chief rebels, said "This is not good, it's a lie!" Here Capt. Abbott properly drew his pistol to shoot the scoundrel down, but the general turned round to him and said, he desired Capt. Abbott would "not fire on his own men."

Again Capt. Abbott addressed them, and a second time the *jemadar* told him *he was a liar,* and ordered his men to "prime and fire!" In an instant, with a rattle, a pistol was in each man's hand, and the timid general and his mortified staff not half a dozen yards from them! Instead of firing, they turned and fled, and the general then rode behind the guns, where Capt. Woolcomb stood pointing one at them. There was the port-fire ready, one word and they would have been blown into eternity; but the general said, "No! there are good men among them."

They had now gained their horses, and were impudently mounting them only some 250 yards off. Woolcomb now went to another gun and pointed it, but he was not ordered to fire, even though the general was being thus bearded; at last he cried out, "May I fire, sir?" Again no order came.

In another moment they were all mounted and away like the winds! By-and-bye came a feeble order that Capt. Woolcomb might fire; but they were off, and of some thirty rounds fired, only a few donkeys, horses, and a poor *ghorawalla* were killed!

They had cleared the lines, and then drew up upon the maidan, out of range of the shot. The 14th Dragoons were then ordered to charge, but before the 14th could close with them, they turned and were off east, west, and south. The dragoons cut up some dozen only. Capt. Abbott was with the dragoons, and as he had not marched 40 miles that day like them, he overtook a native officer and would have sabred him, but the fellow prayed for quarter with his sword in his mouth. Abbott, like a Christian and a good soldier, stayed his hand, and spared his life, but as he passed the fiend drew his pistol, and discharged it at Abbott's head. The ball flew past, and the rebel escaped for the time. He was caught towards evening, and paid the penalty of his treachery the next day. The remainder of the corps was then paraded and disarmed, and the bad characters imprisoned for trial. The audacious *jemadar* escaped *in toto,* with some sixty others.

Now, it is quite clear that had the general acted in a decisive, bold manner, as his position and the exigencies of the case warranted, he would have quelled the spirit of turbulence at once and in a never-to-be-forgotten manner, but his indecision marred the whole transaction. It became a subject of no light remark. The courts-martial ceased, and on the morning of the 7th July, at 530 A.M., there was a parade of the whole troops.

We all marched onto the ground in silent expectation of something awful. We formed three sides of a square, thus: the Hyderabad Infantry and Cavalry on one side; the 14th Dragoons and the 25th Bombay N. I. the side opposite the open; the Artillery and Sappers formed the third side, facing the Hyderabad Contingent; the fourth was open and occupied only by a solitary gun, with the port-fire burning beneath.

Three prisoners were then marched into the square by some twelve sowars. Their names were then read out, their offences, and the sentence of the court. Two were to be shot by musketry and one blown away from a gun.

Up to this moment they were ignorant of their fate. The two were speedily blindfolded and placed in a kneeling position, when twelve dragoons dismounted and marched towards them. There was a sharp rattle of musketry, and they fell down like logs of wood. The third was then tied to the muzzle of the gun blindfolded. Fire! and in an instant he was blown to atoms. His head flew up into the air some thirty or forty feet—an arm yonder, another yonder, while the gory, reeking trunk fell in a heap beneath the gun. Scarcely had the head and arms fallen to the ground before the carrion birds were glutting themselves upon the warm and mangled flesh, and the whole air was tainted with a most sickening effluvium. Such was the fate of those who sought to welter in the blood of the unoffending!

Such a lesson ought to have wrung their comrades' hearts— perhaps it did, but nothing less than such a fearful example could then be thought of. It was woeful to witness for the first time, but in such times and in such scenes justice, indeed, should be blindfold; and we should thank God that war with all its horrors only lasts for a time, otherwise the better feelings of our nature might become almost extinguished.

After the terrible scene of the morning parade, I strolled into the town of Arungabad, and afterwards paid a visit to the very beautiful Taj in its vicinity. The city, once extensive and beautiful, and still renowned, presents a truly marked picture of desolation, poverty, and fallen greatness. Like most large Hindu towns, little remains now to interest the sightseer, while there is much to disgust and hasten his departure. Squalid poverty sits squatted in rags beneath many a time-worn, elaborately-carved portico, through which the proud and gaudy Musselman once strode; houses, once inhabited by the wealthy Mahrattahs, are now fallen to ruin, their ornamental carvings alone remaining to show where opulence once dwelt; mounds of ashes and filth lie in every street; children scream at your presence, and astonished adults peer out of their miserable abodes upon you with lustreless eyes, while the Pariah dogs start from heaps of ashes, howling as they disappear among the gullies and huts of their owners.

Having stayed long enough to satisfy my curiosity, I returned to camp to find that we had to march on the morrow to repair a road over some hills about fourteen miles from Arungabad.

There was no doubt now about our movements. Brigadier Stuart, of the Bombay army, joined and assumed command, and everything was life and expectation. Paper after paper came into camp burdened with accounts of the fearful political condition of our Northern territories: to balance this was the good news of what our few Europeans were doing and could do. Neil and Havelock, and Barnard at Delhi, seemed working miracles against the overwhelming odds, and at such a season of the year, too!

In a short time we were all excitement about the march up to the pass of Chowker, and this particularly as we were to go in advance of the main body of the column. On the evening of the 8th we left Arungabad, and having made the pass fit for artillery, we returned on the 10th, rather an unnecessary step, as we all marched off from that city on the 12th instant. During our temporary stay at Chowker we kept a sharp look out to the north, shot hares and peacock in the jungle for the evening's dinner, and otherwise took it very easy, considering the times.

On the morning of 12th July the column left Arungabad at an early hour. It was a remarkably fine sight to witness the ascent of the troops over the rough pass of Chowker, which had been repaired a day or two before by the sappers. We had a bullock battery of the Hyderabad Contingent with us, and what through stupidity of drivers and unwillingness of bullocks, it was not surprising to see gun, tumbrel, ammunition-wagon, and bullocks too, go headlong over the side of the road into a deep gully beneath. The *biles* backed, and snorted, and looked wild, when they ought to have done the reverse; and at this moment their drivers, who sit upon the yokes, jumped off and ran away, while the biles turned round, got their heads out of the yokes and their legs into them, and otherwise tied themselves into most perplexing knots, and down went the whole, gun and bullocks together.

Then followed the unyoking, the unchaining, the patting, and coaxing, and gentling, and re-yoking—a pitiable business, and enough to tire and disgust the most patient Job. This kind of thing generally occurs in most unwished-for places. Fancy our artillery being left to the mercy of such beasts as a team of bullocks in these days of progress, whose intelligence is about their least point of recommendation!

On the evening of the 15th July we arrived at Adjuntan, famous for its ancient caves, and encamped on the south side of the town. Around this fine old town is the very *beau-ideal* of an Indian fortified wall, with fine imposing bastions and magnificent old gateways.

19th July, we reached Edulabad in the evening, where Captain Keatinge kindly entertained us. On the other—the northern—bank of the river Poorna he had pitched tents for us, and had a bazaar in readiness.

On the 20th we encamped at Anthoolee on the south bank of the river Taptee. Cholera broke out in the camp at this place, and in a few hours many men, Europeans and natives, died. Major Follett, commanding the 25th Regiment Bombay N. I., died here about 9 p.m. He was a fine man, and much beloved by his regiment. About 1 a.m. the column marched for Boorampore; we had to cross the Taptee. When we arrived at its banks we found it little above knee-deep, and the whole troops and baggage soon crossed. The natives remarked that "God was evidently fighting for the Sircar, for everywhere the roads were good and the rivers almost dry, although the season for the rains was far advanced."

I know no sight more pleasing to the eye than that of a force crossing these Indian rivers in the cool of the morning. Horsemen in advance soon cross and appear on the opposite banks among the brushwood and trees, while the column moves slowly on, filing down the narrow road that leads to the ford. Once upon the shingle at the water's edge, the infantry commence taking off shoes and stockings to cross, some mount upon each other's backs like schoolboys, having tossed up for the ride over. Then there's the joke; hundreds stay to drink of the clear cold water, native and European mingling together, then quietly wade across and form up upon the opposite bank; then down comes the artillery, gun after gun, dashing the stream about in a thousand rainbows as they pass through; there are the dragoons and gaudily-dressed irregulars in groups quietly watering their horses; there *dhooly*-bearers carrying the sick men across, sprinkling their heads and *dhoolies* with the precious water as they go; yonder is a long line of camels jingling with bells, stalking over; and there is the great unwieldy elephant sucking up gallons of water for his capacious stomach (with a huge bunch of leaves tucked up between his trunk and tusk), or blowing it over his heated body and limbs. When he has quenched his thirst, he takes down his leaves and fans the flies away as he carefully moves off.

Both banks are lined with men, horses, and followers, and droves of sheep, goats, and bullocks; all, and every animal, seem delighted with the river. I wonder not that natives worship rivers in this country, for no one can too highly estimate the value of clear, cool, running water, wherein all may wash and be clean, quench their burning thirst, and cool their heated, weary frames after a march over an arid country and through clouds of choking dust.

We passed through the town of Boorampore and encamped on the north side. Here the body of Major Follett was buried; and as a proof of the love his men bore for him, they carried his body, dug his grave, and heaped up a rude mound of stones over the spot when the ceremony was ended; and these were *high caste* men, too! But that this regiment should do such an act seems only natural, they are such fine soldiers, and commanded by such superior officers.

22nd July. We encamped about seven this morning on the north of the Fort of Asseerghur, in a little plateau surrounded by dense jungle. Towards evening Mrs. Durand, Mrs. Keatinge, and Col Durand, who had found their way thus far south, came into camp from the fort.

23rd July. Parade of the troops at 6 a.m., for the execution of three mutineers of the 6th Infantry, Gwalior Contingent. They were tried by drum-head court-martial the evening before, and sentenced to be shot by musketry. They were a havildar, a private, and a *bheestie*. A similar disposition of troops to the Arungabad execution; the criminals were placed near a hill, twelve dragoons dismounted, and blindfolded them, and in another instant they rolled to the earth to be buried where they fell.

The rattle of the carbines had scarcely died away when screams were heard outside the square. They came from a poor woman, who was running through the camp to the scene of death. She was the wife of the havildar, and evidently had never dreamt that she was thus to be robbed of her husband, so soon, too, and for ever.

24th July. We marched for the Berwai ferry on the river Nerbudda. In this march to the Nerbudda we passed through a considerable amount of jungle. The land on either side of the road was but little cultivated, although light and loamy, and capable of producing everything useful to man and beast. During the march up thus far I had taken the precaution to administer every evening small doses of quinine. True, every encamping ground was tolerably well-cleared of brushwood, but I am inclined to believe that this precaution kept us free from fever, while it sustained the nervous power, and thereby rendered us less likely to suffer from the effects of over-fatigue and malaria, of which there is no lack all over the district between the Taptee and Nerbudda.

On the evening of the 28th the whole of 3rd Hyderabad Cavalry, under the command of Capt. S. Orr, joined us. We were now upon the south bank of the Nerbudda at the

Berwai ferry. The river was rising very fest—indeed in a few hours it rose several feet. High and large boulders rapidly disappeared; the current increased in rapidity, while huge trunks of trees, bushes, and logs of wood came floating down. All this was a sufficient warning to us. The sooner the force crossed the river the better, for rains had certainly fallen, and heavily too, in the hills, and we might expect them ere long. Large boats of a rude description were ready, and upon these our troops, artillery, and baggage crossed over.

Here, also, several fugitives came into camp—the worse for flight, and painful apprehensions. A little fellow of the telegraph department had been beaten about the head sorely; and those who had escaped unhurt looked very woebegone and anxious. In the bungalow on the north bank of the Nerbudda were Capt. Waterman of the Bheel corps, and Mr. Theobalds of the Geological Survey Department. These gentlemen had had a long run for their lives, and scarcely boasted of an article other than what they stood in. They accompanied us to Mhow.

1st August. We marched to Simrole through the exceedingly picturesque *ghaut* of that name. The bed of the valley torrent was then dry, but I can fancy how beautiful it would be when filled with water. The scenery all through this pass is very charming. It also abounds in game of every description. Very heavy rain fell all night.

2nd August. The morning was fine and cool, and we now commenced our last march to the relief of Mhow. We had pitched our camp in and about nice smooth-looking fields of fine black loamy cotton soil In the morning, after the intensely heavy rain all night, the whole camp was a mighty sheet of soft mud. It was difficult to march through, more particularly for the guns. The elephants sank knee-deep into the mire, but this was nothing to them.

It continued fine, and the column went along quietly. At length we sighted the cantonment and town of Mhow, and as we neared it, fresh horses came out to assist the artillery along the still heavy roads. As we drew nearer there was the sound of a heavy gun, another, and another, until twenty and one were counted; "What could this be for? Has Delhi fallen? It must be so!" But no, though perhaps it was an equally important thing to the people here; the salute was fired from the fort, for the "relief of Mhow."

This timely succour was, indeed, equivalent to a victory in this part of India, for all around were enemies—every hand was against us from Neemuch to Saugor, from Gwalior to Mhow. Indore, only twelve miles off, was full of sedition—of evil people only biding their time for our destruction. The rains had held back for us, and we attained our object, and by this we established a centre of effective operations of an offensive kind; re-opened communication with distant parts that had long been closed to us; re-established the electric telegraph, the wires of which had been cut and stolen; and now showed a menacing face to the boastful cowards who had long defied the pent-up Europeans of the station.

Not only had they need to rejoice at the presence of a relieving force which dissipated their fears, but they were now able to escape from the millions of fleas and other vermin, which formed no very agreeable society to them while shut up in the fort, and to re-occupy the bungalows, the barracks, and other buildings, which had escaped the incendiary, in safety. So they fired the salute, and rushed out of the fort, like prisoners whose chains had been loosed, and we marched into Mhow, the 25th band playing rejoicingly, and severally took up our quarters in such bungalows as were not burned, glad that a period of rest had at length arrived.

It was indeed a Sabbath, a harbinger of long repose to both man and beast, during which the energies of all were husbanded for the long and daily trials soon to be encountered upon the battle-field.

Mhow was for the time being a strong basis of our military

operations, but to denude it of the troops and leave it in a position similar to that in which we found it would have been impolitic in the extreme.

To obviate this, and to give it an air of real military strength, the wretched thing that had gloried for years in the name of *the Fort* had to undergo extensive alterations. An earthwork was thrown up all round it, deep and wide ditches were dug, and batteries established in an admirable style. A strong battery faced the gateway, looking towards the cantonment to the north; others of equal strength looked south and west; a covered way was run out from the fort wall, south, to a well, there being no water in the fort; the angular corners of the old tumble-down walls, forming the quadrangle of the so-called fort, were built against from without and within, and large guns mounted thereon, pointing over cantonment, town, and country; the four walls were heightened and loop-holed all round for musketry; and at length this badly placed stronghold —for it is commanded on three sides—assumed a really imposing feature, and looked as though people could confide in its strength if necessity should compel.

During the whole of our sojourn in Mhow, from the day of our arrival in the beginning of August to the middle of October, every preparation was being made for the coming struggle to be commenced as soon as the rains permitted the movement of troops, with all their unwieldy paraphernalia. Very heavy rains fell almost incessantly up to the week before we marched to take the field; many of the cattle of the force drooped, emaciated, and died; but the men generally seemed to pick up an almost robust state of health.

Fortunately for our force the rebellious regiments had only destroyed some eight or nine bungalows on the night of their mutiny; they were too anxious to get away with their blood-stained plunder, and Hungerford's guns were too quick and terrible to tempt them to complete the horrid work of destruction they had commenced, so that our troops were well housed in good buildings, the native lines being all tiled. Our sick were placed in admirably built bombproof hospitals; and the artillery lines and barracks of the Bengal cavalry remained as before the outbreak.

The library, with its well-stocked shelves of goodly tomes and maps, and the prettily built church, escaped the firebrand, while the chaplain's house hard by, with all his worldly goods, was burnt to the ground; where the mess-house once stood was a heap of ashes, with a tumbling pillar here and there; further on, on either side of the road, the blackened walls and fallen pillars of destroyed bungalows showed the march of the mutineers, as they fled from the cantonment they had plundered and partially destroyed to join the other reckless masses all pouring upon Delhi.

It was a sorry spectacle to look at; and when one gazed upon the graves of Platt, Harris, and Fagan, who lay buried in a remote corner of the fort, and remembered that even a service of nearly forty years with a regiment was requited by foul murder, it cannot be wondered at if unrelenting revenge filled the bosom!

On the night of 4th September a troop of the 3rd Cavalry H. C. came into cantonment, unchallenged by a soul, and picketed their horses. An enemy might have done the same. After this a little more vigilance was observed. All this time most distressing reports came into our camp from north and south, east and west. Mutiny among Bombay troops, sedition and conspiracy in Poona, rebels increasing in force in Malwa, Holkar's remaining troops—some 10,000—more than distrusted, and here were we, immoveable on account of the rains, while Pandy was getting more powerful and mutiny more universal.

An anxious eye was cast towards Madras and the Nizam's people, but no great manifestation of sympathy or sedition was apparent. Everywhere terror had stricken our homes, and I doubt not more safety and strength was felt in the camp than in the city; in either case one's position was not an enviable one; real security and life were upon mere lease.

To live in India now was like standing on the verge of a volcanic crater, the sides of which were fast crumbling away from our feet, while the boiling lava was ready to erupt and consume us!

On the evening of the 19th considerable excitement was occasioned in Mhow by the sound of artillery firing at Indore. After the first few sounds, the dragoons had saddled their horses, and the Bombay artillery, under Capt. Woolcomb, were all in readiness for action. Boom after boom came over the distant hills, one after the other, like the commencement of an action, and then they died away. It was the salute of the Maharajah's people on the beginning of the Dusserah, and so our excitement quietly subsided.

On the morning of 27th September, just as service at the church was over, a salute from the heavy guns of the fort was fired in honour of the capture of Delhi! This famous stronghold was again in our keeping. It had fallen by assault some thirteen days before. This news was known in the native bazaar two or three days prior to the official announcement, when twenty-and-one guns poured forth their loud voices on the still air of a bright Sabbath morn proclaiming the glorious achievement of General Wilson's army. I hesitate not to say that every soul felt grateful for what this noble army had endured and effected. A burden seemed at once to be lifted from the heavily oppressed hearts of the British, and now they could breathe more freely and again exult in their prowess.

From June 8th up to the memorable day of assault and capture of Delhi our little army had done nothing but conquer. They were assailed from the city in their front, and from fresh arrivals of the enemy in their rear; daily attacks were made by vast masses, but our brave band stood each and all unvanquished; many, of course, perished in these affairs, but how so many escaped is the wonder, for not only had they to combat an ever vigilant enemy by night and day, but there were the sun, the terrific falls of rain, fever, anxiety, isolation, privation, and cholera—a legion of evils—besetting both body and mind! For nearly fifteen weeks our troops endured what were almost fabulous to relate; deeds of gallantry worthy of the Curtii were performed. Never, perhaps, did an army achieve so much or display such brilliance of conduct individually and as a body as that brave band commanded by General Wilson in the capture of this enormous city against such overwhelming odds.

# Cawnpore to Lucknow

## W. O. Swanston
Lieutenant, 7th Madras Native Infantry
and the Volunteer Cavalry

# Cawnpore to Lucknow

On the 9th of June, 1857, I had left the Salone *kacheri* (where everything had been going on much as usual, with this exception that the crowd of suitors had for several days gradually decreased) about 3.30 p. m. for a few moments, when, just as I reached Capt. Barrow's (Deputy Commissioner) gate on my return, I met Capt. Thompson (Commanding 1st Oudh Irregular Infantry at the station) talking to a Sowar,[1] who appeared to have just come off a journey. On asking what was the matter, he said, that he had just escaped from a party of the mutineers from Allahabad,[2] consisting of a wing of Infantry, two troops of Cavalry, and two guns; that they where marching on to Salone, and were then within five miles. This looked rather too close to be pleasant; so we took the man down to Capt. Barrow, where, after again interrogating him, we decided it was time to prepare for the reception of any mutineers who might come. Capt. Thompson turned out his Regiment, and, loading two old guns we had there with grape, he stood ready for anything that might occur. We

---

1. About sixty men of the third Oudh Irregular Cavalry had been sent from Lucknow to Salone to strengthen us, as it was the general opinion that the Irregular Cavalry would stand firm, after the Infantry had gone. How much we have all been deceived has been shown by the issue.
2. The first intimation we had of the outbreak at Allahabad was from one of our Thannadars, who reported that he had secured two or three of the prisoners from the Allahabad jail, who had escaped, and brought the news that the Regiment stationed there had mutinied and released all the prisoners, and that all the Europeans had taken refuge in the fort.

on our part turned out (what was then called) the new levies—about one hundred and fifty men enlisted in our Police, whom we had armed and were drilling. At the same time we sent out some trustworthy men in the direction the Allahabad mutineers were said to be coming, and also towards Sultanpore, from whence another body of mutineers were said to be marching on us. We waited in this state of readiness for about an hour, when our spies returned, and reported that the road was clear in both directions, and that there was no sign of any mutineers: so we turned in the Regiment, and, having set guards of the new levies all round Capt. Barrow's house and placed the lying Sowar in confinement, we went home. The truth was, the mutineers in our own station had thought that by causing an alarm of "they are coming" to be spread, they would make us take suddenly to flight, and so leave them in quiet possession of our treasure, consisting then of some 500,000 *rupees*. But when they found that their plan did not answer, they had recourse to another, *viz*. open mutiny.

It must be remembered that at this time the Regiments at Lucknow had mutinied; Fyzabad and Sultanpore were (as the expression then was) "gone," and Futteypore likewise; at Allahabad all the Europeans had retired into the Fort, the native Regiment (6th B. N. I.) having mutinied; that the whole country was up in arms, and Cawnpore in a state of siege. We were therefore quite surrounded by mutineers: all the *dawks* (except that direct to Lucknow, which we managed to keep open) were closed, and every road of escape seemed to be shut against us; but we never lost heart. We hoped, almost against hope, that we should be able still to weather the storm (and if we did, what an honour!), and we put our trust in Him, who had hitherto kept us in peace and quietness.

We all dined together at Capt. Barrow's that evening; and, with the exception of Capt. Thompson and Lieut. Chalmers, who slept in the lines with their men, we slept at Capt. Barrow's also—thinking that if anything did take place we ought to be together, and as near the only lady (Mrs. B.) as possible.

The night passed off quietly enough, but the next morning showed us we had not much longer to remain. The sepoys of the Regiment were all moving about, armed and accoutred, and were sending their luggage out of the place; and about six o'clock Thompson came and told us, he could do no more, for his men were in open mutiny. We had a long consultation, and determined that we had remained at our post as long as we could, and that we had nothing left but to provide for our own safety.

While we were consulting together, one of our most influential Talookdars, Hunnowant Sing, came in and informed us, that the game was up (which we knew before), and that we must go that day, or we might be sacrificed; that, if we could leave at about 4 p. m., he would meet us about a mile out of the station with some of his men, and conduct us to one of his forts, where for the present we should be safe. This we agreed to do; and he left us to make preparations.

I may here mention, that this man Hunnowant Sing, in accordance with the policy brought into play at the annexation, had been deprived of the greater part of his estate, which was in the King of Oudh's time very valuable, had consequently been reduced from a very wealthy and influential position to quite the contrary, and had even, under instructions from the authorities, been confined in our jail for not paying up part of his revenue. Notwithstanding all this, he had, I think, a personal friendship for Capt. Barrow, for he was a quick enough man, and saw that Barrow was acting up to orders, and much against his own judgment. It was in a great measure to this friendship that I attribute Hunnowant's conduct, though the old man may have had an eye on the future when he thus acted; for he all along believed that we should be back in Oudh some day. Had our annexation policy been different, I think we should have had many friends where we had enemies. We hoped to make friends of the new men we raised up, but found, to our cost, that in the time of need they were wanting. The truth was they were not strong enough to hold their own, much less to assist us; though I believe many, for their own sakes, would have done so if they could.

At about eleven o'clock, Thompson came and told us that his native officers had come to him, and promised faithfully that, if he would give the whole Regiment six months' pay out of the treasury, they would march with us, colours and all, to Allahabad. At first, we would not hear of such a thing, it seemed so like bribing our own servants to remain faithful: but when we considered the matter again—that the treasury was in the hands of the mutineers, who could help themselves without any asking, and that if, by giving six months' pay we could save the rest of the treasure and the Regiment, it would be worth doing so—we determined on trying it.

The Regiment had no sooner received the money than we found upon what a reed we had been leaning. The guard at the jail left, and all our prisoners escaped; the men became more sullen than ever; and (what was worse than all) the detachment of Harding's Cavalry now came and claimed six months' pay, the same as the infantry had received; and, after them, our police would doubtless have come. We had made a false move, and were suffering from it: but our position was such it was very difficult to know how to act. We determined to pay up all our establishments, and then quit. I had been down to the treasury for money two or three times that day, and, thinking that perhaps the guard over the Treasure might not like me to take any more, I took one of the native officers down with me to show the guard, that *it was by permission of those then commanding* that I was drawing the money. When I arrived at the treasury, the sentry called for the Jemadar on duty, who came and at once permitted me to open the cash chest; when he saw the other native officer with me, he asked why he had come, and, on being informed, turned to me with tears in his eyes, and asked if he had ever hesitated in permitting me to take money. I tried to explain it away, but did not succeed very well: the old fellow seemed really hurt—and yet he was a mutineer and a rebel at heart.

As soon as we paid our people, they immediately all forsook us; our police, who had sworn to stand by us, leaving us also, and among the first a man whom I had got promoted to be a Jemadar, and who, an hour before, had with tears in his eyes sworn to stick to me through thick and thin. At about 4 p. m. we prepared to start, Mrs. B. and two children in Carnegie's buggy, and the apothecary's wife and his family in another buggy: the Sergeant Major (who had been very ill) with his wife and family were to go in Barrow's bullock coach, and we men on horseback. Our party was seventeen in number, nine of whom were women and children. We started, *all* our servants having forsaken us, except Capt. Barrow's three Madrassies, with the clothes on our backs and our swords by our sides, not knowing how long we might have to live, as now, that we were obliged to go, every man's hand was against us. We had some twenty-four of our new levies, about the same number of new jail Burkundazes, and one Jemadar, one Havildar and five Sepoys of Capt. Thompson's Regiment with us—and this was all out of thousands, who a week before would have followed us cringing and bowing to the ground! We had to go right through the Regimental lines, which of course was a rather dangerous thing to do: but, as it could not be avoided, we put a bold face on it, and went straight through them. The men were standing armed and accoutred in groups, looking very sulky; the two guns were drawn up, so as to sweep the road we must go, and the men were standing with lighted port-fires in their hands. This was probably for show, and done with the idea of frightening us; but I do not think it made any of our hearts beat faster by one stroke.

About a mile out of cantonments we were met by our old friend Hunnowant Sing, with about 200 as funny looking a set of men, as could be well imagined; and, after a long ride of about fourteen miles, we arrived about 1 o'clock at night at Dharoopore, where our kind host gave us a hearty welcome and made us as comfortable as he could for the night. Thus ended the memorable 10th of June 1857, the 6th anniversary of my wedding day, to which auspicious event I attribute our having escaped so easily—but, joking apart, we had very much to be thankful for: we had *all* escaped with our lives from Salone, and I think, with one or two exceptions, we were the only body so fortunate. At Sultanpore, thirty-seven miles off, the Deputy Commissioner and his assistant had been killed, also the officer commanding and the 2nd in command of the Regular Cavalry corps (13th). At Fyzabad the Commissioner and nearly all the officers of the 22nd native Infantry, the officer commanding the artillery and the Adjutant of the 6th Oudh N. I. had been murdered. At Lucknow three had been killed.

Cawnpore was in a state of siege, the end of which is too well known. At Futtehpore opposite to us on the other side of the Ganges, the Judge, Mr. Tucker, had been killed. At Allahabad some eighteen or twenty had been killed, and the remaining Europeans had been shut up in the fort: but we had escaped, and were now in the hands of a man, who had given us his "Bhân," the most solemn oath a Hindu can take, to see us safe to Allahabad, or any other place, which the Europeans still held. He was, however, a native, on whose most solemn oath we could hardly depend, if Allahabad fell. The natives had all an idea that our rule was at an end; and although our host, who was clever enough, did not, I think, really believe as much himself, still he was evidently playing a double game, trying to keep friendly with the Rebels, and still to preserve us from harm—a difficult game to play, but one which he carried through very well: and though be has been, and is now, fighting against us, still I should be very glad to see him forgiven, and shake him by the hand again.

Next morning we heard that C. was at Kalikunker, another of our host's forts, on the banks of the Ganges, where he had taken refuge, after having been robbed of everything he had by the Thannadar and police at Manikpore. This Thannadar had been appointed by C. himself.

I forgot to mention that on the night of our arrival here, Hunnawant Sing's son had gone to Alladgunj, where one of our Tahsilees was, and had not only rescued the Tahsildar who was in danger, but had brought in with him all the money then at the Tahsilee, *viz.* Rs. 12,000, which he gave over to Capt. Barrow, and which he took with us into Allahabad, and delivered to us there before leaving us.

Immediately our host heard of C's position he sent him down money, told his servants to take care of him, and the next day started off himself to bring him to us. He left at about 4 p. m. on the 14th, and returned with C. and his cousin, who was with him on the night of the 15th. We, as I have mentioned, all left with nothing but the clothes on our backs. Mrs. B. had brought a small supply of wine and beer, some forks and spoons, and had a regular little kit in a cowry basket, which, however, never reached us—the coolie carrying it having bolted. The day after we got to the fort, the bullock coach which had been left behind was brought in by Capt. B's Afghan servant, and in it were some few things for Mrs. B. and her children.

It was good fun seeing us sitting down to our meals, our dinner consisting of fowls, lamb, curry and rice, *dal* and *chapattis*, placed in earthen *chatties*, or rather earthen saucers, and put on a *charpoy*, round which on the ground we all sat. I think we each had a spoon, but there was only one knife—so we had to use our fingers pretty well: but we got on famously. Old Hunnowant kept up our supplies; and, as far as we could be, we were very comfortable.

It was very hot in the day time, and what we all felt extremely was the want of employment, as we had come away without any books. We were badly off for clothes of course, but here again our old friend came to the rescue, got us cloth and *durzees*; and we soon turned out as regular natives.

About the fourth day of our being in the fort, a man, named Chând Khân, came up where we were, and commenced making enquiries about a horse that he said had been lost by Lieut. Grant's party from Sultanpore. After having made his inquiry, instead of going away he remained hovering about in a mysterious manner; at last he came to Capt. Barrow, and put a letter into his hand, which proved to be from Grant, who (with some twenty-nine, most of whom were women and children) had escaped from Sultanpore, and was then under the protection of an old man, named Ajeet Sing, who was not very powerful, though very willing to do all he could. It appeared that this party, from there being so many women and children, and their protector being not very powerful, were really in danger, and altogether in a sad plight; so after talking the matter over, we determined to trust our host, and see if he could and would do anything for them. He at once set to work, wrote to a relation of his own, whose *illaka* was in that direction, and also to Goolab Sing, and took their "Bhân" from them for the safety of the party. Grant eventually reached Allahabad with the whole of his party in safety, under the escort of his host alone.

About this time all our jail Burkundazes and sixteen of our new levies, who had followed us, asked permission to go to their homes: so we allowed them; we had now only eight of these men and seven of Capt. Thompson's with us. We lived in an upper story of the house, and used to walk on the roof, when not too hot, and, when up there, very often people came for the purpose of looking at us, as if we were wild beasts. This became so unpleasant that we were obliged to ask our host to put a stop to it, which he did at once by placing a couple of sentries at the staircase leading up: but before this was done, a man had been up, carrying in his waistband a very nice duelling pistol, evidently the property of some English Officer. On interrogating him, he told us that he was a Jemadar of Police under Capt. Thurburn, who had given him his pistol; that the Regt. at Fyzabad had mutinied and all the officers had escaped in boats, and that the civil officers with their families had taken refuge in Raja Maun Singh's fort, where they then were.

We immediately wrote to them, and, promising the Jemadar a present if he delivered the letter, persuaded him to start for that purpose: about four days afterwards he returned with a long story that they had left. This at the time we did not believe, for there was something in the man's manner not straightforward, and we imagined he had never gone. I now think that his story was so far true that he knew they had left Maun Singh's the first time he came to us, but had concealed it for some purpose; and, when the reward was offered him, he determined to absent himself for a few days, and then bring us the right tale, which he might have told us at first—namely, that this party had gone to Maun Singh's and, after remaining there three or four days, had been sent by him down the river in boats. Eventually after much suffering they arrived at Dinapore in safety.

We now became rather anxious about ourselves: we had been upwards of a week in the Fort, and could gain no information of what was going on at Allahabad. We heard reports of large forces of Europeans arriving daily, which kept us in good spirits; but we could not manage to get a letter conveyed there for us, and although our host continued his attentions, still we began to fancy he was throwing obstacles in our way on purpose. At last two men of our new levies came and said that they would try to get into Allahabad with a letter: so we promised them a large reward if they succeeded, and they started.

While they were absent, our friend Chând Khân again made his appearance, with a letter from the Collector of Allahabad, and one from Grant, who with his party had arrived there safely. So at last we found out what was going on, and that the road was quite safe. We then sent for our host's son, he himself having gone on some excuse or other to his other fort, told him the news we had heard, and insisted on leaving as soon as possible. He replied that he could do nothing without his father, but that he would send off a messenger immediately for him. This be did; and next evening the old gentleman made his appearance, and, after a good deal of talking, promised to collect a number of men to escort us, and to start on the third day from that time, as that was a lucky day. Well we did not like to push him too hard; so we consented.

Next day our two messengers, dressed as *fakeers*, returned with a letter from Allahabad; and they were again sent off to tell Court[1] when we were to start, so that he might have boats ready for us at the ferry, the bridge of boats having been destroyed. On the day decided on, we left the fort at about 5.30 p. m.—all the women and children in *doolies*, and we on horseback. We had a large escort of our host's followers, and, after a tiresome ride of about twenty miles, arrived at Dhunnâwâ, a small fortress belonging to Shudat Singh, a small landholder in our district.

We reached this at about 2 o'clock a. m. and had to lie down outside the fort under a tree, as the owner would not, or really could not, receive us inside. Next morning we went to look at the house, to see if we could not get some accommodation in it, but found it in such a state of dirt and ruin that we preferred to remain under a large banyan tree just inside the walls, under which Shudat Singh, pitched a small tent for Mrs. B. and the children; so that we got on pretty well on the whole. We were well supplied with eatables and milk by our host. Our old host, Hunnowant Singh, on being consulted as to our future movements, told us, that we must pass through the estate of a man (whose name I now forget) who was not favourably inclined towards the English, and that it would be necessary to take his "Bhâñ," and that he should have to go himself for that purpose, which would cause a delay of some hours, so that we would not be able to start before 12 at night.

There were two roads for us to go, one about twelve miles to the Pâpâmow *ghât*, and the other about twenty

<hr />

1. The Collector of Allahabad.

miles to the bridge of boats. We wished of course to go the shortest road; but Hunnowant was so decided about taking us the other route, that we were obliged to give in; and he left us to get the Bhàn from the man he had spoken about. He returned at 12 at night, but had now altered his mind about the road we were to take; so that we went the short road after all. As the old gentleman wanted something to eat after his long ride, we did not get off much before 2 o'clock in the morning, and just at daylight we came in sight of the river Ganges, where we met two men, with a note from Court, telling us not to go to the bridge of boats, as that road was not safe, but that he had boats and carriages ready for us at the Pâpâmow *ghât*: so on we went, rejoicing to get so near the end of our troubles.

We arrived at the river, put the horses and ourselves on board the different boats, and wished our kind host a hearty farewell telling him, that ere long we should be back at our old station, when we should not forget his devoted kindness. I must here mention that we could not persuade our old friend himself to cross the river with us, or to allow any of his followers to do so. They had an idea that whoever once got into Allahabad, did not get out again, except as a Christian.

When we offered him some pecuniary reward for all he had done for us, he decidedly refused to accept it; nor would he allow any of his men to take any, although we offered him Rs. 5,000 to divide amongst them. "No," he said, he wanted no reward then: he only wished us to remember him, when we again got into power; and as for his followers, they were his servants, and were paid for doing as he told them:—and so we parted. May he get his reward! More than one heart blesses him, for having saved our lives; for there is no doubt that, had he not come forward, we should have found great difficulty in getting to Allahabad, as every man's hand, even those of our own police, was turned against us, and we were a small party to fight our way through, with the women and children we had with us. But One, mightier than the mightiest rebel, was with us, and watched over us. He brought us in safety through our enemies. May we never forget His goodness in this, as in all things, and may it be the means of drawing us closer to Him.

We found Col. Neill of the 1st Madras Fusiliers, with about 200 men, in possession of the fort, the Seikhs having been turned out and encamped under the walls. Every house had been nearly ruined, and such a scene of destruction as met our eyes, I suppose never was seen, and I hope never will be again—all sorts of furniture and clothes lying about—all, or nearly all, perfectly useless, as the mutineers seem to have taken a delight in destroying everything that belonged to the Europeans: even the lining of the *punkas* was all torn out.

Daily arrivals of Europeans soon filled the cantonments with white faces; and on the 30th June a small force, consisting of 200 of the Madras Fusiliers, 200 of H.M. 84th, 250 Seikhs of the Ferozepore Regiment, 2 six-pounder guns, and 1 twelve-pounder howitzer, with some 60 Sowars of the 13th Irregulars and 3rd Oudh Irregular Cavalry, who were supposed to be staunch, started under the command of Bt. Major Renaud of the Madras Fusiliers towards Cawnpore, in the hope of being in time to relieve our gallant countrymen, who were besieged there by the rebels under the Nânâ.

On the 1st July, another party of the Fusiliers, about 100 strong, under Capt. Spurgin, left in a steamer to endeavour to make their way up by the river to co-operate with the land force.

On the 26th of June, Brigadier General Havelock, who had been put in command of a moveable column to be collected at Allahabad, arrived with his staff; and, finding the great want of Cavalry, obtained permission from the Government to raise a Regiment to be called the Allahabad Volunteer Cavalry. Capt. Barrow was put in command. He made Lt. Grant of the 3rd M. E, Regiment his adjutant, and gave Lt. Swanston the Quartermastership. We got about 18 men to join us, amongst whom were Ensigns Brander, 37th B. N.

I. Ramsay, Stuart and Hare, 17th B.N.I. Pearson, 27th N. I., Woodgate, 11th N. I. and Cornet Fergusson of the 8th B. L. C. All honour and praise to these boys, who were the first to offer their services to the Government they served. Many of them had never even joined their own corps, and none of them had been more than eighteen months in the service. We had also some eight young men, who had been engaged on the railways, but had of course been now thrown out of employ. Altogether we mustered, I think, eighteen, when we left Allahabad with General Havelock's force on the 7th of July 1857.

Nothing occurred till the 12th. The whole road was deserted, the villages empty and all in ruins, and every here and there bodies were seen hanging from the branches of trees. These had been executions carried out by Renaud's force. On the night of the 11th we made a forced march, and came up with Renaud's force at about 4 a. m. on the 12th. We then marched on some five miles to a place called Belinda, about four miles from Futtehpore, where we intended to encamp, and had commenced pitching our tents when we were ordered with the Irregular Cavalry to move on towards Futtehpore to reconnoitre, as the General had been informed that some of the mutineers had possession of it, and intended disputing the advance (as they thought) only of Renaud's force; so off we went, and were followed by a company of the Madras Fusiliers with their Enfield rifles.

We got within about a mile of Futtehpore, when we saw the enemy collected just outside. So we were told to halt, and Capt. Barrow and the Quarter-Master General rode on ahead to within about a quarter of a mile of where the enemy were. At first they were not perceived; but when they were, bugles sounded, drums beat, and out came a cloud of Cavalry after them; so they galloped back to where we were. We waited for the enemy, but they took good care not to come too close. As we were too few to fight, and had only come to see what was going on, we got the order threes about, and fortunate it was so, for we had not got half a mile off when down came the artillery and opened on us. This was my first experience in real warfare—the first time I had heard balls flying in earnest; and, I must say, I did not like it, though outwardly, I dare say, I looked brave enough, and called to our gallant volunteers to be steady, (as they were all young at it like myself). I then thought I should never get accustomed to the *whizz* of a bullet, or the sing of a cannon ball; but I have learned that art, and can now hear them all about me, and not even wink an eye.

We retired gracefully, the rebels trying to hit us, but not succeeding; the Cavalry in crowds (or clouds, I believe, is the proper word,) trying to get round us, and cut us off from our people: so we pulled up, and the rules commenced a little practise on them. They evidently thought they were well out of range, and so they were of old Brown Bess; but when they saw two or three of their saddles emptied at nine hundred yards, they turned and never came within range again: and ever since, as they have improved their acquaintance with the Enfield, they have increased their distance, till now they seldom come within 1200 or 1500 yards.

When the enemy's guns first opened on us, those "faithful gallant Irregulars," the black chivalry of India, tried to bolt, but were stopped by Barrow. I have now seen these men fighting both for and against us, and, on all occasions, I have seen them behave in the most cowardly way one could imagine. I always had an idea that the irregular Cavalry would do anything, but I now disbelieve it. No doubt they will gallop after men who have been beaten, and are running away like sheep; but in a charge to break the enemy I believe they are useless.

At last we got safe back to our camp, and General Havelock turned out the force to meet the enemy. We had altogether about 1,400 Europeans, and 550 natives, 8 six-pounder guns, with 2 twelve-pounder howitzers. These were in the centre, with Infantry on each side, and on the left flank the Volunteer, and on the right the Irregular, Cavalry: the enemy had between four and five thousand.

Our guns opened and so astonished the enemy, that they soon turned; and we then advanced, took twelve of their guns, among them 1 twenty-four pounder, and 1 twenty-four pound howitzer, and drove them through Futtehpore. Our fire was very good, and to a new hand like myself seemed splendid. General Havelock in his despatch said Capt. Maud's firing perfectly electrified the enemy. After driving the enemy through Futtehpore, we encamped on the other side, and the town was given up to *loot* and afterwards nearly destroyed. Thus ended my first battle.

On the 14th we marched about twelve miles; and on the 15th, at Aong, a small village about four miles on, we met the enemy again. Here they had entrenched themselves, and stood for some little time; but we soon drove them out, taking two guns. We had a few killed; and amongst the number of the wounded was Bt. Major Renaud, who was hit in the thigh: his leg was amputated, and he eventually died. After we drove them out of this, we advanced about four miles further, and again met the rebels at a bridge over a small river called Pundu. They had two large guns here (which we took) in position, but our gallant 1st M. F., with their rifles, advanced in skirmishing order, and regularly silenced their fire with the rifles. Here we encamped for the day.

We were now within fifteen miles of Cawnpore, and all anxious to go on and save our unfortunate fellow countrywomen there. We little knew what was then taking place! Next morning we advanced about eight miles, and then halted under a tope of trees, where we remained till the men had got their breakfasts; and then on we went about a mile, when we made a flank movement to the right, so as to come round the enemy, who had, we heard, a number of guns in position to keep us from advancing along the road. As we advanced to the right we came under fire of their guns, which, however, they did not seem able to move; so as each Regiment passed, they received a round shot or shrapnel among them: at last we all passed this, and got right round the enemy's position. They had managed by this time to turn their guns upon us, so we had a little game at long bowls, in which the rebels delight so much; but soon we got the order for the general advance.

It is impossible for anyone to give an account of what has happened to every Regiment in any engagement; but it is much more impossible to give a description of the battle of Cawnpore, opposed as we were, a small band of about 1,500, to as many thousands. Every Regiment had its hands full. The enemy had taken up several different positions, so that as fast as two guns were taken from them, we found two more open on us from another direction.

The first guns I saw taken, were two which were opposed to H. M.'s 78th Highlanders; and the splendid way in which this Regiment rushed up under a heavy fire of grape, and took these guns was the admiration of all. This rush was headed by Lieut. Moorsom of H. M.'s 52nd, who was in the Q. M. General's Department of the force. I do not mean to say that he led the Regiment, for it was led (as it always is) by its own officers; but the cool way in which Moorsom cantered up, waving his wide-awake, must have astonished the natives.

Two other guns were taken about the same time in another direction by the 64th. As all these guns were taken, they were spiked: for we could not take them on with us, till our work was done. The consequence was, that the rebels, who regularly swarmed all round us, retook two guns, and were unspiking them, when the Seikhs were sent to retake them; which they did in their usual gallant style.

It is impossible to mention everything that each Regiment did on that day; but all was well and gallantly done. The Volunteer Cavalry were too few to do much; so they were kept to support a company of the Madras Fusiliers, who were on the right of all skirmishing. While thus employed, the Deputy A. A. Genl. Capt. Beatson rode up, and asked Capt. Barrow "what he was doing?" adding, "There are the enemy." Of course there was nothing for it then but to go at them.

*There they were,* certainly, in thousands, Infantry and Cavalry; and *here were we,* eighteen in number. But as at Balaklava, the order was given, and Englishmen knew their duty, and charge they did, right into the thick of the rebels.

But what could eighteen sabres do among so many? What could be done, was done; and then the little band had to pull up, to find their loss to be one killed, one wounded, two horses shot dead, and two wounded. How we escaped so well, God knows. The bullets rained upon us: but He who had been with us all along was with us still. We pulled up, as we could not, so few of us, pursue too far from our Infantry. When they came up, each Regiment as it came cheered the little band; and our brave old General, riding to our front, said, "Gentlemen Volunteers! You have done well. I am proud to command you."

We all pulled up here, (on the Delhi road) thinking the day was ours, when we suddenly found guns opening upon us again in another direction. These had to be taken at the point of the bayonet; our own gun-bullocks being regularly knocked up with the long march and hard work of the day— and so it went on till dark, when we could see no longer.

We bivouacked as we stood. All our baggage, food, and everything of that sort, were five miles behind. We had nothing to eat, and a very little dirty water to drink; but we were all so tired, that we were glad to lie down as we were, and sleep with our horses' bridles in our hands. We took in this engagement twelve guns of sizes. I was roused up during the night by my *syce*, who had found me out, and, having a little flour with him, had mixed it with some water, making a sort of paste, which he could not cook for want of fire: this the poor fellow offered me, but I could not, hungry as I was, eat it.

Next morning at daybreak we were all on the alert to find where the enemy were, but none were to be seen. The rumbling of cart and gun-wheels had been heard by the pickets all night. The truth was our enemy had bolted, and left Cawnpore. About 7.30 p. m. a tremendous explosion took place, which turned out to be the magazine, which they had blown up. A small party under the Q. M. General was sent in to reconnoitre. They found the place deserted by the rebels; so, after getting up our baggage, we marched into Cawnpore, and encamped on the *maidan* in front of the Cavalry stables, and not far from the spot where poor Wheeler's force had made their stand.

How intently the thoughts of every one of us were bent on the pleasure of releasing our poor fellow-countrywomen, whom we knew to be in the hands of those wretches, can be more easily imagined than expressed—and how deep and bitter was the curse hissed through the lips of many a hero that day! Had those cowardly brutes heard the oaths of vengeance sworn, they would have turned white with fear: and, oh, when we came to *see* the place where our poor sisters and their little children had been barbarously murdered, the very blood in our hearts turned cold, and then again boiled up with thoughts of vengeance.

I have often thought whether we are right to think of revenge; for we are taught, *"Vengeance is mine, I will repay", sayeth the Lord*: and then I have eased my conscience by thinking that I was an instrument in His hands. If I am wrong, may God forgive me; but it is hard to think of what our unoffending women and children suffered, and not have feelings of revenge rise in one's heart. "Mercy, mercy," cries the *Sepoy,* when, seeing death certain, he throws away his musket, and pleads with clasped hands. *Cawnpore!* is hissed at him, as the sword goes through his vitals.

And is it a wonder? Who could look upon that little enclosed yard, reeking in blood as if 100 bullocks had been killed there—see the long tresses of some once fair lady's hair lying in handfuls—and above all the small mark of the little children's feet, printed with their mothers' blood on the floor—and then look down *that* well upon the naked bodies of our poor countrywomen, evidently only rendered lifeless the day before, and not feel that he would never forget it? No! never shall a Sepoy receive his life at my hands; and had I the power I would never forgive a mutineer. If it took fifty years, I would hang every Sepoy that was caught. I would make India feel that England would never forgive such insults and such barbarity, as have been heaped upon her daughters.

On the 18th, General Havelock made over forty Infantry men to Barrow for his Cavalry, and ordered us to take all the horses' saddles and arms of the Irregular Cavalry, who had behaved so badly, to fit our men out with; which we did, and next day we were sent, thus fitted out, to Bithoor with a small force to take the place. It was the headquarters of the villain Nânâ. We went there, and found it deserted. We took twenty guns, a number of camels, elephants, stores, &c. &c. and returned; and from that day, till we re-crossed the Ganges after our first advance on Lucknow, our men never had a day's rest, riding generally for we had picked up a few hunting saddles) in native saddles with native swords as arms, dressed in any clothes they had. They certainly were a funny looking set of Cavalry; but the way they did their duty was the admiration of the whole force.

Sixty Cavalry were about a proportionate number to the 900 Infantry; and, with these we used to go upon long reconnoitring expeditions of twenty miles and more, and the cowardly enemy were afraid to come near us. How easily they might have cut us off, we all felt; but God was with us, was fighting for us; and the cries of murdered women and children at Cawnpore were still fresh in His ears.

Besides the continual duties of reconnoitring and pickets, the Volunteer Cavalry were constantly called upon to furnish parties for escort duties of all sorts, and now and then to assist the Commissariat Department in procuring bullocks for slaughter. Whenever such a party was required, the order would come for a Sergeant or Corporal, and party from the Volunteer Cavalry immediately: so the party was mounted and off; and it used to afford us much amusement at first, before we were well known, to see the faces of the officers to whom we had to report ourselves on these occasions—how puzzled they used to appear, when they saw a gentlemanly looking man come up and report himself as Sergeant so and so, with party of Cavalry.

I remember one occasion especially, when Capt. Thompson (an officer of seventeen years' service, who had commanded the 1st Oudh Irregular Infantry), who was a Sergeant in the Volunteer Cavalry, had to report himself to some young sub-altern commanding the Infantry of the party going out—the perplexed look of the young fellow, feeling convinced that Thompson was a gentleman, and not knowing how to address him: but that wore off, and we were soon known.

On the 22nd we commenced to cross the Ganges in order to relieve Lucknow; the river was running strong, boats were few and we were in the middle of the rains: it consequently took some time crossing the force over, and those who went first were for some days encamped in a low swampy plain, where cholera soon broke out, and many a brave man laid his bones there.

At last all were crossed over, and on the 27th we advanced about five miles to the village of Mungawarrah, situated on the crest of a rise, and commanding the country for some distance in both directions. Here we remained on the 28th, on which day, we, the Volunteer Cavalry, were sent to reconnoitre as far as Busseerutgunge, where the enemy were said to have two guns in position, which we were to have taken—if we could—of course. Busseerutgunge is about fourteen miles from Mungawarrah, a small fortified place. On the road we passed through the large village of Onao, once the headquarters of the Poorwah District in Oudh, where we were received kindly by the villagers, who gave us milk to drink, and lights for our pipes, for which no doubt they suffered afterwards from the rebels.

When we got to Busseerutgunge we found the place strongly fortified and guns in position sweeping the road; and noticing the enemy's Cavalry galloping in swarms round our flanks to try and cut us off, we thought it wisest to retire, which we did, and arrived all right at our own camp.

Next morning, 29th, the force moved in advance. Before we had proceeded two miles, the Volunteer Cavalry as usual leading, we found the enemy in force ahead of us. They had taken possession of the village of Onao, and defended it, as they always do walled places, with determination. Here Lieut. Bogle of the 78th Highlanders received the Victoria Cross. The fire was very severe, and we were detained for some time before we could clear out the village; and only succeeded by burning it over our enemy, who at last left. Lieut. Seton, Madras Fusiliers, Aide-de-camp to General Havelock, was here wounded, and Lieut. Richardson of the same Regiment killed: here also Lieut. Brown, Adjutant of H. M.'s 84th was wounded, and while having his first wound dressed, received two others, from which I am happy to say he has since recovered.

We got through the village, at least the head of the column did, the Volunteer Cavalry this time behind—when *bang, bang* we heard milling again, and "Volunteer Cavalry to the front" was passed from mouth to mouth; and they were not long in getting there, you may be sure, notwithstanding one man had a hole shot through his helmet.

When we got up, we found our men deploying in a tope of trees, and the enemy in thousands deployed just ahead of us, and pouring in grape and canister, which came crashing through the trees most unpleasantly, I can assure you. Our guns soon opened, the enemy's gradually ceased; and then there was a general advance, with constant cries for Volunteer Cavalry to go and secure two guns here and two there, till we had taken twenty of their guns, and sent them flying as usual before us. We halted here for two or three hours in the hot sun, each man receiving his tot of rum, and a biscuit: when that was done, the Volunteer Cavalry again were sent on to see where the enemy were. We soon found them in position in Busseerutgunge about five miles off: so back we came, when the whole force advanced for another mile.

I was sent out with a few men on the right flank to see what was doing there, and we actually got right behind our foes, and saw in the distance, over their heads, (for they were lying down under mounds of earth, or wherever they could, to get protection) the glitter from the bayonets of our jolly Infantry—the stand-by after all of our glorious army: so we thought it advisable to go back and report, and, by the time we did so, we found the engagement had commenced, and a very pretty game at long bowls going on, which soon ended as usual in the general advance, the retreat of our cowardly foes, and the capture of the village with two guns. We went through the village, and encamped for the night; and next day for a change blew a couple of men away from guns, and hanged a third.

I think we must have had in this engagement some 25 or 30,000 opposed to our 1200, of whom about 900 were Europeans. When God is with us, who shall be against us?

We remained where we were on the 30th; and on the 31st were ordered to march: but what was our surprise when instead of turning to the right we turned to the left, which took us back again to where we had started from! We retired to Mungawarrah, and encamped again. During the week all our sick and wounded were sent over to Cawnpore; and on the 4th, the Volunteer Cavalry were sent on to reconnoitre again, and returned having found the rebels as before at Busseerutgunge. They were ordered to halt on the road; and the whole force at a moment's notice ordered to strike their tents and march away. When we were all formed upon the road, the General had a letter from the Governor General, thanking; us for what we had done. This he read out to us, and then said:

"Men, yesterday two guns and a small reinforcement joined us, and I told them to go from the right down to the left of the line, and in every man they would see a hero. You have heard what the Governor General and Commander-in-Chief have said. I shall have to write to His Excellency again tomorrow: and it depends upon you what I write. Tomorrow we meet the rebels again in the field."

The order was then given to advance; we marched through Onao and encamped for the night. Food and grog for next day were issued, and we lay down where we could, knowing that we were on the eve of another fight, and hoping that we were really *en route* to Lucknow. Long before daylight we were all formed up; and just as it broke we advanced.

When the Volunteer Cavalry, leading as usual, got close up to Busseerutgunge, the enemy, who were in thousands, opened out with blank ammunition from two small guns they had in position, and commenced yelling and making a tremendous noise—to frighten us, I suppose. We remained where we were, and the line was formed behind us. On the road were two very ominous looking things in the shape of two twenty-four pounders. Our guns opened; after the first two shots from the 24s, there was dead silence among the enemy. After a couple more, the lines advanced; but the rebels had as usual bolted.

While a working party was levelling a wall the enemy had built across the road, we amused ourselves by watching the effects of some shots from the 24s at a lot of the enemy on our left: among whom was a grandee on an elephant, which latter animal, finding the shot rather too close to be pleasant, bolted off as hard as he could, whether with or against his master's will I know not.

We advanced through the village; and here for the first time I saw bodies lying mangled by shot and shell. I shall never forget my feelings, sickness of heart and stomach too, so much so that I almost vomited: but how soon one gets used to these sights!—when we returned through the village, I could look at them without a shudder. We advanced through the village, had a little more play at long bowls, took two guns, and then pulled up to breakfast or *tiffin*, whichever you like. As we lay on the grass in the hot sun (well I remember it, as I had a most splitting headache) we were as usual talking over advance or no advance. All elated as we were, we would one and all have gladly pushed on: but our gallant old leader thought differently, and we were ordered to retrace our steps. How we all abused him, and what grumbling there was then! But now we have learned to appreciate his generalship, and to feel how judiciously he acted.

The Volunteer Cavalry in the retreat of course had again the post of honour, *viz.* behind all: so we had to keep up all the stragglers, and see that none of the baggage fell to the rear. When we got about two miles from Busseerutgunge, we came up with an elephant that had thrown its load, consisting of the men's kit, which is generally tied up in small long bundles—an elephant carrying some forty or fifty of them. We pulled up and assisted in reloading the beast, and then set off with it; but we had not gone half a mile, when the brute threw its load again. The way he managed it, was this—he stood still and lifted two legs on one side off the ground, then the two on the other side, and so on, giving himself the motion of a ship rolling on the sea, till at last the ropes, which tied the bundles on his back, became loose, and the whole thing came to the ground. Well, this was too much of a good thing: we saw if we went on loading in this way, we should never get on; so we each seized a bundle, and putting it in front of us, rode on, leaving a small party to bring the elephant on: and so we arrived—a sort of land transport corps—at our old encampment of Mangawarrah, where we found our pots steaming with grub. Thus ended our second advance and retreat.

How these retrograde movements affected me, I cannot, I am afraid, clearly explain. I always felt a sinking at heart, an utter despondency, not at all pleasant, and at the same time a mixture of anger and rage, at being obliged to turn my back on such cowards as we had to deal with. I know when we were obliged to leave Salone, I could not have spoken to have saved my life. It was not fear. I, never during those times had any other feeling than that we should all get safe out of it; and still I felt so enraged and disgusted at being obliged to fly from our post, that I could really have cried.

On the 9th, a mysterious order came round to send all sick and wounded men over to Cawnpore, and also all spare baggage, tents and horses; so all was sent, and as it was generally supposed that we were all to re-cross the Ganges next day, I was ordered to go and take charge of the horses and baggage, and prepare for the reception of the Regiment. On the morning of the 10th, I went and remained there till the evening of the 11th, expecting the force; when I suddenly heard that it had again advanced towards Busseerutgunge. It was too late for me to follow them very well, and I could not find out what was intended.

The officer commanding Cawnpore, General Neill. was perfectly in the dark, and advised me to remain where I was. I felt very much inclined to go, for although I thought it hardly possible, still I imagined they might be going on to Lucknow, and I would not have missed that for anything; but it was fortunate I did not go, for if I had I should have had a long ride of twenty miles to catch them up, perhaps when the engagement was over, and then to ride back all the way with them again.

The third advance on Busseerutgunge was much the same as the 2nd, and the fight the same as usual, except that the enemy had thrown up a small field-work about two miles on the river-side of Busseerutgunge, from which they poured into us a heavy fire of grape and canister. The Volunteer Cavalry appear to have had the full benefit of this; though as usual no one was hit, except Young Fergusson, scratched by a piece of a shell. So hot was this fire, and so well directed did it appear to the rest of the force, that, when the affair was over, several men rode up to us, to see who had been knocked over, or rather who had escaped. In this engagement we had 600 Europeans and some 200 Seikhs—no large force to do what they did, *viz*. lick some 10 or 15,000, and take two guns.

Our force returned after the fight to Mungawarrah; and then next day with the assistance of the steamer the whole of them crossed to the Cawnpore side of the river, and were housed in the few houses that remained unburned.

Thus ended our first advance across the Ganges to the relief of our fellow countrymen in Lucknow. How sick at heart we all felt I leave you to imagine, as we knew reinforcements could not reach us under a month, if so soon; and we were under the impression that the garrison at Lucknow were then on half rations, and could not hold out so long. But what could we do? We left Allahabad 1500 strong, and had received perhaps 400 men more since we left: and we were now reduced to 600 European fighting-men of all arms, fit for duty, or rather who could be spared for duty across the river. As Cawnpore had to be held, we felt it was hopeless to attempt it, in face of the countless hordes we had to meet. Although we were unable to proceed to Lucknow, there is no doubt that we relieved the little garrison very considerably, by drawing a great part of the besieging force away from Lucknow to meet us in the field; and, even when we re-crossed the Ganges to Cawnpore, they were obliged to keep a considerable force to watch us: so that, as we afterwards heard when we got to Lucknow, we had actually relieved them in a great measure: and, although it must have been very heart-sickening for them to hear of our retreat, still they knew that friends were near them, and that we should advance again directly we were in a position to do so.

On the 15th August, in the evening, we received an order to be ready to march at four next morning: so we were all immediately on the *qui-vive;* and at the time appointed we took our post where ordered, and found the whole force ready to march, consisting of about 1400 men and fourteen guns, two of which were 24s—a larger battery than we had ever had in the field. We soon found our destination was Bithoor, where the rebels had again taken up a position; and, as it was rather too close to Cawnpore, our gallant old leader determined to drive them out.

In this he certainly appeared to know the rebel well. Never let him rest. If you have any force to move with, follow him up; otherwise he immediately fancies you are afraid, and either attacks you in countless numbers, or sets to work with labour to any amount at his disposal, and strengthens himself in some position. He is like a jackal: if you leave him alone, he goes sneaking about, doing all the damage he can: but just gallop after him, making as much noise as you can, and you soon run him down.

It was a beautiful day: the country all round was looking nice and green, and it was pleasantly cool with a fresh breeze blowing. As we rode along the hard well made and well known road, we discussed the probability of the rebels making a stand at a bridge about half way, which from its position offered every facility for a good defence: but on, on, we went, our advanced guard and flankers still going quietly on, till we sighted the bridge, came up to it, and passed over it. No! No enemy: they had neglected, as they often did, one of their best chances: but they have done this so often, that one cannot help feeling that our God has blinded their understanding.

When we arrived within about a mile of Bithoor, our advanced men gave signs of the enemy at hand, and soon we saw their Cavalry arriving in hundreds on our left flank. When they had pulled up well out of rifle-shot, and had collected together a little, *bang, bang* went a couple of doses of shrapnel into them, and then it was 'the devil take the hindermost.' Just then a number of them came straight out of Bithoor down the road, as if they were going to indulge in a charge: but seeing the blue *topees* of the dreaded rifles, they too turned tail and bolted.

Our line was formed, and on we went. Tytler and Moorsoom, H. M's 52nd, rode on in advance to try and find out where the guns were; which they soon enough did, as the rebels opened on them with round shot. This being all they wanted, they returned, and the enemy found out that sniping at single horsemen with nine-pounders is not so easy as it looks. Steadily our line advanced, till we got well within range, when our guns opened, and after a short time we saw the Highlanders tumbling in through the embrasures of a little work the rebels had raised to their left. Two guns were taken. On the extreme of our right, the gallant blue bonnets (1st Madras Fusiliers) got right amongst the enemy with their bayonets, and bayoneted a number of them—the first time we had that pleasure: but they could not follow up their advantage. They were exhausted with the twelve miles' march, and the fight after it. Had the Volunteer Cavalry been with them, they might have done something; but they were on the extreme left, watching the Cavalry. The enemy here gave us more trouble than they had ever done before. They had a very strong position, and the fields being at this season high with sugar-cane and grain of different sorts, they found good shelter there, and made use of it accordingly; for a native certainly does know how to fight behind cover. But this as usual ended in our driving the enemy out of their position, and taking their guns. We then advanced through the village, and halted in different topes on the other side.

The Volunteer Cavalry, having thrown out videttes, lay down to await the arrival of their mess-kit; which had left Cawnpore, through some blunder, three or four hours after the force. Suddenly *bang* went the vidette's piece. Two or three of us were soon in our saddles; and there, to our surprise, we saw a native officer and a Havildar of Cavalry in full uniform, looking at us within a hundred yards of us! They looked just as much astonished as we did, but soon got over it, when they saw the rush made at them: but being on better and fresher horses than we were, they soon distanced us, and so, giving them a parting shot, we returned. What they had come up so close for I know not, unless they really did not know we were there, as we were quite hidden in the tope; or perhaps it may have been the Quartermaster

General of the rebel army come to reconnoitre our position: however, we never saw anything more of him.

We waited, and waited patiently, or perhaps not very patiently, for our mess servants to come up, to get some of our rations cooked; but none came: so we had to do the best we could on biscuit and steaks fried on the embers, and our tots of rum. Hunger is the best sauce, says an old adage; and we certainly did justice to the victuals. A twelve-mile march, with a fight afterwards, does not decrease one's appetite.

We remained at Bithoor that night, and returned next morning to Cawnpore. About two miles out of Bithoor, the non-appearance of our mess-kit was fully accounted for, by the remains of broken boxes, plates, &c. &c, which we recognized, and also the dead bodies of two or three of our mess servants. Poor fellows, they had started late, and had been cut off by the enemy's Cavalry. We arrived in Cawnpore late in the afternoon, and took up our quarters in the houses again, where we remained two or three days; and then were ordered to encamp on the plain in front of Wheeler's entrenchment.

For the first day or two all went on well enough; but then it came on to rain, and we soon found ourselves in a regular swamp. Nothing would keep the water out of our tents. It seemed to soak up from the ground: and the only thing we could do was to put all our things on the chairs, or tables, and ourselves lie on our beds. This state of things could not last long: cholera broke out, and the men, weakened by exposure and hard work, gave in one by one and died. We were then ordered to leave our tents standing, and take possession of some sheds there, which fortunately sufficed for the whole force. But it was too late. Cholera had got among us; and certainly and quickly it did its work. We, the Volunteer Cavalry, lost ten—six of whom died in twenty-four hours; many more had slight attacks and recovered. Those whom death had marked as his own, were taken; and then gradually the dire disease left us.

We then set up foot-games, and races of different sorts to

keep up the men's sprits, and turn their thoughts from the late melancholy events. We of the Volunteer Cavalry set to work to clothe ourselves and the men in something like uniform, and also to get them proper saddles and arms; and by the time General Outram arrived with reinforcements, on the 17th September, (I think it was,) we did look a little respectable, and could move about somewhat in order, and, when we charged, looked rather formidable to the rebels.

On the 17th September, General Outram arrived with the 90th and 5th, some heavy artillery, and some sixty (supposed to be staunch) Cavalry (Native) of the 12th Irregulars under Lieut. Johnson of the Bombay Army. On the 19th, we crossed the river over the bridge of boats, which had been built, under great difficulties, by Captain Crommelin, Bengal Engineers; and, driving the advanced guard of the enemy before us, we encamped behind a ridge of sand, which runs along the banks of the river about half a mile off it. On the 20th, the Volunteer Cavalry were sent to reconnoitre: and that evening the order of march was issued for next day.

At daybreak on the 21st, the whole force was in readiness, and formed up: after advancing about a mile, we deployed in order of battle, and marched on to the enemy's position. The balls began to fly about as usual; but our. line steadily advanced. H. M's 5th, on the left, advancing in skirmishing order, soon drove the enemy right back. On we pressed, when down came an aide-de-camp with "Volunteer Cavalry will advance". Off we went, and soon came up with General Outram, who, riding stick in hand, headed us. Round we went to the right and took the rebels in rear, and then commenced the cutting up in good earnest. The pouring rain soon drenched us; but as it also did the same to the muskets and matchlocks of the enemy, rendering them useless, we were rather thankful for it. Down, down went the wretches. "Cawnpore, my lads, remember Cawnpore," was the battle-cry: and woe to the black skin that came under our swords.

At least 250 must have been cut up. Our gallant leader,

General Outram, not deigning to draw his sword, kept hitting the enemy as he came up to them with his stick, leaving it to those behind him to kill—and you may be sure they spared no-one. Two of the young officers, who had been doing duty with the 6th Native Infantry at Allahabad, and had escaped the massacre, recognized the drill Naik of that Regiment. One of them called him by name. He immediately threw down his musket, turned round with clasped hands, and crying for mercy, said, "Yes, sir!" The only reply he got was two swords through him.

Our Sergeant-Major Mahony, of the 1st Madras Fusiliers, got badly wounded in taking the Regimental colours of the 1st Bengal Native Infantry from the hands of two men who were defending it. For this he was named for the Victoria Cross; but I am sorry to say he has not lived to receive it: he died of cholera in October at Alum Bagh.

We took the whole of the camp of one Regiment, the 1st Bengal Native Infantry, all their drums and pots, &c; but, being unable to carry them off, we destroyed as much as we could, and then, dashing on again, came up with the enemy in full retreat. We succeeded in taking two large guns, and numbers of camels and carts. There were several elephants; but we could not succeed in getting any along with us, the drivers having either bolted or been shot down for refusing to bring the beasts on. As we were riding along, we came up with a man walking quietly along the road, covered with a blanket. One of the officers was going to kill him, when General Outram said, "Oh, do not; he is only a villager:" so the officer pulled the blanket off the man, and exposed a full blown sepoy, musket belts, and all, of the Oudh police. You may be sure he did not escape to tell the tale.

As I said, we got two guns, limbers and all, and having yoked bullocks to them, off we started back to our force, where you may be sure we were hailed with delight. We met them at Onao, and having halted there for half an hour, got our tots, and some roasted Indian corn, and off we went again, feeling as jolly as possible. We advanced on to, and right through, our *ultima Thule* of the former advance, Busseerutgunge, and encamped in and about it for the night. Next morning we marched again, having to pass through the dreaded Nawab-ganj, which on the former occasion had always been held up to us as something very dreadful. However this time we passed through it quite safely—not a soul being seen in the village.

On, on we went towards Bunnee, wondering whether we should find the bridge broken and the enemy there. At last the bridge came in sight, and on either side what looked very like embrasures; but no guns belched forth on us. On we went, crossed the bridge, entered the village, passed through the village, no-one! Our advanced men suddenly made signs of enemy; so up we galloped, and saw a number of Sepoys bolting out of a house. They were too quick for us, and we only killed a few of them: but we succeeded in taking all their kits, among which I found the leave chit of a Sepoy of the 22nd Bengal Native Infantry. Two Commissions of Bombay Native officers were also found there. What a day this was—pouring with rain in torrents, so that often we could not see 50 yards ahead of us. Most fortunately a kind friend at Calcutta had sent me a waterproof coat, which kept me dry—no small thing on these occasions, as you are often unable to get a change, and have, as we had this time, to sleep in the clothes we had on. Such a night too—no tents and no cover of any sort, the rain pouring in torrents. You may fancy how jolly we were.

You, who are comfortable in your homes, and read of the gallant deeds of the army little know what the poor soldier has to go through. To him, we officers owe all the honours we get—but how little this is thought of when, at a well spread board, healths are proposed and speeches made, and General This and Captain That are praised to the sky for gallant deeds: yet it is the poor Private, through whom all this has been done. We forget our Privates too much on these occasions; and, with some few, but glorious exceptions, are too prone to take all the credit, as if we had done it all ourselves.

At dark that evening we fired a salute of 21 guns from the 24-pounders to give notice to our friends in Lucknow that we were coming, and during the night several fancied they heard a return salute: but this turned out to be a mistake, as the garrison in Lucknow had not heard our guns. Well do I remember that evening, when, looking in the direction of Lucknow, we heard the fire of guns every now and then. How anxiously we talked over the meeting with well known faces, the joy we should be received with, and the certainty that there were some still left, as proved by the firing we heard. It was indeed a time of anxious pleasure, after so many trials to be at last within fourteen miles of our gallant fellow country-men—a most pleasurable feeling, mixed though it was with a tinge of grief, knowing as we did that many must have been cut off during the time they had been shut up.

Next morning the 23rd, we had breakfast in the open air (the rain having cleared off), and marched about 9 o'clock. When we had got about five miles I was sent back with half the Europeans and half the Native Cavalry to protect the bag-gage, as the enemy's Sowars were seen hovering about our flanks. This was rather unfortunate for me; for a soldier always wishes to be to the front. However, back I went, and pulled up under a tope of trees about half way down the line of baggage, which extended, I should think, two miles along the road; and, having thrown out my videttes, we dismounted to smoke.

We had not been long seated, when up came a couple of men with baskets of cakes of all sorts, fresh from Cawnpore. I at once seized on them all, and gave them to the men, as I think a soldier on service ought to eat whenever he can, for he never knows when he may be able to get his next meal. About the same time up came a man with what the soldiers call *pop* (ginger beer), which we likewise bought; so we had a very fine *tiffin*. When the last of the baggage had passed us, we mounted and rode along, the line till we got about half way to the front, and then we pulled up again; and so on till we arrived on our ground.

All this time our forces had not been idle. A battle had been fought, which, as I was not there, I can't describe, but which ended as all the others have done, in our taking several guns and licking the rebels out of the field. The fight lasted till dark, and the firing appeared to us behind very heavy.

When our services could be spared from the baggage, we rode on to the front; and the first man we met gave us the glad tidings of the fall of Delhi, or of that part of it which so commanded the rest of the city, that no doubt remained as to the speedy completion of that business. Our usual luck attended us. No one was hurt, though several had narrow escapes; one man got a graze on the head, another on the leg, from grape. We got up just at dark: the rain had commenced again to pour in torrents, and the country, which was very flat, soon bore the appearance of a wide swamp. Where-ever we turned, the water was up to the ankles. How to pitch tents and make the men comfortable was the difficulty. First of all I had to find the tents, which were carried on elephants: but, in a pitch dark night, among about 150 elephants, it was no easy matter to find one's own, especially as every one was howling and screaming as loud as he could. Perseverance at last succeeded; and I found the beasts, and at length got our men and ourselves under cover, though the ground inside the tents was not particularly dry.

But that was not the worst part of it. We could get nothing to eat, and no fires could possibly be lighted: so we had to content ourselves with dry biscuit and the never-failing tot of rum. However, we tumbled to sleep, hoping that tomorrow would see our toils at an end and our brethren in Lucknow relieved from their troubles.

Morning broke—a fine day: the camp was regularly pitched, and we found we were not going on that day: so we set to work to get our kits dried, which were all pretty well soaking. Suddenly about 11 o'clock we heard cries of, "The Cavalry are wanted immediately to the rear. The enemy are attacking the baggage."

We were not long in getting into our saddles, and having been joined by the staunch 12th Irregulars, off we went; but we were too late. The enemy's Cavalry had come down among the baggage, and having at first been mistaken for our own Native Cavalry, had got well amongst our men before the alarm was given. They succeeded in killing some seven or eight of our men and one officer; but they left 17 of their number dead on the road, and then had to fly. While they were riding down the line of baggage, they came upon some 19 prisoners who had been taken, who called out to be released: the Sowars passed the word down to some Infantry, who were supporting them, and they advanced and succeeded in releasing them. So much for taking prisoners, and so much for having staunch Native Cavalry with us, who are constantly getting us into trouble one way or another. I can safely say I have never seen them do a single thing yet for our good: they always appear to me to be looking out for the first opportunity to bolt. Well, we got up to the scene of action: a company of rifles was moved forward and two of Olphert's horse guns, with which we advanced; and after giving the enemy some few rounds, which soon sent them, green standard and all, to the right about, we returned and had a quiet day of it.

The morning of the 25th September, 1857, at last arrived. Ever memorable will that day be, for although no great despatch was written about it, the results of that day's fighting, though at so great a cost, may well be looked back to with pride, not only by those engaged, but by the whole of the British Army: for a handful of Europeans forced their way through a densely populated city, every house of which was loop-holed, and filled with an enemy thirsting for their blood. Had there not been a great end to gain, this deed might have been put down as one of the most rash ever undertaken by a General: but knowing as our Generals did the imminent danger our fellow-countrymen and women were in, it was a deed of which we may well all be proud.

Early in the morning orders were given to send the whole of the sick and wounded, and all baggage and camp-followers, into the Alum Bagh. This Alum Bagh was a large garden surrounded by a high wall; in the middle of the garden stood a large house, and the entrance to the garden was through a large archway. The force was told to take nothing with them but their rations in their haversacks, and the commissariat to take two day's rations. We were all soon formed up; and, about 10 o'clock, the first Brigade, headed by General Outram, advanced.

The firing from the enemy commenced at once, and for some time it was kept up with much spirit. They had guns so placed that they regularly raked our force while advancing: but, notwithstanding this heavy fire, our men steadily pushed on, and gradually the enemy's fire slackened and receded. The second Brigade also advanced on the left; and, as usual, our brave troops carried everything before them. We were kept behind today in the rear guard—the first time we were not in the advance. While standing under some trees waiting for the order to advance, one of the enemy's round shot came crashing in amongst us, and struck the bough of a tree just over the head of one of our men, who was lighting his pipe. The man never moved; he did not even cease lighting his pipe, but turned his head up to see where the ball had struck the tree—it was one of the coolest things I have seen.

At last the order was given, "threes right," "advance by sections of threes," "walk, march:" and off we went. Little did any of us think what we had to go through;—we were all pretty new to street-fighting. We went on slowly, and, as we advanced, many a poor fellow was taken back past us in a *dooly*, and here and there we passed the bodies of our own soldiers, as well as of the enemy, telling too plainly what the fighting had been. We advanced without any interruption till we arrived at the Char Bagh, a very large garden surrounded by a high loop-holed wall, just on the outskirts of the city. As we rode along, our heads and shoulders appeared just over the wall, giving a very good mark for the enemy, who were there waiting for us. They opened upon us; and, I am sorry to say, one of our young Volunteers, by name Erskine, was shot in the side. He was one of three young fellows, who came all the way from Calcutta to join us. Poor boy, well did he do his duty! He died three or four days before we got out of Lucknow. He leaves a widowed mother in Calcutta to grieve for him. I hope the Government will do something to show that it appreciates the services of her gallant boy, who gave his life for them in their time of greatest need.

We were ordered to dismount and walk, and thus were completely covered from the fire of the enemy. As we got up to the bridge over the canal, we came across more and more dead and wounded. Here was the place where the Madras Fusiliers so gallantly charged and took the enemy's guns placed in position at the head of the bridge; and in this charge it was we lost so many of our officers and men. When we came up, we found a house just across the bridge occupied by the gallant 78th Highlanders. The remainder of the force had turned down to the right, and proceeded along the banks of the canal, so as to avoid going right through the city. The baggage (what little there was,) and *doolies* bearing their loads of wounded men, were moving on as fast as possible: but the road was bad, and some of the ammunition carts had stuck; so we were told to advance and go past them; which we did till we came to some brick kilns, where we found young Havelock, Deputy Adjutant General, with a few rifle-men standing on the top of a high mound of broken bricks and rubbish. Here we were ordered to halt and dismount till the whole of the wounded and baggage had passed us.

The enemy, seeing a number of us standing on this mound, commenced to fire on us with their rifles, and succeeded in wounding one of the men. At first we thought it must be our own men firing on us by mistake, as the *whiz* of the bullets sounded very like that of the Enfield: but we soon found out our mistake. The enemy were round us like a swarm of bees. Gradually all the carts and *doolies* passed us, and there remained only one cart behind. It was loaded with round shot, and had stuck in the road, so that it was impossible to move it. Every exertion was made, but without avail, and we were losing men so fast from the fire of the enemy, who seemed to concentrate their fire on this unfortunate cart, that we were ordered to leave it. During all this time the Highlanders had not been idle. Surrounded as they were by thousands of the enemy, they had to do their best to keep down their fire till the whole of the baggage had passed.

The rebels, finding they could not dislodge them, sent out fresh troops and two guns to try and turn them out. Our gallant Highlanders charged these guns through a withering fire, and succeeded in spiking them: but in doing this they had three officers and thirty men placed *hors de combat*. All the baggage having passed on, they were ordered to follow. They passed us, while, with a Company of the 90th, we were doing our best to keep the rebels back from the kilns. At this time a troop of ours was ordered back, (why, no one can tell: as Cavalry in a narrow road with the enemy lining the hedges is not of much use). But back we went, and there we lost two men shot dead and Lieutenant Lynch wounded severely.

I was standing looking down the road by one of the kilns, when *bang* went a musket out of a house on my right, and *whiz* came a bullet right across my throat, and killed a man standing on my left. I had a narrow escape—as it was, the skin of my throat was only slightly cut. All having passed, we were now ordered to move on. We had no sooner turned our backs on the enemy, than they swarmed round us like ants: every house and hedge belched forth its deadly fire.

On, on we went, passing dead bodies of horses and men, and the guns, which had been taken, spiked and left behind. At last we got into the broad street leading up to the Tara Kotee (Observatory) where the Deputy Commissioner's *Kacheri* used to be held. As we went along, no one knowing whether we were taking the right road or not (we had *not,* as it turned out, though it led us to the advance part of our force), we were everywhere met on all sides by such a fire as I hope I may never see again. How many men were knocked over I cannot say: but I know that nearly every one of our horses carried two men that day: for as a man was wounded he was immediately put up behind one of us. Many of these poor fellows were again hit and knocked off the horses.

On, on we went, the Infantry officers gallantly leading their men, rushing first at one house and then at another, and oh! how many a poor fellow was killed—hit in the back. The 78th, who, when they had passed us at the brick kilns had pulled up for us again, lost on this day, I believe, 120 or 130 men. At last we got, to the corner of the Tara Kotee compound, just opposite a large gateway leading into the Kaisarbagh or Chief Palace of the Royal family of Oudh; and here we had to pass so close to the houses, that the enemy, who were in hundreds on the tops, actually flung stones down on our heads and spat on us, as we passed. One of our young fellows was knocked down and badly hurt by a stone thus thrown at him. Just as we arrived at this corner, we were delighted to see the blue bonnets of the 1st Madras Fusiliers, several of whom, on seeing us coming, had rushed out. to try and keep down the fire of the enemy in the houses; and we saw our own Sikhs coming along a road to our right.

It turned out that, instead of following the main body, we had turned up the broad street to the left past the Tara Kotee; instead of going on as they did towards the river and passing the Tara Kotee to the right.

When we got up to where our men were, we found them Infantry, Artillery, Cavalry, *doolies*, and camels—all huddled together in a small square space, just outside the wall of the Ferad Bux Palace, close down by the river Goomtee: and there we remained for an hour and a half, the enemy every now and then firing round shot at us from one of the guns we had spiked and left behind us, and from another they had on the opposite side of the river. Fortunately they fired too high; and so the balls went over our heads and probably in among their own people.

At last the order was given for the advance—the 78th in front this time, and we in the rear. It was now night, and as we passed through the streets, we found them quite deserted: but the fighting had been severe. It was here that General Neill was killed. We got into the garden of the Tara Kotee, where we were obliged to halt, as the guns were all pulled up by the ditches, which had been cut across the streets—at last, about 2 o'clock, we got into the entrenchment, and so ended this memorable 25th September, 1857. When we came to count our numbers, we found we had 75 men fit for duty out of 110.

Next day we had to get our heavy guns in, which had been left at Martin's house, with the 90th to guard them: and, in getting them in, we suffered very heavy loss from the enemy, who at first had retired, but had returned in great numbers. Major Cooper and Lieutenant Crump here met their death: and here it was where so many acts of gallantry were displayed by our soldiers. One man, Ryan, of the 1st Madras Fusiliers, refused to leave the wounded, who were in a house surrounded by the enemy; and kept up, with some two or three other men, such a fire that the enemy could not effect their purpose of getting into the house to murder the wounded. For this Ryan is to get the Victoria Cross. Here also other men in equally small numbers defended themselves till burned out by the enemy: and here one of the 5th Fusiliers was by mistake left asleep, when the rest of the men were withdrawn. When he awoke in broad daylight, he found himself alone and surrounded by the enemy—but, nothing daunted, he cried out, "Come on, my lads; here are the *saipoys!*" and, rushing out, cut his way right through them. We lost on this day thirty-one officers and 541 men, out of 2,500 of all ranks; which will give an idea of what the fighting must have been.

We were now within the Bailly Guard, and there was no use in mincing matters—we were in for it. As Cavalry, we were of course useless: but our horses had to be fed, and the Commissariat Department were unable to give them any grain: so all we could do was to get grass; and this, surrounded as we were by the rebels, was no easy matter. Our grass-cutters had to go out for it during the night, and, poor fellows, many of them never returned. Every day, I had men brought to me either shot dead, or wounded, in endeavouring to get grass for our horses; and my heart smote me whenever I had to order them out, as I knew it was to almost certain death. Why they did not desert us I cannot imagine—as inside with us they had barely sufficient to keep them alive, with the chance of being killed or wounded every night. Our horses of course gradually fell off: several died of starvation; numbers were shot by order; and a great many were killed by the enemy's shot and shell, which used to come in pretty thick now and then—so that, when we did get out of Lucknow, out of a hundred horses we took in, we had about fifty-two to take out with us—and these so miserably thin that few of them could be ridden.

On the evening of the third day after we got into the Bailly Guard, the Volunteer Cavalry got orders to hold themselves in readiness to move during the night: and about 10 o'clock, some fifty of the Volunteer Cavalry (all we could muster), with all the native Cavalry, started under Captain Barrow, with Lieutenant Harding to show the way, with the intention, I believe, of endeavouring to cut our way through the enemy to Alum Bagh. Had we succeeded in getting out, we should have been of great use to the little garrison there, and have relieved the Lucknow Commissariat of so many mouths requiring to be filled. We started. How many of us were to get through had to be proved, though we all felt it would not be many.

It was a bright moonlight night: the enemy consequently could see our every movement. We were ordered to keep along the bank of the river for some way; but before we had gone far we were met by such a heavy fire from the other side, and right in front, that our leaders deemed it prudent to pull up. The whole camp of the enemy was on the alert. Bugles blew, drums beat, and sepoys howled. We had two horses wounded, and two men hit, though not much hurt.

One man was saved by having two biscuits in his pocket, which turned the ball. We returned—and how thankful we were, I leave to the imagination: for we all felt how desperate was the undertaking.

As we were of no use as Cavalry inside the entrenchments, we had a post assigned to us, known as Innes' post, close to the Church—one of the most exposed posts of the works. The enemy were constantly peppering into it with round shot and shell, and no one dared show his face anywhere, but *whiz* came a bullet past it. We had several men shot there—a number of them hit in the hand. One of our Volunteer Officers, Lieutenant Hearsey, was very fond of going potting at the enemy; and always, after firing, he used to look to see the effect of his shot. He had often been warned that while he was looking at one enemy, there were three or four looking at him: but he never would take the advice given him, till one day, while peering about to see what damage he had done, *whiz* came a bullet, and wounded him in two places in the arm. Poor fellow, it was fortunately only a flesh-wound: but instead of getting any pity, everyone burst out laughing. It was a great shame; but he came in looking the picture of misery, and holding up his arm in such a funny way, we could not help it. He has gone down to Calcutta and, I am glad to say, is doing very well.

One day while we were sitting at breakfast at Innes' post, *bang* came a 24-pound shot right through the roof, and very nearly fell on one of the men, who was lying down, covering us with dust at the same time. We jumped up, and found out that it was one of our own 24-pounders, which we had been firing at some building over our house; but, through the bad practice of the officer firing, it had hit us by mistake; so we sent him up the ball with our compliments, and a request to fire a little higher next time.

The enemy were all along the south and west sides of the entrenchments, within (in some places) fifty yards of us; and their constant practice was to make false attacks almost every

206

night. These attacks used to commence with a tremendous fire of musketry, followed by heavy cannonading and loud shouting. At first we imagined that they were really coming on: but we very soon found out what it was, and hardly deigned to notice them. Not a shot used to be fired by us: for our men had received strict orders not to fire unless they saw the enemy—which they seldom did, as they used to sit behind loopholed walls, and blaze away as fast as they could, up in the air, or anywhere, without taking any particular aim, except that the bullet should fall within the Residency.

The consequence was that, although few men were hit while at their posts on the walls, numbers were knocked over by the bullets and cannon shot, which used to be flying all day and night in all directions No place was quite safe: bullets used to come into the most out-of-the-way places. Men used to be hit while lying in bed, or sitting down to dinner, inside the houses. One officer, while asleep, had his pillow torn from under his head by a round shot; and a lady, who was sitting outside her door, safe, as she thought, had the chair carried away from under her. Notwithstanding all this, it is wonderful how few were killed and wounded. Children used to play about, and women and men were constantly walking about, so accustomed to the *whiz* of the bullets that they never paid any attention to them.

It certainly was a dreadful thing to see a cannon ball come rushing through a number of men and horses. I have seen two horses, one tattoo and three men, killed by one shot; and I remember on another occasion seeing the top of a man's head taken off, while cleaning his horse—the ball killing the horse and another next to it. The suddenness with which this happens impresses one very much: you may see it a hundred times, and, I think, the hundred and first time you would have the same feeling—a feeling of awe at the nearness of death.

The rebels were very short of shell and shot:—the latter they got by picking up what we fired at them, or by beating iron into something like shot, and now and then they used to send any odd thing they could get. Once they sent a smoothing iron. They were most persevering. We had taken most of their large guns from them; but instead they had countless small guns, carrying a ball of 2 or 3lbs. These little guns they used to place on the tops of houses, or anywhere else where they had a good command of us; and certainly they did annoy us considerably. Often, after they had fired three or four rounds, one of our large 18 or 24-pounders would open upon them—but immediately the smoke from our gun had cleared away, out would pop the little gun, and, as, if in defiance, belch forth in its shrill broken voice another round. It was of no use wasting shot on them—they used I believe to do this merely to draw some of our round shot out of us, of which they were much in want.

Their shells were the most extraordinary things—now and then when our shells which we threw at them failed to burst, they used to send them back again: but otherwise they had no 8 inch shells, though they had the mortars: so they used to make up shells of two small hand grenades, round which they used to put tow filled with powder. The consequence was, that when these things fell among us, there were always two reports—the first that of the tow round the hand grenades, which exploded and burst, so leaving the grenade free—and then the second explosion of the grenade itself. At first, before we discovered this, we were near coming to grief, as when the first explosion had taken place, we thought all was over, and so used to rise up and perhaps rush to the spot.

Then again the rebels used to make stone shells, which never did much damage; and now and then you would hear something coming singing through the air, like a small barrel-organ or a large Humming bird—*hoo, woo, woo, woo, woo, woo, thud*—it would fall close to you, and you'd find a large block of wood about two feet, or 2½ feet, long and a foot thick.

I remember, one morning, while talking to a friend of mine not in the army, seeing something coming through the air in our direction, which burst high up, and did no damage:

but it was the, most extraordinary thing in the shape of a war-like missile I have seen. When it burst, four or five things flew out of it in different directions, and went whizzing about like one of those English crackers we used to have at home:—but what amused me so much at the time was my friend's face and the way he went dodging and wheeling about, trying to escape from each individual piece which he imagined was coming after him: and when he returned to where I was standing—his face red and warm-looking, and panting with exertion—I thought I should have died with laughing.

We had been in the entrenchments about three weeks, when the news were whispered, "Tomorrow only half rations." Living on fall rations is hard enough, when you are suddenly brought down to it without rum or liquor of any sort—but to be reduced to ½lb. meat, ½lb. wheat, ½oz. salt and a pinch of rice, was rather unpleasant to think of. When the time came, we (who had been long in India) did not feel it so much as the Regiments who had just come out from England—men with appetites like horses: but, poor fellows, it could not be helped; and I think those who were not wounded owe their health to their not being able to get too much to eat or any spirits to drink. The people who felt it, were the sick and wounded. For them there were no comforts—nothing but the hard beef and coarse *chupatties*: and when the little stock of rum and beer that was kept for the hospital was expended, they were indeed badly off.

Many a man sunk into the grave for want of stimulants: hardly a single case of amputation ever succeeded; and I do not think there is more than one (a drummer boy in H. M's 32nd) who lost leg or arm and lived. Many men died from mere scratches—the slightest almost to a certainty proving fatal: hospital gangrene invariably supervened, and the patient after great suffering died. Poor Major Stevenson of the 1st Madras Fusiliers was hit by a spent ball on the pit of his stomach. He had a *kummerbund* on at the time; so that the skin was not even raised, and still in a few days it turned into a sore, became gangrenous, and the Major died. Then scurvy broke out; and indeed the hospitals were a melancholy sight. Everything that could be done by the Medical Officers, was done; but, without medicines or means of any sort, it was hard to fight against disease.

The two Generals used to be constantly among the sick, holding out hopes of speedy relief, and doing their best to make the men comfortable. There were others also, who did their utmost to relieve the sufferings of the brave men, who had fought for them. I have seen fair and delicately nurtured ladies, when bullets were flying about like hail, when round shot and shell were common visitors in their houses, when many of them were bereft of husband, children, brothers, and all that they held dear, rise above their own misfortunes, and devote themselves to works of charity and love. When rations had been reduced as low as they could be (and women's rations at the full are much less than those allowed men), I have seen them taking from their own small shares of flour and tea, making delicate *chupatties* with their own hands; regardless of the bullets, carrying them to the sick and wounded in hospital; and, lest their hair should fall down and annoy those on whom they were attending, they have cut it off. Above all, I have seen them moving about the sick, holding out promises of love and forgiveness and hope through the blood of our dear Saviour out of that Book which we are, many of us, I am afraid, too apt to neglect in the time of our good fortune and ease. As long as English women are such, so long will English men be only too willing to die for them.

The defence of Lucknow will be handed down in history as one of the most memorable events upon record. A few hundred Englishmen, hampered with women and children equal in numbers to themselves, their sick and wounded daily, almost hourly, increasing, cut off from all communication with friends outside, indeed for some time not knowing whether there were any friends nearer to them than

Calcutta, surrounded by a countless host of bloodthirsty enemies, under ceaseless fire of cannon and musketry, (for before the first relief under the late Sir H. Havelock reached Lucknow, the fire was such that no one dared show a finger out of cover) gallantly held their own; and not one step did the rebels gain upon them.

If the natives of India are capable of taking a lesson, they will long remember it, and feel how hopeless any attempt would be to drive the English out of India. In the audacity of their pride, pampered as they have been, lauded up to the skies as they always were, they forgot that, in all the deeds of arms in which they had been engaged, they had always been led by the Europeans. Their thought was, *"We* have conquered the Punjab; *we* have won and held India for the Sirkar; now that we are tired of them, we who have done all this, will turn them out and set up a king of our own colour." But they calculated without their host. They found it very different fighting *against* the despised *Feringees*; and they have now re-learnt a lesson, which was taught them a century ago by Clive. May they remember it!

No-one, who has not seen the Residency at Lucknow, can form any idea of the fire the garrison were under. Houses breached (almost) with musketry were never before heard of in warfare: but so close were the enemy, that they had actually loopholed our own walls, and used to fire in on our garrison through these holes. They had recourse to every sort of expedient to overcome us, but never succeeded. Mining was tried; and, with the command they had of labour, they could sink any number of mines. When we had to countermine, we had no labourers; and officers as well as men had to take their turn in the mine. But British pluck and endurance beat them.

They were beaten at everything. They had our sappers and miners, taught by us; they had our artillery men—all these, and countless numbers. We had no labourers, and so few artillery men that they had to run from one battery to another as required. Still we beat them.

Of course this continual wear on the energies of the men told after five months' siege. How anxiously we used to look for despatches from Cawnpore, which were brought in to us with the greatest difficulty! How many of our messengers never returned; and how excited everyone was at the first newspaper being brought in in a bundle of grass! How well thumbed that paper was! No-one, who has not been shut up for months, can realize our feelings.

At last the joyful news was spread that the Commander-in-Chief would be at Alum Bagh on the 15th inst. Then we began to count the days, and then when it did arrive and we heard the firing, how anxiously we watched from the different look-outs to see how our force was advancing. Next day we saw the fighting advancing towards the Dilkhoosha—then up went the Jack on the Martiniere, and, we knew our Chief was so far on his way to us. Next day pounding commenced again; and gradually the smoke advanced, till we saw the British flag waving on the mess house. We had not been idle those three days: mines had been exploded, sorties made, and positions taken up in advance of our old position; so that when the mess house was taken, the relieved and relieving forces were close to each other.

The Chiefs meet. The relief is complete: and in gallop two men, one Col. Berkeley of H. M's 32nd Regiment, the other Mr. Cavanagh, the head Clerk in the Chief Commissioner's office, who, three days before, had made his way out of Lucknow right through the enemy's camp to the Commander-in-Chief with despatches from General Outram—one of the most daring feats performed during these troublesome times. He will no doubt get his reward: he richly deserves it.

We were relieved. Arrangements were made for taking the women and children, the sick and wounded, in safety out of the place—as it had been decided that Lucknow must be vacated for the present. Five months of hard fighting and toil, such as had never been undergone before, were thus to be thrown away: and many a man—sick as we all were of the place—would willingly have remained, rather than let the rebels get in and exult over their imaginary victory. But that it was a wise step, all must acknowledge. Cawnpore was threatened, and the sick and wounded required a large number of troops to convey them in safety out of Oudh.

Finally orders were issued that nothing was to be taken except a small bundle of necessaries: and then commenced the destruction of property, clothes of all sorts, silver, and books—some of these no doubt old friends—and the burning of which caused many a tear: but all felt it was better to destroy them, than to leave them to our cowardly foe to gloat over.

On the night of the 22nd, all the women and children and sick and wounded having been sent in safety to the Dilkhoosha, the garrison commenced its evacuation of a place they so well knew how to defend, and had so nobly defended. By 3 a. m. the place was empty; and next morning we arrived at Dilkhoosha, where we remained as the Chief's rear guard during his march to the Alum Bagh. On the 25th, we marched and reached it; and there we are now, watching the enemy, and the enemy watching us.

I have thus brought my account of what I did and saw down to the 25th November, 1857. I have said nothing of the siege before General Havelock's force forced their way into Lucknow. I have not said much of what we did after we got in, as it was much the same, day after day—a continual watching the enemy, something like a cat watching at a hole for a mouse (we being the cat), with, for the first week, a sortie now and then, in order to destroy houses which commanded the entrenchments.

The first thought that strikes one regarding this rebellion is that the general rising of the Bengal Army has been caused by a fear that we were going to interfere in some way with their caste—in fact, that it was entirely a matter of caste. I think it has, and it has not—if that can be understood. I have little doubt that the principal instigators will be found to be Mohammedans, and Mohammedans in power, connected with the King of Delhi and the ex-king of Oudh. There is no doubt that as long as there was a king of Delhi, acknowledged though in ever so small a way, and as long as there remained a Delhi for that king to live in, so long would the Mohammedans all over India hope and pray to see him once more seated in state on the throne.

The annexation of Oudh, though, I believe, a wise and necessary measure, has been no doubt the straw that has broken the camel's back, though in a way we never expected. The sepoys, as a body, had nothing they could justly complain of: and it was imagined that they, above all, would be benefited by the annexation of Oudh, as so many of them are drawn from that province, where their families are tillers of the soil, and that by the orders issued during the settlement many of these men's families would be replaced in possession of their old landed rights—and so they were. But annexation also affected the sepoys in a way which they did not like. It made all the people of Oudh British subjects equally with themselves. Formerly if they had any grievance, they got an *arzee* signed by their commanding officer, which was sent to the resident: and the mere fact of the applicant being a sepoy of the Sirkar Engréz Bahadoor was sufficient, if the man had any right on his side, to gain his cause. After the annexation he found every man in Oudh, even the poorest, had an equal hearing with himself. He did not like it, and so, I have no doubt, cried out against annexation. That their prejudices were not interfered with is too well known: for these were allowed to interfere with the discipline of the Bengal army.

The sepoys no doubt, and indeed others besides sepoys, thought that we were going to do away with caste. This idea was confined perhaps to the uneducated: but I think we have brought it on ourselves by thinking and talking so much about caste. Had the Bengal sepoy been taught duty first and caste afterwards, we should not have had so many against us. I do not for one instant urge that we ought to hurt their feelings as to caste: but I do strongly urge that every sepoy on enlistment ought to be told that he would have to perform his duty as a soldier notwithstanding his caste. It is so in Madras and Bombay, where there are many men from Oudh, of the very men composing the Bengal army, and you never hear caste named as an excuse for not performing any duty. If the high caste men do not like to enlist with such an understanding, there are numbers of others who will. The plea of caste was a false one, though no doubt it took at the time.

That we have, as a nation, been greatly to blame in this matter, no one who thinks on the subject but must see. Caste has been raised above our own religion. Anyone might endeavour to make converts, or do what he liked for his faith, except the Christians. "Oh, those missionaries!" how often does one hear, "they ought to be turned out of India; they are the cause of this mutiny:"—and indeed I have heard an officer say, that he would place any missionary in jail whom he caught in his district, preaching or trying to make converts; while another officer present said, "If things had been carried on as they were fifty years ago, this mutiny never would have happened." Thank God, things are not as they were. Then no doubt officers did know more of their men, and perhaps were better liked by them: but why? I leave to others to answer.

Let us, ere it is too late, mend our ways, lest God in His turn deny us. Though we have gone through much suffering, we have been most graciously preserved—God, even our God, fighting for us. Often in our engagements has that beautiful verse in the Psalms recurred to me—*If it had not been the Lord who was on our side, now may Israel say: if it had not been the Lord who was on our side, when men rose up against us: then they had swallowed us up quick, when their wrath was kindled against us.*

There has been a very apparent difference between the effects of the rebellion in our old Provinces and in Oudh—in the former there has been much more maltreatment of the Europeans by the villagers than in Oudh, and again they (the villagers) have settled down to their old occupations and resigned themselves to their old rulers (the British) much sooner than the people of Oudh. In the Provinces there were no men of weight or influence, who, however they might have wished it, had the power to assist the Government, or individual Europeans. The whole community was broken up into small brotherhoods. Our system had entirely ruined and almost wiped away the old lords of the country: so that when the sepoys got possession of any district, the villagers found themselves powerless to resist, and unable to protect.

That the villainous and barbarous deeds committed have, with few exceptions, been perpetrated by the Mohammedans there is little doubt: and however guilty the Hindu soldiery may be, the Hindus as a race have generally been the people to save and protect the Christian.

In Oudh we on annexation systematically set to work to ruin and reduce the gentry and nobility of the country. To the honour of most of the District Officers be it said, they protested to the last against this policy. We were, however, forced to carry it through, with a view, as was stated, of restoring to the real proprietors their rights to the landed property: hoping that by so doing, we should raise up such a body of friends, as would hold the dispossessed men in check. How miserably this failed we all know. That it must have done so, all who studied the matter were convinced; and now we appear surprised, that all these gentry, whom we ill-treated and ruined, should fight against us! So evident was the falsity of the policy, that at the outbreak of the mutiny these very men whom we had so treated were told, that if they would remain faithful and assist the Sirkar, they should be restored to certain of their lands from which we had dispossessed them.

With one or two exceptions, these men, the Talookdars of Oudh, have behaved well. Wherever any of the British officers in Oudh were saved, it was these men who protected them. True, they have been in arms against us; but is that to be wondered at? Had we treated them better on annexation, we should have had many of those who are now opposed to us, on our side: and I am sure that even now they would come in, had they any hopes of being well treated. If they do declare for us, the work in Oudh will be easy enough. We shall be able to; govern the country through them: but, without them, it will be no easy matter to get things settled down.

Through the whole of these advances and engagements of General Havelock's small force, the want of Cavalry and horse artillery has been sadly felt. We have taken guns without number, and have always beaten the enemy; but we have never been able to inflict such a punishment on them as to make them remember it. They were always too quick for us. Their flights were certainly marvellous: we never could get up to them. Had we had even one good troop of Cavalry, we should have given them much severer lessons than they received. The only time we had enough Cavalry to do anything, was, when we crossed the river the second time. At Mungurwarah the Volunteer Cavalry, about 110 strong, followed them up and took two guns: and it was owing to this that the enemy never stood again till we reached Alum Bagh—whereas, had we been unable to follow them up as we did, they would, no doubt, have stood both at Nowabgung and Bunee, at both which places they had evidently intended to make a stand.

*********

And now, before I close, I must say a few words on the Volunteer Cavalry, to which, I am proud to say, I have the honour to belong. On our first starting from Allahabad it consisted of about eighteen men and officers. On the road four more officers joined us; and this was our strength through the whole of the engagements till we crossed the river Ganges the first time, when we were strengthened by the addition of forty men from the different Infantry Regiments; and while encamped at Mungurwarrah, we were joined by some six or eight Volunteers, some of them officers.

I sincerely hope the Government will take some notice of the services performed by those composing the corps, and show that they appreciate them. New to the country, new to the service, unaccustomed to roughing it, brought up accustomed to every luxury, and led to believe that on their arrival in India they would have the same, these young officers willingly threw themselves into the thick of the work, often without a tent or cover of any sort to shelter them from the rain or sun, with bad provisions and hard work. Side by side with the Privates, they took their turn of duty: and side by side with them they fought, were wounded, and some of them died.

When we got into Lucknow, and were useless as Cavalry, they cheerfully took the musket, and night and day at one of the most important posts did sentry duty with the men. It must not be imagined that, in saying this, I am blowing my own trumpet. I was fortunate enough to be made an officer at the raising of the corps; therefore I have not had to take the duties of a Private, as these gentlemen had. But I am, and shall ever be, proud to say, I have served with them in the field. Well and nobly they did their duty: and if Her Gracious Majesty shall grant us a medal for what we have, under God's Providence, been able to do, proud may those boys be, when they point to the medal on their breast and say, "I won this, while serving as a Private in the field."

*Alum Bagh, 26th September, 1857*

# The Siege at Arrah

John James Halls
Civil Administrator

# The Siege at Arrah

There are perhaps comparatively few in England who have any very distinct ideas upon life in India; fewer who know what is life in India at a civil station; and fewer still who are conscious of the existence of a modest little civil station, an episode in the history of which we are now about to relate.

Life in India—without entering into luxurious disquisition on *tiffin*, curry, and *brandy pawnee*—we shall content ourselves with describing as a life of excessive laziness, alternating with the most wearying exertion—the former injurious to the mind, the latter too often to the body; the transition from the one state to the other being often sudden, and dependent on unforeseen circumstances. The intense heat and relaxing nature of the climate give but too specious an excuse for sloth to the indolent; while to the impetuous and energetic man, unless he be gifted with a fair amount of prudence, they bring—and sometimes with fearful rapidity—disease and death.

Life in India at a civil station is, or rather was, an existence of easy leisure, with intervals of employment of the dullest and most uninteresting nature. The amount of labour daily varied according to the character of the individual, his capacity for business, his physical temperament, and a variety of other circumstances. The work was always routine; the recreations were routine likewise. A Government servant daily got up, had his *chota Hazree*, his walk, his bath, his breakfast, went to his *cutcherry*, and perhaps to the billiard-room; took his wife to the one drive of the station, ate his dinner, and after a cup of coffee retired to bed—if insensible to heat and mosquitoes, possibly to sleep. The same course had to be traversed on the morrow, the same the next day, the same for weeks, months, and years; a man was like a wheel—perpetually going through a succession of turns; getting over the ground indeed towards promotion and pension, but slowly and imperceptibly wearing away his life. The wheel will sometimes break down on the road; the civilian also was carried off by dysentery or cholera at his post, as the damp and mildewed monuments in the European burial-grounds abundantly testify.

Arrah, the little civil station above mentioned, is situated in the district of Shahabad, near the junction of the rivers Ganges and Soane, at about ten miles distant from the former and eight from the latter, which intersects the road to Dinapore and Patna, Arrah being distant from Dinapore about twenty-four miles. To approach Arrah by the Dinapore road, after passing the Keimnirgger bridge, which spans a stream of some size, and traversing about a mile and a half of very bad road, the traveller proceeds for a considerable distance between thick groves of mango and other trees, when a new and somewhat imposing mosque meets his eye on the right, and beyond the native town commences. The old houses, with their quaintly carved balconies and balustrades, many of them in a very tottering condition, give a picturesque appearance to the scene; but the open drains, the mud walls, the dirt and wretched appearance of some of the inhabitants, give ample evidence of a darker side to the picture; indeed it would be difficult to find more miserable habitations than the huts of the poorer community in this and other native towns, or fitter nurse-beds of contagion and disease.

After extending for about a mile, the main street makes an abrupt turn to the left, and becomes widened into a broad straight road or market-place, flanked on either side by the houses of the Mahajuns (bankers) and richer natives, and terminated at one extremity by the Judge's Compound, and on the other by the road leading to the jail, the abiding place of 400 or 500 of the worst characters in the district.

A short distance beyond the market-place is the Cutcherry Compound, a fine large open space of green, enclosed for the most part by trenches, and about a mile in circumference. Here tokens of superior civilisation and European comfort take the place of mud huts and broken-down galleries in the prospect, which is now not without pretensions to a certain amount of beauty. The eye wanders over a large expanse of brilliant verdure to the pretty little English cemetery at the bank of a handsome tank, while on either side the Government offices, the new school-house, and the European bungalows and gardens give, with some fine large trees, importance and variety to the landscape. Beyond the Cutcherry Compound the road passes by a small mosque and some tombs of Mussulman saints towards Buxar, distant forty miles, and the station may be said to terminate at the pretty rural bungalow of the sub-deputy opium agent, built by himself and surrounded by a garden such as is rarely seen in India, tastefully arranged, well stocked with fruits and English vegetables, and abounding in curious shrubs and graceful creepers.

Such was the aspect of Arrah at the commencement of the Sepoy mutiny in 1857; perhaps even now its appearance is comparatively unchanged. A storm however, created by the evil passions of man, has swept over it, and tranquillity and confidence exist there no more, perhaps never will reappear.

The European inhabitants of Arrah and its neighbourhood, at the beginning of 1857, consisted of the usual officials attached to a civil station, with their families and several railway engineers and inspectors; there were also some Europeans in Government employ. The usual routine works went on; the ladies rode and drove about the station in the evening, and frequently travelled alone by *palankeen dák* to other districts, though the native population was of a fierce and turbulent character, and disputes and fights were of every-day Occurrence: desperate wounds and loss of life frequently attended these *rencontres*; the services of the civil surgeon were in continual request.

Yet, in spite of these warlike propensities of the natives, the Europeans remained unmolested throughout the whole extent of the district, and the very name of an Englishman, though its prestige had already from various causes somewhat diminished, was still a sufficient passport for security of life and property, and for the most part commanded a certain amount of respect. The white man was everywhere master, and held the position of, though not in effect, the lord of the soil.

This state of things was, however, not destined to endure. The great Sepoy mutiny burst forth like a thunderbolt over the length and breadth of the land; and like, alas, too many other districts, Arrah became in its turn the theatre of a lawless insurrection. The treacherous and fiery element, hitherto concealed from motives of interest or fear, but always inherent in the bosom of the Asiatic, was suddenly let loose, and nourished by the lust of plunder; and, impelled by stormy fanaticism, spread its scorching flame over the country like the all-devouring fires of the American prairie.

It was not till May 1857, after the Meerut mutiny and the massacre at Delhi, that the Europeans at Arrah discovered that they too were standing on the brink of a volcano; and even for some time afterwards the full extent of their peril was not recognised by all, and yet that peril was no slight one. They were by themselves, in the midst of a warlike native population, composed for the most part of Sepoys and their relations. Three or four hundred prisoners were in the jail; the Najeebs, or jail guard, were distrusted; more than suspicions were entertained of the disloyalty of Koowar Singh, the greatest Zemindar of the district, and looked up to by the Rajpoots as their chief; while twenty-four miles distant, at Dinapore, were three regiments of Sepoys whose mutiny might daily be expected, and whose direct route lay through Arrah to the north-west.

The only signs of excitement at first observable in the station were the frequent congregating of the Europeans on the course at the time of the drive and little evening gatherings in the doctor's garden, where the events of the times were discussed. There was, however, a restless desire on the part of all for the latest scrap of news from Delhi, Calcutta, or Dinapore; and to satisfy this craving, telegraphic notices, extracts from newspapers, and even private letters, were in continual circulation; creating more or less anxiety, according to the importance of their several contents.

During the greater part of May and afterwards, constant official communication was kept up by the authorities with the neighbouring districts. On the 8th of June, a letter was received from the commissioner of Patna, stating that an outbreak among the native troops was expected to take place at Dinapore. In consequence of this intelligence, the greater part of the Europeans at Arrah assembled together, and passed the night at the Judge's house, two or three only remaining at their own homes; and on the morrow a meeting of the male European population of the station and neighbourhood was held at the magistrate's house.

At this conference the only decision arrived at was, that the women and children should at once be sent away to Dinapore, where the presence of 600 men of Her Majesty's 10th Regiment would ensure their safety; the magistrate (Mr. Wake) having beforehand provided ample boat accommodation for the whole of the defenceless party to proceed via the Ganges, which was thought safer than the direct route. Various opinions, nevertheless, were offered as to what further steps should be taken in the emergency.

The Government officers having declared their intention not to abandon the station, some few individuals desired that a house should be temporarily fortified, and that the residents should therein abide the result of the expected revolt. Others again proposed that the Europeans should form themselves into *extempore* cavalry corps, to fight, skirmish, reconnoitre, or fly, according to the process of events. Their opponents, on the other hand, suggested, with some show of reason, the possibility that the horses might not stand fire; that the unpractised cavaliers might do them or themselves a mischief with their own swords; or that if, during the anticipated flight or skirmish, an unfortunate fell from his horse, there would be considerable difficulty to pick him up again. These cavaliers however, it must be confessed, had not been accustomed to ride across country; their arguments, therefore, were treated with becoming contempt by the equestrian majority.

In short, nothing was determined.

When the magistrate at length asked, "Who will remain and act with us?" but one voice replied, "I will."

"Thank you, Sir," said Mr. Wake; "what is your name?"

"My name is Cock."

The appropriateness of the cognomen caused a smile, and in the sequel the speaker proved himself a thoroughly game bird. No others followed his example, and the meeting broke up without satisfactory result.

All of the non-officials there present, with exception of two hereafter to be named, made the best of their way, some by boat, some on horseback, to Dinapore, carrying with them a formidable battery of double-barrelled guns and revolvers, and leaving the party at Arrah reduced to eight men, who afterwards took up their abode together at the Judge's house. These eight were Mr. Littledale, the judge; Mr. Coombe, the officiating collector; Mr. Wake, the magistrate; Mr. Halls, the civil surgeon; Mr. Colvin, the assistant magistrate; Mr. Field, the sub-deputy opium agent; with Messrs. Kelly and Tait, of the Civil Engineers; the last two, though compelled by no duty, having voluntarily remained to support the Government officers, and assist in preserving order in the station.

In the evening, the ladies proceeded in buggies and carriages to the place of embarkation, whence, escorted by Mr. Boyle and accompanied by some other fugitives, both male and female, who had previously arrived at the river, they departed in the guard-boat to Dinapore, which they reached in safety, and were kindly received by Lieut.-Colonel Fenwick, of Her Majesty's 10th, and the Rev. Mr. Burge, the chaplain of the district.

The departure and safe embarkation of the ladies and children removed a great. weight from the minds of the few men who remained at Arrah, in the Judge's house; and on the 10th of June, had any stranger seen them assembled at the dinner-table of their hospitable host, he would scarcely have suspected the serious nature of the crisis which had brought them together.

Their numbers were increased on the 11th by the return of Mr. Boyle (the resident railway engineer) from Dinapore, Mr. Armstrong, the assistant sub-deputy opium agent, having previously arrived from Patna. This last, though he had met the whole band of heavy-armed fugitives in full retreat on his road, still pressed on alone to Arrah, to share the fate of the other officers of the station, who, in acknowledgment, conferred on him a brevet rank, and always addressed him by the title of *General*; his presence added greatly to the cheerfulness of the little circle, and much regret was felt by all when, after a few weeks, he returned to Patna by Government order; he was succeeded by Mr. Anderson. A more serious permanent loss was also sustained by the departure of Kelly, the Ajax of the garrison, "himself a host," who, the danger of the revolt at Dinapore becoming seemingly less imminent, was compelled by his duties, as railroad engineer, to leave the station. With the exception of the above arrivals and departures, the party at Mr. Littledale's remained unchanged.

Our limits will not allow us to take more than a brief survey of the manner in which day after day of painful suspense passed by at the Judge's house. Yet the period must not be left unnoticed, for to the exertions and watchfulness of that little band, sometimes eight, sometimes nine, and never more than ten in number, and to the untiring energy of the superior officers, are due the preservation of the town from plunder and anarchy, the retention of the prisoners in the jail, the restraint upon the disaffected jail-guard, and the continuance of public business for more than six weeks; for up to the time when the arrival of a hostile army and the rebellion of almost the entire district forced this little band of Europeans to cast away all considerations but those of self-defence, property remained safe, and disturbances were unknown in the station.

The first step taken by the magistrate was to secure a regular and rapid communication between Arrah and Dinapore on the one side, and Buxar on the other. For this purpose *eckas* (light bamboo carts) and messengers were stationed at different parts of the road in addition to the usual Government dâk.

The next point was to prevent panic and disturbance in the town; this was attained by carrying on the public business as usual during the day, and at night by an increased force of native police and watchmen, and by a vigilant patrol of Europeans. To these last, this nightly patrol was, owing to their paucity of numbers, most wearying. The night was divided into four watches of two hours each, commencing at nine o'clock p.m., when two of the party, armed and mounted, went over all parts of the town and about three miles of the Dinapore road; a fresh pair relieved these at eleven p.m., and so on till five a.m., the first couple having frequently to take the last watch in addition to their own; besides this arrangement, one or another kept watch in the house throughout the night.

The natural result of these *pervigilia* displayed itself by a considerable tendency to sleep during the day, at all hours of which some of the garrison might have been seen courting repose in every possible attitude, in every practicable locality, and in every variety of undress: the weather being oppressively hot, the nearer the costume approached to the primitive "Adamite" the greater seemed the contentment of the individual. Letter-writing, reading, and, as a desperate resource, float-fishing in the tank, filled up any intervals of leisure till the dinner-hour, when all met together and formed generally a cheerful, if not a joyous party.

One of them writes of their condition as follows:

*Judge's, June 11th*
Here we are all right and very comfortable! W——'s arrangements are perfect. We get information from all sides. The Sikhs (sent from Patna for the treasure) came in this morning, and we knew of their approach many hours before their arrival. L—— is most kind and hospitable. We have horse patrols throughout the night. I myself, not being an equestrian, promenaded round the station on foot, visiting the collectorate and jail. The table in what was the billiard-room bristles with weapons of all descriptions. We had a merry dinner yesterday; your letter (the first news), telling of the safe arrival of you all at Dinapore, tended much to promote our comfort. What a night you must have had of it in that abominable boat! B—— came in this evening. I always expected him back. The town is quiet, the Mahajuns in a stew, and the population generally in a state of excessive curiosity, crowds staring into the Compound when the gates are open. Fifteen or twenty horses are tethered to trees and bamboos in the said enclosure, so that there is some life in the scene.

Similar extracts to the above, and a portion of a diary which has been kindly submitted to our perusal, enable us to give a brief sketch of the principle incidents which occurred while the party remained at the Judge's house; one day, however, passed much the same as another, and long ere their period of probation had concluded, all were heartily weary of the monotony and uncertainty of their position.

At one a.m. on June 12th, 100 Sikhs, who bad been sent from Patna for the purpose, escorted thither treasure to the amount of five *lacs* of rupees. The Arrah party were glad at the time to get rid both of the money and men, little imagining that, at a future period, the steadfast and gallant behaviour of those very Sikhs or their comrades would be mainly instrumental in saving the lives of all the Europeans in the station.

It was some time about the middle of June that rumours were first heard at Arrah of the taking of Delhi, as well as of the mutiny of the 6th Bengal Native Infantry at Allahabad; unfortunately the bad news proved true, and the good false. Information, too, arrived that a rising of the Sepoys at Dinapore was expected on the 15th; it being said that another "lucky day" for them would not occur for two months. "We are therefore," says a letter from Arrah dated June 14th, "keeping good watch, and obtain intelligence from all quarters, thanks to W——, who is a most active and efficient officer, and well fitted for the emergency. Twenty irregular cavalry arrived here today, *en route* for Buxar, to take care, I suppose, of the stud; our people there have entrenched themselves in a bungalow near the river, the old fort being too large for them to defend. There is no occasion for you to tell us to keep up our spirits, for there is no lack of them among our little party."

Our narrative has hitherto treated of what took place at Arrah immediately after the first alarm of mutiny at Dinapore, and it will hereafter be seen how the bold determination of the few gentlemen above named to remain from the very beginning at their posts—a determination nonetheless bold because the expected emergency was for a time delayed—enabled them afterwards to form the nucleus of that small body of men, Europeans and Sikhs, whose defence at Arrah against the overwhelming force of a savage and merciless foe is already an episode in history.

The 16th or 17th June saw the completion of a work which afterwards exercised an important influence on the fate of the few residents at Arrah, and indirectly on the future of the entire district. As has before been stated, it was the opinion of a small minority, that a house should be put into a state of defence, and that in the event of mutiny or disturbance, the Europeans should take shelter therein and endeavour to make a temporary stand; this proposal being negatived, at the time, by the majority.

There was, however, fortunately one of the party who holding the above opinion had the resolution to act upon it, and *singly,* possessed the means of carrying his plans into effect. This was Mr. Boyle, the railway engineer, who collected several cartloads of new bricks, and built up with them the veranda arches of a small two-storied building, originally destined for a billiard-room, and distant sixty yards from his own house. The new walls, though without mortar or cement of any kind, were artistically constructed, and formed a very sufficient defence against a musket-bullet. The low arches beneath were, with the exception of rather a spacious loophole, entirely bricked up, while on the upper floor, between the pillars, a sort of breastwork was formed, upon which numerous sandbags were placed, having intervals left between them for the guns of the besieged. Other arrangements were carried out in the interior. Into this extemporised fortification, Mr. Boyle conveyed a large supply of rice, grain, biscuits, and water, with a small quantity of brandy and beer.

It was then proposed that the party should change its quarters from the Judge's house to this building, or, at all events, to Mr. Boyle's residence, so as to be prepared for any emergency; but there were many and reasonable objections to such a proceeding, independent of a general unwillingness on the part of all to leave the comfortable quarters where they had experienced such kindly hospitality.

First, the sudden migration of the Europeans would probably have led to panic and disorder in the town, which contingencies had hitherto been prevented as much by the central position of the Judge's house, as by the continual nightly patrol.

Secondly, the situation of the new fortress was singularly uncalculated for defence against superior numbers, commanded as it was in front by the large dwelling-house in its vicinity, and hemmed in on the other sides by trees, outhouses, and garden-walls, behind which the besiegers could carry on their measures for the destruction of the garrison with entire security to themselves.

The sequel will show that the latter of these objections was not unfounded, but it will also testify how Mr. Boyle's enterprise and forethought proved of signal service to his companions, and his imperfect fortification one of the many providential circumstances which, in the end, secured the safety of them all.

For some weeks after the construction of the little fortress, all things went on as before. On June 20th, a letter arrived from the Commissioner, stating that the treasure at Patna was about to be removed, and that there was apprehension that an *émeute* would then take place among the Sepoys. Reports also were rife that Koowar Singh was tampering with the 40th Native Infantry; while letters from Buxar stated that numbers of Sepoys were flocking at that side into Shahabad.

The 21st of June brought chequered news: there had been a signal defeat of the rebels before Delhi, with the capture of twenty-five of their guns; but in the Santhal district, Sir Norman Leslie had been murdered by his own men, and two of his officers wounded. Mirzapore had been abandoned by most of the European residents. There was disastrous news from Neemuch: mutinies at Peshawur, Shahjehanguuge, Futtehpore, Tusedgunge and Sultanpore in Oude. Alarms, too, of danger in the more immediate neighbourhood of Arrah were abundant: on June 22nd, as Messrs. Littledale and Field were just starting on their usual patrol, they met an express with letters, stating that reports were in circulation that a simultaneous rising of the Sepoys and Mohammedan population would take place in all quarters of the district on the following day, and that several influential natives at Patna and Chuprah (about sixteen miles from Arrah) were implicated.

The morrow, however, although the centenary anniversary of the battle of Plassey, passed off quietly at Arrah, with the exception of a furious dust-storm, which filled the houses with dust, and almost choked the inmates. Every day now brought its budget of intelligence, by turns exciting indignation, pity, and admiration.

A dreadful massacre of Europeans was reported from Cawnpore. The ladies and children from Fyzabad, after suffering incredible hardships, had arrived in a state of utter destitution at Dinapore; and the gallant Tucker, of the civil service, had fallen gloriously at his post, after having singly killed twenty of his enemies. Each post brought news of fresh disasters; but bright examples of woman's uncomplaining fortitude and man's devoted heroism were of every-day occurrence. The Anglo-Saxon gloried in his race!

The 1st of July brought tidings to Arrah of the decease of Mr. Garrett, the opium agent at Behar, a kind-hearted, straightforward man, brother-in-law to the Lieut.-Governor of Bengal. The event threw a gloom over the spirits of several of the Arrah garrison, who knew his worth, and had experienced his cheerful hospitality. The excitement consequent on the anticipated insurrection at Patna, and the constant worry and annoyance to which he was exposed, no doubt accelerated his death.

On the night of the 3rd, Dr. Lyell was murdered, and his body disfigured by sword-cuts, in the streets of Patna. This gallant gentleman, on hearing of a disturbance in the town, rode at once to the place, and, being considerably in advance of the Sikh police who accompanied him, was at once surrounded and cut down by the fanatical mob. Many of the villains, however, afterwards paid the forfeit of their crimes.

After hearing of the above catastrophe, the duties of the night watchers in the streets at Arrah appeared more dangerous, for there was no safeguard either against the desperate fanatic or the concealed assassin, and they might be shot down at any moment on their rounds. The patrol, however, continued as before. Between two and three o'clock in the morning of July 8th, a tremendous tumult and shouting was heard in the town, apparently in the direction of the jail. All the Europeans at the Judge's promptly got up and armed themselves, thinking that the decisive moment had arrived, and that the anticipated insurrection had commenced. The judge and the magistrate rode at once to the jail to see what was the matter, and soon reappeared with intelligence that the prisoners in some of the wards, for no other cause than their own amusement, had set up this horrible outcry; that these turbulent gentry were safely locked up, and that the town itself was perfectly tranquil.

This little alarm served to keep the garrison on the *qui vive,* and was consequently not without its use, for a sense of security and weariness of what seemed unnecessary watchfulness began to creep into the minds of all, and the cry of *wolf! wolf!* from Patna and Dinapore having been so often heard without the appearance of danger, began after a time to be almost disregarded. Still the peril was the same as before. The three Sepoy regiments still threatened from Dinapore; the crisis was in fact approaching; and the *wolf* at last came.

After breakfast on the morning of the 17th, an anonymous communication was found on the table in the Judge's office; and, singularly enough, all the information contained in it afterwards proved to be correct. The letter stated that Ali Kurreem (a noted zemindar of Gya, who had latterly made his escape from Patna, in consequence of the discovery of a treasonable correspondence between him and. a police jemadar in Tirhoot) had arrived at Jugdeespore, the dwelling-place of Koowar Singh; that Koowar Singh himself was concerned in an intended rising of the Sepoys, which was *certain* to take place on the 25th of July; and that if the house of his agent, Kaleeprosad, at Arrah, were searched, letters confirmatory of the latter part of this story (about the bribes, &c.) might be found.

On receipt of this intelligence Messrs. Littledale, Wake, Colvin, Halls, and Tait at once started off in a dog-cart through the town, to the house named. Kaleeprosad was absent; many of his papers, however, were seized and inspected, but proved to be of no importance.

On the 22nd, news arrived of the occupation of Cawnpore by General Havelock, and of the second horrible massacre of women and children by the infamous Nana Sahib.

On the evening of the 25th, the following laconic epistle, directed "by express—urgent," was received by the Judge:

*To the Judge or Senior Civil Officer, Arrah*
*Dinapore, 25th July, 1857*
*Sir—*
A revolt among the native troops at Dinapore is expected to occur this day. Stand prepared accordingly.
Your obedt. servant,
*W. Lydiard*
Major
A.A. General

This looked serious, but the party at Arrah still had hopes that the Sepoys would be not only hotly pursued, but that they would not be able to cross the Soane, which river, as before stated, intersected the road between Arrah and Dinapore, and was now considerably swollen by the rains. A railway engineer, who resided on the river's bank, having promised the magistrate, in the event of a rising, to destroy all the boats. These hopes, however, proved fallacious.

The revolt took place, the boats were not destroyed, the Sepoys were un-pursued, and early on the morning of the 26th (Sunday) accounts came in that the rebels were crossing the river, and had fired upon a messenger of the magistrate. Later in the day (about ten o'clock) Messrs. Delpeiroux and Hoyle, two railway inspectors, who lived on the Arrah side of the Soane, with another man, came spurring into the Judge's compound. Their story was brief, that the Sepoys had passed the river in force, were then engaged in burning and destroying the railway works and neighbouring bungalows, and that they themselves had fled for their lives; the number of the mutineers was not known, nor any particulars of the outbreak.

The Judge and the rest, still not wishing to abandon the station, determined to proceed at once to Mr. Boyle's fortification; accordingly the dog-cart was once more put into requisition, and the greater part of the arms having been deposited therein, was driven through the town to the rendezvous, escorted by the Sikhs and a few Europeans on horseback. An attack was somewhat apprehended, but none was made, though, as the little troop marched through the streets, the population gazed in crowds, indifferent and careless spectators, or awed by the appearance of the armed force.

The Europeans afterwards assembled at Mr. Boyle's house, where they remained a few hours engaged in writing letters to friends both in India and England, and sending a few extra stores into the fort: among these was a five dozen case of port and sherry belonging to the doctor, which, not having been unpacked, was taken in at the eleventh hour, and its contents afterwards conduced not a little to the health and spirits of the garrison, worn out as both frequently were by heat, impure air, and exhaustion. The Sikhs also took in a supply of water for their own use.

Early in the afternoon two or three European women and children who had unfortunately returned to the district, sought shelter with their husbands at the station; the Judge and magistrate determined that these should at once be sent in *palankeens* to the boats, the road on the side towards the Ganges being still open. This was a most judicious decision, for had the women remained, their situation would have been most wretched, for, besides the impossibility of giving them a separate apartment, or indeed any privacy, fright, privation, and disease, would probably have put an end to their lives ere the termination of the siege.

The Europeans and Sikhs were joined at Mr. Boyle's by Mr. Cock and Messrs. Godfrey and Da Costa, and by Syed Azimoodeen Hossein, a Mussulman gentleman, the deputy collector of Arrah, who, with a rare fidelity, resolved to enter the fort with the Europeans; a young boy, his servant, refused to leave him, and together with another native (Mr. Anderson's bearer) was afterwards most useful in cooking such provisions as the besieged could command, and in general attendance upon all.

In the evening the whole party, Europeans, Eurasians, and Sikhs slept and watched by turns in the little fortress. The following account of their proceedings therein, and of some subsequent events, is extracted from a private letter, written a few weeks after the scenes which it describes:

We were altogether nine Europeans, six Eurasians, and one native (the deputy-collector); there were also fifty Sikh police with us, whom we *hoped* were true men, but could not at first be sure; afterwards they proved themselves to be real sterling metal. . . . That night, (Sunday, the 26th of July) we went into our fortified billiard-room and bricked ourselves up. Had the Sikhs who were with us been treacherous, they might have eaten us up for a breakfast. On Monday morning up came the Sepoys; they broke open the jail, looted the treasury of 70,000 rupees, and were joined by the jail guards, prisoners, and hundreds of bad characters from the neighbouring villages.

It afterwards appeared that the bulk of the three native regiments, the 7th, 8th and 40th, had, through the apathy, to call it by no harsher name, of the general and his advisers, been deliberately suffered to walk off unmolested with their arms and ammunition, and that too in the face of three or four large guns, and six hundred European troops.

All these assembled on a rising ground about 600 yards from and in full view of our position by sound of trumpet, and then moved down steadily towards us till they got within 200 yards, when their trumpets sounded a charge, and down they came at the double quick, shouting like demons, and firing as fast as they could.

Our side, however, soon began to reply from their double-barrelled guns, and the carbines of the Sikhs, and some of the rascals were soon knocked over. This brought the multitude to a standstill; and some more being hit, the greater part of them retreated into and behind a large house situated, most unfortunately for us, at sixty yards' distance. The others took skirmishing order on our flanks and rear, where they were well sheltered by trees, outhouses, and garden walls, whence they kept up a continual fire all day, and occasionally throughout the night. The first rush of the vast force was certainly the most fearful; and, judging of the feelings of others by my own, I suspect few of us had much hope beyond that of selling our lives as dearly as possible. Indeed, had the rebels had the pluck to advance, they might have kicked down our defences, or have scaled the walls and overwhelmed us by their weight of numbers. Fortunately, however, they had *not;* and, when this their first attack had been repulsed, our hopes began to revive, especially as we all escaped providentially without a wound, and expected that relief must shortly come from Dinapore.

A most dirty-looking set were we after this attack; and for several successive days, most of us in shirts and trousers covered with plaster and brick dust, knocked over us by the hailstorm of bullets; for, though all of us were unhurt, yet there was scarcely one who had not experienced two or three narrow escapes. Three inches difference in a bullet's direction, on two separate occasions, and I should not be writing to you now: on a third, a brick behind which I was squinting, to get a shot at a Sepoy, was shivered by a ball, a great quantity of the fragments and brick dust flying into my face and eyes, making me for a second or two fancy myself hit. Many others of our party could tell similar stories.

After the first day but few of our opponents were killed, and those by long rifle shots, or by snap shots from the top of the building, when a sepoy-looking arm or leg was for a moment visible. They did not, however, give many chances of this kind. During the entire siege, I should think that some twenty or thirty of the villains might have been put *hors de combat*. I should however add that I speak under correction, for I believe that some of the fire-eaters on our side claim nearly that number as their individual share of the slaughter.

Wake, the magistrate of Arrah, was, from the buoyancy of his spirits, the life and soul of our party, and a great favourite with the Sikhs. Though often exposing himself more than necessary, he only fired off his gun twice, being, as he said, quite disgusted with his performance as a fusilier.

The enemy harassed us by occasional shots throughout the night, and in the morning astonished us by a loud taunting shout, followed up by a formidable bang and a splintering of bricks. They had in fact brought two small cannon (4-pounders) to bear upon us, and again for awhile we thought all was up.

After a shot or two, we got more accustomed to them, as we found our main walls tolerably proof, and the bricked-up intervals were not hit more than once in a dozen times. Still it was not agreeable to have two cannon firing at us in cross directions, while the rascally gunners had a complete shelter, formed by bricks, earth, and our own tables and chairs. One gun was sixty yards distant, the other about 150; the balls from the latter scarcely hit the house at all, but went over with a *whizz* and concussion that shook every part. Afterwards they made a hole in the garden-wall behind us, and through it got one of the guns to bear at sixteen yards; even then, however, the shot did not penetrate the main walls, and only hit the loose bricks occasionally, which were not always beaten down, as we had strengthened them from within.

Finally, on the fifth day of the siege, the fellows hoisted up one of the guns on the top of the large house opposite, which was rather serious, as a shot could now be sent over our defences right into the middle of us. But they were not good shots and were not permitted to take aim at leisure, Boyle, Field, Anderson, and others of our best marksmen being continually on the top of our fortress, blazing away on and about the said piece of artillery. We found, nevertheless, a good many of the larger shot, both at the time and afterwards, both inside and embedded in the walls. If the fire from the cannon had proved very serious, there would have been a sally to spike them, if possible, though a large *ascites trocar* was the only spike procurable, and such a use of it entirely *unprofessional*.

Such is the history of the cannons which were brought against us, and which were continually fired during the whole siege, except for a few hours at night.

About midnight on Wednesday we heard regular vollies of musketry and a continuous dropping fire about two miles off, and we knew that relief had arrived; I myself, however, was not sanguine, as the night was pitch dark, and the sound of firing did not seem to approach, indeed rather the contrary. It soon ceased altogether. In fact, as we afterwards learnt, 400 men who had been sent in pursuit of the rebels from Dinapore, had, through the heedlessness of their officers and a too ardent desire to press on to our rescue, suffered themselves to be surprised and surrounded by ten times their force, as they were coolly walking into the town of Arrah, without having taken the precaution of sending out scouts to the right and left, and that too on a dark night. The enemy, who were under cover of thick groves of trees, put one third of the relieving force *hors de combat* by the first volley, and utterly disorganised the whole.[1]

The captain commanding and four other officers were almost immediately killed; the rest retreated as well as they could to the river, harassed all the way by the rebels, and obliged to leave many of the wounded on the road. The remainder of the party finally reached Dinapore

1. See endnote.

in a pitiable state of dejection and fatigue. One of the Sikh police, who accompanied the force, contrived by stratagem to pass the rebel sentries, and was drawn up by ropes into our stronghold. From him we learnt that the English had been surprised and driven back, but hoped that the check was only temporary, and that they would come on again after waiting perhaps for guns or reinforcements.

Had we known the full extent of the catastrophe and afterwards how entirely our case had been given up as hopeless by the Dinapore and Patna authorities, we should, I think, have despaired of relief, and perhaps sallied out in a rash endeavour to get away. Rash and fruitless indeed must such an attempt have proved, for we were watched from all quarters, and when once outside, must have been surrounded and cut up. Indeed had any so escaped, it would have been only by good fortune and swiftness of foot; the slow, sick or wounded, must have perished, and been abandoned where they fell. Happily we did not know the worst, and so determined to hold out while provisions lasted, and then, as a *dernier ressort,* to try to break through and escape.

I cannot give you a detailed account of the events of the whole week; some time, however, about Wednesday, we found that the insurgents, under shelter of some outhouses, which came up close to our walls, were commencing a mine. What did some of our gallant Sikhs do? They stealthily stole out at night and brought in the mining tools, and as we were pressed for water, conceived the idea of digging a well inside the house. This well, eighteen feet deep, was completed in twelve hours; plenty of water was obtained, and all of us, Sikhs and Europeans, had a regular wash, an inadmissible luxury before. The water running down on the outside of the house must have somewhat astonished our foes, if they expected to reduce us by thirst.

To proceed: every night we were on the lookout. Almost every morning, the wretches had some new contrivance for our destruction. One time they tried to smoke us out by burning capsicums to the windward; another time, in the middle of the night, they startled us by a horrible shout, '*Maro! maro!*' (Kill! kill!) and we frequently thought they were coming to the assault.

Luckily for us and for *some* of them, they did not venture on a close attack.

The thing which gave us most apprehension was the mine, which we knew was advancing, but could not prevent its progress, though we countermined under the foundation of the house, and, as we afterwards found, our excavation was immediately beneath that of the enemy. The last day or two of the siege, the mutineers confined themselves to firing a few rifle shots from the top of the opposite house, and to keeping up a pretty constant cannonade; no one of us, however, was hurt, though an Englishman, Mr. Hoyle, was struck on the chest by a spent bullet, which had previously passed through a thick door and a mattress; he was considerably surprised for the moment, though the ball failed to scrape the skin.

The discomforts of our situation were much aggravated by the vicinity of four dead horses, which, when living, some short-sighted mortals had tied up to be ready in case flight were practicable. The poor animals were at once shot by the Sepoys, and the effluvia, arising from their rapid decomposition, was most horrible; had the wind blown from their quarter, we could scarcely have escaped serious illness. Fortunately, the wind came thence for three hours only, but then the stench was deadly. I said, 'This is the worst enemy of all, we shall be struck down with fever or cholera.' However, I administered a dose of port wine to the garrison and took one myself, and as the wind soon changed, we got rid of some portion of the smell; what remained, however, was sufficiently pestiferous and the concomitant plague of flies very troublesome and disgusting.

I may here mention the terrible retribution which befell one of our adversaries, who was shot within seventy yards of the house; his companions did not dare (or care) to carry him off. The man was not quite dead, and for nearly two days we could see him feebly endeavouring to scare off the kites and crows, which appeared however to disregard his efforts; he died at length, but who shall analyse his bodily and mental sufferings ere death came to his relief.

At last, when we almost despaired of succour, one night a voice called out from behind the trees that there was 'some news' and at the same time requested us not to shoot. Two men then, on our invitation, came under the walls, and informed us that the Sepoys had been defeated about six miles off, towards Buxar, by Major Vincent Eyre (the Cabul man), and that, doubtless, our deliverers would arrive in the morning.

This news brought joy into our hearts, though at first we were doubtful of our informants; as one of them, however, suffered himself to be drawn up within our walls, and as the enemy seemed to have left the spot, things looked more cheerful and reassuring.

About midnight a sally was made by some of our party, who found no Sepoys, but brought in the two guns which had so long annoyed us, also a large quantity of powder. They discovered that the enemy's mine extended up to our walls, and that the powder and fuse were prepared, so that, had the relieving force been delayed a few hours, the house probably would have been blown about our ears, for though our mine was immediately beneath that of the besiegers, yet it was very possible we might not have heard their proceeding in time to anticipate the explosion.

The mine was of course at once destroyed, as well as some outhouses which had afforded shelter to our foes, and we remained on the watch till morning, when, about seven o'clock, two of the volunteers who were with Major Eyre rode in, waving their hats. Their advent opened our mouths, and we gave three hearty cheers.

Numbers of the townspeople, servants, and others, soon appeared, bringing in arms of all sorts, some wounded Sepoys and other traitors, and two more cannons, which had been just mounted on our own buggy wheels.

We now certainly heard that some friends at Buxar (the Hon. Captain Hastings and others) had persuaded Major Eyre's *non invitum* to deviate from his course up the river, and come over with three guns, a few artillerymen, and 150 men of Her Majesty's 5th Fusiliers to our rescue, and that this gallant little band, with the aid of a dozen mounted volunteers from Buxar, had twice defeated the enormous odds opposed to them.

It appears that the rebels thought to entrap this party, as they did the poor fellows from Dinapore; but they reckoned without their host, the gallant major not being the man to be caught asleep. They did, however, nearly surround the English, and our deliverers were for some time in great peril; the fire was hot and sustained, and the enemy made an attempt or two to get at the guns. At this crisis the soldiers were ordered to charge, and the wretches dared not abide the onset, but bolted in all directions, collecting finally at Jugdeespore, in the heart of the jungle, the stronghold of Koowar Singh, whom I have mentioned before.

That morning was a cheerful one for us all, and it was very gratifying to hear the comments of the officers, and to exchange hearty shakes of the hand; some of them declared that our defence was 'the finest thing they had ever heard of'. In the course of the day the Sepoy prisoners were tried by court-martial and hanged, after which we all bivouacked in the collector's house and garden, abandoning the place which had so long sheltered us, the major thinking the spot unfavourable, even for our increased force.

It was thought probable that we might be attacked in the night, or, at all events, in the morning, for the insurgents still outnumbered us in the proportion of twenty to one, and we did not know how completely they were for the time disorganised.

After this we rested for a day or two, and lived in a very primitive style, having very few chairs, very few bedsteads, no *punkahs*, and only some stray knives, forks, and plates, of many and various patterns. It was sad to survey the interiors of our several houses; outside they were untouched, the scoundrels having preserved them with a view of permanent residence.

Every article of furniture was, however, taken away or destroyed; the floors were covered ankle-deep with torn books, papers, and pictures. Out of about two hundred and fifty volumes which we possessed, not one remained uninjured. Glass and crockery were found smashed in all directions; our horses were all stolen, and most of the carriages. I found my brougham in a dilapidated state, two of the wheels having been taken off to form a gun-carriage; these I afterwards recovered, and sold the whole concern at Dinapore for 13*l*., thinking myself lucky to get even that.

The little plate we possessed was saved: I had given it in charge to a table-servant, who buried it in his hut. All my old engravings and my father's drawings were torn up and destroyed. In fact we were all stripped of everything; even of clothes we had a *very* scanty supply, and were obliged both to borrow and lend.

After a day or two, the wounded were sent on elephants to Dinapore, and Major Eyre was kind enough to give me the charge of them, so that I had an opportunity of getting a glimpse of L——, who, as you may suppose, had been in some *little* anxiety about her unworthy husband, on whom, however, she was again destined to set eyes. She must tell her own story.

Everybody at Dinapore had given us at Arrah up for lost, excepting L—— herself, who had *one of her pre-sentiments* that I (I suppose being a bad shilling) should turn up again. I did not remain long at Dinapore, thinking it my duty to join the three or four Arrah civilians who remained with Major Eyre. Accordingly on the second evening I started back again, and arrived just in time to join the party, now reinforced by 200 of H. M's 10th Regiment, and to proceed with them to the attack of Jugdeespore, it being my first campaign.

The first day of the march we started at two p.m., and encamped for the night on a tolerably open plain about eight miles from Arrah. The next morning we got up at sunrise, and proceeded along some very bad roads, often covered with mud and water, through which it was slow and laborious work to drag the guns, till our advanced guard reached a brook, near which and on both sides of us the enemy were assembled in force, though for the most part concealed by a thick jungle and their entrenchments. After a round or two of grape from the guns in advance, the interchange of shots became pretty rapid, and the Sepoys' fire gradually extended on both sides to the entire length of our line of march, fortunately without very good aim; the bullets nevertheless often *whizzed* very uncomfortably near us, and several soldiers were wounded.

This state of things, however, did not last long; our advance, about 100 men of H.M.'s 5th Regiment, charged at a run, in skirmishing order, while 100 of the 10th, with a screeching shout, turned the flank of the rebels, and sent them flying into the jungle. On our rear, Sergeant Melville, of the Bengal Artillery, by two or three admirably-aimed shells from a howitzer, completely scattered a large body who were trying to get behind us; and the whole Sepoy force shortly made a rapid retreat. They maintained a running fight for a short time, through a dense jungle and the streets of a village, which they ought to have defended against ten times our number, and at last disappeared altogether, leaving the large village of Jugdeespore and the house of Koowar Singh in our hands.

From that day we never saw them again, but afterwards found that they had at once rapidly decamped in the direction of Sasseram. We remained several days at Jugdeespore, principally, I fancy, for the sake of the wounded, some of whom were seriously injured—indeed, two or three afterwards died—perhaps also to give the major time to communicate with the authorities at Dinapore. We then, after hanging a few more rebels, blew up and destroyed Koowar Singh's palace and a new Hindu temple in its vicinity; set fire to the village in several parts, and departed, following the route of the rebels towards Sasseram.

Orders, however, I believe, came to Major Eyre to return to Arrah; whence I and some of the civil part of the community went to Dinapore; our brave commander and the soldiers proceeding *via* Buxar to Cawnpore and Lucknow, where, under the veteran Havelock, they have again and again been victorious. God bless them all! So much for my campaigning, by which I was considerably knocked up, having had to march on foot the greater part of the way. My *palankeen* was given up to an officer who was lamed temporarily by a kick from a horse.

The foregoing narrative gives a tolerably correct sketch of what passed at Arrah from the arrival of the mutineers to the departure of Major Eyre. Being a private correspondence, it may appear to treat rather of personal adventure than of the doings and sufferings of the whole party; as, however, it was written while the events it relates were yet fresh in the memory, it is perhaps a better description than, writing at a later date, we are now able to give. Some omissions, indeed, we shall endeavour to supply, and make a few brief remarks upon the whole affair.

All who were shut up in the little fort shared the peril, work, and privation pretty equally among them. There were no recognised leaders, though, from their respective offices, the Judge and magistrate were held in greater consideration than the rest; Mr. Boyle's opinion, too, from his engineering skill and resources, carried great weight in all matters connected with the defences of the place.

The Judge was undoubtedly the superior officer, but as for the six weeks previous to the siege, the bulk of the labour, all the executive arrangements, the intelligence department and the management of the Sikhs and police, had, by virtue of his office, fallen to the share of the magistrate, the former gentleman forbore to take the lead to which his rank in the service entitled him, or to interfere with Mr. Wake's measures; he gave, however, his cordial support, and set a good example to all the garrison; wherever hard work was to be done, wherever additional risk was to be incurred, there the Judge was among the foremost. He accompanied Major Eyre afterwards as a volunteer, and, if his name has not been more prominently mentioned in connection with Arrah and Jugdeespore, his own modesty must bear the blame. Had Antony been Brutus, and Brutus Antony, such had not been the case. It would be superfluous here to speak of the merits of Messrs. Wake and Boyle; they have made themselves known to the world, and enough may be gathered from the foregoing pages to show that, whatever reward may be bestowed on them by Government, such can scarcely be in excess of their deserts; but it is no less true that other names ought not to be forgotten.

Throughout the siege, Mr. Field's double-barrel was continually at work, and with fatal effect, both from above the breastwork and the more exposed roof of the building; one Sepoy he shot through the head, just visible at the corner of a wall; another, whom he severely wounded, was, while yet alive, attacked by the kites and crows, his miserable fate afterwards forming one of the foundation-stones of the fanciful superstructure of Anglo-Indian cruelties, recently built up by an antiquarian architect.

Of others we may also speak; of Mr. Colvin, who, as Wake says in his despatch, "rested neither night nor day, and took on himself far more than his share of every disagreeable duty;" of Mr. Cock, always strong, active, and cheerful, ready alike for the musket or the pickaxe, for the loophole or the well; of M. Delpeiroux, who worked, fought, and talked, with the buoyant vivacity peculiar to his French extraction; and of several more: but, where all did their best for the common cause, it would be invidious, if not difficult, to institute comparisons.

Nevertheless, the gallant and simple-hearted Sikhs must not be passed by, whose conduct redounds as much to their own credit as to that of the gallant officer[1] by whom they were enrolled, and whose name they bear. Of a separate race and religion, with different sympathies, with every inducement, pecuniary, or otherwise, held out to them to be faithless, they remained true to their salt and their European comrades. While their countrymen in the upper provinces were instrumental in the preservation of India, these manly fellows stood by the Arrah Europeans in the hour of peril. Independent too of their fidelity, some of the most important measures for the safety of the garrison were originally designed and carried out by the Sikhs. By their stealthy sallies at night, some sheep were procured, and the enemy's own mining tools turned against him. They discovered the hostile mine, and countermined beneath it, and finally dug the well, the happy completion of which tended, perhaps, more than anything to the successful protraction of the defence. Their Jemadar (sub-lieutenant) Hooken Singh, a fine bearded fel-

1. Major Rattray.

low, six feet two inches high, was everywhere active, *Kooch-purwa nahin!* ("No harm done, no matter!") was his laughing sarcastic ejaculation after every unsuccessful cannon shot; and on one occasion he carried his contempt of the enemies so far as to pitch brickbats at them from the top of the house. He was slightly wounded in the hand.

Another Sikh, too, on the second day of the siege, was struck by a musket bullet, which glanced from one of the lower loopholes and entered the back of his head, fracturing the skull and lodging on the brain; he apparently did well at the time, but died two months after at Dinapore. This was the only serious casualty which occurred among the besieged. Others were struck by bricks, and cut by falling glass; and the Judge got a nasty wound on the face by the recoil of his own gun, while firing almost perpendicularly from the top of the house.

Provisions, though tolerably plenteous, were not remarkable for quality. Feverish, jaded, bitten by mosquitoes and flies, each man rose at early dawn from his couch on the floor (Sikhs and Europeans slept cheek by jowl), after having taken his share of watching during the night; he next generally proceeded to a corner where tea was preparing, by means of a patent lamp. If fortunate, and among the first arrivals, he perhaps got a good half cup of tea; but as the pot was continually being filled up with water, without a corresponding supply of the *herb*, the last applicants had to content themselves with little better than the pure element. A few biscuits, some parched grain, and a cheroot completed the breakfast; when the enemy's fire generally commenced for the day.

Dinner, at three o'clock, was an improvement on the former meal; rice and date, with a little chutney, forming a filling, if not very nutritive repast. To this was added on two days a portion of mutton; and each man had a quarter of a bottle of beer, the moment of drinking which was, perhaps, the most luxurious of the twenty-four hours. Plates being scarce, four or five only could dine at once. The dining-room, a sort of pit formed by a small staircase, the lower end of which had been bricked up, was for some time thought the securest place in the house; till one day the diners were astonished by the appearance of a brass piano-castor, which had been fired from one of the cannon, and came smashing through the thin wall, an unexpected and unwelcome guest. Providentially no one was hurt, the usual occupant of the stair opposite to where the missile penetrated being that day late for dinner.

During the progress of the siege, every means that could be suggested were put in execution to heighten and strengthen the defences. The outer breastwork was built higher, doors were taken off their hinges, and with them and some mattresses, the three windows in front of the house were completely blocked up, and rendered tolerably proof against bullets fired from the top of the opposite dwelling.

The mud from the well was used to strengthen the lower defences, and became a most efficient defence even against the cannon.

Some thousands of bullets and cartridges were also made and many new loopholes cut for purposes of offence. A daily narrative of events was written in pencil on the wall Of the little fort. This diary originated thus: after the failure of the relieving force, from Dinapore, two of the garrison, while conversing, expressed a wish that in the event of their own destruction (then considered more than probable) some record should remain of the defence; and one of them suggested the above journal, adding his fears that the Sepoys would not suffer the inscription to remain. Mr. Wake, however, who was passing at the time, caught at the idea, and at once commenced the brief chronicle, which we believe is still in existence on the dilapidated wall.

To analyse the feelings of the besieged Europeans, during that painful week of peril and suspense, would be a vain endeavour. All, upon several distinct occasions, must have thought their last hour at hand; once when they beheld the multitude of foes who rushed to the first attack; once, when they knew of the discomfiture of their friends from Dinapore; and many times when a regular assault was expected. At such moments men keep their thoughts locked in their own breasts. Seasons of depression, both physical and mental, were doubtless common to all, but in the hour of action, one determination, to resist to the last, animated the whole party, and, however apparently hopeless their situation, hope never totally forsook them.

Had they no thoughts of a higher nature, no trust in an all-pervading Providence? Surely yes! Outward demonstration there was none; but they knew that to whatever straits they were reduced, there was *One* above, whose arm is always omnipotent to save; and to Him, who knoweth the secrets of the soul, many an unspoken prayer ascended in their troubles, and afterwards many a heart was silently lifted up in gratitude to that God who delivered them out of their distress.

We now take our leave of the Arrah garrison; but how shall we speak of that glorious band of fearless and true-hearted Britons, who, despising every danger, overcoming every obstacle, deaf to every timid suggestion, perhaps even to the orders of a superior, still pressed onwards in their path of deliverance; twice fought and conquered an enemy twenty times their number, and accomplished the rescue of their countrymen! Gratitude forbids us to be silent, though well aware that all we can say must fail to do justice to the dauntless perseverance and military genius of an Eyre, to the valour and social virtues of such men as Hastings, Jackson, and L'Estrange, to the hardy intrepidity of the Volunteer, or to the world-known fame of the British soldier. Names are rushing to our pen! Scott, Oldfield, Lewis, Mason of the 5th, Eteson, and Melville of the Artillery, Siddale of the Stud, Wylde, Kelly, Nicholl, Barber, and Burrows of the Volunteers, with some 200 others, shared the perils of that brief campaign, and participated in the happiness of the result—happiness, we say, for however grateful the moment of succour to the besieged, however pleasurable their emotions, the feelings of their deliverers must have been still more enviable at the successful issue of their noble and chivalrous exploit.

Many and great events, rapidly following one another in triumphant succession, have almost obliterated from memory the less stirring incidents which form the subject of the preceding pages.

The fall of Delhi; the two reliefs and final capture of Lucknow; the taking of Jhansi, Calpee, and Gwalior, both from the magnitude of their results and the number of British lives involved, have secured great and deserved distinction at the hands of the historian; while the melancholy catastrophe at Cawnpore preserves *that* name forever from oblivion; yet, such grand achievements excepted, there are perhaps few events that, considering all the circumstances of the case, and relative numbers of men engaged, were more productive of immediate and tangible benefit to the British rule in India, than the successful defence at Arrah, and concomitant victories of Major Eyre. This is a bold assertion, but the following considerations will go far towards its support.

The time was the very crisis of the rebellion. All the available European troops were being hurried in small detachments, both by the river and the grand trunk road, to join the small force under Neill and Havelock. Delhi had not fallen; the whole of Behar and a great portion of Bengal was defenceless; 600 men of Her Majesty's 10th Foot barely sufficed to protect Dinapore and Patna, the large Mussulman population of which and the surrounding districts was ripe for a revolt. Several native regiments too, both horse and foot, some of which afterwards took part in the rebellion, were scattered about Behar. The gain or loss of a day was of vital importance to either party.

Suddenly the three regiments at Dinapore revolted and crossed the Soane with their arms. They were joined by Koowar Singh and his retainers, and an army of from 7,000 to 10,000 men arose as if by magic in Shahabad. Several courses were open to the Sepoys: to plunder Gyah and overrun Behar; to threaten Patna and Dinapore; to obstruct the communication and passage of troops on the grand trunk road;

or to march up at once to co-operate with their "brothers" at Lucknow. Any of these plans carried into effect, might have added much to the difficulties of Government. A rapidly increasing hostile force was in fact placed between the English army and its resources.

It is now profitless to speculate upon the amount of mischief that the rebels, under Koowar Singh, at such a time and in such a position, might have been able to effect but for the delay caused by the obstinate defence of the few civilians at Arrah, and the repeated victories of Major Eyre, which completely confounded the mutineers, and finally forced them from the district.

The efforts of a few hundred men, and the military genius of their commander, restored security to the district of Behar. Other native regiments afterwards revolted, and Jugdeespore was again occupied by the Sepoys; but these were then looked upon rather as dangerous marauders, destined to be destroyed when it should be found convenient to attack them, than as threatening the future tranquillity of the district. Neither was the moral effect of the campaign at Arrah on the minds of the natives insignificant, to whom successful revolt against the British Government must have indeed seemed hopeless, when they saw the host of their countrymen kept at bay for seven days by a few civilians and Sikh police; while the British troops, though numbered by scores, were more than a match in the field for almost as many thousands of the mutineers.

As a story, the defence at Arrah lacks the romantic interest which the presence of women and children has imparted to other episodes of the rebellion; nor is the sympathy of the multitude excited even by a melancholy list of killed and wounded; but though the besieged, by what almost seems the special intervention of a merciful Providence, escaped many horrors which had prevailed elsewhere, yet the actual peril to which they were exposed was imminent in the highest degree, while the danger was, in part at least, *voluntarily* incurred, the path of escape being open to the last. The battered condition of their diminutive fort bears ample testimony to the severity and perseverance of the attack, and abundant evidence exists to show how hopelessly desperate their position was considered by the European community in India.

In England intelligence was received of their total destruction, and for a brief period many were mourned for as dead by their friends.

Nor, in considering our subject, should the character of he besiegers be forgotten; for these were not alone the off-scourings of the bazaar and the refuse of the jail, but the warlike population of the Rajpoot villages, headed by perhaps the bravest chieftain who has appeared on the side of the rebellion. Added, too, to the retainers of the veteran Zemindar, was the bulk of three of the best disciplined native regiments—the only ones ever successful in the field against British troops—some of these same Sepoys, by the fierceness of their attack upon the 93rd Highlanders and the Naval Brigade, afterwards added much to the renown of Sir William Peel and his brave companions, by whom, after a hard-fought action, the mutineers were defeated and beaten back.

The above is a tolerably correct account of the proceedings of the Europeans at Arrah, during the period immediately preceding, and subsequent to the revolt of the Sepoy regiments at Dinapore. We have been hampered in our relation, on the one hand by a fear of not doing justice to our countrymen, and on the other, having ourselves participated in the scenes described, by a desire to avoid the appearance of self-glorification in our description. It has, however, been our endeavour to give the reader a just impression of the facts related, and, if he be inclined to bring against us the accusation of egotism and vanity, we would reply to the first charge that our own part in the above transactions was not prominent, and that consequently, in the foregoing pages, we have spoken rather of the actions of others than our own: to the second charge, we plead guilty; we *are* proud to claim a brief association with the defenders of Arrah and the captors of Jugdeespore; nor are we disposed to deny that, hereafter, when looking back upon past events and talking, perhaps by an English fireside, of what then will be the great bygone Sepoy rebellion, when telling of the hairs-breadth escapes of some, the steadfast defence of others, and the perils or anxieties of all who bore a European name in India, it will be no small gratification to us to be able to add, though without the boast of the Trojan leader, *quorum pars fui.*

********

## Note

The following letter, taken from one of the journals of the day, gives a graphic account of this disastrous expedition:

### The Disaster At Arrah

*Patna, July 31.* I thank God that I am alive and well, and able to write you once more. I have been in great danger, and never expected to reach this place alive again, but God has been most merciful to me. As I dare say you would like to hear the whole story, I will begin at the beginning.

About a week ago, as we have long anticipated, the three native regiments at Dinapore mutinied. The general, an old man in his second childhood, managed the whole affair very badly, or rather did nothing at all. No one knew who was in command of the Europeans, no one knew whom to look to for orders, the general was not to be found, and the consequence was that the three regiments managed to get clear off with their arms and ammunition, and almost without losing a single man! The general was advised and asked to send men after them, but this he altogether declined to do, and determined to keep every European in Dinapore, to keep good care of himself.

A day or so after the mutineers left we heard that they had gone to Arrah, where they were attacking poor Wake and party, consisting of about twelve or thirteen Europeans and fifty Sikhs. Wake had strongly fortified a *puckha* house, and laid in lots of ammunition and food. Directly we heard of this, and that they were holding out well, Mr.—— wrote to the general to send out aid to them. At first he refused, but after receiving a strong letter from Mr.——, he consented, and sent off 200 Europeans in a steamer. The next day we heard that the steamer had stuck in the river, and that the general had sent orders to recall them.

Of course, as Englishmen, we were in a great rage at this— leaving a number of poor fellows to their fate; so off——and I started at twelve o'clock at night on Tuesday night to pitch into the old muff. When we got to Dinapore we found that he had been made to change his mind, and had consented to send another steamer off, which luckily happened just to have come in. In this started 150 Europeans and fifty Sikhs; we altogether made up a force of 400 men.

As Wake is one of the greatest friends I have got, I determined to give him a hand if I could, and so volunteered with seven other fellows, five of whom are dead. Well, I was up all that Tuesday night, and at daylight on Wednesday, off we started. We reached the nearest point to Arrah, on the bank of the Ganges, at about two o'clock, and were beginning to get dinner ready (so as to start with a good feed, as we could not expect to get anything on the road), when we heard our advanced guard firing. We immediately all fell in, and went off to the place about two miles off, where we found them drawn up before a large *nullah* (river) about 200 yards wide, firing away at some Sepoys on the other side.

The Sepoys, when they saw us coming, ran away; and then, as we had got so far, we thought we might as well go on. After a delay of two or three hours in getting boats and crossing over, it was nearly seven o'clock before we got well off. From the villagers we heard that Wake was still all right and holding out, which was confirmed by the firing we heard in the direction of Arrah of big guns.

It was a beautiful moonlight night, the road a very bad one (a *kutcha* one in the rains), and wooded country on both sides of us. We did not see a soul on the road, though we passed through several villages, until we came to within five miles of Arrah, where we saw a party of horsemen ahead of us, who galloped off before we got within shot. About eleven o'clock the moon went down; however, as we did not expect that the mutineers would face us, we still went on till we came within about a mile of the fortified house.

We were passing a thick black mango grove to our right, when all of a sudden, without any warning, the whole place was lighted up by a tremendous volley poured into us at about thirty or forty yards' distance. It is impossible to say how many men fired into us—some say 500, some 1500.

The next thing I remember was finding myself alone, lying in the middle of the road, with a crack on the head, and my hat gone. I suppose I must have been stunned for a minute. When I recovered there were several men lying by me, but not a living soul could I see. There were lots to hear, though, for the bullets from right to left were whistling over my head. I was just thinking where our men could be, and which way I should run, when I saw the Sepoys advancing out of the grove with their bayonets within a dozen yards of me. I fired my double-barrel right and left into them, and then ran towards our men, whom I could hear shouting on the left, under a tremendous fire from both parties.

Everything now was in a most dreadful confusion; the men were all scattered in groups of fifties and twenties, firing in every direction, and, I fear, killing each other. At last a Captain Jones, a very fine fellow—our commander was never seen again after the first volley—got hold of a bugler, and got the men together in a sort of hollow place, a half-filled pond. There we all lay down in a square. I was in the middle, with the doctor, helping him to tie up the wounds of the poor fellows, and bringing them water. The firing was all this time going on. The enemy could see us, as we were all dressed in white, while they were nearly naked, and behind trees and walls. However, the men fired about at random. At last the poor doctor was knocked over, badly wounded. It was dreadful to hear the poor wounded fellows asking for help.

I shall never forget that night as long as I live.

We held a consultation, and determined to retreat, as the enemy was at least 3000 to 4000 strong, and had besides several cannon. Directly morning dawned we formed order, and began our retreat. The whole distance, sixteen miles, we walked under a most tremendous fire; the ditches, the jungles, the houses, and, in fact, every place of cover along the road was lined with Sepoys. We kept up a fire as we went along; but what could we do? We could see no enemy, only puffs of smoke. We tried to charge but there was nobody to charge; on all sides they fired into us, and were scattered all over the country in groups of tens and twenties.

Dozens of poor fellows were knocked over within a yard of me on my right and left; but, thank God, I escaped in the most wonderful way. The last five miles of the road I carried a poor wounded fellow, who begged me not to leave him, and though we had had nothing to eat for more than twenty-four hours, and I had no sleep for two nights, I never felt so strong in my life, and I stepped out with the man as if he had been a feather, though he was as big as myself. Poor fellow! The men, most of them more or less wounded, were leaving him behind, and the cowardly Sepoys, who never came within 200 yards of us, were running up to murder him.

I got the poor fellow safe over the *nullah*. I swam out and got a boat, put him in, and went over with a lot of others. The poor fellow thanked me with tears in his eyes. At the crossing of the *nullah* we lost a great many men; they threw away their muskets to pull the boats and to swim over, and were shot down like sheep. I never before knew the horrors of war; and what I have gone through I hope will make a lasting impression on my mind, and make me think more of God and His great goodness to me. I am sure God spared me because He knew I was not fit to die; and I pray God that He will prepare me, for we can truly say we know not what a day may bring forth.

I had several extraordinary escapes; one bullet went between my legs as I was walking, and broke a man's leg in front of me; another bullet hit me on the back of the head, knocking me down but hardly breaking the skin.

Everything here is quiet as yet, but people are in a great panic. I cannot say that I am. Out of the 400 fine fellows that started for Arrah, nearly 200 were killed, and of the remainder I do not think more than fifty to sixty were not wounded; out of seven volunteers five were knocked over, four killed and one wounded. This has been the most disastrous affair that has happened out here. I hope, however, we may soon get some more troops again from Calcutta, and get back our name.

I cry to think of the way we were beaten, and of the number of poor fellows who were killed. I will send this letter at once, for perhaps the *dak* may be stopped, and I may not be able to send a letter in a day or two. I will write again if I can; but do not be alarmed if I do not. The crack on my head hardly broke the skin, and is nothing; the bullet hit me sideways, and the folds of cloth I had round my hat saved me.

*August l.* I have just heard that about thirty men came in last night who got separated from us in the dark, and wandered to the river, where they got off in a native boat. The authentic return I have just seen; 150 men killed, the rest wounded, except about fifty men who escaped untouched. I suppose such a disastrous affair was never heard of before in India—most dreadful mismanagement throughout. Of course we did not relieve poor Wake and his garrison. Poor creatures! We heard that they were still holding out up to two o'clock on the day we left. I am sure, my dearest mother, all your prayers to God for me have been answered. All through that dreadful night, the horrors of which I shall never forget, I felt sure that God would protect me, and bring me back in safety. I will write again; but don't be anxious about me. God will order all for the best, and I feel sure will take care of me, as He has done.

# The Siege at Lucknow

Henry Metcalfe
Private, H. M. 32nd Regiment of Foot

# The Siege at Lucknow

And now I may safely say the Great Siege of Lucknow commenced and history I suppose has faithfully chronicled how it was carried on and how it was ended, with its vicissitudes etc., but a few incidents pertaining thereto and which came under my own observation I hope may not be out of place.

Well, on the morning of the 2nd July my Company were posted at a place called Dr. Fayrah's, and that post was to be the headquarters of the Company while the siege lasted, but occasionally we sent parties to form outposts to more exposed places, and indeed, these posts in too many cases proved forlorn hopes to many a fine young fellow. However, we had to take our chances and trust to God and our weapons, which we had a good supply of the latter. On the morning of the 2nd July our position was attacked from all quarters and indeed very determinedly, but we repelled all their efforts on that day, and you may depend we were very glad when they took it into their heads to retire within their position for that day at all events.

And now about Sir H. Lawrence. On that day, while sitting with his staff in his room in the Residency, a shell was fired into his room but without doing any damage, except the hole it made in the wall. His Staff urged him to leave his present quarters for fear of any harm occurring to him, but he treated the circumstance very lightly, saying, they will never fire another shell into the same place, but on the next day a shell came into the exact place and exploded, and a splinter of said shell hit Sir Henry in the groin and terminated his earthly career, which was not only a noble but a Christianlike and useful one, and the country lost not only a brave but a valuable servant, and the Garrison lost its right arm, indeed, only for the foresight of Sir Henry, I am almost sure we would never be able to hold our position as long as we did, for by his judgment and tact he could see what was coming, and he set about provisioning the place from all sources, and well it was that he did so, and his loss cast a gloom on the whole Garrison. He, when he found his end was near, sent for Colonel Englis of my Regiment and Major Banks—handed over the entire Command to Colonel Englis and the Commissionership (which he held himself) to Major Banks. The latter was killed during the Siege and the former survived the Siege and was promoted to Major-General and K.C.B. all in the space of five months. Quick promotion you will say, but it was nothing extraordinary in those days. Well, the last words he uttered were—

"Dear Inglis, ask the poor fellows who I exposed at Chinut to forgive me. Bid them remember Cawnpore and never surrender. God Bless you all."

And thus ended the life of a gallant soldier and a true Christian. He is in Heaven.

By this time and by some means the authorities heard of the dreadful massacre of Cawnpore and all the Garrison of Lucknow proved how well they kept their promise never, with their lives, let the women and children in their charge fall into the hands of the enemy. How they kept that promise the world knows.

And now to mention a few incidents which occurred during the siege.

One morning in the early part of the Siege, I was sitting in the veranda of the house where we were stationed. A gentleman came out of the house and held a beautiful white terrier dog by a chain. He asked one of our men if he would shoot the dog as he had not the wherewithal to feed the dog as he was only a lodger in the Doctor's house, and he had not time to bring anything with him into the Residency and had to live on the bounty of strangers. Well, this man (I mean the soldier) said he would shoot the dog as he wanted to empty his piece for the purpose of cleaning it, and he would have done it had I not interposed and asked the gentleman if he would let me have the dog to keep, and he said I would not be able to keep him as my allowance was too little for myself. I replied it did not matter, I would share my little allowance with the dog if he would let me have it. He consented, and the dog's life was spared, and a valuable one it proved to me, which I will explain as I go along. The gentleman who owned the dog proved to be the Church of England Chaplain, the Rev. P. Harris, whose good works during the Siege was highly spoken of and mentioned in Sir John Englis despatch of the Siege of Lucknow.

Well, I kept the dog and shared with him my scanty allowance of food which he, the poor dog, seemed to appreciate. Well, after a few days the gentleman called me to him and told me the history of the dog. He said that when he was stationed on the Frontier, himself and his good lady were in the habit of attending the sick soldiers and were very kind to them, and one man in particular of the 75th Regiment. Well, this man did not know how to properly show his appreciation of their kindness, but asked the lady if she would accept of a little white terrier puppy and be kind to it. She took the puppy and promised the dying soldier that she would not part with it except through sheer necessity. The soldier died and the lady kept the dog to that day, and that was the dog that I became possessed of.

"And now," said Mr Harris, "if you and Mrs Harris and myself survive the siege, will you promise to give the dog to Mrs Harris again," and I promised that I would, and I kept my promise.

And now to show what soldiers generally think of worldly matters in war time, and your humble servant in particular,

Mr Harris on this occasion said he would never forget me, and I believe he has not, and said anything that he could do for me he would, and I am certain he would keep his word too if I troubled him. He asked me then if there was anything he could do for me. I considered for a while and came to the conclusion that I wanted a pipe, as the only one I had was taken from me by somebody who thought he had a better right to it than me. Consequently I considered he would be conferring a great favour on me by getting me one. Accordingly I asked him for a pipe. He stared at me, and everything considered, well he might, for when he was considering how he could forward my worldly prospects, I only thought of the worldly pipe. Well, he said, "Metcalfe, you have almost stunned me, for I was thinking of something else, but I must see if I can get you one. I don't smoke myself or I might have no difficulty in getting you one."

However, he went into the house and told his tale about me and the pipe, which caused a general laugh. He could not obtain the pipe however, but instead he presented me with a box of beautiful cigars. After this, the dog accompanied me wherever I went, both day and night, and indeed, it was a good job on some occasions, for when on sentry at night and when the least sign of drowsiness came over me, the dog was sure to notice it and catch my trousers between his teeth and shake me to keep me awake, for it was very hard indeed to keep from getting drowsy considering being belted and under arms day and night, and never had our boots from off our feet for five months. But more about the dog anon.

The Siege continued without intermission. Constant firing and alarms both day and night, till the 20th July when we had an intimation that the enemy were about to attack us from all quarters, and the Brigadier went round all the posts to see that everyone was on the alert. The Officer commanding my Company was having his breakfast at the Officers' Mess and I was ordered to go and apprise him of the Brigadier going round.

I did so and as I was coming back who should I meet but the Brigadier and staff. Of course, he must ask me what I meant by being absent from my post when there was an attack expected. I told him the reason, which turned his wrath from me to my Captain, and as the Brigadier passed me I thought I would wait and see the upshot of the meeting between him and the Captain, so I stepped behind a clump of bamboos and had not long to wait, for on the Captain coming from the Mess, the Brigadier met him and the language between the two was very hot indeed. However, about 10.0 o'clock the game commenced, and a stiff game it was.

The enemy opened the Ball, by blowing a mine which was laid for the Redan Battery, so called after the Great Redan in Sebastopol, but of course, nothing to be compared to the latter. However, they miscalculated the distance and a good job for us, for their intention, to use a nautical phrase, was to board us in the smoke. Well, on they came like so many demons in human forms—all round the position with their bands playing all our National airs, their bugles sounding, flags flying, etc. Scores of times they advanced to the charge and of course, on each occasion were beat back. They kept this game up all day till we were nearly fagged out, and indeed we thought they would force us, but God ordained it otherwise. About 5 p.m. they gave up the job.

Now the position of the Residency was almost divided by a road from the Baily Gate, and on this road we placed a battery of 4 light field pieces, so that if the gate was forced we could play on the party who would force it. If this gate was blown down or burnt, the communication between the positions would be partly cut off, for they had a battery immediately in front of this gate, and the fire from it would completely sweep the road that divided the position. However, this did not occur, but they tried to burn the gate, and indeed almost succeeded, for the gate took fire and there was volunteers asked for to extinguish the fire. I was one who volunteered for this job, which was rather tough whilst it lasted.

They kept up such smart fire of musketry while we were engaged in putting out the fire. We succeeded with only two men slightly wounded. Well, after this to prevent a repetition of the fire we had another loophole cut in the side of the wall so that we could see if there was anyone approaching from an opposite direction.

Well, on the 10th August about 5 p.m. I was sitting on the veranda conversing with a young lady, the name of Alford, whose father was Colonel of one of the regiments which mutinied. She told me she was only just after coming out from England after finishing her education, when the mutiny broke out. Rather a fiery reception for her, you would say, but such was the case. However, she said to me she believed the enemy would force their way in in the long run. Yes, she went as far as to say that they would attack us that night. The Baily Gate would be the place to be attacked. Whether she had a presentiment or not I don't know. I told her that if they made the attempt it must be done while I was on sentry at the new post, for after my time the moon would be risen and the attempt would not be made.

Well, I went on sentry accompanied by my dog. I sat down on an empty case with my firelock between my knees, thinking over the conversation of the afternoon. Just now the dog gave me the usual signal by biting my trousers. I looked through the loophole and sure enough, there was two of my sable friends. One had a bundle of tarred wood on his head, the other was after planting a bundle against the gate. I got my piece through the loophole and took deliberate aim at one of my friends. I could not fire at the two at once. They were not in a position. However, I knocked one over, and the other did not remain to be accommodated with a like dose. However, the gate was saved and remained so till the relief, and I may say that the dog was partly instrumental in saving it.

Next day there was a very severe attack, which lasted a considerable time. In one or two places they effected breaches and were just on the point of storming the breaches when they were routed by hand grenades. Some got under the walls and placed the ladders against the walls with the object of scaling, but their hearts failed them. Then they were afraid to run back for fear of being killed on the road, thus remaining to be treated with hand grenades, which medicine did not agree very well with them. We beat them off on that occasion, and had a short respite for a few days.

During this time Havelock was making rapid strides towards our relief, but owing to sickness and paucity of numbers was forced to retire and await further reinforcements.

*Hope deferred maketh the heart sick* was truly applicable to us. However, on we kept, hammer and tongs, day and night. One time chilled with heavy rain, another scorched with the sun. In the meantime, sickness and bullets were making sad inroads in our numbers, and things began to take on a very gloomy aspect, especially when we found out that Havelock was obliged to retire. They were continually mining and our people counter-mining, and indeed, our people and the enemy miners on more than one occasion met and had hand to hand conflicts, in which our people were victorious, and destroyed their mines.

I am now about to mention a few miraculous escapes. This is one instance. One evening a comrade of mine came to see me, and asked me if I could obtain a tot of rum. Well, I did not care for my rum on that occasion, and I knew if I wanted it I could get it from my friend Mr Harris, so I let him have my tot of rum. He put it in a small bottle, and said this will do nicely, for when I am going on sentry. He left me in a little while for it was a hazard to be absent from your post for any length of time.

Well, about 10 o'clock at night I was on sentry on a heavy siege gun. It was a beautiful night, as calm as possible, and very little firing for a wonder. Just now I saw a shell being thrown from the enemy's position and going in the direction of the tot of rum. I remarked at the time that the shell was going in the direction of Jem, meaning the rum chap—and sure enough it did. It landed at the exact spot, exploded and pitched the rum chap into the trench. Smashed the little bottle which contained it, and which was under his head, for he was lying down at the time, also tore the pillow which was under his head into fragments; wounded Major Low and one or two others, and strange to say, never hurt the individual who it pitched into the trench, except stunning him for the time being, and when he came to himself his first enquiry was "Is my dram of grog all right?"

One of the officers who heard this, laughed, and said, " I'm afraid not, my man, but never mind, I will give you one since that's all you care about."

You will wonder perhaps about me seeing the flight of a shell, but it was quite easy for a spherical shell fired from a mortar does not attain the same velocity as the elongated shell of the present day, and besides, the fuse which is attached to the shell to explode on its arrival at its destination emits sparks all the way in its flight, so that you may easily trace its direction.

I felt rather uneasy on account of my friend's safety, so I paid him a visit the following morning when the above tale was told to me, he remarking at the time that he would never be killed after that. It would just as well if he had been for the poor fellow was reserved for a more painful and lingering death. That night as he was on sentry close to the same spot, he was hit, with a round shot which completely shattered his leg. Of course, the leg had to be amputated above where it was hit so as to come at the sinews, and there being no chloroform, the poor fellow could not bear up against his sufferings and expired in great agony.

Another narrow escape from a shell. This to myself. I was one day at an outpost accompanied by the dog as usual, and also a Sergeant by the name of Varney. We were looking from loopholes and taking an occasional pot shot at some fellows who were employed in cutting at trenches at some distance from our position. Sometimes we could only see their spades when they threw up the earth. I was just after returning my rifle from the loophole but never shifted my position, when in came a shell, right through the loophole and struck the wall in rear of me and exploded, knocking bricks and mortar about the place. You may be sure I was startled and the dog barking like mad. At last he found me covered all over with bricks and mortar. I looked more like a miller than a soldier.

The officer shouted, "Is there anyone hurt?"

The Sergeant shouted, "Yes, I think young Metcalfe is killed," for he thought it was impossible to escape.

However, I shouted that I was alright, and when I presented myself I looked such a picture that I was jolly well laughed at. I thought this was rather queer sympathy, but my faithful quadruped showed me plenty as far as licking and pawing went. How I escaped on that occasion I cannot tell. I only had a few scratches from fragments of broken bricks. I suppose the Almighty thought proper to spare me for more hardships.

I will mention an instance of the foolhardiness of some soldiers, and I may say flying in the face of God. We were one day resting after a very heavy night engaged in burying dead battery horses, for fear of sickness arising from the stench caused by them. Well, we were resting, when the cry of "Turn out" made us all start, sick, lame and lazy just as we were, and none too soon, for they were making for the battery. We had two guns in this battery and one of these was very soon disabled. The other they got off the platform, and we had hard work to get it right again. We had only one artillery man with us for I may say that the greater part of our artillery men were either killed or wounded, so that we had to learn to fire and load the guns ourselves, so that we sometimes found ourselves in the double capacity of artillery and infantry.

Well, on this occasion we had only this one man of the artillery. His name was Barry, which bespeaks his nationality. The bullets were *whizzing* both thick and fast and the men were ducking from them, although when the *whizz* of a bullet is passed that bullet has passed also, but indeed, he must be a very self-possessed man who will not duck his head occasionally. However, this old artillery man rebuked the lads for ducking so to musket shots. He said you should never duck to anything under a 9 pound shot. While he was going on at this rate a fine young Grenadier was shot through the head with a musket ball. This hardened old gunner made remark—"Ha, that fellow has ducked to musket ball at all events," and he said, "if ever I am to be killed in action, I hope it will be from a cannon ball and right in the head, so that my death may be soon and sudden." And indeed his wish was complied with, perhaps sooner than he anticipated, for the next day and at the same hour and the same place, he was accommodated with a round shot right in the head. I need not say his death was soon and sudden.

One more instance and then I will stop and I may say what soldiers are callous to danger and good natured and generous when out of it, perhaps sometimes to a fault. We had a man by the name of Tomlinson who, when he had his allowance of grog no one could stop his tongue from wagging. So much so that, he got the soubriquet of "Chatter-box". Well, one day after he had his allowance he must have a look over the parapet to see how his friends the rebels were getting on, and to show your head was the signal to get a bullet through it. Well, this poor individual showed himself and of course received the usual pill in the head, which of course put an end to his career.

Upon this his comrade remarked, "It serves you jolly well right, you confounded ass. I often told you you would be served like that before you were done and my words have come true." After considering a while and contemplating the corpse of his comrade he burst out crying and said, "Well, I am sorry poor Jack. You were as good a comrade as ever a soldier had," and it was hard to see this generous hearted soldier shed tears. But so it was, from recklessness to tears and from tears back to recklessness again, and so on.

One more. I cannot resist it, and I hope you who read these lines will not take exception to it. It happened in this way. My friend, the Rev Mr Harris, was in the habit of having

Divine Service in the house in which he stayed every Sunday. Indeed, this was about the only way in which we could tell the day of the week, for every day was such a sameness that they all appeared alike to us. Well, on this day Mr Harris came to us and said: "Well now, boys, I am about to have a little Divine Service, and any of you who wish to join me you will be very welcome to come and attend, and those who don't care to come, I hope you will keep quiet and not disturb us."

Well, we all went, with one or two exceptions.

Now, I may state here that the rebels practised all sorts of schemes to alarm the Garrison, and amongst them they had recourse to the following. They would dig a hole in the ground with an angle of say 45 degrees. Place some loose gunpowder, then place a great round stone or a great lump of wood on top of this powder, and the angle in which this hole was cut gave this missile whatever it might be, wood or stone, a certain amount of elevation, so that if there was sufficient powder placed in the hole, when ignited it was sure to land in some part of our position, and it would come on with a tremendous *whirr* and noise that would almost set a person crazy.

Well, when Mr Harris was in the midst of his service with his thoughts bent, not on the rebels, but on something more worthy of his calling, one of these interesting bombs, *i.e.* a large block of wood, came *whizzing* through the air. Just then in rushed a young fellow who had been watching the arrival of this thing. In he rushed into the room where the good Chaplain was engaged in prayer, and without the least warning shouted out, "H—y Japers—Boys, the devils are firing cook houses at us." You can imagine the commotion this caused. The man never gave the Parson, or what he was engaged in, a thought, but when he realised his position you can imagine his feelings.

About this time another gloom was cast on the garrison by the sad end of a gallant young officer by the name of Birch. This young officer was a Lieutenant in one of the Seatapore regiments. I believe his father commanded one of the regiments, and I believe was killed in the Mutiny. He had a brother and two sisters in the garrison, and the sisters were continually in the hospital tending on the sick and wounded (like Mrs Nightingale of Crimea fame), and were consequently almost worshipped by the soldiers. This young officer volunteered to reconnoitre the enemy's position at night, and orders were given accordingly so that the sentries were to be on the look out for his return and not to fire on him on his return.

I don't know how it happened, whether the order was neglected or what was the case. He was returning by the battery at Gubbins bungalow, when the sentry, seeing a man outside the position and not knowing who it was, he fired and shot this gallant young officer, and when falling he cried out, "Oh my God, sentry, you have shot me."

The sentry, you may be sure, felt a great shock. He immediately jumped over the parapet and at the risk of his life brought the body of the young officer in to the position. It seems strange that the officer should be fired on by one of his own men, but that is easily explained. We considered that everyone outside our position were enemies, and the fact that we never challenged anyone at night especially, and also the sentry not being apprised of the fact of the officer being out on that occasion, I think you will say that the sentry was blameless which I am sure he was.

However, the poor fellow fretted so much over the occurrence that he wasted away to skeleton, and for a long time could not be comforted, and he could never be persuaded to accept of promotion. As for the Corporal whose duty it was to acquaint the sentry of the officer being out, I believe he lost his stripe and met with a sad death years after at the Cape of Good Hope.

This family of Birches were very unfortunate. The father killed, the brother killed, and one of the sisters killed with a fragment of an exploded shell when attending on the sick and wounded in the Hospital. The younger brother, who was then a young Cadet, rose to the rank of Major afterwards, and I read was killed when gallantly leading his regiment at the storming of the Fort of Alimessgid in the Khyber Pass during the last Afghan War. I know the place where he fell very well.

And now a little anecdote in connection with an officer of my regiment by the name of McCabe. This was one of the most indefatigable officers in the garrison and one in whom the Brigadier placed great confidence, and indeed which was well deserved. This officer was an Irishman and who was promoted from Sergeant to a commission for bravery displayed at a former campaign.

Well, this officer was continually bobbing about, as the soldiers termed it, and one night he went outside a certain post and it so happened that an Irishman was on sentry on this particular post, and for fear of another mishap he was made acquainted with the officer being out and likely to pay this man a visit. Well, this soldier was rather hot-tempered, but a good soldier. Nevertheless, the officer was a little hasty also. Well, in came the officer right enough without being challenged, and the spirit of discipline being uppermost, he held forth in the following manner.

Officer—"Are you the sentry?"

Sentry answered, "I am, Sir."

Officer—"And why the d— didn't you challenge me?"

Sentry—"Because I knew it was you Sir, and that you would be coming this way."

Officer, very severely, "You should have fired, sir. You are not supposed to know anyone outside of your post, especially at night, sir."

Sentry—"Then by J— C— the next time you will come the same way at night I will accommodate you. I will shoot you right enough."

The officer took no further notice, and did not trouble the same sentry again.

Another about this officer. I was stationed at an outpost called Segoes Bungalow and was very near the enemy's position, so much so indeed that we could hear them giving and receiving orders. One day there was a severe attack commenced by the enemy blowing up a mine. Two of our men were blown into the road and in the smoke they escaped into the position again.

Well, on these fellows came very determinedly, and we had very hard work to keep them out, so much so that I was despatched to this officer for help. I went. The officer said: "Well Metcalfe, what's the matter at Segoes?" meaning the post.

I said, "We are attacked and I am afraid greatly outnumbered, and am sent to you for help."

"Well Metcalfe, I can't afford you any help from my post. We are as bad off as yourselves. Go back and tell your officer that he must keep the post at every risk," at the same time asking me who the officer was and, when I told him, said, "Well, I think I will go with you myself," and indeed that was something for he was really a host in himself and the men thought so much of him that they thought he was as good as twenty men. However, back we ran as fast as we could.

In the meantime our poor fellows were very hard pressed, and on our way he encountered one of the half caste young men on his knees praying away for himself. As soon as the officer saw this, and knowing that the fellow should be helping our men, he gave the poor fellow a cuff in the ear and knocked him off his knees, and said, "What do you mean, you d—d swab. Now is no time for praying when the position is nearly in the hands of the rebels."

We did not wait to see how the poor fellow took it, but scampered on and only just arrived in time. Well, the gallant McCabe was equal to the occasion. He had recourse to a ruse which succeeded admirably. We made such a hubbub in running to the help of our comrades, the officer shouting as if he had a whole regiment with him. He shouted "No. 1 will advance, No. 2 support, No. 3 reserve, Charge," as loud as he could, which had the desired effect. I need not say that the enemy waited for the sham charge, but at night we had to be reinforced, for if the enemy found out the ruse, which most surely they would, I am afraid we would have hard work to withstand their attack. However, they did not trouble us afterwards.

And about McCabe, had he lived he would have been made a Bt. Lieut. Col., but it was not to be. Poor fellow. He was mortally wounded leading his fourth sortie. I was with him on the occasion. I believe that when the Commander-in-Chief heard about him he asked as a favour that he might be allowed to retain his regulation sword as a souvenir of his bravery, for he said there did not exist a braver soldier. The Commander-in-Chief also recommended that this officer's mother might receive a pension, as this, her son, was the sole means of support, so that being a brave soldier and good officer, he was also a good and dutiful son. His mother got the annuity and if alive is drawing it now, and may she continue to do so.

Well now, Havelock and his brave band are approaching. We hear their firing at Allenbaugh, or Allen's garden. We are ordered to be on the alert. All day we are at it, hammer and tongs. This is on the 25th September in the afternoon. Their attacks become more vigorous, the distant cannonading becomes more distinct. The attacks become less frequent. At last we hear the shouts. The most beautiful of sights. We see the head of a column, and at the head rides the bravest of the brave, gallant Havelock, and by his side his gallant and generous comrade Outram. Oh, what welcome, what joy. Comrades shaking hands, rough soldiers embracing and kissing little ones. Women asking for absent friends etc., but why prolong? Suffice it we are saved, and under God, Havelock was the means, his rapid advance and his glorious entry into Lucknow on the 25th. Had it not been for this, I say that not a man, woman or child of the famous Lucknow garrison would be alive on the 27th to tell the tale, for the place was thoroughly undermined, the trains laid and everything ready to blow us into the air.

This was ascertained after Havelock had been in the Residency a few days, and then and not till then the sad tale of the Cawnpore massacre was verified, and the news caused a sort of reaction, so to speak, in the Garrison, for there were a great many who had relatives in Cawnpore.

There was one young lad in the Band named Symes. His mother, stepfather, sister and brother were butchered at Cawnpore. I was by when he heard the news. I thought the poor young fellow's heart broke on the spot. However, he made a sort of vow that when he had a chance he would neither spare man, woman or child on account of his family being slain. However, on the morning after Havelock's force came in there were volunteers asked for, to go and clear the position of any of the enemy who were thought to be still in position around us. Well this young lad happened to be of the party, as also myself.

After we had been out some time I missed this young fellow. I asked if anyone knew what became of him. One man told me he had seen him rush into a house close by, pointing to the house. I thought, strange, that the young lad did not come out of the house again, so I made a rush towards the house and I heard a scuffle going on. I rushed in and saw the lad in a very awkward position. A huge *sepoy* had a hold of the lad's musket and was in the act of cutting at him with his *tulwar*, or native sword. I just arrived in time to save him.

He said to me, "Oh, Harry, I am a brute."

I said, "How is that Jack?"

He said, "Oh, I said when I came out I would spare no-one, and I fired at a young woman and I am afraid I killed her, and by so doing I have placed myself on a par with the rebels by me killing her. I will not get my own relatives restored to me and consequently I am not fit to be called a soldier or a Christian."

I rallied him on it and said perhaps he had not killed her, but it was no use. I asked him to point out the spot where this took place. He did so, and on going towards the spot we saw some of our men stooping over someone who was laying down. When we got to the spot we found it to be the young woman who the young lad had fired at. She was slightly wounded and had fainted, and in this position our men had found her, and seeing her seemingly alright this young lad almost jumped for joy at the thought of him not killing her. A few men brought this poor young native woman into the garrison and had her wound dressed, and she was then sent about her business, a striking contrast to the way our poor women and children were treated, but then we were soldiers—they were fiends.

Well, this young lad rallied a little and seemed a little more settled, and on our advance we saw a mosque, or native temple, from which temple the rebels had used to keep up an incessant fire on our position.

The officer said, "Now lads, we must take this sammy-house at a rush." He placed himself in front, waved his sword.

That was enough. The thing was done before we knew where we were, and in overhauling the place we found a quantity of loose powder which I suppose they were about to destroy when we suddenly burst upon them and made them change their plans. We asked the officer to let us destroy it, but he would not allow it without superior authority.

Well, this young lad came into the place and without noticing the powder, or perhaps not caring, threw himself down to rest as he felt rather jaded and out of sorts. In the meantime the officer had planted a sentinel at one of the windows to look out, and on the sentry seeing a *sepoy* running past let fly at him. Well, a portion of the lighted paper was blown into the place where the powder was strewed and where the lad Symes was lying, and the consequence was an immediate explosion. The powder blew up and with it the poor lad, and a frightful spectacle he presented. He was taken in and placed in the hospital, where I remained with him till he died in great agony that night.

I forgot to say that he had two sisters in the garrison, both very respectable young women, and married, one to a Colour

Sergeant, and the other to the Drum Major. About 10 p.m. the two sisters came to see him. He was then, poor fellow, very low indeed, and the poor sisters, whose husbands were out in the City with a sortie party, and they did not know whether they were dead or alive. I say that seeing these dear sisters talking about their loss at Cawnpore and their dying brother (the last prop of their family), why, it was simply heart rending, so much so that I had to beg of them to leave us and not to embitter the poor lad's last moments. They left, poor things, on my promising to let them know when he was on the point of death.

Well, they left and they had scarcely gone when the poor lad breathed his last. I went to fetch the sisters, and when we got back there was no signs of the remains to be found anywhere. We searched high and low, but no trace could we find. We enquired of the doctors. They could not tell us anything, only they supposed he was taken away to be buried. Well, we started for the graveyard, and it was a beautiful moonlight night, so clear that you could see to pick a pin up, as the saying is, for in India the moon shines with far more brilliancy than at home in England.

The reason that I mention this was that, strange to say, during our tour round the graveyard not a single shot was fired at us, and at other times you could scarcely show your nose there without having dozens of shots fired at you, so much so indeed that the dead were generally buried under cover of darkness, and you may be sure without much military pomp or ceremony. A few hasty prayers, a few shovels full of earth, and all was done.

Well, we could not find what we sought for and so had to retrace our steps to the hospital, for the sisters would not relinquish the hope of having a last farewell look on the remains of their dear brother. At last we found where the remains were deposited. We ran rather than walked and arrived just in time to see two native attendants sewing the remains up in his *guthery*, or native rug. The sisters wanted to have one more look and natives would not let them because it involved the re-opening of their work and going over the whole thing again. They offered money, but no, they were resolute. At last the sisters appealed to me. I could not withstand the appeal. I asked the natives to let them look. They refused. I then showed them a horse pistol I had with me and said I would blow their brains out if they did not comply. This had the desired effect. They let them look, and I was very sorry after that I got them the privilege, for the scene that ensued I won't attempt to describe. However, I had almost to drag them away, almost more dead than alive, and thus ended this little affair.

Well after Havelock came in, of course he thought he would have nothing to do but withdraw the whole of the force from Lucknow and march back on Cawnpore, but he reckoned without his host. On this account he left all his stores and provisions at Allenbaugh and when he came into us instead of being able to go out he and his force were forced to remain, until finally relieved by Sir Colin Campbell, and consequently reduced our small stock of provisions to one half.

Well, you know self-preservation is the first law of nature, and so it was with your humble servant and his faithful dog, who you have no doubt lost sight of for some time, and in whom you will be a little interested.

You know our very small allowance of food and that small allowance being rendered beautifully less by having more mouths to consume it. You may be sure there would be but a very small amount come to the faithful dog's share, so that I thought, and very reluctantly indeed, the best way out of the difficulty would be to give him back to Mr Harris. So I accordingly brought him the dog and told him that I thought I had fulfilled my part of the compact on account of the dog. I said I thought we had survived the siege and that I had much pleasure in returning the dog to Mrs Harris safe and sound. I did not like to tell him the real cause, but I believe he guessed it. He took the dog back, and by God's help we all survived the siege—Mrs Harris, Mr Harris, Metcalfe and the dog.

But the siege was not over just then. It lasted until finally relieved on the 22nd November by Sir Colin Campbell, and the first thing he did on forming the communication was to send to each man of the beleaguered garrison a small loaf of bread and a dram of grog, both of which I need not say were very much appreciated by us poor half famished wretches.

However, before the final relief we had to undergo not a little hardship, what with starvation, sickness, attacks, etc. We had plenty to occupy our time. Indeed, we had no time. I asked a comrade of mine one day how he was getting on. He said, "all right."

"Why, I heard you were very sick Jim."

"Sick be hanged man, a fellow hasn't time to get sick now."

About the 28th September I was one of some volunteers who were called on to storm a house called Johannas Bungalow. This was a house on the very border of our position, and which we stormed once before and beat the enemy out of it, but owing to our paucity of numbers we were not able to occupy it, and the Brigadier thought that after being thrashed out of it once they would not have the cheek to occupy it again, but he was deceived. They occupied it again the same night. I was wounded in both legs on this occasion, and the same place happened to be the scene of a little affair which was nearly proving fatal to your humble servant.

Those fellows who occupied this place for the second time proved very troublesome to us, and the Brigadier determined to make another attempt, and after taking it, to blow the place up with gunpowder. Consequently, volunteers were called for again. Well, I volunteered again, my former wounds being nearly well. About this time anyway I considered I was all right. Well, there happened to be a great tall soldier of the Grenadiers with the party. There were two ladders placed against the two windows, and the word "Forward" was given. We all rushed off together, and whether me being light or small, or what, I reached one of the ladders just as the tall Grenadier reached the other, and it was a race between him and me, and although I reached every rung of my ladder as soon as he reached his, still he seemed to be higher than I was, and so he was, and I never allowed for his height. However, I believe he got in at his window before I got in at mine, but when I got in I could not see anyone in my room. Consequently I concluded that the enemy did not wait for us but took to their heels as soon as we rushed forward.

Well, I looked round the room to see if there was anything worth laying hands on in the shape of provisions etc. Well, there was a very large box, something about or nearly resembling a large flour bin. The lid was partly up so I threw it entirely up, and what was my astonishment to see three of my sable friends sitting on their haunches in this big box. Well, I shot one and bayoneted another, but the third was on me like mad and before I knew where I was he had hold of my musket by the muzzle so that I could not use the bayonet at him.

So there I was, he chopping away at me with his native sword, and me defending myself the best way I could by throwing up the butt of my musket to protect my head and trying to close with him, which I knew was my only chance. In doing this I received a chop from his sword on the left hand which divided the knuckle and nearly cut off my thumb. Well, he had his sword raised to give me, I suppose, the final stroke, when in rushed the tall Grenadier. Tom Carrol took in the situation at a glance and soon put an end to my antagonist by burying the hammer of his musket in the fellow's skull, and when he saw me all covered with blood he shouted out a great hoarse laugh and said, "You little swab, you were very near being done for."

And indeed, so I was. I then showed him the box and its contents, and I can tell you it rather astonished him.

I was laid up with my hand for a few days. About a fortnight after this we had another sortie, and that was to try and capture a heavy Houtzer from the enemy. Now, there were three of this party who knew the position of this gun.

That was a man the name of Ryan, another by the name of Kelly, and myself, and the man who would be first at this gun would be recommended. Well, we all of course would vie for this honour. Well, this Ryan took a circuit on purpose to be first. Well, there was a single brick wall presented itself to us in the way of an obstacle. The other man Kelly knocked the bricks out with the butt of his musket, and as soon as I saw room enough I darted through, and not waiting for anyone I ran off in the direction, never giving it a thought what danger there might be attached to it, and indeed I must admit it was very foolhardy on my part. Be that as it may, there I got before anyone else and lo, the gun was gone. Well, I had time to scratch my initials of my name in the wheel tracks, left there and got into a yard where the old King kept his game fowl. Well now, I upset two of the baskets that contained the fowl. I got two of them and tied them together before the others came in. Well, I went into a shed and got a *chatty* full of flour. I emptied this flour into a turban that I had round my cap.

A bugler, by the name of King said, "Harry, you had better throw away that flour."

I said, "Why, George?"

"It might be poisoned Harry, you know."

"Poison here or poison there George, I will stick to it. I might as well die of poison as die of hunger."

Well, after all this the officer recommended Kelly as being the first man at the place where the gun had been, but Kelly manfully enough repudiated the recommendation in my favour (indeed he could do no other) for there was proof positive in my favour, but the recommendation came to nothing then, but perhaps afterwards it did, but I got no cross, which are getting as common as dirt nowadays.

Well, we got back to the Garrison about 5 p.m. after taking and blowing up a few places, and when I got in I was asked how much I would take for the fowls. I mentioned some fabulous sum, and the parties were only too willing to give it, but I declined. I gave one fowl to Mrs Harris and the other I gave to a lady who had four or five little ones, and little ones who were reared in the lap of oriental luxury, but who, poor little things, were deprived of them during the siege.

To do these people justice they did not want to deprive me of the fowl, but I made them take them, and I have no doubt they enjoyed the morsel, and as for the poisoned flour, I tell you it made about the sweetest bread I thought that ever I tasted, and my comrade nor me, well we were not poisoned.

And with this I will wind up the Siege of Lucknow as far as I was concerned.

# The Siege of Delhi

George Bourchier
Captain, Bengal Horse Artillery

# The Siege of Delhi

The rain had been falling heavily and the clouds were lowering. At 3 o'clock p.m., on the 30th of July, we started, and without mishap arrived within sight of Balachore by daylight The Himalayas were looking very majestic; we began to think our *cicerone* right; all seemed *couleur de rose:* but on arriving at the staging bungalow, alas! all our hopes were dashed to the ground. A fat, and, strange to say, blue-eyed native official, of the Mohammedan tribe, rushed to the house to tell me that we must return immediately; and, if possible, by a cross and unfrequented road which led direct to Phillore, as, in consequence of some disturbance at Lahore, orders had just been received to destroy all the boats on the Sutlej, and that it was impossible we could cross at Rooper.

To me he imparted the additional pleasing intelligence that if, as he suspected, the regiments had mutinied at Lahore, they would, in all probability, make for Balachore.* The latter I did not at the time communicate to my wife, but the anxiety I felt at every moment's delay I cannot describe.

No sooner had we made preparations for a fresh start than the rain came down in torrents; a stream close to the bungalow became impassable, and the whole face of the country assumed the appearance of a lake.

At 2 o'clock p.m. the rain ceased; the river, which, like all streams near the Himalayas, fell as quickly as it rose, became

---

* The 26th N. I. had the day before mutinied at Lahore, killed their colonel, and deserted in a body.

passable, and we determined to make a start; anything I felt was better than remaining where we were, with the chance of falling into the hands of ruffians who never had shown mercy, even to women and children.

Although the stream had somewhat subsided, the waters were still deep; for ten miles I waded above my knees, the axles of the carriage being under water, never knowing for a moment that it might not be precipitated into some hidden stream or deep hole. To do the bearers who dragged the carriage, and the servants who accompanied as, justice, they worked like slaves; although poor creatures they had had little to eat, and saw little in the prospect to encourage them.

At one time I despaired of reaching our destination, and thought we must have stopped until the waters had become less. It became deeper and deeper, and at one time we had eight inches of water inside the carriage. Everything in the shape of clothing for the poor children was drenched, many things floated away, and the few biscuits we had for them were reduced to pulp.

Ladies under trying circumstances are far better sufferers than men. History cannot show greater heroism than they have evinced during this terribly eventful year, although in many cases tried to the utmost.

From the commencement of the mutiny, although surrounded by events calculated to excite alarm, not a murmur had I heard from her whose only thought was for the little ones who were so entirely dependent on her care.

By degrees we extricated ourselves from the lowlands near the river, and proceeded in comparative comfort for some hours, until night set in, and with it the rain began to fall. Thankful that the dear ones in the carriage, fairly exhausted, had fallen asleep, we pushed on slowly until about two o'clock in the morning; when, as a crowning point, the rain put out our torch, which, up to the present time we had, by dint of great care, preserved alight. Without its friendly aid it was impossible we could in any way proceed. In hopes that some village might be near, we all halloed for assistance. No response was given, the track was nowhere visible, and we determined to halt until the return of day. Each crouched where most shelter was procurable, to indulge in an hour's sleep.

As day dawned we discovered that it was indeed well we had halted. The ground for some distance had been slightly cut up, but further ahead it was a mass of ravines; the road, if so it could be called, taking a tortuous course through them, and in many places the water was very deep. We got on slowly, arriving at Phillore at twelve o'clock in the daytime. Here we found that the column, delayed by the very heavy rain, was just crossing the Sutlej. Colonel Dawes' troop of Horse Artillery had been ordered to remain in the Punjab, much to their disappointment. Our friends supplied all our wants, and we arrived at Loodiana, at 9 p.m., to enjoy a night's sound rest—a thing we had not known since leaving Lahore.

Once again upon the beaten and frequented road, our troubles were comparatively at an end. We started at 7 a.m. on the morning of the 2nd of August, and arrived at the foot of the Himalayas on the morning of the 4th, and at Simla on the afternoon of the 5th.

Having spent three happy and quiet days with my family, and been enabled to settle them with every comfort around them, I was obliged, on the morning of the 8th, to make a rush down, calculating to catch the column at Kurnal.

A couple of good strong ponies carried me forty-four miles to the foot of the hills in eight hours. There I learnt that General Nicholson had pushed on by forced marches, and that I should have difficulty in overtaking him. Sooner would I have lost my commission than have allowed my battery to march into Delhi without me.

The good bustling old landlady of the Bull Inn, at Kalka, "a thorough old soldier," sympathising fully with my distress, fastened me down to cold chicken and a bottle of beer, while she went out herself to raise the post-office officials to give me an express cart Her arguments and entreaties prevailed; in she rushed with the glad tidings of her success, with the mail cart at her tail. In went the bundle, up I jumped, and after a severe fight with the ponies at starting, away we went at the rate of eleven miles an hour, over as rough and rocky a road as one could well imagine.

The first forty miles riding down the hills had taken it pretty well out of me; but the cart, devoid of its usual ballast in the shape of mail bags, fractured nearly every bone in my body. At 10 at night we arrived at Umballah, as the Loodiana cart with the mails from the north arrived at the post-office.

Little dreaming of any opposition to my onward progress, my bundle, as much bumped about as its master, was being transferred to the new vehicle, when a sable-countenanced apothecary appeared upon the stage, and at once disputed my right to the vacant seat, he having, as he stated, been waiting for three days. An argument, not of the gentlest kind, immediately sprang up as to whether the inflictor or healer of wounds was most urgently required at Delhi. He was positive that his advent would be hailed with joy, while that of a captain of artillery would be but a matter of indifference. Perhaps he was right: be that as it may, while he stormed I adjusted my seat and started, leaving my little black friend vowing that all sorts of pains and penalties should attach to my devoted person.

Nature borne up by strong excitement can bear an immense deal, particularly when the conviction is clear that a certain thing must be done. The first three stages of the road, from Umballah to the Markundah river, were so bad that sleep was out of the question, and even to hold on was a matter of difficulty; but beyond, where the road was well made, after three times rescuing me from falling from my perch, the driver found that it was impossible to keep me awake. A broken spring, to which previously he had appeared perfectly indifferent, was his excuse to transfer the mails and my sleeping self to a covered van, known as "a penny a miler;" the transfer I just remember, but nothing more, until the execrations of the driver at his done-up pony, awakened me to the fact that the once large but now deserted station of Kurnal was in sight. Here I had hoped to have found the column; but *ignis-fatuus*-like it had fled; my horses were laid upon the road for a twenty-mile ride: a cup of tea and a Newfoundland dog sort of shake was all I had time for.

At 7 a.m. I again started, and found myself two hours afterwards at Paneeput with my old comrades, chattering round the mess-table of my battery, after travelling 168 miles in the preceding twenty-five hours; sixty-four miles having been done on horseback, the remainder on the mail cart.

We were now within sound of the guns at Delhi: morning, evening, and noonday, their thunder penetrated to our camp, and all were burning with anxiety to witness for ourselves what was the state of affairs and the position occupied by our force.

Some few of us thought we knew Delhi, but found afterwards how painfully slight was the knowledge of that wonderfully strong position. General Nicholson had preceded the column and gone into Delhi, sending back orders that on the following day (the 10th) we were to march to Lursowlee.

There were to be seen the first signs of that deadly struggle we were about to enter upon. The town was held for us by the Jheend Rajah, who had undertaken to keep open our communication towards the Punjab. Across the road and extending far right and left were field-works furnished with guns. The Rajah's force being encamped within this line of defence.

On the 11th we halted at Lursowlee, to allow Captain Green's Punjab regiment to swell our ranks, and on the following day encamped at Raie, where General Nicholson again joined the column.

Expectation was on tiptoe to hear his opinion as to the state of affairs. He told me that the tide had turned, but that we should have some tough work; and that General Wilson had promised our column a little job, to try our "'prentice hands," to dislodge a body of troops who had taken up their position with some guns in the neighbourhood of the Ludlow Castle.*

On the 12th we marched to Raie, and as we approached nearer, curiosity and expectation knew no bounds: a native trooper who came with letters from the camp, was squeezed dry of every idea he possessed. "Batteries," he said, "we should find extended further than the eye could reach, shot and shell were ordinary compliments, and a night's rest was a thing we none of us must again hope for."

The 13th brought us to Alipore, not more than seven miles from the camp; with our glasses we could discern the Flagstaff Tower on the top of the ridge, and at night the flashes of the guns, not few or far between, told that they were "making a night of it." Through our nasal organs we were most painfully made aware of the scenes we were about to enter upon. From Alipore to the camp, death in every shape greeted our approach; even the trees, hacked about for the camels' food, had a most desolate appearance, throwing their naked boughs towards heaven as if invoking pity for themselves or punishment on their destroyers.

A messenger was sent express to our camp to intimate that we might expect an attack, and that a force had been sent out from Delhi to prevent our junction with General Wilson.

Nothing seemed more likely. Our greatest safety from surprise was the state of the country: five yards on either side of the road (except exactly the ground on which we were encamped) was a swamp, impracticable for artillery or cavalry; but on this occasion, as in most others during the mutiny when head and combination were necessary, the enemy signally failed to take advantage of their position.

Although fully prepared for an attack, none was attempted. On the morning of the 14th of August, having passed the

---

* The gnus proved so annoying to the troops at the Metcalfe picquet, and also to the camp that their capture could not he delayed. Brigadier Showers took the party completely by surprise, and brought four guns into camp.

strongly fortified position of Badulke-*serai*, where the mutineers made their first stand against, the Commander-in-Chief, with our bands playing, and hearty cheers, we joined General Wilson's force, which had for so long a time withstood the brunt of the mutiny.

## The Force Before Delhi

The Delhi field force has been compared in many respects, on a small scale, to the allied armies before Sebastopol; in some points there is a resemblance: both drew their supplies and reinforcements from their rear, and from a great distance; each was unable, from its great inferiority in numbers, compared with the besieged, to invest the fortress; while in each case the besieged had the command of an unlimited supply of ordnance and ordnance stores.

The position of the army might more correctly have been called an entrenched camp, holding the forces within the city in check, and from time to time repelling their numerous sorties; keeping up a constant fire from a series of batteries erected on a long rocky ridge, which formed a natural protection to the front of the position, while on the right, at a high mound, was formed a strong picquet to protect that flank of the camp.

I write but of what took place at Delhi after our arrival, and therefore can give no detailed account of the numerous engagements which occurred prior to the arrival of the column; suffice it, that for the two first months, from the 8th of June to the beginning of August, seldom a day passed without either a real or a feigned attack: every detachment of reinforcements, as they joined, had to prove their fidelity to the Mohammedan cause by a decided engagement.

Yet, although so tremendously overpowering in numbers, but once did a few cavalry troopers penetrate into the camp, and few of them returned to tell the tale.

At the time we arrived things were remarkably quiet, and the morning and evening game at long bowls, was our only occupation; but still, although no further reinforcements were expected, it was necessary to wait for the siege train, now *en route* for Ferozepore, before the actual siege could be commenced upon.

General Wilson, from the time he took command on the 17th of July, had apparently determined to leave nothing to chance; he must have known full well that failure would be disastrous, not only to his force, but to India at large. The Punjab, up to the present time tranquil, was in a state of vacillation; placards of an inflammatory nature were posted in every village; the Bombay army was shaky; a rising which cut off our postal communications with Bombay at Gogaira had already taken place; and, to use the words of the Judicial Commissioner in the Punjab, "India seemed to be slipping through our fingers:" and so it was.

Every day's delay to the siege train was of vital importance; but a line of carts, eight miles long, travels slowly, and it was many days yet before it could be expected.

But to return to Delhi. General Wilson had determined to remain as much as possible on the defensive until the train arrived. The position was strengthened by connecting the batteries with walls on the ridge, and the ridge with the Subzie Mundie and Sammy-House, our right rear and right front posts, and providing more effectual cover for the guns and picquets.

The troops were relieved from duty as much as possible; no bugles, save the "turn out" and "alarm," were allowed, and then only as a preparatory measure; no movement was allowed without positive orders from the generals of division or their brigadiers.

Thus we found things at Delhi. Far from being in a dispirited state, as it was supposed, the greatest confidence as to the final result existed, and when off duty, there was no lack even of amusement: quoits, and sometimes football, in the headquarters camp, made the evening pass merrily by.

The body of troops which left Delhi on the 13th or 14th,

with the apparent view of preventing the junction of General Nicholson's force with the main army, was still unaccounted for; and as it was pretty certain they were up to some mischief, either by cutting off our communications with the Punjab, or attacking our camp in the rear, Lieutenant Hodson, with a body of cavalry numbering about 300 sabres, was sent to watch their proceedings.

On the first morning he came upon a party of cavalry, who were surprised, and all but annihilated. He then pushed on for Rohtuck, and from the reports which reached the camp, serious apprehensions were entertained for his little band; they were happily unfounded. He returned on the 22nd August, after having dispersed and driven back towards Delhi the whole force; which had, it was discovered, been sent to raise revenue in the Rohtuck district.

The enemy were supplied with the best information, and were well aware that the train, which was but slightly escorted, was *en route* from Ferozepore.

On the 24th of August, a force, with about eighteen guns, was detached from the city to intercept its progress. This move from the "castle" was met by a "knight," who allowed no difficulties to hinder the attainment of his object.

With a column consisting of sixteen Horse Artillery guns, four squadrons of cavalry, and about 1,600 infantry; General Nicholson started on the morning of the 25th.

The track he had to travel was off the Grand Trunk Road, and on account of the deep swamps, all but impassable for artillery; but Tombs, who commanded that branch, had as little idea of an obstacle being insurmountable as the General himself.

In many places, axle-deep in water and mud, the guns had to be extricated by hand, and by dint of undaunted perseverance. I must here trespass on Major Norman's narrative for a detailed account of this enterprise and engagement.

At Nangloe, nine miles from camp, intelligence was received of the enemy's movements, and the troops were immediately pushed on towards Nujjufghur. Arriving there at about four in the afternoon, the enemy were found occupying a position about a mile and three-quarters in length, extending from the canal bridge to the town of Nujjufghur. The baggage was left behind, protected by a detachment of the 2nd Punjab Cavalry and 120 Punjab Horse.

The strongest point of the enemy's position was an old *serai* on their left, in which they had posted four guns; nine more were between the *serai* and the canal bridge. By 5 p.m. the troops were across the ford, and advanced to the attack of the *serai*; with the intention, after its capture, of sweeping down to the left, along the enemy's line, to the bridge.

One hundred men from each corps formed the reserve. The 61st Foot, 1st Bengal Fusiliers, and 2nd Punjab Infantry, were formed up with the artillery on either flank, supported by the 9th Lancers and Cavalry of the Guide corps.

After a few rounds from the guns, the Infantry charged, carried the position, changed front, and swept down the enemy's line. The rebels fled over the bridge, while the guns were playing on them. Thirteen pieces of artillery, with a large quantity of ammunition, was left in our hands.

The 1st Punjab Infantry cleared the town of Nujjufghur, and were sent to take a village in their rear; where the resistance was so obstinate, that the 61st Foot were sent back in support The village was evacuated during the night.

The troops bivouacked upon the ground without food, having been either fighting or marching all day.

The Sappers mined and blew up the Nujjufghur bridge.

The column returned to camp on the evening of the 26th of August The enemy, having quite given up all idea of going to our rear, were in full retreat on Delhi.

On the morning of the 26th, the mutineers, believing that the force left in camp after General Nicholson's departure was very small, attacked the right of the ridge, and opened guns from the Ludlow Castle and a battery lately formed on the opposite bank of the river.

The attack was not of a serious nature, and was soon repulsed, the enemy suffering much from the Artillery fire. From information subsequently obtained, it is certain that the King of Delhi, from the dates of General Nicholson's junction with General Wilson, and the loss of his guns at Nujjufghur only a few days afterwards, felt that all chance of success against the British force was at an end.

Such was the dread in which the wrath of this pseudo king was held, that the result of the Nujjufghur expedition was for a time concealed from him, and a fictitious story circulated, that not only were their own guns being brought back by the country people, but those also which had been captured from the British; that scarcity of provisions had obliged them to return without their guns, which were delayed in consequence of the swampy state of the country.

This story, so improbable, was current but a short time; and when the truth came to light, the rage of the imbecile monster is said to have been excessive. The Commander, Bukht Khan, a *subadar* of artillery, who had been chief among the mutineers, and had raised the standard of rebellion in Rohilcund, was dismissed from the presence in disgrace. The Council was harangued in no measured terms as to their duplicity and unvaried failure in every attempt against the handful of British troops, and terms were sought, clandestinely, by members of the Royal family.

The reply was the only one a British General could give. That it would be delivered at the ridge at a certain hour; at which time every gun opened upon the city, and told plainly the terms that might be expected.

The first act of the Delhi tragedy may here be said to have terminated. The train was at hand, and to save a day's delay was of the utmost importance, not only to the country in general, but more especially to the Delhi Field Force.

The season was approaching when a low fever became prevalent, of a most debilitating nature; the hospitals were filling daily, more and more rapidly, and cholera seemed on the increase. On the 3rd of September, supported by two squadrons of the 9th Lancers, No. 17 Battery left Delhi for Rhei, distant about sixteen miles, to reinforce the Belooch Battalion, which formed the only escort to the siege train.

The stink of dead cattle along the road for the first seven miles, was even worse than when we came into Delhi three weeks before; the rest of the trip was like a holiday, the contrast of the fresh country air being grateful to the senses after the tainted atmosphere we had been inhaling.

We had not long to wait before the line of guns, howitzers, and mortar carts, chiefly drawn by elephants, soon "hove in sight," followed by a train of carts drawn by oxen, extending over a distance of eight miles, loaded with shot, shell, and ammunition of every kind and description. Poor *pandy*,* what a pounding was in store for you.

At half-past 5 p.m. on the 3rd, we started on our return to camp. It was a wearisome trip, but without adventure; the train was safely brought into camp on the morning of the 4th, when operations were commenced in earnest.

About this time a far more destroying enemy than the enemy's shot and shell attacked my company. Cholera in its worst form broke out among them. It was almost a matter of certainty that every corps as it arrived went through a course

---

* From the adoption of the word *pandy*, as the cognomen of a mutinous *sepoy* in general, it has been supposed that the rising was acknowledged as a Hindu insurrection; *pandy* being the designation of a caste of Hindus. The first two men hung at Barrackpore were *pandies* by caste, hence all *sepoys* were *pandies*, and ever will be so called.

of this terrible disease. H. M.'s 52nd and 61st, who arrived at the same time, suffered also severely. The attacks of the disease seemed to justify the theory that certain constitutions taking in a certain amount of miasma, the result was cholera and death. Hardly a man taken escaped, and out of seventy-five, in the course of a few days, seven were lying in the graveyard.

Personally, I took little part in the work of the trenches. It was General Wilson's wish as much as possible to keep my Battery (No. 17) in reserve, to form part of the column which, immediately after the assault, was to follow the enemy in pursuit. This was an arrangement little to our minds, and I fear our feelings were of a kind little less mutinous than those of the *sepoys* within the city. In fact, I am not sure that it was not suggested that we should walk over to the enemy, battery and all. We were only told to obey orders, like good children; so we sulked quietly in our tents, or from the ridge watched the storm below.

The batteries on the ridge formed a base on which our siege operations commenced, and may be said not only to have formed a protecting rampart to our position, but a first parallel of investment; while a ravine running nearly parallel to it, and extending up to the Ludlow Castle, at a distance averaging from six to seven hundred yards from the walls, was our second parallel, and saved an immense deal of labour and loss of life.

The first operations were commenced early in September, prior to the arrival of the siege train. A trench was dug on the left of the Sammy House (our most advanced position on the right of the ridge), and in this trench a battery was erected for four 9-pounders and two 24-pounder howitzers, having for its object the prevention of sorties from the Lahore or Kabul Gates which, passing round the city walls, might have annoyed our breaching batteries, while at the same time it assisted in keeping down the fire of the Mooree Bastion.*

---

* Nearly the whole of the siege operations have been compiled from Major Norman's narrative, and "Felix," an engineer officer's account, published in the *Lahore Chronicle;* omitting only some minor details, and here and there amalgamating the information contained in each.

On the 6th of September, the last detachment which possibly could be expected had arrived in camp. The effective strength of the whole force, including Lascars, artillery drivers, and newly raised Sikh levies, amounted to 8,748, while 2,977 were sick in hospital, and the numbers of the latter were daily increasing.

The strength of the British troops was:

Artillery    580
Cavalry      443
Infantry  2,294
**In all    3,317**

The native forces in camp amounted to 5,431. On their fidelity we could only depend so long as their interests were ours, and the prospect of plunder was before them; added to which, no support was nearer than Lahore, distant 300 miles. From this it will be seen that General Wilson's position was one to try the strongest nerves.

Felix thus describes the siege operations.

We had from the first no choice as to the front of attack; our position on the north side being the only one that could secure our communications with the Punjab, whence our supplies had been drawn.

Whether the city might or might not have been carried by a *coup de main,* as was contemplated in June and July, is needless now to inquire. But, judging from the resistance afterwards experienced in the assault, though we were greatly reinforced, it appears fortunate that the attempt was not made.

The strength of the place had been greatly undervalued, and it was never supposed to consist in its actual defences. Every city is, from its nature, even when without fortifications, strongly defensible; and within Delhi the enemy possessed a magazine containing upwards of 200 guns, with an inexhaustible supply of small arms and ammunition of all sorts, while their numbers were never less than double those of the besiegers.

Few will doubt that the General exercised a sound discretion in refusing to allow a handful of men, unaided by siege guns, to attack such a place; knowing how disastrous would be a failure.

The Artillery force, at the commencement of the siege, consisted of:

Four Troops of Horse Artillery
Two Light Field Batteries
Forty heavy guns and howitzers
Ten heavy mortars & twelve light mortars

The means of the Engineers were very restricted, 120 trained sappers only being available; but with the aid of some companies of Sikhs newly raised and rapidly trained, and superintended by Lieutenant Brownlow with untiring energy and activity, 10,000 fascines, as many gabions, and 100,000 sandbags, together with scaling ladders, field magazines, and spare platforms, were prepared and ready for immediate use.

The north face being the side to be attacked, it was resolved to hold the right in check as much as possible, and to push the main attack on the left. 1st, as the river completely protected our flank as we advanced; 2ndly, as there was better cover on that side; and 3rdly, after the assault the troops would not immediately find themselves in narrow streets, but in comparatively open ground, on which to form.

The front to be attacked consisted of the Mooree, Cashmere, and Water Bastions, with the curtain walls commanding them. These walls had been greatly improved by our engineers, and presented a succession of faces and flanks, with regularly constructed embrasures. The curtain walls were twenty-four feet above the plain of site, eight feet of which was a mere parapet three feet thick, the remainder about twelve feet thick; outside the wall was a *berm*, and a ditch sixteen feet deep and twenty feet wide at the bottom. The escarp and counterscarp walls were steep; the latter unreveted, the former reveted with stone, eight feet in height. A glacis covered ten feet of the wall, rendering it impossible to breach that portion of it from any distance.

On the evening of the 7th of September, No. 1 Battery was traced in two portions, at a distance of about 700 yards from the Mooree Bastion: the right to contain five 18-pounders and one 8-inch howitzer, intended to silence the Mooree, and prevent its interfering with the left attack; the left portion for four 24-pounders, to hold the Cashmere Bastion partially in check.

Early on the morning of the 7th, both portions of this battery were completed and armed; its flanks being connected with the ravine in its rear, which protected the guards of the trenches, and the litters for the wounded and sick.

For some time the fire from the Mooree on this battery was most harassing, and also from musketry from a trench below the ridge; but as the guns came into full play, the enemy's fire was completely overpowered, and the Mooree on the 9th was but a mass of ruins. This battery was known as Brind's Battery, having been worked by Major Brind during the siege; or rather until, having done its work, its services were no more required: and, strange to say, only a few hours before dusk, when it was intended to dismantle the battery, the left portion was accidentally ignited, and utterly destroyed.

To our surprise we had been allowed to take possession of the Ludlow Castle, within six hundred yards of the city walls, without opposition; the enemy doubtless thinking that the assault was intended from the right, where our batteries had from the first been erected on the ridge; and the attack on the Mooree Bastion confirmed this belief.

On the 8th the Ludlow Castle and the Koodshah Bagh were occupied by strong detachments of infantry; Nos. 2 and 3 Batteries in front of Ludlow Castle, and on the left, were traced and commenced on the same evening, and on the morning of the 11th opened fire and were soon in full play.

No. 2 Battery, like Major Brind's, was constructed in two parts: one immediately in front of Ludlow Castle, for nine 24-pounders, to open a breach between the Cashmere and Water Bastions; and by knocking off the parapet right and left of the breach, to destroy all cover for musketry. The second portion was some two hundred yards to the right, in which were mounted seven 8-inch howitzers, and two 18-pounders; their object was to aid the left half of the battery and work to the same end.[*]

A flank was afterwards added, and in it an embrasure constructed for a heavy howitzer, intended to counteract the effect of guns brought by the enemy in the neighbourhood of the Kissengunge and Talewara suburbs.

The first salvo from this battery from nine 24-pounders showed what might soon be expected. The Cashmere Bastion attempted to reply, but was soon silenced, and became almost as great a wreck as its twin brother the Mooree; neither were portions of the curtain walls in a much better plight.

Simultaneous with the construction of No. 2 Battery, No. 3, on the extreme left, was commenced and executed in the boldest manner possible, within 180 yards of the Water Bastion, in which it was intended to form a breach. It was built behind a small ruined house in the Custom House compound, and under such a fire of musketry as few batteries have ever been exposed to. It was for six 24-pounders, which opened on the forenoon of the 11th, commanded by Major Scott, who most effectually performed his task.

No. 4 Battery, for ten heavy mortars, in the Koodshah Bagh, and some lighter ones behind the Custom House, opened on the 12th. The former were commanded by Major Tombs, the latter by Captain Blunt.

From this time until the moment of assault, the continuous roar of fifty guns and mortars pouring shot and shell into the devoted city, warned the enemy that retribution was coming on apace.

It must not be supposed that although no opposition was made to our occupation of Ludlow Castle and the Koodshah

---

[*] Major Campbell commanded the left half of No. 2 Battery, and Major Kaye the right. When Major Campbell was wounded on the evening of the 11th, Captain Johnson assumed command and held it until the assault.

Bagh, that the batteries were unmolested. On the night of the 8th, a sortie was made on No. 1 Battery; and although repulsed with slaughter to the enemy, yet it required constant showers of grape from Captain Remmington's battery at the Sammy House, to clear the broken ground of skirmishers; while guns which had been brought out from the city into the suburbs, enfiladed our line of batteries and did much mischief.

Three guns with the same view were in battery on the opposite side of the Jumna, and a continual fire was kept up from the Selimghur, a fort on the Jumna side of the city.

On two occasions, sallies were made from the Cashmere Gate before No. 2 Battery was in full play; and the heavy covering parties of infantry kept in the trenches were constantly at work keeping down the musketry fire, which was opened from a trench running parallel to, and three hundred yards from, our left attack, and was kept up until the morning of assault.

On No. 3 Battery, on the left, a tremendous fire of musketry was kept up from the city walls and the Water Bastion: the *mantlets* on the guns showed scarcely an inch without a dent Captain Fagan, of the Artillery, whose gallantry and energy had won for him the admiration of every officer in camp, was killed by a musket-ball through the head, while looking over his gun to see the effect of the fire. A kind friend and a gallant soldier, his loss was deeply felt by all who that evening followed him to the grave.

## The Assault and Capture of Delhi

So well had affairs been conducted in camp, that although naturally enough every one was aware that the time for the assault was at hand, it was late on the night of the 13th before (the breaches having been declared practicable) orders were issued for the assault on the following morning. All necessary preparations were at once made, and at 4 a.m. of the 14th of September—a day none present will forget—four columns were collected at their respective parades, preparatory to moving to the attack. They were composed as follows:

First column commanded by Brigadier-General Nicholson, to storm the breach near the Cashmere Bastion, and escalade its face.

| | |
|---|---|
| H. M.'s 75th | 300 |
| 2nd Punjab Infantry | 450 |
| 1st Bengal Fusiliers | 250 |
| **Total** | **1,000** |

Second column, Brigadier Jones, to storm the breach in the Water Bastion.

| | |
|---|---|
| H. M.'s 8th | 250 |
| 2nd Bengal Fusiliers | 250 |
| 4th Sikh Infantry | 350 |
| **Total** | **850** |

Third column, Colonel G. Campbell, H. M.'s 52nd, to assault by the Cashmere Gate after it should be blown open.

| | |
|---|---|
| H. M.'s 52nd | 200 |
| Kumaon Battalion | 250 |
| 1$^{st}$ Punjab Infantry | 500 |
| **Total** | **950** |

Fourth column, Major Reid, Sirmoor Battalion, to attack the Kissengunge from the ridge, and enter the city by the Lahore Gate. This column consisted of the Sirmoor Battalion and Guides, with the picquets from the ridge: strength about 850. Besides these, there was the Cashmere Contingent.

Fifth column (the reserve), Brigadier Longfield.

| | |
|---|---|
| H. M.'s 61st | 250 |
| 4th Punjab Infantry | 450 |
| Belooch Battalion | 300 |
| Jheend Force | 300 |
| H. M.'s 60th Rifles | 200* |
| **Total** | **1,500** |

This column subsequently was brought into the city after the assault.

---

* H. M.'s 60th Rifles had for some days been in the advanced batteries covering the artillery, and keeping down the musketry fire of the walls. This regiment covered the advance of the storming columns.

Three Engineer officers were attached to each column, and it was intended that a couple of guns should have accompanied each also; but the drawbridges being broken, the guns were drawn up near the Ludlow Castle.

The morning was still and sultry; not a sound was to be heard save the continued roaring of the batteries, which to the last poured their deadly salvos into the city. General Nicholson, who at his especial request was selected to lead the assault, soon passed-on to the road leading to the Cashmere Gate, and was followed by the remainder. It was the last time I ever saw him, and knowing the honourable but terribly dangerous post he had selected, as we shook hands, I felt that we had parted for life.

It seems a pity that a man with such administrative capacity was allowed to do what fifty others would have done equally well, and whose loss would have been less a national calamity. Felix thus admirably describes the assault:

> Everything was ready. Nicholson, whose excellent arrangements elicited the admiration of all, gave the signal. The Rifles dashed to the front with a cheer, extending along and skirmishing through the low brushwood which extends to within fifty yards of the ditch. At the same moment the head of No. 1 and 2 columns emerged from the Koodshah Bagh, and advanced steadily towards the breach.
>
> Our batteries had maintained a tremendous fire up to the moment of the advance of the troops; and not a gun could the enemy bring to bear on the advancing columns. No sooner did they emerge into the open, than a perfect storm of bullets met them from the front and flanks, and both officers and men fell fast on the crest of the glacis.
>
> For ten minutes it was impossible to get ladders into the ditch to ascend the escarp. The determination of British soldiers carried all before it, and *pandy* declined to meet

the bayonet. With a cheer and a rush the breaches were won, and the enemy fled in disorder.

In the meantime the explosion party advanced in front of the three columns, straight upon the Cashmere Gate.* This band of heroes (for they were no less) had to advance, in daylight, to the gateway in the very teeth of a hot fire of musketry from all sides. The powder bags were coolly laid and adjusted, but Lieutenant Salkeld was *hors de combat,* with two bullets through his body.

Sergeant Carmichael attempted to fire the fuse, but was shot dead. Sergeant Burgess then attempted it and succeeded, but paid for the daring act with his life. Sergeant Smith, thinking that Sergeant Burgess had failed, ran forward; but seeing the train alight, had just time to throw himself into the ditch and escape the effects of the explosion. With a loud crash the gateway was blown in, and through it the third column rushed to the attack, at the same moment that the other columns had won the breaches. General Wilson has since bestowed the Victoria Gross on Lieutenant Salkeld, Lieutenant Home, Sergeant Smith, and on a brave soldier of H. M.'s 52nd, who stood by Lieutenant Salkeld to the last, and bound up his wounds.

So far, all was as successful as could be wished—both breaches and the Cashmere Gate were in our hands. But a scene was passing outside that no pen can properly describe. For the reasons before assigned, General Wilson had ordered the light artillery which he had intended to accompany the columns, to form as much protection as possible near the Ludlow Castle. It was, indeed, a time of breathless anxiety. The breaching batteries, having done their deadly work, had ceased; nothing but the continued rattle of musketry was

---

* On arriving at the Cashmere Gate a horrible right awaited them; a European soldier (doubtless a prisoner) had been chained outside the gate, and been killed by the shot from our batteries.

heard, save the booming of the guns from the Selimghur Fort The long, long line of litters commenced to return to the field hospitals from the scene of strife, with their mangled burdens; the dead, dying, and wounded in every state, were passing by, showing how deadly was the struggle.

Though little separated from the scene of action, none could tell us what had been doing, or what was the state of affairs. Over and over again the same questions were asked, "Were the columns inside? Were the breaches gained?" None could reply. The intense anxiety of that hour made it like a week, until that cheer which no Englishman can mistake proclaimed that the victory was ours, and that the day of retribution was at hand.

Major Norman thus describes the operations within the city, after the actual assault:

Nos. 1 and 2 columns having effected an entrance, proceeded round the walls to the right, capturing a small battery and tower between the Cashmere and Mooree Bastion, the Mooree Bastion itself, and the Kabul Gate. All attempts to take the Burn Bastion and Lahore Gates failed.

The troops had to advance up a narrow lane swept by grape and musketry; and in one of these attempts General Nicholson received his mortal wound.

Up to the Kabul Gate our position was secured, and the Artillery on the Mooree Bastion turned upon the city and Kissengunge suburbs; the gorge being secured by sandbag parapets.

The 3rd column, after storming the Cashmere Gate, proceeded through the town towards the Jumma Musjid. It was conducted most gallantly by Sir T. Metcalfe, who had volunteered for the service; his local knowledge being of the greatest assistance. Taking a circuitous route, little opposition was met with, until reaching the Chandnee Choke, possession was taken of the city police station.

The lanes leading to the Jumma Musjid here became more intricate, and the men began to fall fast It was found impossible to capture the Musjid; the gates being strongly closed, and neither artillery nor powder-bags being at hand.

This column eventually fell back to the neighbourhood of the church; which, with the adjoining buildings, it occupied with the reserve.

Major Reid, with the 4th column, had in the meantime advanced from the Subzi-Mundi into the Kissengunge, the Cashmere Contingent operating on his right The latter, however, were so sharply attacked by the insurgents, that after losing a great number of men and four guns, they were completely defeated, and fell back to camp.

The most strenuous opposition was offered to Major Reid's column in the Kissengunge. Many men and officers were *hors de combat;* the enemy were strongly posted among gardens and walled enclosures. The commanding officer being severely wounded, Captain Muter, of H. M.'s 60th Rifles, the next senior, withdrew to the ridge; covered by the guns which had been left in the Crow's Nest Battery on the extreme right.

Brigadier Grant, with the cavalry and Horse Artillery, effectually prevented any annoyance to the flanks of the assaulting columns; but suffered so severely from the guns and musketry in the suburbs, that General Wilson ordered No. 17 Battery to move up in support and aid Major Tombs' troop, which, with that officer's usual gallantry, had been in the thick of the engagement, and suffered so severely in men and horses that it was with difficulty he could drag his guns from the ground when relieved.

The steadiness of the 9th Lancers and Carbineers was the subject of admiration. File after file was shot down; yet, in the quaint language of General Grant's despatch, "the spirits of the men seemed to rise as their ranks were thinned."

Gradually the fire of the Kissengunge became less, as the heavy guns from the Mooree Bastion were brought to bear on that quarter; and in the afternoon, it haying nearly ceased, and no fears being entertained of an attack from that direction, General Grant's force was withdrawn to the Ludlow Castle, with picquets towards the ridge.

Thus ended the siege and assault of Delhi. The actual loss on the day of assault, in killed and wounded, was 66 officers and 1,104 men: nearly one-third of the number engaged; while the casualties which occurred from the opening of the batteries to the moment of assault, amounted to 327 officers and men. The loss to the enemy must have been severe. The best idea was the one which could be formed from the statement of Colonel Burn, the military governor of Delhi, that when he commenced to try and clear the houses, he seldom came upon one in which there were not eight or nine dead bodies.

For the complete success that attended the prosecution of the siege, the chief credit is due to Colonel Baird Smith, the chief engineer; and to Captain Taylor, on whom, consequent on the former being early wounded, devolved the superintendence of the attack. The plan of the attack was bold and skilful. The nature of our enemy was exactly appreciated. *Pandy* can fight well behind walls, but here he was out-manoeuvred: his attention was directed from the real point of attack until the last moment, when the cover, which would have been of such annoyance to us, had been seized and turned against him.

To enable the siege batteries to be fully armed, most of the heavy guns had been withdrawn from the ridge. Such only were left as would secure the position, while two light guns were, on the morning of the assault, added to the rear picquet.

The Foot Artillery, though never once relieved from the commencement of the actual siege, were quite insufficient to work the whole of the heavy ordnance: nearly all the officers and men of the Horse Artillery were sent into the batteries; these even were insufficient, and parties of volunteers from H. M.'s 9th Lancers and 6th Dragoon Guards, hastily trained, rendered most hearty and valuable service, while many officers, having undergone previously an apprenticeship on the ridge, rendered important assistance.

Not a man on the batteries was once relieved from the time of opening fire until the assault. In like manner the Engineers and Sappers were continually under fire, and without relief.

The 14th of September ended, if not with the full success that was anticipated, certainly with as much as the handful of troops engaged had a right to expect.

## Fighting Within the City

Although the first day's operations were most satisfactory, yet on the evening of the 14th September nothing but the city walls and bastions, extending from the Kabul Gate to the Water Bastion, and the open space round the church, college, and Skinner's house, were in our hands; and it was clear that the enemy intended to dispute every street, foot by foot, with us.

Unfortunately, that terrible license invariably consequent on the capture of a besieged city, was deeply indulged in. At the very entrance were large stores filled with wine, beer, and spirits, in the greatest abundance; and for a time, our tenure of the position we had gained was deeply imperilled. Our guard fell victims to their vice, and were all murdered at their posts; while champagne was taken by the followers outside the city to the Ludlow Castle and sold for about 3d. a bottle.

The most vigorous efforts were at once made to destroy all the liquor in the town. Thousands of dozens were broken up by guards placed at the disposal of the Provost-Marshal, and order was once more restored. Yet although the passions of the troops were, by drink and revenge, worked up to burning heat, not a case, it is believed, was heard of a woman or child having been intentionally hurt—all credit to them.

No sooner was the Cashmere gate open* than a tide of

---

* Several men were caught going out of the Cashmere Gate disguised as women, and were hung; while several *bheesties*, or water-carriers, detected bringing in drugged liquor for the troops, were likewise disposed of.

women and children poured out towards the British camp: a noble testimony of the estimate they placed on the national character. For hours and hours the stream passed up the Ludlow Castle road; the numbers were such that their remaining in or near the camp was impossible, and a large deserted village was told off for their especial use. Although the women and children were protected by the British, their own relatives and friends set much less value on their lives. We had adopted an ingenious method of discovering whether in the next street there were any riflemen, by putting out a hat at the corner on the point of a bayonet; it seldom returned without a bullet in it. These ruffians, trusting to the Europeans not firing at them, generally pushed forward a woman or a child as a feeler. Near the Lahore Gate this was especially remarkable, and it is only wonderful that several were not shot.

Although much delayed in advancing by the conduct of the troops, the 15th did not find us idle. The guns and mortars of the Mooree Bastion kept up a fire upon the city; others were brought into position for the same purpose; while the Water Bastion and a battery erected at the left of the college garden were opened upon the Selimghur, and two guns of Major Scott's battery made a breach in the magazine walls from the college square. The church, which was exposed to heavy fire from Selimghur, was also put into a more defensible state; the ordnance and engineering stores being brought within the churchyard enclosure.

On the morning of the 16th, the magazine was stormed and carried; but every building was fought for.

Towards the afternoon, an attempt was made to recapture it, as also the adjoining workshops, covered by the fire of some guns placed in front of the palace gate.

As far as the workshops were concerned, it was partially successful; but the enemy were soon driven off, and endeavoured, as they retired, to set fire to the roofs with torches.

Lieutenant Renny, of the Artillery, on this occasion exhibited the greatest coolness and gallantry, by mounting the roof and pelting the enemy with shells; which were handed up to him, with fuses alight. On the same morning, the Kissengunge was evacuated, being entirely commanded by the guns from the walls: naturally a strong position, every means had been taken to improve it; and it was indeed fortunate that we were not obliged to dislodge the enemy from the numerous fortified positions it contained. It would only have been done with great loss.

On the 18th, our positions were advanced in the centre, towards the canal; and on the left, the Bank House was taken possession of. The line of the canal may be said to have been our front: on its bank some light mortars were posted, to clear the neighbourhood of the Lahore Gate; while light guns were posted at the main junctions of the streets, and sandbag batteries erected to prevent the possibility of a surprise.

The whole of the heavy mortars were at work in the magazine, pouring a continuous flight of. shells into the city and palace;. and it became apparent that, although no post was given up uncontested, the resistance was becoming less, and that the abandonment of the city had commenced.

On the 19th, the Burn Bastion was captured; and on the following morning, the Lahore Bastion (which had twice before resisted our attacks) was assaulted, and, together with the remainder of the city walls, was held by our troops.

A column, hastily formed, pushed along the Chandnee Choke, and took possession of the Jumma Musjid, which was but slightly defended. A second was formed at the magazine, for a simultaneous attack upon the palace. When the latter arrived at the gateway, the palace was found to have been evacuated; save by a few fanatics, who fired from the walls, and were subsequently bayoneted by the troops. The gates were blown open, and General Wilson's headquarters were there established. The Selimghur Fort had likewise been evacuated; a royal salute was fired from its ramparts, and the British flag was flying from the palace walls.

Thus ended one of the most severe struggles history has

on record. At the first it was the passive resistance of a handful against crowds of enemies. Our force, it must be remembered, had to contend with every disadvantage, not only of climate and sickness, but of circumstances of a still more discouraging nature. Reinforcements of every kind for the enemy were arriving day by day, crossing the bridge of boats before our eyes; but it was so far distant that the destruction of the bridge was impossible: several attempts to burn it were made, but in vain. Disastrous accounts were also received as to the state of the country. Mutiny after mutiny, massacre after massacre, were recorded; and the storm about July loomed so black, that it appeared certain nothing but Providence could save the vessel of the State.

Yet, under these circumstances, the little band before Delhi never desponded. All behaved nobly; but it may be permitted to allude to those corps most constantly engaged—the 60th Rifles, the Sirmoor Battalion, and the Guides Corps. Probably not one day throughout the siege passed without a casualty in one of these regiments. But the losses in action, compared with their original strength, show the nature of the service.

The Rifles commenced with 440 of all ranks, and a few days before the assault they received a reinforcement of 200: their casualties were 389.

The Sirmoor Battalion commenced 450 strong, and were reinforced by 90 men: its casualties amounted to 319.

The Guides Corps, 550 strong, lost 303 of their number.

The 1st Bengal Fusiliers, and, in fact, all the regiments, were severe losers. The 52nd, which arrived in Delhi only a month before the assault 600 strong, could only muster out of hospital on the day of assault 242 men of all ranks.

It only remains to say something of the appearance of Delhi on entering after the assault.

The demon of destruction seemed to have enjoyed a perfect revel. The houses in the neighbourhood of the Mooree and Cashmere Bastions were a mass of ruins; the walls near the breaches were cracked in every direction, while the church was completely gutted and riddled by shot and shell: its gilt cross was still untouched, and, as seen of a bright morning from the ridge, glittering in the rising sun, seemed beckoning us onwards, with the full assurance that the religion of the Cross should still, even in that city, soar high over Mohammedan bigotry and cruelty. In the Water Bastion the destruction was still more striking. Huge siege guns, with their carriages, lay about seemingly like playthings in a child's nursery. The palace had evidently been hastily abandoned. The tents of Captain De Teissier's battery, stationed at Delhi when the mutiny broke out, were left standing, and contained plunder of all sorts.

The apartments inhabited by the royal family combined an incongruous array of tawdry splendour, with the most abject poverty and filth. The apartments over the palace gate, formerly inhabited by Captain Douglas, who commanded the palace guards, and Mr. Jennings, the clergyman, were denuded of every trace of the unfortunate party which had inhabited its walls; and with whom, not many months before, I had spent a happy week. It was with a sad and heavy heart that I paced its now empty rooms, which could tell such terrible tales of the scenes there enacted.

On the morning of the 21st of September, the cleansing of the city was commenced. Although previously every effort had been made to destroy the dead bodies, it was in a dreadful state. A military governor was appointed, guards were distributed, the light artillery were withdrawn to Ludlow Castle, and No. 17 Battery received orders to leave Delhi, under the command of Colonel Greathed.

# After the Fall of Delhi

E. W. Churcher
Indian Civi Service

# After the Fall of Dehi

WhenDelhi was retaken I was much worried by rebels making their way into Oudh, and on to Lucknow. The prisoners I took used to tell me that the mutineers were all of one opinion as to what would become of them when peace was established, that is, that they would all be blown away from guns. I was tired of making prisoners. They gave me most thrilling accounts of the siege of Delhi, and of the discord that reigned amongst them.

The King's wishes they said were never consulted, and only small sums of money were doled out to them, as the King's treasures were all buried deep underground, by people who were kept prisoners in the palace, and who were killed immediately the work was finished, in case they should divulge where the treasure was hidden. From what they said no one person was in supreme command in the city. They complained of the utter demoralization which prevailed, and of the want of food, which alone would have driven them to capitulate. I questioned many of them about Begam Shumroo's palace, situated in the Chandni Chowk, which was occupied before the mutiny by the Delhi bank, of which my brother Harry was deputy manager. They all assured me that it had not been destroyed. All the inmates of it had of course been killed, and amongst them was my brother.

The Hindu portion of my prisoners bewailed the mistake they had made, and put the mutiny down to the machinations of the Mahomedan portion of the army. They used to entreat me to find some means for their reinstatement, but of course that was impossible. The jail was full of them, and could receive no more. With the exception of the Mahomedans it ended in my letting them all go to their homes, which I have no doubt they did, for they seemed to have had enough of fighting. The Mahomedans were released later on.

The mutineers were occasionally seized in the fort, which they entered as labourers. They could always be detected by their walk. When walking ahead of me I used suddenly to call out "tention", down would go their arms to their sides, and that betrayed them.

I was much relieved when Captain Murray joined me with some Jat Horse he was raising, though he had then with him only about 150 men. We encamped near the Kutchla Ghat, in my district, with a hundred of my own men. A considerable body of rebels were encamped across the Ganges; we used to ride to the banks of the river, and fire into the enemy, and they into us. This went on continuously for a few days.

One morning we saw a body of about 1,000 infantry and 300 cavalry cross the river at a ford, and come towards us. They were too strong for us to tackle, so we beat a retreat. Paddy Hennessy, a young man of great promise, the son of General Hennessy, had been attached to the Jat Horse, and McKellar was their doctor. We retreated into a defile, and called a halt. Paddy, with two men, watched the enemy from the top of the ridge. All at once a partially blind old Jamadar of Murray's horse, mistaking Paddy and the two men with him on the ridge for the enemy, threw his turban on the ground, drew his sword, and started at full gallop, shouting to the men to come on if they were not women. Away went the Jats by twos and threes after him, and when we joined in the melee they discovered their mistake.

Paddy, thinking that Murray had given the order to charge, started at the head of the two men. We decided to go after them. Paddy was not far from me. I saw him swerve off to the right, and foolishly go at one of the enemy close by, who had been unhorsed. He cut at him, but missed him, not so the man, for he gave Paddy a nasty cut on the elbow of his sword arm. I noticed that Paddy checked his mare Ruby with difficulty. He then went at the man a second time, he missed him again, and again the man cut him near the first wound. Ruby was then galloping towards me, with the man after her. He evidently expected to see Paddy fall. After finishing him, if he only had the time for it, he would have jumped on Ruby, and ridden off.

Paddy was falling from faintness. The man cut at his head, but his helmet had steel bars, and that saved him, and before he could use his sword again we killed the assailant. We put Paddy on Ruby, and sent him to the rear.

We could do little with so large a body of the enemy, but show them a bold front. They burnt two villages, and then re-crossed the river. My men were somewhat accustomed to this sort of thing, and came off scathless, but we lost about thirty of the Jats, including the old Jamadar, who was more courageous than intelligent, his loss was not regretted. The Jats had seen nothing of the kind before. Their horses simply ran away with them. After the enemy had gone we sent men with stretchers to bring in our killed and wounded.

The Jats, although a brave set of men, were very inexpert horsemen, as they had only lately been enlisted. They are good agriculturists and cart-men, but, without training, are not horsemen. Karak Sing, a fine old Jat, was Murray's *risaldar*. He carried a bullet in his stomach for long afterwards, which he got in that scrimmage. Paddy was sent off to Mussoorie, a hill station, to recover from his wounds.

When we assembled for our midday meal Murray asked us what we thought of the behaviour of the Jats. We were unanimous in saying that they had done splendidly. Murray reported the matter, and by return post he was instructed to raise the Jats a thousand strong, and they are now the 17th Bengal Lancers.

It was in the month of December that news was brought to me that a *sahib* in disguise, was in a village near the Grand Trunk Road. I rode to the village, and to my surprise found that the information was true. It was difficult to understand what could have brought a European, all alone, so far away from protection. I was told that he had betaken himself to the roof of one of the houses. On going to the house I called to the man, saying that I was there to protect him, and that he was to come down. It was a great pleasure to hear the cry of delight which came from him.

He lost no time in making his appearance, and then, to my surprise, I found that he was Mr. A. M. Layard, Her Majesty's Minister at Madrid, commonly known as Nineveh Layard. He said that he believed that the road from Allyhur was tolerably safe, and that he would get through disguised as a native. He was dressed partly as a native, and had made his complexion somewhat dark. I took him home, and he shared my last bottle of beer with me.

Hearing that a British force was approaching Fatehgarh from Cawnpore, I began to get anxious for news of my brothers, whom I had left at Fatehgarh. A column commanded by Colonel Seaton entered the Etah district, to join the Commander-in-Chief's (Sir William Mansfield) force, on its way to Fatehgarh. I made all necessary arrangements for an absence of a few days, and joined it, with Mr. Layard.

Before we could get much further we had three engagements with rebels who had arrived from Shumshahad, that is at Sahawur, Puttialie, and Gungeerie, where we took ten guns. Captain Hodson, with his horse, was with the column. After their defeat at Gungeerie the rebels took shelter in tall elephant grass, where great numbers were speared.

We saw the rebel commander escaping on an elephant. Hodson, myself, and some of our men, overtook the animal; we rode ahead of him, turned about, and received him at the point of the spear, but he gave a loud snort, swung his trunk about, and so frightened away our horses. As the elephant driver would not stop the animal, he was shot, and so was also the rebel commander, on his silver howdah. The elephant was then quieted, and taken to Hodson's tent, where he was made to sit down. No money was found on the fat commander, which was a great disappointment to the men. They treated him with contumely, and carried him away to some ditch. The silver howdah was taken into Hodson's tent, and the elephant was sent to the commissariat officer, who paid Rs. 800 for the animal.

On reaching Fatehgarh I left Mr. Layard with Sir William Mansfield, who had routed a large body of rebels, with the Nawab of Furrukabad at their head, at Khodajunge, a little way out of Fatehgarh. The town is called Furrukabad, the station occupied by Europeans, distant three miles from it, is called Fatehgarh.

On getting to my brother's house I found it in ruins, with the exception of two rooms. Soon after my arrival two servants appeared; they told me that my brother Thomas had been killed in one of the boats, in which the survivors from the fort at Fatehgarh had started, with the intention, if possible, of making their way to Cawnpore. The gallant defence of that fort, by a handful of men, for three weeks and more, against large numbers of mutineers, and the Nawab of Furrukabad's men, is too well known to need repetition here. The fort was vacated when it was impossible to hold it any longer.

I was informed that my brother David was alive, and that he was in hiding in Oudh. Also that he had been protected by a native landlord named Luljoo Sing, in a village called Karhar. I started for that village soon after my arrival, and found my brother, but at first I did not recognize him.

He was sitting on the ground with his back to a wall, and a black blanket was round him; his hair, beard, and moustache were also much grown, and he was quite sunburnt. He had been twice sun-struck, and did not know me, but when I spoke to him his face, after a little, became animated, and he looked up in wonder and amazement, and then we knew each other. I had him carried to our late brother's house, and made him as comfortable as I could in the two rooms.

It was difficult to get him to speak of all that he had witnessed and gone through; he had a scared and unhappy look, and was perfectly listless. Before I returned to my work he told me of the tremendous odds they had against them in defending the fort. His story was somewhat as follows:

As it was impossible to hold out any longer they started down the river in boats. When the massacre in the boats took place his friends, Major and Mrs. Robertson, the latter with her infant in her arms, and other men and women, threw themselves overboard. My brother dived after his friends (he was an expert swimmer) and came across Major Robertson, who clung to him. He was a stout man, and unable to swim. With much difficulty he got Robertson to release him, by giving him the oars of those killed which were floating by. He pulled him away a distance of about a hundred yards, when a bullet struck Robertson high up on the hip, and quite disabled him. He continued to pull him down stream, and did so for a distance of about three miles, when he got him under a high sand bank, where he left him, after pulling him out of the water. He then scrambled up the bank, and laid down in heavy rain, quite exhausted; with his small towel round him he fell fast asleep, and awoke to find the sun shining brightly. He looked down the bank, and threw sand at Major Robertson, who then spoke. Thankful that he had riot been dragged away by an alligator during the night, he told him that he would endeavour to get assistance. Help was eventually procured, through a native who saw him, he communicated with Luljoo Sing, the landlord of Karhar, who arrived with some men and had them both carried to the village, and placed in a sugar cane crop for fear of rebels, where they were fed upon unleavened bread.

Here I must introduce a few details about the landlord, Luljoo Sing. He and his brother Hurdeobux were at great enmity with each other. The latter had taken Mr. and Mrs.

Probyn and family under his protection, Mr. Probyn was the magistrate and collector of Fatehgarh, and it was told Luljoo Sing that if, when peace was established, it was found that he had done nothing to protect the Europeans, his brother Hurdeobux would denounce him as a rebel, and the chief instigator of the massacre of the people escaping on the boats. That was the real reason why Luljoo Sing sheltered my brother and Major Robertson.

My brother could not be persuaded to leave his helpless friend, when offers of escape were made to him. He attended to all his wants, and watched over him for about three months, and then Robertson died. My brother buried his friend and comrade, and then existed as best he could for a further period of four months, when I brought him away. He was quite a wreck of his former self, and was always glad to be left alone. I have made the above notes from a narrative of my brother's, which I took down from his own lips a short time after his rescue.

I will close my narrative of the occurrences at Fatehgarh by relating the following sad story. A lady, the widow of Major De F., whose full name I need not disclose, lived at that station, with her daughter, then in her teens. The Nawab of Furrukabad, a most licentious individual, insinuated himself into their good graces. He drove them out daily in his carriage and pair, and sent them *dollies* (baskets of fruit, flowers, and sweetmeats). The authorities remonstrated with the man and the ladies in vain. At last their conduct became so scandalous that the authorities sent the young lady to an establishment for girls in Calcutta, called Kidderpore.

The people in charge of that establishment were in the habit of giving balls, to which young military men, just arrived in India, and other people, were invited. This was done with a view to getting the girls settled in life. In that way Miss De F. became engaged to a young military man. In a few days they were married, and most unfortunately for them the young officer was posted to the 9th Native Infantry, stationed at Fatehgarh. Soon after their arrival the widow, who had kept up her acquaintance with the Nawab, informed him of the fact, and he drove down to see the young lady.

Her husband, on return from parade, finding them in close and earnest conversation, and having been warned by his brother officers about the Nawab, ordered him out of the house, but as he demurred, he kicked him out of it. The Nawab, who could talk a little English, swore that he would be avenged. Two months after the mutiny broke out.

The first thing the Nawab did was to send some armed men to take off the young officer's head, and to take it to him, stuck on a pole. This was speedily done, and then the young wife and her mother were driven to the Nawab's palace, where they were found when the Commander-in-Chief arrived. Mr. John Power was appointed magistrate and collector of Fatehgarh, soon after Sir William Mansfield had cleared the district of rebels. He telegraphed to the Governor-General for permission to hang Mrs. De F. and her daughter, but in reply he was told that there had been enough bloodshed of the kind, and that the Governor-General could not sanction his proposal. After an engagement with the Commander-in-Chief's force at Nawabgunge, the Nawab escaped to the Turraie jungles and was never again heard of.

The day of my arrival at Fatehgarh, as I was preparing to start to seek for my brother, I received a message from Sir William Mansfield that he wished to see me. I went at once to him. He said that Colonel Seaton had informed him that I knew the Nawab of Furrukabad by sight, that he had news that the Nawab was in hiding in the city, and that as I knew the city, and the man, would I accompany a small force, then in readiness to march, as civil officer, and help to seize him. I was of course only too pleased to do so. I had two companies of Europeans and a squadron of horse.

We surrounded the Nawab's palace, and placed pickets in other parts. After a most careful search we found that the Nawab had escaped to the Turraie, on the day of his defeat. In searching some underground closets I suddenly came upon Nawab Gazaffar Hosian Khan, a brother of the missing Nawab, a most bloodthirsty individual, and an arch rebel. I knew him well; had it not been for him I believe the Nawab himself would not have treated the English prisoners with cruelty. We communicated with the Commander-in-Chief, and were ordered to hang the man I had seized, which we did. In blowing up a portion of the fort in the city, the debris rolled into the Nawab's garden, where a large tiger was caged. The debris destroyed the cage, and the tiger escaped. He ran into the earthwork which had been blown down, and was shot in it. I gave the animal to the officer who commanded our little force; he also asked for a gold amulet which encircled the arm of the Nawab who had been hanged. I had it taken off, and gave it to him: a strip of thin paper, about an inch in breadth, and a foot and a half in length, was found in it, on which were extracts from the Koran, in red ink.

It was now time for me to return to Etah. The district was quiet, and there was little or no fighting to be done. In a letter I received from the officer in charge of the treasury in the fort of Agra he informed me that the treasury was being emptied fast of money, that the refugees in the fort had for a long time been living on subsistence allowances, and that he would be glad if I would collect and send in some revenue. I made great efforts to get in money, and succeeded in doing so. A large sum, under a strong guard, was sent on elephants to the fort.

The difficulty was to convince the landlords that it was imperative on them to pay up the revenue instalments then due, for seeing nothing more of the British Raj than what I represented, and being persuaded in their minds that the rebels might return any day, and require money from them, they were very reluctant to pay up. A few strong measures however convinced them that the matter could not be shirked, and then the revenue began to come in. Dawur Ali, the revenue collector, and Najaf Khan, the civil judge, were indefatigable in this work.

The country had never been disarmed, and numbers of armed men were constantly met with. I considered it necessary to disarm the more turbulent portion of the population. It was a most difficult task. The subterfuges adopted to avoid surrender, and the manner in which the weapons were secreted, caused much amusement. The natives cling most tenaciously to their weapons. The scenes which took place were often more painful than amusing to witness, especially amongst the old people, for they kissed their weapons, and hugged them, and wept over them, as they would over a pet child.

Later on I had to disarm the whole of the district. I obtained guns of many peculiar makes, swords, some with pistols attached to the handles, and pistols innumerable, and some cannon. They were all laid in heaps, and broken up by blacksmiths. Had it not been for natives spying upon each other, the difficulty would have been much greater.

I can never forget a native informing me that a large brass cannon, with the muzzle shaped like the mouth of an alligator, had been buried in a well a few miles from my camp. I rode to the spot with some of my men, and had the well dug about, but there were no signs of a cannon. Two days after the man accosted me again, saying that the cannon had indeed been in the well, but had since been removed to another place: he offered to show me the spot. He was so very earnest about it (evidently because of enmity between him and the Mahomedan landlord, who was said to be the owner of the cannon), that I went with him.

He took me to a large copse of trees, in which were some Mahomedan graves. He poked about the ground with an iron ramrod, and finding the earth soft over one of the graves, he assured me that the cannon was there. I had the grave opened, and to my astonishment, on the top of some human bones, the cannon was found. I had it taken to camp and destroyed: great was the joy of the spy that he had succeeded in exposing his enemy's cunning. I took no further notice of the matter, and was content that the search had not been fruitless.

We used to amuse ourselves in trying to burst a small cannon I had found. It was filled half-way with powder, some paper wadding was then rammed in, and over that damp mud, up to the muzzle; it was then buried, muzzle downwards, a depth of six feet, and fired. It shot up a great height, but was always found to be quite sound when it came again to earth.

In the month of March General Penny's force took up a position at Puttialie, in the Etah district. After a short halt it crossed the River Ganges. On the march from the river inland, owing to want of necessary precautions, the General and others lost their lives. I was near at hand. No scouts had been thrown out. The force entered a road with large trees on either side, when loud reports of cannon were heard, and before anything could be done the General and others were killed. The column immediately left the road, and flanked it on either side. The enemy were soon driven off, and we took their cannon. I remained behind, and had a rough coffin made, got together the General's remains, and had them buried in a spot I marked. Some time after, at the request of his widow, the General's body was exhumed, and sent in a *dak garrie* (a horse conveyance) to Meerut, where it was interred.

# Agra

### George Bourchier
Captain, Bengal Horse Artillery

# Agra

Never did boys escape from the clutches of a schoolmaster with greater glee than we experienced on the 21st of September, when we received our orders to proceed on the following morning to the plain in front of the Ajmere Gate, where a column was to be formed under the command of Colonel Greathed, H. M's 8th Foot, destined to scour the Gangetic Doab. Its presence would restore confidence, by instilling into the native mind the fact that not only had the siege of Delhi come to an end, but that British rule was again in the ascendant; by administrating "vindicatory justice" upon those who had aided and abetted in the rebellion; and also bringing to battle the brigades of mutineers who were attempting to cross the Doab, like rats escaping from the empty house, and pushing their way towards Cawnpore and Oude.

The trouble taken by these ruffians to impress upon the country the belief that the fall of Delhi was a fable, was most successful. It was long ere the provinces could realise the fact that the imperial city was in possession of the handful of British which had invested it.

The neighbourhood of Delhi and Meerut, for years notorious as the hot-bed of *dacoity* and misrule, was now a scene of anarchy.

The Goojah tribes, by whom unheard-of atrocities had been committed on the unhappy fugitives who escaped the fangs of the Palace officials and *sepoy* assassins of Delhi, were still in open rebellion; and a roving commission, with unlimited powers and martial law, was the only likely method of bringing the Doab into subjection. Well had it been if Colonel Greathed had been able to exercise these powers: as assuredly was intended. The civil power, which at the first outset of the mutiny in the North-West had suddenly collapsed, sprung up with mushroom-like rapidity the moment the column crossed the Jumna. Villages tainted with rebellion and murder were spared, only from fear that the coffers of the State might suffer a temporary deficit.

It remains to be decided whether any deficit would not have been preferable to allowing the whole country to be infested with gangs of villains who had witnessed the tragedy of the mutiny, or who, having been released from gaol by thousands, joined in its horrors.

So well known was the state of the country, that not a civilian would venture beyond the sound of our trumpets. Ere many days had passed, however, Mussulmen armed to the teeth, appeared at every village: men who, from their position and creed, could not have existed during the crisis, but as bowing the knee before the Mohammedan idol they had set up, now appeared as our devoted slaves.

The troops detailed to form the columns were as follows:

|  | European | Native |
|---|---|---|
| Remmington's Horse Artillery, 5 guns | 60 | |
| Blunt's Horse Artillery, 5 guns | 60 | |
| Bourchier's Battery, 6 guns | 60 | 60 |
| Sappers | | 200 |
| H. M.'s 9th Lancers | 300 | |
| Detachments 1st, 4th, 5th Punjab Cavalry and Hodson's Horse | | 400 |
| European Infantry, H. M.'s 8th and 75th | 450 | |
| Punjab Infantry, 1st and 4th Regiments | | 1200 |
| Totals of Each | 930 | 1860 |
| **Grand Total** | | **2790** |

The column broke ground on the morning of the 24th of September, bidding adieu to the "city of the dead." Our road from the Ajmere Gate to the bridge lay through the Lahore Gate, and passing along the Chandnee Choke.

Not a sound was heard save the deep rumble of our gun wheels, or the hoarse challenge of a sentry on the ramparts. Here might be seen a house gutted of its contents, there a jackal feeding on the half demolished body of a *sepoy*; arms, carts, shot, dead bodies lay about in the wildest manner. Outstretched and exposed to the public gaze, lay the bodies of the two sons and grandson of the wretched King; they had been captured and executed the day before near Humayoon's Tomb. The King's life, however, was guaranteed to him. The sight was one to be remembered: it was the first step towards that vengeance which Providence has ordained against those who, so foully and with treachery of the blackest dye, had broken his laws.

But, let us pause a moment and consider, was it ever to be expected that Mussulmen, after it suited their interests, would keep faith with' those whom they consider infidels; when to be instrumental in their destruction is a meritorious act in the eyes of their accursed religion? The only comfort one of these miscreants possessed was to this effect: "I die happy: I have seen English women polluted in the streets of Delhi."

The air of the city seemed dense and uncomfortable to breathe; but the bridge once crossed, every moment brought us into a fresher atmosphere. It was wonderful in how short a time the spirits of all were raised by the change. Major Turner, who commanded the Artillery of the column, and who had suffered severely from the sun and fever during his exposure in the batteries, told me that the delight of escaping into fresh air made him inclined to sing.

But to return to our route. Our first march was to the banks of the river Hindun; it was crossed by a suspension bridge, which early in the campaign had been partially destroyed by our engineers to cut off that line of communication between Delhi and Meerut, and afterwards most ingeniously repaired by the rebels.

Our encamping ground was at Gazeeoodeen Nugger, General Wilson's first battlefield, when, leaving Meerut early in June, he effected a junction with the Commander-in-Chief. Our mission was indeed a noble one: in fact nothing more or less than again taking possession of the country which had slipped from our grasp.

It has been well said that for months we possessed no territory in the North-West below Delhi and Meerut, except just the ground on which our troops were encamped. Such indeed was the fact The town of Gazeeoodeen Nugger was deserted, and the inhabitants of the village had fled, knowing what they ought to expect; and, conscience stricken, they doubted whether we came as friends or foes.

Our baggage cattle, which had for so long a period been on scanty and bad forage in Delhi, were in bad condition: the camels especially could scarcely carry their loads, and many died daily. It was the evening of our first march before the whole had arrived in camp, and it was necessary, in consequence, to halt the following day. It being found that the camels were overloaded chiefly from the quantity of plunder and trash that the camp followers had brought out of Delhi, a certain time was given them to dispose of the surplus loads; after which a search was ordered, and whatever was found in the shape of plunder was burnt.

On the 26th, with a sensible difference in the baggage, our camp moved to Dadra. There a quantity of property belonging to Europeans was found concealed in the villages; and as the inhabitants had been notoriously disaffected, the villages (which had been deserted previous to our arrival) were burnt.

Our next march was Secundra, only the previous day evacuated by a body of cavalry detached from Walidad Khan's force at Malaghur Fort, which had for months been held by the rebels.

The town and surrounding villages were in a terrible plight The inhabitants, quiet cultivators of the land, and a race opposed to the Goojahs, flocked out to meet us and to implore our protection. Every house had been gutted and destroyed; their property of every kind taken, and their bullocks, the only means of drawing water for irrigation purposes, driven away.

It was no difficult matter to discover who were for us and who were against us. The British rule brought peace to the labourer, while its discipline controlled the savage propensities of the Mussulman; who, while to gain his end he would invariably cringe in abject, nay loathsome, servility before his master, yet let him but attain his object and a little power, and he will twirl his moustaches and laugh in his sleeve at the credulity of those who fancy that aught but interest and pay kept him in the employment of Feringhee heretics.

On the morning of the 28th, we left Secundra for Bolundshur, a civil station forty-two miles from Meerut, and about five from the fort of Malaghur.

From the latter place it was to have been our business to unearth Mr. Walidad, a relation of the King of Delhi, and make him pay the penalty of his sins.

About daylight the advanced guard arrived at four cross roads about a mile and a half from Bolundshur; one of which led to Malaghur, another straight ahead to the civil station and town.

A picquet of the enemy's cavalry which had been placed on the junction fell back at our approach, and it was ascertained that they had possession of the station in force, and intended there to make a stand; having their guns in battery commanding the entrance, the houses, gardens, and offices being occupied by, the infantry, while bodies of horse were hovering about, ready for any mischief that might turn up.

The advanced guard was strengthened by two of Captain Remmington's Horse Artillery guns, and were soon within range of the enemy; who opened at once down the road. The column in the meantime were being collected well in hand. A reserve was formed, under command of Major Turner, at the junction of the four roads before alluded to, for the protection of the baggage; which was, as anticipated, attacked, in flank by cavalry and guns. These were quickly driven off with loss; the infantry were formed, and. the artillery collected on the left of the road.

Remmington had not been idle: his two guns had opened on the enemy, and he was reinforced by the remainder of his troop; while my battery took up its position more to the right, supported by a squadron of Punjab Cavalry, and a portion of H. M.'s 75th.

The enemy were not slow in turning a portion of their attention towards us, and plied their guns with a will; while from the high crops and the surrounding gardens a. sharp fire of musketry was kept up. The infantry, forming on the right and centre, commenced an. advance among the gardens. This was exactly the style of fighting *pandy* enjoyed; his guns behind walls and his infantry concealed, while the attacking force was necessarily exposed at every step.

By the crossfire which was kept up upon the enemy's battery, their fire was subdued; an advance was then ordered. A few salvoes of grape cleared the front, and the commanding officer being anxious that the position should be secured, ordered an immediate advance of the artillery. Lieutenant Roberts, of the Artillery, who seemed ubiquitous, brought the order at a gallop. The guns charged and took the battery, the enemy scampering before us as we came up to it Lieutenant Roberts was first at the guns. A second burst, after clearing our front with grape, brought us to the goal; the enemy flying before, us like sheep.

While affairs had thus been successful on the right, a second column, consisting of the greater portion of the cavalry, with, two guns of Captain Blunt's troop, under Lieutenant Cracklow, were busy on the left; and having advanced into the town, were for some time exposed to a most, severe fire in the streets. Four, men out of one gun's crew were wounded, and the gun was worked with difficulty. The conduct of the cavalry was conspicuous: under most disadvantageous circumstances they charged and defeated several bodies of the enemy far their superior in numbers.

The 9th Lancers, under Major Curry and Captain Drysdale, cleared the town. Their, loss alone was three officers wounded, six rank and file and twenty-one, horses *hors de combat,* before they extricated themselves from their position.

Three, guns, an immense, quantity of baggage and ammunition fell into our hands; and had the localities-been better known, the loss to the enemy would have been, much more severe, and the pursuit more speedily followed up: as it was, not fewer than three hundred could have fallen.

The action commenced about 7 a.m. and terminated at about 11, when the camp was pitched on the Annoopshur road, on the banks of the Kalee Nuddy. The fort of Malaghur was reconnoitred, and the cause of the stand at Bolundshur became apparent under its cover; the fort had been evacuated, and Walidad had made good his retreat to the Ganges!

A few guns of native manufacture were taken in the fort, from which a royal salute was fired, and a large manufactory of gunpowder was destroyed. Gun-carriages were being built, and models of guns were on the lathes ready for casting. The place was crammed with stores, plunder, and furniture of every description; the property of officers who were at the station when the mutiny broke out, or which was in transit to the north-west.

Preparations were made for destroying one of the bastions of the fort by mining, which was most effectually carried out on the morning of the 1st of October; but, in superintending the operation, Lieutenant Home, of the Engineers, was unfortunately blown up and killed on the spot He was one of those officers who so greatly distinguished himself on the morning of the assault of Delhi, by igniting the train which blew open the Cashmere Gate, under a heavy fire, and had been promised the Victoria Cross for his gallant conduct. His untimely death cast a gloom over the whole camp. The exact cause of the accident is not known; it is supposed that he used a native-made port-fire to ignite the train, a spark from which may have ignited the mine itself. Only the morning before we had been standing together unpacking powder stowed on carts in every shape imaginable, from the carefully packed barrel with four hoops fresh from the Delhi magazine, to loose cartridges and powder strewed all over the place; and close by, two men of the dragoons were quietly sitting smoking their pipes, while they were examining different articles in the carts. Poor Home's invective at their conduct, and the careless manner in which powder was generally handled, makes me feel sure that the unexpected explosion of the mine was the effect of accident, which no care on his part could have prevented.

On the morning of the 2nd of October the camp was shifted to the Allyghur road, and a proper escort having been secured, the sick and wounded were sent into Meerut.

On the 3rd the column marched to Koorjah, the junction of the Delhi and Meerut roads—a town said to have been the hotbed of mutiny. If the fact of the utter destruction of Secundra and plunder of its inhabitants was a sign that they had no sympathy with the mutineers, the perfect protection afforded to the town of Koorjah was evidence of a contrary state of things.

As the column entered, a tall Mohammedan *subadar*, formerly of the Gwalior Contingent, and now a pensioner of the Government, came forth to meet us, mounted on his well-conditioned and caparisoned steed, his whole appearance displaying the consummate insolence of his race; he was known, by many officers formerly connected with Gwalior, as a most influential member of that force (now in open mutiny, and which had at Gwalior perpetrated such atrocities), and to be able, if required, to raise recruits for the cavalry branch of the contingent to any extent. Was it likely then that a man so well-known, living within thirty miles of Delhi, in an important town not a stone of which had been touched—whose inhabitants instead of flocking to welcome our approach, hid like toads in their holes—was it likely, I ask, that this man had been living an immaculate life devoted to our service? Was it in the order of things that he could have remained neutral? No-one but men tainted with the weakest of political opinions which prevailed in the north-west, would have dreamt of such a thing.

Had the column been accompanied, for political purposes, by a civilian of the Punjab stamp—men who, taking their cue from Sir John Lawrence, indulge in a little common sense, and possess the feelings of soldiers as well as collectors of revenue—or even had Colonel Greathed been left to his own judgment, the advance of the column would have been of more essential service to the State, and punishment would have been administered where it was merited. Will it be believed? As we entered Koorjah, a skeleton was stuck up on the roadside, exposed to public gaze, against a wall. The head had been severed from the body, and cuts: in the shin bones were apparent, inflicted by some sharp instrument; and in the opinion of. a medical committee, this skeleton was that of a European female. But still the town paid a large sum yearly to Government, and on that account, in the opinion of the collector, was to be spared.

But the history given of the skeleton by "our faithful Mohammedan pensioner," showed, that after finding himself at large and unscathed, he considered any amount, of humbug would pass current. His account was that "the skeleton was that of an old man who had died from hunger some time ago, and his body had not been removed!"

Was anything more absurd? Did anyone ever hear of a Mohammedan or Hindu corpse being allowed to rot in the streets of a town; and that, apparently, a well-regulated one? But before many hours had passed, a still small rumour flew through the camp that the town was not wholly filled with innocents; and towards evening it was well known that a number of armed men had barricaded themselves in their houses, and civilly declined to give up their arms. Mark the consequences!

Colonel Greathed was well aware that a number of rebels of all sorts—butchers, bakers, men let loose from the gaol, others who had fled from Delhi, in fact, a miscellaneous armed mob—were awaiting our arrival at Allyghur, distant only about thirty miles; and that the Bareilly Brigade, commanded by the *subadar* Bukht Khan, who had raised the standard of rebellion at Bareilly, had crossed the Jumna at Muttra, and would try to form a junction with them, in order to seize the Fort of Allyghur, a most important position on the Grand Trunk Road. To send a force into a strange town at night was madness, while it was equally impossible to make any delay and thus risk the loss of Allyghur.

The men who in the morning, armed as loyal police, had sallied forth to meet the collector, had not the power to disarm the rebels in Koorjah; the consequence was that they remained with their arms: the column marched on to Allyghur, and the collector bolted back at full speed to Bolundshur, where the Belooch Battalion, with a couple of guns, were left for the protection of the station. So much for immaculate Koorjah!

Two marches brought us to Allyghur, where, as before stated, we had heard that a number of villains were prepared to resist the advance of the column, believing that it was only a small detachment sent out from Agra; this opinion was strengthened by the advanced guard, composed only of a small detachment of cavalry, falling back (when fired into) upon the main column.

Out came the villains, yelling like a set of infuriated demon; but their *Io Poeans* were of short duration. Major Turner, with H. M.'s 75th, the 4th Punjab Infantry, and some guns, passed round to the right. Captain Blunt immediately came into action, and silenced the fire of a brass gun and several "telegraph guns,"* which were placed in breastworks across the road, and

---

* Guns made out of the sockets of the telegraph posts; a most ingenious but not very safe arrangement.

at the various gates of the city. Major Ouvry, with the cavalry and No. 17 Battery, took a cast to the left towards the cantonments; passing in skirmishing order through the various compounds and gardens, which were chiefly deserted.

After a long detour of about four miles, the two columns met on the opposite side of the town. Like a babbling pack who in heavy cover has lost all scent of *reynard*, each inquired what bad become of the enemy; who, at the first discovery of the grief into which they had fallen, made off at once.

Not a soul in the town seemed inclined to give any information as to their whereabouts, until an old woman, possessing as little the powers of taciturnity as the rest of her sex, let out that their *penates* having been sent on ahead, they had taken the route to Akbarabad, hoping there to fall in with the Bareilly Brigade under Bukht Khan.

Major Ouvry, by whom a chase after *pandy* was not to be resisted, started at once, and after a three miles' trot, we came upon the whole detachment; which, including women and children, amounted to some 500 persons, with thirty or forty carts of household stuff.

The fair riders, with the utmost politeness, were requested to descend, and after an inquisitorial search into the contents of the carts, were allowed to depart. While domestic arrangements were thus being carried on by some of the less active of the party, Major Ouvry had made his dispositions for "a bag."

Unlike a true member of the chase, who loves to see his fox take well to the open, he had headed his game; spreading his cavalry right and left of the road, to beat back the high crops with which the country was covered, and into which the enemy had skulked.

Forming his line precisely as he would have beaten a field of turnips for game, a scene commenced which baffles all description; peafowl, partridges, and *pandies* rose together: the latter gave the best sport. Here might be seen a Lancer running a-tilt at a wretch who unfortunately had taken to the open; there a Punjab trooper cutting right and left as his victims rose before him; while the enemy, who were Goojahs and armed with swords and hatchets, started up as the line approached, and dashed at their nearest opponent.

Two troopers and a horse were our only casualties, while about 100 brace of Goojahs bit the dust. A detachment of the column was left at Allyghur to garrison the fort.

At Akbarabad, our next march, resided two brothers, Mungal and Mytab Sing, Rajpoot chiefs; who, during the mutiny, had made themselves conspicuous by their rebellious conduct The cavalry arrived there at daylight, and surrounded the town; and the two brothers were caught and slain as they were attempting to make their escape. Three guns were found in the town loaded and primed, but such was the surprise, that they had not even had time to fire them. A large quantity of powder and ammunition was secreted in the palace, which was blown up, and the city burnt to the ground. The few inhabitants that were caught were summarily executed; and the bodies of the two chiefs were hung to the boughs of the trees outside, on the public road.

The 8th of October was devoted to a halt; on the 9th the column marched, by a cross road, to Brijghur, a very pretty fortified position, in most flourishing case. Far distant from the great arterial thoroughfares, it had in no way been molested by the mutineers; and an indigo factory, a short distance from the town, had been preserved from destruction. Even the hens, which in these troublesome times had refused elsewhere to supply our breakfast-table, here had conducted their domestic duties in the ordinary routine, and by their cackling welcomed our advent as their best of friends.

At this distance even from Agra, loud croakings were heard: epistles imploring aid, in every language both dead and living, and in cipher, forwarded by Government special messengers, and received by Colonel Greathed, came pouring into camp. Many, like the dreams of Pharaoh, were beyond the interpretation of the soothsayers, and no Joseph was at hand. All, however, that could be made out of the business was, that the people at Agra were in a cruel stew about some enemy supposed to be hovering round the neighbourhood with a siege train. The Cavalry and Horse Artillery, it was insisted, must go on at once; and as Colonel Greathed felt that he had come within the clutches of the hydra-headed powers of the north-western Government, they were despatched on the 8th, at midnight, with instructions to push on rapidly to Agra, a distance of forty-eight miles. The infantry and the field battery followed four hours afterwards, arriving early in the morning at Hattrass, a well-built town, in an apparently flourishing condition, through which Bukht Khan's force had marched a few days previously, levying a heavy fine for its ransom.

As we got nearer to Agra, the plot was getting hotter and hotter. Despatches, more and more urgent, were received by Colonel Greathed. "His credit would be at stake if Agra was attacked, and he so near: they were threatened, and in momentary dread of an attack; in fact, we most push on to the utmost, for if we delayed, we should only find their ghosts to reproach us for their murder."

A few hours only were given us to rest the cattle at Hattrass. The European infantry were carried, on elephants, carts, and camels, and all were pushed on to overtake the cavalry and horse artillery. This being effected, we crossed the Jumna in one body at the bridge of boats, at sunrise on the morning of the 10th, to relieve the garrison of a fort possessing an inexhaustible supply of ordnance and ammunition, amply supplied with provisions, and capable, from its strength, of defying the whole army of *pandies* for an indefinite time.

********

Little did the appearance of Agra give token of the terrible emergency which required that an army, whose infantry, from prior exposure and service, were far from being in good health, should march forty-four miles, with but a few hours' rest, to its succour.

The 3rd Bengal European regiment, neatly dressed, sleek and well favoured compared with the battered state of our regiments, was mounted on the bastion, and cheered us heartily as the force passed under the walls of the citadel.

Ladies were riding and driving about in all directions; yeomanry cavalry were careering in full equestrian pride, while from every hole and corner loomed the ugly muzzle of an iron monster, ready to annihilate any amount of *pandies*.

The fort itself, large and well built, was in perfect repair; and with its high double walls and deep ditch, would have been reduced with difficulty, even by a European force. The appearance outside, however, was deceptive; the holiday-makers were the exceptions, not the rule of the place; and the ladies represented certainly the most cheerful portion of the community. We were kept grilling on the public roads for two hours, while the local executives argued with Colonel Greathed as to whether it would not be more advisable to encamp the column in a series of gardens overgrown with brushwood, where the guns would not have had a range of fifty yards, and where the cavalry could not possibly act, in preference to a magnificent grassy plain, with not an obstacle within three or four hundred yards of our front, and those only a few high crops.

Fortunate indeed was it that Colonel Greathed's better judgment prevailed, as the sequel will show.

It was finally arranged that the force should encamp on the Native Infantry parade. No sooner was the camp marked out, and the horses picquetted, than it was crowded with men of all descriptions from the fort. To our great disappointment, we were positively informed, that hearing of our approach, the enemy had again retired beyond the Karee Nuddee, a stream about nine miles distant.

The baggage was just arriving, there were but few tents up, the artillerymen had obtained permission to lie down in a house hard by, and many officers had gone to see their friends in Agra. All were much knocked up, and in a few minutes most were in the arms of Morpheus; but in a very short time we were all roused to the conviction that something was wrong.

This was confirmed by a round shot coming through the mess-tent; and as I rushed out at one door of my tent, a servant was bowled down at the other by a second round shot. All were instantly on the alert: the conduct of our troops was beyond praise; that stern discipline which war alone teaches, stood us in good stead. A shower of round shot from a battery of twelve guns on our right and front, came dashing into camp, spreading terror among the camp-followers, and still greater alarm to the sightseers.

Such was the terrible panic among the latter, that those officers who had gone into the fort, and were eager to get back to their posts, could not stem the torrent of affrighted beings: an officer of the Dragoons in attempting it, was fairly carried off his legs and borne back with the crowd. Not satisfied with legitimate means of escape, the gun horses in many cases were seized as they were being led to the guns, and were found next morning in the fort.

In the meantime the troops had not been idle. The artillerymen, having, no time to think of their accoutrements, rushed to their guns, and from the park opened such a fire upon the enemy's position, as led them to see that they had found their match. The horses were soon put to, the cavalry in their saddles, and the infantry awaiting orders on parade.

It was evident that the sooner an advance was made the better. Camp-followers and horses were falling fast in camp, and the native grooms, panic stricken, loosed from their picquets many horses, which were galloping about in all directions. The distance of the park from the enemy's position was too great to hope to silence their guns, which were of heavy metal. Captain Remmington's troop, supported by a portion of the infantry and Punjab Cavalry, was directed to advance on the right; three guns of No. 17 Battery, being of heavier metal than the Horse Artillery guns, were left to cover the advance from the centre, supported by the guard left for the protection of the camp; while the remainder of the battery, with Captain Blunt's troop, supported by H. M.'s 9th Lancers, and detachments of H. M.'s 75th Foot and 2nd Punjab Infantry, advanced from the left towards a mosque, round which the greater portion of the enemy's guns were posted. The Agra Battery and the 3rd Europeans subsequently joined on the right; the column being thus formed into two divisions. The infantry were soon busily at work, dislodging the enemy from the gardens in which it had been suggested that we should encamp; and which were even then in the hands of the enemy.

A large body of cavalry was completely routed by the Punjaub Cavalry in gallant style, under their leaders, Captains Probyn, Watson and Youngbusband, three guns being captured in the charge; while the fire of the remainder of the enemy's artillery was sensibly diminished. The practice of Captain Remmington's troop was particularly effective: three ammunition wagons were exploded by his shot.

On the left, however, a large body of cavalry which had been for some time observed hovering about, made a dash into camp. Captain Blunt, with his guns and a squadron of Lancers, fell back as a reinforcement to the guard left for its protection, meeting the cavalry as they came in; a splendid charge from the Lancers, in which unfortunately Captain French was killed and Lieutenant Jones dangerously wounded, dispersed the enemy's cavalry as a body, and eventually (but not until they had executed a large amount of mischief) they were driven from the camp or destroyed in it.

Steadily our whole force advanced, supported by the infantry, until the enemy's fire was entirely silenced and the position near the mosque, with several guns, captured.

It being evident that the enemy were in full retreat towards the Karee Nuddee, a pursuit by the artillery and cavalry was immediately ordered.

About four miles on the Gwalior road, sheltered by two villages, was the camp of the enemy. Apparently, both divisions of our force came within sight of it at the same time, and arrived at the same moment Forming line, we together flew through its streets, driving the enemy before us.

Only once did they again make a stand; a few rounds of grape, however, scattered them in all directions, and the cavalry were soon among their flying ranks, doing great execution. For seven miles the road was one continued line of carts, guns, ammunition wagons, camels, rushing about without their drivers, and baggage of every description; all of which fell into our hands. Not a gun or cart re-crossed the stream; all became a prize, owing to the rapidity with which the victory was followed up on the opposite bank: a few cavalry troopers made their appearance, but soon disappeared, after a few rounds from the Horse Artillery. Thirteen pieces of ordnance, with an enormous quantity of ammunition, were brought into camp; much that was useless was destroyed, and the enemy's camp, with the villages on which it abutted, were burnt.

Seven of the captured guns were of native manufacture, and in many parts covered with Persian and Hindu inscriptions. Three were of enormous weight, though only eighteen and 12-pounders: these had been brought from Dhalpoor, for the purpose, doubtless, of attempting to breach the walls of Agra; but they had not a mortar with them.

The force returned to camp at about 7 o'clock, having marched sixty-six miles, and fought a general action in thirty-nine hours: nine miles of the route had been done by the cavalry and artillery, at a trot, through high crops and ploughed fields.

Truly we had reason to be thankful to Providence for the successful issue of our day's work; which at first looked far from promising. As it turned out, nothing could have been more successful, or better managed; but the culpable ignorance of the Agra authorities—who summoned a force to their rescue from a distance, and on its arrival allowed it to be led into an ambuscade, by repeated assurances, up to within half an hour of the attack, that the enemy had retired beyond the Karee Nuddee—seems hardly credible. It could have been no sudden thought of the enemy, or the work of a moment, to have brought their guns such a distance, and crossed them over a river with a stream scarcely fordable, flowing over a bed of deep sand: it must have been the work of many days, and of unremitting labour. The presence of the enemy's camp within four miles of the fort, and their possession of the actual ground on which the Agra authorities wished us to encamp, shows how painfully little the latter were aware of what was passing so close to them.

That the surprise was mutual there can be no doubt. The enemy believed that the reported arrival of a column from Delhi was only an imposition, and hung the spy by whom our arrival was chronicled: they imagined that the Agra force had crossed the river during the night, and marched back again in the morning. The small number of tents pitched, and the little show the camp made, strengthened this belief, and led to the attack upon our position.

For political reasons, it was said, the town of Agra was spared: no fine, even, was levied upon it; although it was well known that the inhabitants were cognisant of the presence of the enemy, whose camp had been supplied with provisions and sweetmeats from the city.

Scenes the most ludicrous passed before our eyes as we returned to camp. First, came a fat old gentleman, on as fat an old horse, who requested Major Ouvry to give him a certificate to the effect that he had been under fire, he being the commandant of some volunteers of whose whereabouts he was in total ignorance; next came a truly perspiring hero, jogging along with his bridle and drawn sword in one hand, while in the other was a fan of enormous size, which he managed with dexterous address; while further on might be seen a corpulent clerk, brandishing his stick over a fallen *pandy*, ever and anon starting at his own temerity.

David wisely says, "It is good for me that I have been in trouble," but it is doubtful whether the benefit extends to Englishmen incarcerated in a fortress, be it even as strong as Agra; certain it is that affairs were in a most gloomy state within its walls, and to those who had been at Delhi at the very worst of times, it seemed incomprehensible. The real state of the country now was comparatively *couleur de rose,* but the black clouds of despair seemed to have settled down at Agra like a pall. So different too from the Punjab, where all were, even at the worst, hopeful; here it was continually instilled into our minds that the worst was not yet come; that Gwalior and Lucknow had still to be subdued, and that although Delhi might have fallen, &c., &c.: in short, we were in a bad way.

The ladies, poor creatures, were most to be pitied; several said that night after night they had to listen to the croakers indulging in wonder as to whether in the morning any of them would be alive, and would gladly, had it been permitted, have risked the dangers of a march with us to Cawnpore, to have escaped from their present imprisonment.

Our men and cattle being much in want of rest, the 11th, 12th, and 13th October were halts. The ammunition was filled up from the fort, and our two 5½-inch mortars were exchanged for two 8-inch. The wounded were sent into the hospital which had been established in the Mootee Musjid, where they were attended not only by the medical officers, but by the ladies; many of whom visited the wards daily, administering little comforts to the sick and dying. It was indeed a touching sight to see our fair countrywomen, many of whom were themselves bowed down by affliction, seated by the bedside of the wounded soldier.

Of course we all visited the Taj, which has been so often described, that the less now said about it the better; it is certainly very beautiful: in fact the most beautiful building in India. Many ladies flying from the gloomy captivity of the Fort, made it an excuse for a morning's holiday, fluttering about in all the weakness of "the last new muslin," and seeming to enjoy themselves like larks escaped from a cage.

To see their happiness was ample reward for the fatigue we had undergone on their behalf.

# The Siege at Dhar

Thomas Lowe
Medical Officer, Madras Corps
of Sappers & Miners

# The Siege at Dhar

The news of the fall of Delhi gave a fresh impetus to our forces, and we heard the hundred and one guns fired at Indore, when their festivities ended, without alarm.

Everything was now progressing fast with us for a move against the rebels in the neighbourhood of Dhar. The hammer and the forge were going night and day in the fort, gear for elephants and siege-guns was making, untrained bullocks were being taught the draught of guns, and commissariat stores were being prepared.

October 12th news came into Mhow that a body of *rohillas* was about to move on Mundlaisir to plunder the treasury there. The 3rd and 4th Troops of the 3rd Cavalry, Hyderabad Contingent, under Lieut. Clark, were ordered off forthwith to the village of Goojeeree to intercept this project of the enemy. They had been burning and pillaging several places in our neighbourhood, and only ten miles off had destroyed the *dâk* bungalow at Mânpoor. Another detachment of the 3rd Cavalry was sent off to Mundlaisir to Capt. Keatinge, the political agent there.

About 1.30 a.m. on the 14th instant an order suddenly came from the Brigadier directing three companies of the 25th Bombay N. I., three guns, and fifty dragoons of H. M. 14th L. D. to proceed without delay to the support of Lieut. Clark, of the Hyderabad Cavalry, at Goojeeree and Mânpoor. The 25th went off with their excellent commanding officer, Major Robertson, and now to us, who remained behind in

Mhow, there was only the excitement of a speedy movement in the same direction to comfort us.

October 16th more ammunition was sent out to the force under Major Robertson; and on the 19th orders were issued for the force to march, and all Europeans left behind to go into the fort. The cantonment was to remain in charge of a detachment of H. M. 86th, a portion of the 25th N. I, and the detachment of the Bombay sappers under Lieut. Dick, Bombay Engineers.

On 20th half the B. Company, Madras sappers, with the 86th, under Major Keane, Woolcomb's battery and the remaining troopers of the 3rd Cavalry H. C, and a squadron of dragoons marched out for Dhar. Early the same morning two companies of the 2nd Infantry H. C, a squadron of the 1st Cavalry H. C, and three guns of the H. C., under the command of Captain Speed, arrived from Simrole.

The remaining portion of the Madras sappers waited till the morning of the 21st to conduct the siege train from Mhow to Dhar, We were up about 2 a.m., and started about 6˙30, a.m., and arrived at Juswunthnugger about 7 p.m., a distance of only ten miles having been accomplished. But this was not to be wondered at considering the bad state of the roads, the stubbornness of the bullocks, and the fragility of the tackle. Almost every fifty yards the bullocks refused to go; pricking, and twisting of tails, and yelling, availed not; and not until the willing elephant came to the tug could we extricate the guns from the many holes and heaps of mud they got into. This occurred more or less every mile of the country we had to travel over, until we sighted the fort of Dhar.

The coercion we were obliged to use to induce the bullocks to move was most cruel, and yet what could be done? The heavy guns were wanted at Dhar and must be conveyed there, by hook or by crook, by these untutored, unwilling brutes. The labour was most trying to the officers and men, as well as to the animals; and when we arrived at Dhar our faces and hands were blistered by the heat of the sun.

Lieut. Christie of the Bombay artillery, who was in charge of the siege train from Mhow to Dhar, was most unremitting in his exertions and labours to expedite the transit of these unwieldy machines across this broken, muddy country. The *rohillas* had all retired from their predatory pursuits on the approach of our force into the fort of Dhar. On October 22nd our forces had arrived there. The enemy left the fort and came out to attack us. They had planted three brass guns on a hill south of the fort, and from this battery they extended in force along the east face, skirmishing in splendid style.

In this instance the 25th Regiment behaved admirably. The guns were charged and captured, and the 25th speedily turned them round and fired upon the enemy. The 86th Regiment, with the sappers, were in the centre with Woolcomb's and Hungerford's batteries, the dragoons on our right, and the native cavalry on our left. The enemy made a move to get round to our baggage, but were frustrated. They soon retired to the fort, leaving some forty of their brethren upon the plain. We had three dragoons wounded by sabre cuts, one *jemadar* and one *sowar* of the 3rd Cavalry H. C. killed, and two wounded.

The siege train arrived at Dhar on the evening of the 24th. As we passed down into the valley wherein our camp was pitched, the enemy opened fire from the fort upon a picket. We continued to move onward, and by-and-bye were greeted with vociferous cheers from the Europeans, who longed for the arrival of the "big guns," that they might breach the fort walls and drive the villains to the winds.

The camp at Dhar was pitched about one mile and a half from the fort, on the south side, in an enormous ravine surrounded on all sides by heights broken by gigantic fissures. From the neck of this ravine was a gorge, through which ran a road towards a beautiful large tank surrounded by stately trees, and onward to the town of Dhar. This road was quite hidden from the enemy by hills, and then led into a broken circuitous lane skirting the filthy suburbs of the city. As the camp lay thus snugly protected, it presented a very happy, busy scene.

There was little to be feared from the enemy; they were too safe behind the solid stone walls of that admirably built fort, and the lesson they had just learned taught them better than to venture into the open again. A randomly-aimed shot occasionally flew over our camp, and a few came bouncing into our midst, but nothing was feared. On a hill some two thousand yards south of the fort we had thrown up a sandbag battery, from whence we constantly threw shell into it On the east and on the north faces we had thrown out strong cavalry pickets of dragoons and irregulars, and also of infantry of the 25th N. I. and H. M. 86th. To the west was another tank, or rather lake.

It thus appeared, from the disposition of our forces, and the solitary position of the enemy in the fort, supposed to number about 4,000, that we had arranged a trap from which there was no escape for them. As our reconnoitring parties went out, the enemy always opened fire upon them from the guns on the bastions. It was quite evident the walls of this place must be breached, and to establish a breaching battery a position must be taken up as near as practicable.

This was effected on Sunday morning, 25th Oct., in the following manner. The 86th and Madras sappers marched off about 5 a.m. through the gorge from the camp leading towards Dhar. They turned along the circuitous broken lane skirting the suburbs, and soon found that they could advance almost totally under the cover of natural parallels, huts, and mud walls to within some 500 yards of the fort. A few trees were cut down, miry *nullahs* filled up, and walls knocked down for the field batteries and heavy guns to advance and take up their position.

As our troops neared the fort, a very smart fire of musketry, gingalls, and round shot was kept up by the enemy. The artillery dashed along in splendid style, and speedily opened fire upon the bastions, while the 86th with their rifles subdued the heat of their fire from the matchlock men. Shells from the mortar battery continually poured into the fort, but with little apparent effect. A house upon one of their bastions at the south corner, commanding the road into Dhar from the fort, was a good deal damaged, as were also some of the parapets to the south; but below these, and the crenelations of the curtains, the walls remained as perfect as adamant. An artilleryman was shot through the chest from this corner bastion.

Another line of attack was taken up all along a high mound of earth, extending from this corner road the whole length of the west face, terminating at the large lake. All along this line were houses, protected from the fort by the mound behind them, which rose above them three times their height, and formed excellent cover and accommodation for our troops. At the extreme left of this line was a large open square and a capacious building, and numerous other houses and shops. This position formed the headquarters of the 25th Regiment N. I., and was in every way suited for the occasion, as the men lining this long parallel were easily relieved and comfortably housed.

Facing this natural parallel for offensive operations was the west face of the fort, with the palace at the extreme left, towering high; the intricate, almost impregnable gateway in the middle, flanked by strong bastions on either side, mounted with guns, and a thick zigzag loop-holed wall running upwards from the lower gate to the curtain, and again, beyond this, another loop-holed curtain, another strong bastion, and another similar curtain running to the large corner bastion commanding the road and *maidan* to the south.

The fort is built of fine-grained sandstone, and everywhere was in almost perfect repair. The south, east, and north faces were quite inapproachable from the *maidan*, upon which there was little or no cover, and the approaches on all these sides were almost perpendicular, while the walls and bastions were equally strong, and considerably higher, on account of the fall of the hill on these sides. It was therefore determined to erect a breaching battery upon this long mound facing the west, only some three or four hundred yards distant, and a spot opposite the corner curtain was fixed upon.

All this time, from about 6 a.m. till 12 o'clock, everything was dash, bustle, and clamour. Horsemen rushed backwards and forwards, the field guns were blazing away, while the infantry established themselves in the houses and along the mound, from whence they kept up a continuous rattle of musketry. The inhabitants of this part of the town deserted it almost to a man; one or two decrepit old men and women alone showed themselves at the doors of their miserable hovels. There was a vile effluvium of decomposed skins and putrescent tan liquor in the part occupied by the chucklers; loose goats and sheep were bleating and rushing about between the legs of men and horses; camp followers, in a hundred varied dresses, were looting chickens, pigeons, and the wretched rags they found in these huts; rows of *dhoolies* and their miserable bearers, half frightened out of their lives, were being urged on to the front; red-turbaned sowars and very hairy dragoons came jingling, all heat and excitement, among the stream; quartermasters and adjutants rushed backwards and forwards, threading their way at a walk or dashing onward like messengers of death; obedient, bulky, indispensable elephants, with the needed engines of fort destruction, moving slowly and ponderously along; crowds of Europeans and natives, sappers and artillerymen, the 25th and 86th, all hauling together, hooting and laughing, all very hot, and all aiding the transit of the siege guns to the front. Such a scene, such a din, such semi-serious excitement!

It appeared wonderful that men should have built such a splendid fort, and have left an enemy such extraordinary facilities of capturing it; for nearly the whole way from our camp to the large mound so near to it, and, as it were, placed purposely for the erection of engines for its destruction, our approach was almost a covered way.

About midday some of the enemy, who had concealed themselves in the houses of this part, fired upon Woolcomb's battery. The 86th men, with the Madras sappers, soon despatched these rebels. In some of the houses where they had secreted themselves we found cartouche boxes full of ammunition, caps, cartridges, and other articles of plunder, and muskets with the bayonets fixed.

The site for the battery was selected by Major Boileu of the Madras engineers. The battery was thrown up during the night; the next day it was improved, and the embrasures blinded. The enemy were not idle; we could see them throwing up a battery on our left flank near the palace. This was rendered too hot for them by the excellent practice of Woolcomb's guns on our left, while a mortar battery erected still further to our left, and closer to the gate and palace, sent its deadly missiles among them every quarter of an hour. The effect of this shelling on the palace was terrific, as proved afterwards.

Our heavy guns opened fire upon the curtain of the fort as soon as the battery was ready. For a long time little or no effect was produced, but by-and-bye shattered fragments of stone began to crumble away. The thundering weight of metal continuously battering at one spot had its inevitable result. Little by little the stone-work crumbled as the eighteen-pounders continued to pour their contents upon it. The fearful din of the rapid *bang, bang* in the battery was followed by a sound equally loud when the balls reached the fort wall.

Every time we fired, a shower of bullets and gingall balls replied to us; while here and there, along the whole curtain, might be seen at uncertain intervals a puff of smoke, and then a firing overhead, followed by a sound like "dead," as the ball of the enemy struck a house or a wall hard by. It was great fun to see the bobbing and peeping going on by all in the batteries. If a blue puff was seen to come out from a loop-hole, down went the best and oldest soldier's head while the ball flew past; and there was invariably plenty of time to do so, for the matchlock is not like the rifle, nor does native powder combust so rapidly as ours, consequently the flight of the bullet is slower, although sometimes fatally true, and then, alas! too quick.

On the evening of the 26th, about 9 p.m., the village at the foot of the fort was fired by a party of our force. It was but a partial burning, and the next morning the place looked none the worse for the fire-brand. To proceed upon this work of destruction our men had to descend the front part of the mound we occupied, cross over a portion of the lake running between it and the fort and village, and expose themselves, then and there, to the whole enemy in the fort, as well as any who may be in the village. It was no laughable duty, but they effected their purpose, and returned in safety.

A spy of the enemy's was taken by one of our pickets dressed up as a *fakeer*. He told us some hundred of the enemy were killed and wounded on the day of the action before the fort, and about twenty horses wounded and killed.

On the night of the 27th Oct. a second firing party volunteered to enter the town again between us and the fort, and to attempt a more effectual destruction than followed the first trial. The volunteers were Major Woolcomb, Lieuts. Strutt and Christie, and some men of the Bombay artillery, Lieut. Fenwick and a company of the 25th Regiment N. I. This party was accompanied by a native guide, who trembled like a leaf with fear, although a large reward was to be paid him when the business was over.

They went in silence about 9 30 p.m. It was a bright moonlight night, and we feared lest the enemy should take cognizance of this small body. They crept down from the front of our battery, crossed over the valley below, skirted the water's edge, and were then lost to us among the trees and cottages. A blaze soon sprang up from one spot, then another, and another, and we could see the burning portfire flung through the air to other houses. The conflagration spread faster and faster, and the whole town was enveloped in flames flickering high and broad; then arose a din of voices, amid volleys of musketry, rattling, and screams, and howlings of dogs.

Roof after roof tumbled in, and soon the village was one huge burning pile, overshadowed by curling clouds of smoke dancing high above the flames, and darkening the bright starry sky. It was a gorgeous sight, and if beauty could accompany such a picture, it was there, as every flame, and cloud, and burning timber lay reflected, bright and changing, on the still bosom of the lake below.

They all returned from this errand in safety, after having despatched some of the enemy, and run the gauntlet back to our battery through the scorching, flaming streets.

The timid guide having lost his way and presence of mind totally, our people had to return almost the same way as they went. Lieut. Christie missed his path across the lake, and, while floundering and swimming about to get to the shore, was greeted by a shower of grape from one of his own guns as he rose up all dripping from the water, crying out, "Don't shoot me!" This probably saved his life, as another charge was ready for him.

Our eighteen-pounders and twenty-four pound howitzer had made a considerable hole in the curtain by the morning of the 29th. Enormous masses of stone rolled down after each weighty succussion from our metal. Still the enemy were just as vigilant and annoying to us. Rifle-shooting against such walls availed but little, even from the most patient and practised shot. The sharp report of the rifle was generally followed by a second sound of the lead flattening itself against the walls, while the enemy could walk leisurely along the ramparts inside, take their aim and discharge their pieces in perfect safety. By the time our riflemen saw the puff, and could take their aim, they had sauntered away to some other part; and so twenty men behind walls could thus easily engage the attention and harass hundreds outside. Two men were wounded this day in the battery, one shot in the head the other in the hip.

The breach was widening rapidly, and now we could see the thickness of the walls, which was astonishing.

This evening the brigadier received a letter from the fort requesting to know upon what terms a surrender would be granted. An unconditional one was the reply, to which they said, "Very good, we don't care; you are only destroying the Rajah of Dhar's property, not ours; we have only lost a few men, but our cattle are being killed by the shells." So we went on with the siege.

The enemy now commenced to escape from the north and east faces of the fort in the night-time by means of a rope and basket. We captured almost all of them, most being disguised in some way or other, some as *fakeers*, others in women's clothes. On the morning of the 30th the enemy hoisted the white flag—wily dogs!

For some time there was considerable altercation in our heavy-gun battery about noticing the flag of truce. All the while this fierce war of words, and senior-officership, and commands, &c. was being carried on by the various officers who poured into the battery, the gunners continued to load and fire sharper than ever. The white flag popped up over the parapet, and *whiz* went the rifle at it, but the fellow was too knowing to expose himself; up and down it went, and at length the order to "cease firing" was given; the eighteen-pounders were loaded and must be discharged, and *bang, bang* they went; then all was quiet.

The staff then came up, and a *vakeel* was sent up to the fort gate to hear what they had to say. During the conference of the *vakeel* with the enemy at the gate our men swarmed outside the batteries and along the whole face of this mound; the enemy boldly paraded upon the bastions and parapets of the fort, each with his shield, matchlock, and *tulwar*, walking up and down or quietly sitting to gaze at us; grey-bearded, gaudily-dressed fellows came up to the breach, carefully examined it, and then walked away, and scores of others, all well armed, followed them; they looked down at the rubble and heap of stone-works outside, and then, having thoroughly examined the breach, walked away.

By-and-bye the *vakeel* returned, saying that they requested to know who sent him, when he replied that he was sent by the brigadier; they coolly told him that "they had nothing to do with the *sircar*, nor could they understand why the *sircar* was fighting against them; and that had one of the Rajah of Dhar's officers been sent, they would have conferred with him," and then they drove the *vakeel* away. Of course this was a ruse on their part to gain an opportunity of examining the breach.

They did this thoroughly, and acted accordingly on the following day. The breaching and the shelling from the mortar batteries was resumed with twofold vigour after this instance of impudence. Shell dropped in every part of the fort. The dust caused by one smashing in the roof of the palace had scarcely settled, when another and another followed in its destroying wake, booming loud and terrible when they burst within its rooms. Today Lieut. Christie, Bombay artillery, was shot through the left chest while pointing a gun. The ball entered about an inch below the heart, and was cut out from the back.

On the 31st the firing was kept up unremittingly from all the batteries, but the enemy grew less annoying; most of them, doubtless, had other business on hand. Two corporals of the Madras sappers volunteered to examine the breach for the storming party, who were now ordered to be in readiness for the night. The men forming the storming party were thirty of the 86th under Lieut. Henry, and sixty of the 25th under Capt. Little, and fifty men of the Madras sappers under Capt. Brown.

Corporals Hoskins and Clarke, of the sappers, went off to the breach about ten o'clock; when they arrived at the fort two blank charges were fired from the siege-guns, and they went to the top, made their examination, and returned. The breach was easily ascended.

Immediately after this firing was heard and seen on the maidan to the north-west beyond the lake. Dragoons and irregulars were instantly despatched. The storming party were ordered to enter, which they did, unopposed by a soul. The fort was deserted!

That the enemy had fled was soon known, and dragoons and irregulars were sent in pursuit after them. The remainder of the 25th Regiment, with their band, now entered through its many gates, officers who could get there did, and *dhooly-*bearers; too, with their *dhoolies*. All crowded into the fort, glad that an end had come to the siege. By-and-bye the brigadier and staff were there; everybody seemed pleased with the success, and the band of the 25th accordingly struck up "God save the Queen! "

The night was like day, the music charming, and *lacs* of treasure and jewels were in the palaces! Officers patted each other on the back in a highly paternal-like, congratulatory manner; our good brigadier was very proper; "he did not care for the money, but was delighted the work was done;" and officers went searching about through the pestiferous atmosphere and darkened rooms with lightened cheroots, and, of course, set fire to heaps of loose gunpowder and blew themselves up—perhaps because the enemy had not done so.

In this way Dr. Butler, Bombay artillery, Lieut. Thane, Commissary, and Lieut. Giles, 14th Dragoons well nigh ended their brief sojourn in this wicked world. An enormous heap of gunpowder lay in a room, and was exploded forthwith by this trio. Lieut. Thane was in flames in an instant, jumping in the open air like a wild man, and crying out, "Oh, put me out! Put me out!" There lay Dr. Butler blown down, horridly burnt, listening to this cry of "Put me out," while other grains of gunpowder were quietly fizzing close to him and running away in tiny combustion in various directions—maybe to another heap, which would assuredly bring the building about his inquisitive head. Lieut. Giles was more singed than burnt These gentlemen soon found *dhoolies* in waiting, and were carried out, in a manner they never dreamt of when they entered it, to their beds that night.

The 25th Regiment guarded the palace and the gate and breach, and at some time about the small hours of the morning we retired to our undisturbed beds, the first time for ten days, to dream of the glorious plethoric bags of prize-money promised to the force on the capture of the fort of Dhar, then lying snugly locked up in the huge chests of the treasury of its palace.

That the enemy should have escaped from the fort after what had been said, *viz.*, that " a mouse could not get away unobserved," was indeed a marvel to all The firing seen by us on the maidan to the north-west, at the moment the breach was entered, was only a skirmish with the tail-end of the enemy and the outlying picket of 3rd Cavalry, Hyderabad Contingent. The main body had passed by them and the dragoons wholly unobserved, and were well away before the alarm could be of any avail.

The pursuers, after a hard ride of some twelve miles, only came up with a few wretched stragglers, some of them were slain, others made prisoners and brought into camp. Those who escaped made the best of their way towards Mundasoor, plundering and destroying various places as they fled. The *jemadar* commanding the irregular picket was placed in arrest, but it would appear, from the evidence adduced on inquiry, that he was not much to blame. The trooper sent by him to warn the picket of dragoons, after it was known that the enemy were off, fell with his horse on the way and was at once disabled; at the same time the European picket, which had been there for some days, and knew the whole locality well, happened to have been changed the very day of the escape.

In the fort we found a good number of brass guns—about thirty—of various sizes, most of them wretched pieces, rudely mounted, and so honeycombed and ragged at the muzzles that the wonder is they dared fire them at all. Upon the various bastions were heaps of loose gunpowder and rudely hammered balls of all sizes lying about, here and there a cot, a broken sponge, ragged clothes, cooking-pots, and a dead man. All four walls were particularly strong, varying in thickness from twenty to forty feet. The thinnest part, curious to say, was the spot through which we had effected our breach, and this was upwards of eighteen feet! All around the fort in the thick-est portions of the walls were dwelling-houses and extensive chambers for stores. On the north side was a long casemated building for troops and horses, sundry sheds, detached build-ings, and a gaudy place of worship.

In all of these the enemy had left something or other be-hind them. Little heaps of grain, powder flasks, belts, shoes, hats, and dirty linen, all lay together in confused heaps; in some rooms there were the tawdry tinsel, hand-*punkahs*, bits of silk, and broken bangles of their women; the temple they defiled by cooking in and storing their rubbish. In every spot there were evidences of a precipitate flight and the terrible effects of our shells. Copper pots, drums, spears, matchlocks, muskets, bayonets, *tulwars*, bows and arrows, carpets, tents, wounded horses and bullocks—dying and dead ones—and their own groaning wounded men, conspired to make up a picture of the horrors of war by no means attractive. The palace was literally torn to rags by Woolcomb's admirable mortar practice.

It is scarcely possible to credit the wreck and ruin brought about by a few hours' constant shelling upon one spot. The massive pillars and beams of the building were almost torn into shreds by our shell; and I am inclined to believe that this alone kept the enemy from the treasure known to be there. In the centre of the fort was a large water-tank containing filthy water. This tank was searched, but nothing was found in it. In the inner chambers of the palace was the treasure, and, as reported, the jewels too.

A prize-committee had been elected, and were soon busily engaged in counting out the gold and silver. It was a most grat-ifying spectacle to behold bag after bag disgorging their shining contents of silver and gold! Each bag of silver contained about 2,500 rupees, the bags of gold *mohurs*—large and small—varied in value: I believe there were some £15,000 in gold.

An enormous chest was opened. First there came out some dingy, fusty cloth; then some more, and then a huge piece of faded purple velvet, ornamented with a silver border and silver bells (the remains of an elephant's trappings), then beneath this was a chaos of huge silver basins, dishes, plates, cups, lamps, and vases; and beneath these were several great bags of silver lying at the bottom of the chest side by side, with tightly constricted necks, in solemn repose; they were unceremoniously hauled out to the companionship of their brethren, and at once counted. Each bag contained its 2,500 rupees.

All the time this tedious, yet pleasant business of taking accounts was proceeding, the pick-axe and shovel of the sapper were going deep into hollow-sounding floors and walls. In one dark dusty room we found a large four-post silver bedstead with all its trappings in silver. The posts lay against the mouldy walls in filthy bags, the silver rails, and steps, and bells belonging to the bed, were all lying in a heap upon the floor. The sappers dug and picked about in various places, but no jewels were discovered. They probably lay deeper down in the palatial recesses, or had been carried away by others; we did not find them, although this treasury was said to be rich in jewels, and the amount captured by our force, including elephants, camels, &c, was something less than nine *lacs*; this was sent under an European guard to the fort of Mhow.

The bastions and curtains of the fort were partially destroyed by the sappers.

Our force was now strengthened by the arrival of Major Orr's column of the Hyderabad Contingent. They marched into Dhar on the evening of 4th November, and again moved out on the 7th for Mahidpore, at which station we now learnt that the enemy from Dhar had been joined by the Mahidpore Contingent, and unitedly seized the guns, destroyed the Europeans, and looted and burnt down the cantonment. This was sad news.

Orders were now out for our force to march towards Mundasore, and we started from our encamping ground at Dhar on Sunday the 8th November, at 5 a.m., and by-and-bye entered the territories of Scindiah.

As we marched from Dhar we left that once stately fort behind us a heap of ruins, the palace and gates burning piles. The flames shot up from the crackling masses beneath them in wild luridity, and glimmered upon the departing masses in ghastly beams, as they threaded along in silent tramp beneath the shadows of its dismantled bastions and walls. It was a cold morning, and our men gazed upon it for the last time with a savage, unrelenting satisfaction.

# Battles at Cawnpore

John Adye
Lieutenant–Colonel, Royal Artillery

# Battles at Cawnpore

In the early part of 1857 I was stationed at Cork Harbour in command of a few men on Spike Island, a period of tranquillity after all the anxieties of the great Crimean war. The tranquillity, however, was not destined to last very long.

One day towards the end of May I crossed the harbour to call on a gentleman in the neighbourhood who had just returned from Cork, and on my asking if there was any news, he said that a remarkable telegram had been received from India that a native regiment at Meerut had killed its English officers and was marching on Delhi. That was the first news of the great Mutiny. It also stated that the natives in parts of India were passing *chew-patties* from village to village. What was a *chew-patty*? Nobody could tell us. It turned out to be a sort of pancake; but why the natives should specially pass round pancakes, and presumably eat them, as a signal of rebellion no one could explain.

Week after week the news became more serious, and troops of all arms were sent off in large numbers round the Cape. Towards the end of July, being in London, I received information that the Duke of Cambridge had appointed me Assistant Adjutant-General of the batteries of Royal Artillery, then on their voyage; and about the middle of August I left via Egypt.

Generals Dupuis and Windham, and many other officers, were of the party; and from Cairo we had to cross the desert (about ninety miles) in uncomfortable carriages like bathing machines. There was no steamer at Suez, and we were detained a week at that dismal village of the desert, receiving occasional news that matters were becoming worse and worse in India. The only hotel was crowded with English officers, with little to eat and not a drop of water except what was brought in skins on camels from the Nile, nearly 100 miles away.

At last the *Bentinck* arrived and carried us slowly down the Red Sea, with the thermometer at 96 degrees; in a week we were at Aden, thermometer still rising, and ten days afterwards at Galle. At Madras we heard of the fall of Delhi, and on October 5 our long voyage in the *Bentinck* came to an end, and we steamed up the Hoogly to Calcutta.

Matters were in a somewhat critical condition on our arrival at Calcutta, for although the fall of Delhi had given a severe blow to the mutineers, still we had no force of much strength to take the field; and the garrison of Lucknow under Outram and Havelock, with many women and children, were entirely surrounded, mere scraps of intelligence only arriving from them occasionally. I had several interviews with Sir Colin Campbell, who was very anxious to collect a sufficient force for the relief of Lucknow.

During October troops of all arms arrived in quick succession after a three months' voyage round the Cape, but the great difficulty was transport. The railway extended to Raneegunge, 120 miles up country, but beyond that point our means only enabled us to push forward about 100 men a day, either in bullock carts or by march. Another difficulty was the provision of horses for the artillery. In fact, the whole of Central India from Delhi to Lucknow was practically in the possession of the mutineers, who fortunately had no generals to lead them, and were content for the most part to hover about and pillage as they could. Slowly, however, as our forces in a long thin line marched upwards towards Allahabad and Cawnpore, the tide began to turn, and on October 27 the Commander-in- Chief left Calcutta for the North.

To a stranger landing in India for the first time, knowing nothing of the language or the customs of the people, more especially in the middle of a revolution, there were many minor personal perplexities, especially about servants. Their very titles were embarrassing. *Bearers, kitmagars, dhobies, durzees, bheesties, chuprassies, punkah-wallahs, hookahbadars, syces,* and others. What were their duties? That was the point. Because in India, as we soon found, one man will only do his own mite of work, and scorns the idea of making himself generally useful. Any attempt to enlarge the sphere of their duties would lead, so we were told, to loss of caste. There were, of course, exceptional cases, such as that of the native servant who, on being asked by a newcomer as to his caste, replied, 'Same caste as master, drink brandy sahib.'

Owing to the great influx of officers from home, all in a hurry to be off, servants were especially difficult to find. I was fortunate enough to get an old fellow whose name was Buktum Hassan to take care of me. He could not speak a word of English, and slept away his time on a mat outside my door. I believe he was a bearer, and a Hindu, but he would not come near me at dinner time. Subsequently I procured another servant, who condescended to wait on me at dinner, but I was cautioned not on any account to eat ham in his presence. Curry and rice he did not object to. Two Sepoys, also, were appropriated for my service as orderlies. They were tall, dark, spare men, and all day waited patiently in the corridor in uniform, strictly buttoned up, with belts and boots. The first evening they said something, which being interpreted was that they wished to go home: they then proceeded to take off all their clothes, except a loin cloth, made them up into a bundle, and leaving them in a corner of my room, marched happily away.

The greater portion of the batteries from England having arrived, General Dupuis and his staff followed the Commander-in-Chief up country on November 12. The journey to Benares occupied five days, and from Raneegunge we were conveyed in *dawk gharries* about eighty miles a day, passing on the road every few hours detachments of troops of all arms, hurrying forward, some in bullock carts, some on the march. Portions of the road, especially near the river Soane, were unsafe from the vicinity of straggling parties of mutineers, and we had to be protected occasionally by an escort.

Remaining a few hours in a bungalow outside Benares, we found time to pay a hurried visit to this celebrated city. As an instance of the precarious nature of our long line of communications, it may be mentioned that although its inhabitants were in a restless, disaffected condition, the garrison only consisted of a weak company of infantry and two field guns.

We were rather a large party at the hotel bungalow, some being officers newly arrived and others who had served for years in the country, and who were very good natured in giving us information. Colonel David Wood, of the Horse Artillery, was one of the newcomers, and had a habit occasionally of assuming ignorance on minor points which perhaps was not always genuine. During dinner he turned gravely to one of the old Indian officers and said, 'Can you tell me, what is a *dhobie*?' They all laughed, and it was explained that a *dhobie* was a man who washed your clothes. Wood, still quite grave, said: "Oh, that accounts for the difficulty. I told mine to clean my horse, and he refused. I will discharge him tomorrow.'

The old Indian officer, however, assured him that a *dhobie* was absolutely necessary. Wood replied that he never required washing on active service.

'You must surely have your shirts washed' was the rejoinder.

'Not at all,' said Wood. 'I always wear a flannel shirt in the field, and as soon as it gets dirty or worn out I throw it away and put on another.'

On November 19 we reached Allahabad, an interesting old fortress at the junction of the Ganges and Jumna; but important events were taking place, and we hurried on and reached Cawnpore on the 21st.

On our arrival we found that Sir Colin Campbell, with nearly all the troops available, had left a few days previously for Lucknow, and that serious fighting had taken place there on the 16th and 17th; but the communications were subsequently interrupted by the mutineers in Oude, and for some days no further information could be obtained as to the progress of affairs. It was a critical period of the campaign. As already explained, the garrison of Lucknow, with many women and children, fifty miles distant, had been entirely shut up and surrounded by multitudes of mutineers for weeks past, and was running short of provisions, so that its relief had become a very urgent necessity. On the other hand, the great bulk of our troops, anxious as they were to reach the scene, owing to want of means of rapid conveyance, were still moving up in driblets along the 600 miles of road from Calcutta to Cawnpore. So that when the Commander-in-Chief had crossed the Ganges on his adventurous march to Lucknow, he was only able to take with him about 6,000 infantry and a moderate force of cavalry and artillery.

But that was not all. Cawnpore, his only base, was in a precarious, defenceless condition, and when Sir Colin had left and placed Windham in command of it, there were only 450 infantry remaining for its protection. The defences of Cawnpore were insignificant. A small incomplete earthwork had been made on the bank of the river with a view to protect the bridge of boats, and lying all round it were the ruins of burnt bungalows and a general scene of confusion and desolation; and beyond again, at a few hundred yards, stood the large city, composed, as usual, of a wilderness of narrow tortuous streets, and devoid of any external defences. So that it was not a favourable position to hold, even had a considerable force been available.

The difficulties and dangers of the situation were indeed obvious. No sooner had the Commander-in-Chief crossed the Ganges and marched in one direction, than the Gwalior contingent a well trained force which, joined by other mutineers, amounted to about 25,000 men with a powerful artillery of 40 guns, field and heavy, was reported as advancing in several columns from Calpee forty-six miles distant on the other side.

The instructions given to General Windham were as follows. The force at his command for the time was estimated at about 500 men; and the detachments of troops as they arrived up country were to be sent on to Sir Colin Campbell at Lucknow. Windham was directed to strengthen the entrenchment, and also to watch carefully the movements of the Gwalior contingent; and should it indicate an intention of advancing, he was to make as great a show as possible by encamping his small detachments conspicuously outside the city, leaving a guard in the earthwork. If he should be seriously threatened, he was to communicate with the Commander-in- Chief as to detaining some of the troops arriving, to assist in the defence.

From a military point of view, it is evident that, whilst Sir Colin's position was somewhat critical, that of Windham was far more so. The general, however, lost no time in carrying out his orders. The entrenchment was extended and strengthened with a few guns, and its glacis cleared. The troops were encamped outside; but whether this rather transparent artifice would have much moral effect on the enemy may be doubted, especially as they had ample means of obtaining correct information from their friends in Cawnpore. On the other hand, it was very difficult to procure accurate accounts of the movements of the Gwalior force. In the absence of cavalry, native spies were the only resource; but some of these were caught and mutilated by the enemy; besides which, under the circumstances of the general disaffection, their fidelity could not in all cases be relied on.

The duty of obtaining intelligence was entrusted to Captain Bruce, commonly called 'the intelligent Bruce,' an excellent officer who was also a magistrate. As all the prisons had been destroyed, the only punishments available for criminal natives were hanging and flogging, and in this horrible occupation he was engaged every day. He held his court in the open air in the yard of a ruined bungalow, surrounded by the debris of smashed furniture. Amongst others, he captured a native of rank, a friend of Nana Sahib's, and on threatening him with death, the native reluctantly gave information which led to the discovery of about 10,000 in money and a quantity of jewellery, &c., which had been looted and hidden away.

I paid one or two visits to the bungalow, which had been the scene of the massacre, a few months previously, of the English women and children by Nana Sahib. The well into which their bodies were thrown had been filled up and closed; but on the walls of the house were still remaining some half-obliterated writing and stains of blood, and in the bushes of the garden, fragments of children's clothing.

Events were now hurrying on to a climax. General Windham, a few days after the departure of Sir Colin, sent a message informing him of the rapid approach of the Gwalior contingent, and obtained authority to detain some of the new arrivals, so that by November 26, when the first battle occurred, he had about 1,700 men and 10 guns drawn by bullocks at his disposal. But of these, four companies of infantry and a few artillerymen had to be left on guard in the entrenchments, so that his movable field force was still very limited.

In the meantime, however, the road to Lucknow became closed, and for several days after November 19 no information whatever was received. On the night of the 23rd a tiny note, rolled up and concealed in a quill (which was the method commonly adopted), was brought in by a native from Lucknow. It proved to be from a commissariat officer, who asked for more provisions at once, but said he could give no opinion on military matters, except that they were complicated. The native who brought the note received 50 rupees.

On the other side the mutineers from Calpee were now rapidly approaching in distinct divisions, and had arrived at several villages within a few miles of Cawnpore, and General Windham felt he could no longer remain inactive. On the 24th he advanced his camp a few miles along the Calpee road up to the Ganges canal, which runs across the country, and when its bridges were guarded it served as a wide wet ditch along his front. The Gwalior contingent, however, began to assume the offensive, and spies reported the advance of their main body from Akbarpore to Suchonlee, and that their leading division was on the Pandoo river, only three miles from the British camp.

At daybreak on November 26 our men were under arms, and Windham, with ten men of the 9th Lancers and a few *sowars*, went forward to reconnoitre, and, finding that the mutineers were on the move, led forward his troops at once to the attack. His force consisted of about 1,200 men, being detachments of the 34th, 82nd, 88th, and Rifle Brigade. He also had eight guns, all drawn by bullocks; four manned by natives from Madras, the others by a few gunners of the Royal and Bengal Artillery and some Sikhs—a sort of improvised battery got up for the occasion. The British troops advanced cheerfully to the attack. When these reached the enemy's position, which was on the other side of the almost dry bed of the Pandoo river, the mutineers opened fire from some heavy guns, and poured in several rounds of grape, as we neared them.

Our artillery at once replied.

Nothing, however, could restrain the eagerness of our men, who came on with a rush, cheering as they went, crossed the river, and captured the position. The enemy retreated in haste, leaving three guns and some ammunition wagons in our hands. We followed them for some distance, and Windham, having halted for a couple of hours to rest his men, then withdrew, as he had intended, to his original position outside Cawnpore, taking the captured guns with him.

The mutineers were evidently in considerable strength, and, notwithstanding their defeat, followed us at a distance as we withdrew. Our loss was rather severe, considering the rapidity with which the attack had been carried out. One young officer, Captain Day of the 88th, was killed, being struck by a round shot and knocked down a well.

Our total casualties were:

| | | | | | |
|---|---|---|---|---|---|
| Killed | 1 | officer | 13 | men | |
| Wounded | 5 | officers | 73 | men | |
| Totals | 6 | officers | 86 | men | = 92 |

General Windham on his return at length received the long desired letter from Lucknow. It was a short note from General Mansfield, chief of the Staff, saying that all was well and they were coming back at once to Cawnpore.

November 27 proved to be a very eventful day. Our small field force, as I have explained, was encamped outside the city, not far from the point where the great trunk road crossed that from Cawnpore to Calpee. General Windham naturally hoped that the successful blow he had delivered on the previous day would at all events so far tend to discourage the mutineers as to delay their movements and give time for the return of the Commander-in-Chief. The position, however, was critical. Whilst desirous of presenting a bold front and of protecting the city, it was evident not only that our force was insufficient, but that the right flank towards the Ganges was open to attack and liable to be turned.

At daylight the troops were again under arms, and part of the 34th and 82nd regiments, with four Madras guns, were detached to the flank, to watch the road from Bithoor. Two 24-pounder heavy guns on travelling carriages, each drawn by a string of bullocks and manned by seamen of the *Shannon*, under Lieutenant Hay, R.N., were brought out from the entrenchment to strengthen the position in front. Lieutenant Hay had a difficult duty to perform. In the first place, his guns were very heavy for field work; and the draught animals, though obedient to native drivers, were so timid that if an English soldier or sailor approached, they at once began to bolt, and became unmanageable.

I remember discussing the matter with him in the morning, and suggested that in the event of a fight he should, if possible, bring his guns into action on the high road, as if he were to leave it, and get into heavy ground and were pressed, he might be in difficulties. He quite concurred, and during the battle, which lasted all day, he acted accordingly, and performed excellent service, he himself being twice wounded.

About 10 a.m. a cannonade suddenly commenced away on the right, followed shortly afterwards by a similar demonstration in front. The mutineers were evidently determined to make a simultaneous attack on both points, and although for the time they held back their infantry, their artillery fire was very severe and continuous. Windham, conceiving that the flank attack might prove the more dangerous of the two, proceeded there himself in the first instance, but on his return to the front an hour afterwards, found that matters were becoming serious. Not only was the fire incessant, but there were indications that our left as well as our right was threatened in fact, the enemy were in great strength (in a semicircle) all round us. The battle continued for several hours without signs of abatement, our ammunition was running short, and the bullock drivers began to desert.

Under these circumstances General Windham directed his troops to fall back a short distance, until they found a temporary shelter under cover of some mounds and remains of old brick kilns just outside the city. It seemed now that the position might be held. Still anxious about the right flank, late in the afternoon he sent an aide-de-camp to obtain information, and shortly afterwards directed me to ride through the streets and ascertain the state of affairs.

Whilst threading the narrow lanes, I suddenly met the aide-de-camp coming back in haste, who informed me that the mutineers were in possession of the lower parts of the town and had just fired a volley at him. At this moment Windham himself joined us. Whilst deliberating on the critical position, two companies of the Rifle Brigade also appeared on the scene, as if they had dropped from the clouds. They had been marching all day up the trunk road, hearing firing in various directions, but unable to find anyone to give them information. Windham said a few words to them, and, placing himself at their head, away they went cheering, and soon cleared the streets of the enemy.

It was, however, becoming dusk, and the general, feeling that it was impossible to remain in the exposed position outside the city, especially as his troops were exhausted and the ammunition running short, sent me to General Dupuis, who was for the moment in command at the front, with orders to withdraw the whole force and return to the entrenchment on the Ganges, as otherwise the position might be lost and the bridge of boats destroyed.

The retirement through the streets was conducted without haste and in good order, and was not interfered with by the enemy. It was rather remarkable that although so closely hemmed in by the mutineers, they did not at first take the precaution of cutting the telegraph wires, so that messages were sent to Lord Canning at Calcutta of the results of each day's fighting. During the evening General Windham held a consultation with the senior officers with a view to a night attack on the mutineers, but in the absence of reliable information as to their position the idea was relinquished.

The chief officers of the staff were temporarily accommodated in a bungalow outside the Fort; and late at night Windham came in and stated that one of the heavy naval 24-pounders had been upset somewhere in the streets during our retreat and had been left behind, and he requested me to go out and if possible recover it, giving me *carte blanche* to make any arrangements necessary for the purpose.

It was rather like looking for a needle in a bundle of hay. I went to the entrenchment, obtained the assistance of some seamen under Midshipman Garvey and a guard of 50 infantry, and, with a cart containing a triangle-gyn and the necessary tackle, we prepared to start. Most fortunately at the last moment we found one of the native bullock drivers, who said he knew the position of the lost gun, and on a promise of a few rupees agreed to conduct us to the spot; and so under his friendly guidance we marched off into the darkness.

Our friendly native, however, instead of entering the city, led us for a considerable distance through its outskirts, along the banks of the Ganges canal, and some doubts arose as to whether he was not wilfully misleading and taking us into the enemy's camp. However, there was nothing for it but to go on, and at length, becoming very excited, he turned sharply into the town, and after wandering through some of the narrow lanes, sure enough there was the gun lying upset against a small shop, with its wheel sunk in a narrow, deep, perpendicular drain. There were planks lying about, and indications that the enemy had been trying to extricate it.

Small parties of the infantry were immediately placed at the corners of the adjacent streets, so as to isolate us from sudden attack. Their orders were to keep perfectly silent, but should an attempt be made to force their position they were to fire a volley and charge. As time was precious, and as mounting a gyn with its tackle, &c., in the dark would cause delay, it was decided to try and pull the gun out of its awkward position by main force; and, the seamen having fastened a rope to the trail and working with a will, the attempt succeeded, and so, withdrawing the infantry, we marched back to the fort in triumph. The coolie got his rupees and every man a glass of grog, and thus all ended well.

On returning very late to the bungalow, the staff were all lying about asleep on the floor in the various rooms. The only one who woke was Colonel Charles Woodford, of the Rifles, to whom I mentioned our successful adventure. Poor fellow! He was out at daylight the next morning, engaged in the severe contest which took place, and was killed in capturing some guns from the mutineers in the open plain.

On the morning of the 28th the fighting was incessant it re-commenced on both sides of the city simultaneously, and for the third day in succession.

Away on the left in the open plain, near the ruins of the 'old Dragoon lines,' the Rifles, with part of the 82nd and a battery, after a hard contested fight drove back the mutineers in a brilliant manner and captured two 18-pounder guns. On the right, along the Bithoor road, a second battle was going on at the same time, and continued all day. Brigadier Carthew, with parts of the 34th and 82nd regiments and the Madras battery, held a position somewhat in advance, between the city and the Ganges, and was attacked with overwhelming numbers, but maintained the position until sunset. Carthew was supported by a part of the 64th, commanded by Colonel Wilson, who during the day, in endeavouring to capture some of the enemy's guns, was killed, together with three of his officers and many men.

Our losses during the three days' fighting were 9 officers killed, and upwards of 300 officers and men killed and wounded.

I have thus related as shortly and clearly as possible the general features of the battles round Cawnpore, at the end of November, as they came under my notice; because, in my opinion, much injustice was done to General Windham, who was a brave soldier and an excellent leader, and whose difficulties were by no means understood and appreciated.

General Windham, in anticipation of the return of Sir Colin Campbell from Lucknow, had sent him several messages, pointing out the serious nature of the attack on Cawnpore; and on the evening of the 28th the Commander-in-Chief at length arrived, and with the chief part of his force encamped on the other side of the Ganges. What with the women and children, the wounded (amounting in all to 2,000 people), and the usual accumulations of camp equipage and stores which are inseparable from an Indian army in the field, his line of march extended for about twenty miles; and when the strings of elephants, camels, bullock wagons, *palanquins*, &c., began to cross the bridge of boats the following day, the scene was more like the emptying of Noah's ark than anything else.

The mutineers, who had now full possession of the city and its suburbs, brought some heavy guns to bear on the bridge, and struck the boats several times. However, on November 29 and 30 the whole force crossed the Ganges from Oude and encamped outside Cawnpore, near the 'old Dragoon lines.' Although all pressing danger was at an end on the return of Sir Colin's force, still the Commander-in- Chief had to proceed with considerable caution. His great anxiety, before assuming the offensive, was to provide for the safety of the women, children, and wounded.

On December 3 they were sent under convoy down the road to Allahabad, and the Commander-in-Chief at length was free to act against the mutineers, who, in the meantime, had harassed the camp by occasional demonstrations and artillery fire. Although the enemy were in full possession of Cawnpore, their main position was on the plain outside, and the Ganges canal between us acted as a wet ditch along their front. Sir Colin Campbell computed their numbers as about 25,000 men with 36 guns.

On the morning of December 6 the British camp was struck, and about noon the whole force, consisting of 5,000 infantry, 600 cavalry, and 35 guns, advanced across the open to the attack. The cavalry and horse artillery made a detour to the left, so as to pass over the canal by a bridge a mile and a half distant, and threaten the enemy's flank. The brigades of infantry supported by the artillery, advanced steadily in, line across the plain, but were somewhat delayed at the Ganges canal owing to there being but one bridge within reach. This obstacle and the necessary crowding once overcome, they rapidly regained their formation, and, spreading out like a fan, soon drove the enemy back, and ran into their main camp at 1 p.m., Sir Colin, fine old soldier as he was, riding in front with his helmet off, cheering on his panting troops.

The mutineers were disorganised, the retreat became a rout, and they fled in all directions, being pursued by Sir Colin and staff with the cavalry and horse artillery up to the fourteenth milestone along the Calpee road, every gun and ammunition wagon which had gone in that direction falling into our hands. Heartily tired, we returned and bivouacked that night in the plain outside Cawnpore. I could not help admiring the toughness of old Sir Colin, who rolled himself up in a blanket, lay down to sleep in a hole in a field, and seemed to enjoy it.

The following day Brigadier-General Hope Grant, with the cavalry and horse artillery, followed up such of the mutineers as had retreated by the Bithoor road, caught them just as they were about to cross the Ganges, capturing the remainder of their guns without any casualties on our side. That was the end of the Gwalior contingent as a fighting force.

The loss of the British troops on the 6th was about 100, and 37 guns in all were taken, besides quantities of munitions and stores.

The following is a translation of a Hindustani document issued by the Gwalior contingent, and found on the field of battle outside Cawnpore:

### CAWNPORE

By order of the great rajah the leader. May his shadow never be less.

Let all the lords of the manor and the rajahs of this country know that a dromedary rider, for the purpose of finding out all about the roads, and defiles, and ferries, is about to be sent, in consequence of the departure of the Gwalior contingent towards Cawnpore; that no person is to molest or hurt in any way the above mentioned dromedary rider; and let them, in fact, assist him to the best of their power. . . . It is written on the 3rd of the month of Suffer, and it corresponds with 1274 of the year of the Flight.

# Retaking Lucknow

Vivian Dering Majendie
Lieutenant, Royal Artillery

# Retaking Lucknow

The delay is over at last. The idle halt has come to an end, and the army once more is on its legs. Tents struck, baggage loaded, and away to Lucknow.

We do not move up *en masse,* however, but in driblets, some troops moving forward every day. The monster siege-train, with an appropriate guard of cavalry, infantry, and field artillery, travels in two divisions, the second half being one day's march in rear of the first; far along the road does the straggling line of guns, mortars, howitzers, and *hackeries* loaded heavily with shot and shell, and *tumbrils* crammed with thousands upon thousands of pounds of powder, and ammunition, and diabolical contrivances of war. Far along the dusty road does all this extend; nor are its movements by any means swift owing to innumerable break-downs, and not a little to certain eccentricities on the part of our old friends, the bullocks, who somehow contrive never to have less than about five hundred carts stuck in ditches, or inextricably jammed at one and the same time, so as always to have on hand some very fine specimens of chaos.

It is but dreary work travelling alongside this *train d'équipages militaires,* as the French would call it, but it is still more dreary work travelling behind it in the capacity of rear-guard, when you are of course delayed by and made sensible of every new break-down, or fresh bullockian caprice, more especially when your humour is none of the sweetest from the fact of your having been roused from your couch two hours before daybreak by a heartless bugler sounding the *reveille.*

I wonder if the best-natured man in the world could be agreeable, or even civil at this unearthly hour in the morning. I have noticed that even the cheerfulest and most buoyant of mortals become grumpy and unsociable at this miserable period of their existence. One is generally in a state of vacant stupidity and owlishness from want of sleep; one is probably in a state of moroseness likewise from the barking of one's shins over an infernal tent-peg; of desperate though subdued rage from the tumbling over an accursed and tightly-stretched tent-rope, and of cold perspiration at the recollection of how, in the dark, you had walked up to a horse's heels and narrowly escaped a violent and horrible death therefrom.

All this causes you to foster misanthropy to an extent which is positively terrific; your dearest friend tells you in confidence that he feels "deuced seedy this morning." Ha! Ha! Delightful! You become grumpily ecstatic thereupon; you chuckle over it with fiendish glee, and you make merry at your "dearest friend's" expense!

Lieutenant ——'s *khitmutghar* failed to bring him the customary cup of tea this morning before starting, and he is consequently hungry, and even in a worse humour than yourself. He confides to you with much pathos the sad fact. Confound the man and his *khitmutghar!* What do you care? You are rather glad than otherwise, and you tell him so; and if he chooses to continue a conversation commenced so inauspiciously, why then—*que voulez-vous, mon cher?*—you will disagree with him on every point except that of licking his *khitmutghar* "within an inch of his life," because at the moment that proposition happens to suit your Timon-of-Athens-like mood.

But of all objectionable people to meet at this hour the worst I know is your *lively* man—the man who affects a sort of ghastly merriment and wide-awakeness, which resolves itself into a hideous jocularity and sleepy sort of briskness, which you know must be all a sham at this time of day, or night. Feigning jollity, he calls you "old fellow." Now I have no objection to being called "old fellow" in the middle of the day or after dinner; but when a man deliberately, and of malice aforethought, calls you "old fellow" at 4 a.m. he commits an act which ought to be made punishable by law. You rather hope that he will bring matters to a crisis by slapping you on the back, which would, of course, be an excuse for at once knocking him off his horse.

"Well, old fellow! How are we this morning? Sleepy, eh?" Of course you are sleepy, and so is he, only he pretends not to be. Continued jocularity: "Cheer up old boy" &c. &c.; and so we wrap ourselves up in a cloak of grumpiness and hatred of our fellow-man, and ride gloomily along on our horse, who stumbles—the brute!—at every step.

By Jove! How sleepy we are. We light a cheroot, which of course is a bad one—we watch the grey morning breaking—we watch the black shades of night peeling off, as it were, one by one, and disappearing—we watch the day dawning prettily in the east, and insensibly, gradually, we are humanizing once more.

We watch the little bit of gold showing above the horizon, and growing into a great, glowing, fiery orb, which we know, ere long, will dart out such brazen heat and scorching rays that existence anywhere but in the shade will be impracticable.

We watch the dark masses of troops and guns (who have hitherto been, to our eye, only as huge, shapeless masses of darkness moving mechanically onward) becoming defined and clear by slow degrees, until at last the men's faces become apparent, and you are able once again to behold private John Smith in all his glory as he trudges along, puffing away merrily at his short, black *cutty*, filled with the nastiest tobacco in the world, in an overpowering state of heat, perspiration, and dust.

It is wonderful how dusty everyone seems to have become in that hour or so before dawn, but so it is: in the wrinkles of the men's coats, on their beards and whiskers, and down the junction of their cheeks and noses—about their firelocks—in your horses' ears and your own, and on his smooth, sleek skin—upon the bullocks, yokes—upon the elephants' broad backs—thickly over the heavy guns, from muzzle to breach, in the crevices of their mouldings and carvings, over the carriages, and upon every chain and hand-spike, ring and bolt—as thickly, too, upon the field pieces, and taking the shine out of the harness—wherever, in fact, a grain of sand or dust can cling there will that grain be found, reducing man and beast, and wood and iron, to a sort of neutral, gritty grey.

It is wonderful, too, how with sunrise all sleepiness vanishes; often have I found in a night's march, when I have rolled and lolled about on my horse with very drowsiness the long night through, and would have given all my worldly possessions for a nap—when I have in sheer despair wound the mane round my fingers, and then resigned myself to Morpheus, and the safety of my neck to chance—when, on a short halt being called, I have thrown myself off my horse on to the soft dusty road, and dropping off to sleep before my foot was well out the stirrup have slept with all my might and main until "Attention!" was called, or in case that failed to awaken me, until a good-natured sergeant coming up roused me with "They're a moving off, sir"—invariably on these occasions, when I have been thus overpowered with sleep, have I found that immediately the sun appears, long before it gets hot, does all that drowsiness vanish, and you feel almost supernaturally wide awake—the first few rays as they sparkle and gleam upon you seem to drive away every wink and blink from your eyelids, and leave you with that sort of sleepless, weary Wandering Jew *marche-marche-toujours-marche* sensation which is scarcely more agreeable than the previous one of extreme somnolence.

********

After two or three days' journeying along a road remarkable for its monotony, except when one passed through some walled village, such as Busseratgunge and Nawabgunge, where ragged shot holes denting the old gateways, and making splintered gaps in the rotten wooden gates, showed us the nature of the key which Havelock had used to open them, but which became monotonous after a time from the fact of the keys being all off the same bunch, as we had opportunities of observing at each succeeding village—we arrived at last at the appointed rendezvous for the army, Bunterah, about seven or eight miles from Lucknow.

Here such a force was collected as must have paled the cheek of Pandy's spies when they caught sight of it, and must have made the old Begum tremble in her palace at Lucknow when she heard of its approach.

Magnificent it was to see this vast assemblage of white tents stretching out for miles, and among which went hither and thither some fifteen thousand troops, English and Sikhs, full of ardour, life, and hope. Nor did this force, large as it may appear, include all the troops who were to be employed in the capture of Lucknow; for, at the Alum Bagh, General Outram had some four thousand men, while General Franks was expected in a few days with a force of five thousand eight hundred men, after a long but victorious march through the south-eastern portion of Oude, while I suppose the six or eight thousand exceedingly useless Ghurkhas must find a place in our calculations.

Well, we encamp with the rest at Bunterah; we eat our breakfast (we are no longer "griffs" in the campaigning line); we smoke a cheroot, and then lie down for a snooze in our hot tents; it is nearly mid-day, all is silent as the grave in camp, except when half a dozen well-toned *churrees* (a sort of native gong) clang out the hour—dozing—dozing gradually off—(a snore)—hush—"eh!"

"Hallo! get up!"

"What's the row?—what is that cry?"

"Stand to your arms, the Saypoys is a-coming!"

A hideous clatter, a rushing of men past your tent, a shouting, a neighing of horses, who possibly imagine that the noise is in some way connected with feeding—an unwonted hurry and confusion, and ringing again and again through the camp the cry of "Stand to your arms, the enemy are coming!"

You are in a sort of summery *dishabille* of *pyjamas* (loose cotton trousers) and shirt sleeves, and you find it as difficult to collect your ideas, which have travelled with you from Dream-land, as it is to collect your luggage at London-bridge station after a three hours' journey from Dover; but, *qu'importe?* Py-jamas, shirt-sleeves, or mental aberration, when you are going out to get shot very possibly?

Away you rush, buckling on your sword as you go, and meeting more men in shirt-sleeves, who also cannot collect their luggage—I mean their ideas—and buckling on swords very fast, and swearing gutturally—but I fear earnestly—to themselves, or mounting their steeds in the very hottest of hot haste; and as you pass a tent door you catch a glimpse of a wretched mortal *à la belle nature,* or very nearly so (he having been employed in the operation of "tubbing" when the row commenced), now engaged in an attempt to perform the im-possible feat of getting into a pair of trousers hind-side before, and the fastening round his waist of a revolver at one and the same moment, and vociferating madly for his "bearer," and, of course, swearing desperately.

Elsewhere is another equally wretched mortal trying to get on a boot, tumbling and hopping about on one leg in a manner stupendous to behold, very red in the face, and using exceedingly strong language, and consigning all sorts of peo-ple and things, and himself among the number, to perdition and elsewhere, in a by no means Christian spirit.

I just see and hear these various domestic episodes *en pas-sant* towards the front of the camp, whither soldiers and offic-ers are swiftly hurrying. Everybody says the enemy are com-ing, some men swear they can see them, or very nearly, but they are not quite sure in which direction, nor, in fact, is any-one. Conjecture is at a loss; officers are still galloping to and fro; Sir Colin, on his white Arab, starts off across country with the intention of judging for himself; bullocks and camels out grazing are coming into camp helter-skelter, urged along by their alarmed drivers, and all looks as if, in our joyous expectation of a "mill," we should not be disappointed.

It is pleasant looking at those dense masses of troops drawn up in readiness in front of their respective camps, and none the less fitted for fighting, you may be sure, because the greater part of them have got neither stock nor coats on; it is equally pleasant to look at the long array of guns with the burly detachments *en chemise* standing by them, slow-match lit, and wanting but two words of four letters each—"Load!"—"Fire!"—to cause them to hurl forth flame, and death, and destruction.

A dead silence pervades the camp now, almost oppressive after the noise and confusion, and one could not help thinking, that "Jack Sepoy" would be a sad fool if he chose this moment for making his attack; and I suppose "Jack Sepoy" thought much the same, for he did not put in an appearance that day, and, indeed, I believe he had never had the slightest intention of doing so, the whole being a false alarm.

We returned to our tents, cheroots, and "pyjamas," and heard nothing more of the matter till evening, when an order from Sir Colin appeared on the subject of alarms generally, concluding with a request that on similar occasions staff officers would "not gallop wildly about, vociferating to regiments to turn out, and thereby causing panic;" whereat we who were not on the staff chuckled not a little.

The following morning, March 2nd, at daybreak, a force marched for Lucknow (Sir Colin Campbell himself accompanying it), intended to drive in the enemy's outlying pickets, and open the way for the rest of the army. The 23rd Royal Welch Fusiliers, the 42nd Highlanders, 93rd Highlanders and three troops of Horse Artillery, with two or four guns of the naval brigade, and I believe some cavalry, composed the chief part of this column; and it was not very long before heavy firing told us that they were at it, and in the afternoon of the same day we had the pleasure of hearing that they had occupied the Dilkoosha, with little or no loss, after driving the enemy before them and clearing the Mohammed Bagh, a large walled garden near the Dilkoosha, in which preliminary operations the troops under General Outram had also assisted.

These successes enabled more troops to push on that evening, when the 34th, 38th, 53rd, and 79th regiments, the remainder of the Naval Brigade, and six heavy guns of the Royal Artillery, and possibly a few other troops that I have not the names of, marched to join Sir Colin, and to occupy the ground taken in the morning. The main portion of the park of artillery had not advanced yet, it being most desirable to get a perfectly firm footing before hampering ourselves with heavy guns, and the more so as they could be of but little use yet.

Heavy firing throughout that night and the following morning, and in the evening, March 3rd, the order came for the remainder of the army, with the park of artillery, to march at half-past ten p.m. Oh, what a slow and wearying march that was! The night seemed interminable, and from having to go the whole of the way across country, the riding was none of the pleasantest. As day broke, we found ourselves under the walls of the old fort of Jellalabad, which is the right of our Alum Bagh position; it certainly was a pretty scene, for Jellalabad is charmingly situated, embedded in dark topes of mango trees, about the branches of which skip innumerable monkeys, chattering, jabbering, screeching, hanging now by their tails, now by one leg, and playing the wildest and strangest pranks.

The effect of the scenery was much enhanced by the groups of men, and guns, bullocks and horses, and the thousands of camp-followers, with their wives and ponies and domestic belongings, scattered about over the face of the country for miles, or gathered in picturesque parties among the trees, a sort of ever-changing, many-hued panorama of striking character.

Under one tope of trees, where also is situated a stone well, lay twenty or thirty skeletons—a ghastly sight enough. There they lay in all sorts of unnatural and distorted positions, with their fleshless limbs angularly contorted, and the white teeth imparting a horrid grin to the ghastly skulls. Some of their old rags yet clung to them, the mouldy remains of their red coats and uniforms as decayed as themselves. Many a dainty meal have the jackals and pariah dogs made over these horrible bodies, often have they in the dark nights held high feast and festival over these mutineers' bones, from which they had stripped the flesh, making night hideous with their unearthly yells.

The trees under which they lay bore signs which told unmistakeably the whole tale; deep rugged dents on the trunks, boughs cut and splintered in two, and the wood so chipped and torn that it did not require much experience in such matters to enable one to see, in imagination, the case-shot as it had come crashing through the tope with that partridge like *whirr-r-r-r* peculiar to a shower of this description of projectile, and laid low those wretched men.

I have since heard the tale from people who were present when these men were killed. It was during the time Sir James Outram held the Alum Bagh, and one of the almost daily attacks by the enemy on his position was going on; these men had with some others occupied the tope of trees in question, where, I believe, they had brought two guns into action, which guns we subsequently captured; the enemy were driven back as usual, but these men, either surrounded by our cavalry, or fanatically determined to die, were at. all events so situated that escape became impossible. The cavalry were ordered to ride in and cut them up; but directly they advanced the Pandies climbed up the trees and coolly "potted" our helpless soldiers as they rode beneath them. Thereupon General Outram ordered the cavalry to be withdrawn, and the guns to pour a few rounds of case-shot among the trees; they did so, and the Pandies' hours were numbered; toppling down they came like birds, some shot through and through, others with the branches on which they were perched cut away from under them, and some of their own accord, in the vain hope, perhaps, that there was yet time to escape. *Bang! whirr-r-r-r, rattle, rattle, rattle,* went volley after volley among the old mango trees, and bringing down at once a shower of green leaves, branches, and men, mowing them down wholesale, while those who attempted to flee were cut up by our cavalry. Two of the wretched devils, seeing that the game of life and death was nearly played out, and unable to bear the torture and suspense of waiting to be killed, in a mad desperation actually threw themselves down the well which I mentioned before, and where to this day, when the sun shines into it, you can catch glimpses of the white gleaming bones.

*Allons! en avant, mes braves!*—we leave Jellalabad some miles in our rear, and at last, about ten a.m., we receive orders to halt and encamp. We do so, and then, in spite of the fatigue consequent on our long night march, we stroll out to the front of the ridge whereon our camp is situated in order to look at the view.

What do we see? Immediately beneath us the florid and gilded Dilkoosha (Heart's Delight)—a strangely fantastic-looking domicile it is too—built apparently of nothing but domes, and arches, and points, and peaks, and cupolas in endless and bewildering variety, and reminding one of those crowded collections of chimneypots which one sees exposed for sale in London. Behind it are groups of Highlanders, musket in hand; and close by it is a battery of heavy guns, which is carrying on a duel with the "Martinière," that immense and very extraordinary looking establishment by the river's bank, among the trees. Martine, the liberal founder of this place must have had some odd notions of his own on the subject of architecture, or possibly he may have been possessed of the noble idea of cutting out the Dilkoosha; in which case I must admit that he has succeeded, for even that very peculiar building must yield the palm in point of outlandishness to the Martinière.

A faint *pop-pop-popping* of rifles is going on between the advanced pickets, varied by the heavy boom of a mortar or 18-pounder. Every now and then a little puff of white smoke issues from the Martinière, and while we are watching the tiny cloud expand, curling up, and fading away in the blue sky overhead, we hear a rushing sound like the concentrated essence of express trains passing us at full speed; we duck—yes! I confess it—we duck involuntarily as a something lodges with a dull heavy thud in the bank behind us, and warns us that we have advanced a little too far in our eagerness to see the view. To our right lies the river Goomtee, winding about, serpent-like, in a great open green plain, fringed with dark trees. This evening our engineers will commence constructing a bridge of boats across it.

Beyond the Martinière, which lies directly to our front, we can see the golden minarets and gay domes of Lucknow, with a few snow-white buildings, and some red roofs gleaming and glittering among the bright green trees, which, by their pleasant fresh colour, set off picturesquely the much painted temples and bright looking houses, and give a sort of relief to the otherwise almost too glowing scene. We cannot see much of the fair city, but we can see enough to excite in a high degree our admiration and interest, and our longing to be inside it.

How many of us will never see the inside of that city—how many a gallant heart will lie cold—how many a noble soldier perish in the attempt? There are old battered veterans, there are young, glad, happy boys amongst us now, who will soon be lying dead upon the space there, which divides us from that town—fair young forms must lie writhing in agony as their life blood trickles slowly away—and life must have died and be dying out from what but an hour before, were sturdy healthy men in the full vigour of their manhood—what a sad trade soldiering!

********

And so the big guns were *booming* hoarsely, and rifles, matchlocks, muskets, and small-arms were *popping* briskly, and the bullets *pinged* with a soft, but unpleasant sibilation before the city of Lucknow, on the 4th day of March, in the year one thousand eight hundred and fifty-eight.

And now the time was come, as Sir Colin Campbell worded it in his despatch, "for developing the plan of attack which had previously been determined on," the first step of which was to bridge the Goomtee. Hereat did Engineers, Royal and Bengal, her Majesty's Sappers and Miners, and Sappers from Madras, dusky of hue, big-turbaned, and intelligent, work gaily through the night, and the following morning did the enemy appear in force upon that wide green plain, through which the little river Goomtee flows so snake-like, and they threatened the bridge, and appeared disposed to retard its completion; whereupon were field guns sent down to overawe these gentlemen by their presence, and to bark hoarsely at them, like huge watchdogs suffering from bronchitis, and to play at "long bowls" with other and hostile guns, which they did to their heart's content the livelong day, while the big guns kept on *booming* and the bullets softly *pinging*, and the city glittered and gleamed unconsciously the while in the bright hot sun.

Swiftly did the making of the bridge (or rather of the two bridges) progress, and plank after plank was laid down with a workmanlike and pleasant celerity. With the exception of this operation, the 5th of March was an uneventful day, in the course of which much ammunition was wasted, and many a bullet fell harmless, and artillerymen and sailors grew hot with the exertion of manning the 18-pounders. And some curious specimens of hammered shot, unsightly, and far from mathematically spherical, came spinning into the camp and crashing through the trees, beneath the shade of which the drivers and horses of Gibbon's field battery of Royal Artillery, whose guns were playing at the long bowls aforesaid, were reposing; and but little harm was done.

But this night will a move be made, and at an hour past midnight, in the darkness and the fog which overspread the scene, and silently, without sound of trumpet or bugle, there assembled in front of the camp a dense body of men, who were about to test the efficiency of the bridges that day constructed by crossing over them. It was a strange scene this midnight assembly, and a sort of forced stillness pervaded the whole as the troops moved, regiment after regiment, up to the rendezvous. I use the word "stillness" advisedly, for to those unaccustomed to the noise and clamour usually attending the parading of a mass of troops it would have seemed far from still.

Now the even, measured tramp of men falls upon the ear, and now the dull rumbling of the artillery guns and wagons; here, trotting briskly to the front, comes a regiment of cavalry, their steel scabbards making a light *jingle* as they fall against the stirrup-irons; there comes another regiment of cavalry, likewise trotting, but who *jingle* not as they advance, and who seem to have even muffled their horses' hoofs, so silently, almost stealthily, do they pass by. Why is this? Because these are Sikh cavalry—who know not steel scabbards and their attendant *jingle*, but who wear leather sheaths, wherein the swords do not become blunt and dull, and who, though perchance they might fail to gladden the hearts of those good folks at home, who love the *clatter* and the *clash*, and the *ringing* of spurs, stirrup-irons, and scabbards, and look on them as part and parcel of a soldier, are able, by foregoing these same, to have *tulwars*, with edges like that of a razor—keen, bright, and ready, as many a deep and ghastly cut on Sepoy corpses can testify.

And so this body of troops pressed on through the darkness (with now and again the flash of a heavy gun, or a sharp rattling volley of musketry, to give a sort of zest and piquancy to the scene), finding their way—so it appeared to me—by instinct; for where we were going, how we were to get there, how penetrate the gloom, and, in fact, how anything was to result from all this, it was not easy to foresee; and, in fact, I still have my doubts on the subject, had it not been that we were suddenly favoured by the appearance of Luna looking rather pale from the severity of her struggle with the fog, but radiant with the triumph she had accomplished over the same.

I have a dim consciousness of all this and all these noises—of finding myself with great, big, armed masses of shadow—for such the troops appeared to be—tramping on every side of me; of innumerable halts and delays; of being somewhere on the open plain, and not far from the river; of taking advantage of certain stoppages to curl myself up in my cloak on the ground in the warrior-taking-his-rest style, and snatch a few moments' sleep; of asking and being asked a score of times the question, which was never answered except by vague hypotheses, "Where are we going to?"—of a sort of confused notion that we were going to cover ourselves with glory; of gradually becoming insensible to the romance and picturesque strangeness of the scene which had at first attracted me, and more sensible of the cravings of Morpheus, who refused to be comforted by the light snatches of sleep above mentioned; of crossing the bridge, and of being a good deal squeezed by my fellow-man in doing so; and, moreover, of hearing a good deal of strong and emphatic language, which, as far as I could judge in the dark, sounded very much like swearing; and, finally, of morning breaking, and of a brave and gay *coup d'ail* as one looked and saw between one and the dazzling sun the various regiments composing the force drawn up in column, and beheld how out of the nettle Chaos we had plucked the flower Order.

Ahead are the cavalry and horse artillery, sending out skirmishers in all directions; there are the Queen's Bays, who look, in their scarlet coats, as if they had come out for the express purpose of attracting all the rays of the sun; there are the 9th Lancers, looking as they ever do, smart, neat, and business-like, with their lances slung lightly on their arms; but— with no little red and white flags fluttering prettily beneath the bright gleaming points; for, alas! it must be admitted that the streamers in question, attractive though they be, have not been found to conduce overmuch to the overthrow of our enemies or the quelling of the rebellion, and considering how liable they are to attract the enemy's attention, and to draw down fire upon those bearing them, they have been wisely dispensed with on service.

There are large bodies of Sikh Irregular Cavalry, big-whiskered, monster-turbaned, and, for the most part, slate-coloured as to clothes, while each man presents the appearance of an armoury in miniature, what with the spear, *tulwar*, and pistols *à discrétion* wherewith he is equipped. There are three troops of Horse Artillery, one whereof is Royal, and the other two Bengal, all equally ready to gallop over the stiffest line of country you can point out to them, and to blaze away with perfect and deadly precision afterwards, and these complete the cavalry column, which is halted on the slope of a hill, waiting the order to advance.

Plumes of Highlanders waving gaily, dark coats of Riflemen, the red uniforms of the Royal Welsh Fusiliers, the blue of the Bengal Fusiliers and of the Artillery, and the serviceable *karkee*-coloured vestments of the Sikh regiment of infantry, are clustered pleasantly *en masse* below the ridge on which the cavalry are halted. There is an everlasting glint, and glitter from the bright locks of the rifles, from steel ramrods, and polished belt-plates and burnished buckles, as the sun's slanting rays fall upon them, and the whole makes up a scene in which the pomp and circumstance of war are so blended with its stern reality that it will not readily be effaced from the beholder's memory.

I like to look back upon all the picturesque details of the same, to see in recollection the horses, with their heads deep buried in their nosebags, feeding greedily—the men carving away with their pocket knives at the hunch of bread, or sucking down the "go of grog" which composes their frugal breakfast—the officers gathered in knots round *doolies*, wherein are pieces of cold beef and mutton, pleasant to the eyes of hungry men, but which are rapidly becoming "small by degrees and beautifully less:" while the meat receives a peculiarly racy and *prononcé* flavour from somebody insisting on carving it with the same knife that he uses for tobacco. The tops of innumerable flasks, both wicker and leather, are being unscrewed, and the "dew off Ben Nevis" is fast evaporating, while it is astonishing how many people find it necessary to "correct acidity" by "nips" of "Exshaw's No. 1." There is a large display of cigar-cases, and short, black pipes, accompanied by a strong smell of tobacco, very sweet and fragrant in the early morning air, and——

But why dwell on trifles such as these, and leave unnoticed a very pleasing and prominent feature in the scene? A little to the left are gathered a group of officers "of high degree," and among them is one who, at this moment, is attentively observing through his glasses some of the enemy's videttes and cavalry, who are visible at a distance on some rising ground—a short, strongly built man, black haired, with a keen, twinkling eye, and a cheerful bright smile, and a kind word for all—dressed in a blue frock coat, and everlastingly puffing away at a cheroot—quiet in manner, cool, unwavering, and determined;—one whom neither the hottest and most deadly fire, the gravest responsibility, or the most perilous and critical juncture can excite or flurry—a knight *sans peur et sans reproche*—the "Bayard of India"—General Sir James Outram.

********

By this time the nose-bags are empty, and the maws of the hungry ones are filled—the black pipes have been smoked down to mere ash, and the cheroots are beginning to burn the lips that hold them—and, in short, our hasty meal is over.

"Attention!" and in a moment the mass of men are reformed in their even ranks, the cavalry are upon their horses, and all is ready for a start. It would be difficult to describe the route we took that day without a plan on which to mark it out, and my best course will therefore be, to endeavour to explain the movements we were intended to execute, and the results which were expected to be derived therefrom.

I must first, however, observe that Pandy's knowledge, or at least his practice of strategy and tactics is exceedingly limited; and that, luckily for us, he judges of his opponents by himself, never anticipating any originality of conception on their part, or giving them credit for more than one idea on any one given subject. Acting upon this, therefore, he obtusely imagines that the same operation must on all occasions be performed in exactly the same manner, and that if we wish to fight a battle or capture a city, we shall invariably go through the same steps, over the same ground, and, in fact, set about it in identically the same way as we did last time we attempted it.

Thus, after Havelock had thrown reliefs into Lucknow, the enemy set to work energetically to erect defences along the road by which he had entered the city, so as to foil any troops who might again attempt to enter the place by the same path. Very naturally Sir Colin, when he rescued the beleaguered garrison, sagaciously declined to advance his troops by the way which they had so carefully prepared for his reception, and by making a slight detour to the right, he steered tolerably clear of these defences on which the enemy had expended so much time and trouble. It was scarcely courteous, perhaps, but decidedly wily, and I doubt not Pandy lamented much over the gross incivility which prompted us to decline so fair an invitation, and must have thought the "Feringhees" sadly un-complaisant and brusque when he saw them come bustling in past Dilkoosha, Martinière, Secunderabagh, Mess House, and Shah Nujeef, which fell one by one into their hands till the Residency was reached, the garrison relieved, and the feat of arms accomplished, without ever once troubling his well-prepared fortifications.

No sooner had Sir Colin gone, than the enemy again commenced their old plan of locking the stable-door after the steed was stolen, and vigorously did they work at repairing the unfortunate gap which they had before left open; thus when we advanced for the capture of the city, we found the defences along the line of Sir Colin's former route greatly enlarged and strengthened, and fortifications grown up where previously none had existed.

This was all well and good—Pandy was perfectly happy; in blissful ignorance of the art of taking defences in reverse, or of the many cunning devices and resources of engineers. In the fond hope that this time he was ready for us, he reposed behind his huge mud parapets, or *popped* away from numberless loopholes and embrasures in charming confidence; or threw up trenches, ditches, and batteries in all sorts of sly streets and roadways; and set a thousand traps in a thousand unexpected corners wherein to catch the unsuspicious infidel.

Alas for Pandy, he had quite overlooked one thing; the side of the city along which the little river Goomtee runs (a side against which no hostile demonstrations had been made on former occasions—a fact which, according to Pandy's reasoning, inferred that none ever would be made,) was left bare, naked, and comparatively unguarded. True, there was the river, and was not that a defence in itself? *Nous verrons.* And, in the meantime, my black friends with the black hearts, child-killers and murderers of women, lie calm and happy within your fortified palaces; set your sly traps, and blaze away with matchlock and booming gun, and heap fresh insults upon those two English ladies whom you hold captive within your walls; and be merry, my friends, over the coming fall of the "Feringhees," for have not your *fakirs* and *gooroos* told you that the sun of the infidels is set, and that they shall be confounded and put to shame? And is not Allah great, and Brahma good and powerful?

It was a pity, to be sure, for your sakes, that Sir Colin should have had a head upon his shoulders at all, or that any of our generals should have been capable of logically putting *this* and *that* together, and that it should have occurred to us to make a demonstration on that particular side of the city where the Goomtee is the sole defence. It was likewise somewhat unfortunate that there should have been a general of Sir James Outram's experience and ability to conduct these trans-Goomtee operations. But so it was; and now, reader, perhaps you begin to comprehend why bridges were built, and why the troops crossed over the river as I have above described. It was not, however, with the intention of actually effecting the capture of the city in this direction, but in order to assist it very materially by diverting the enemy's attention; and then by establishing batteries, which should enfilade and take in reverse their line of defences (chiefly erected at right angles to the river), and thereby render them untenable.

This movement had also another important effect—*viz.*, that of keeping the enemy in a state of chronic alarm lest all outlets to the rear should be closed, and all means of escape cut off. Doubtless the bloody scene which had been enacted in the Secunderabagh, at Sir Colin's relief of Lucknow, where two thousand Sepoys were caught like rats in a cage, and whence, I believe, *not one escaped,* thanks to the keen bayonets of the Highlanders and Sikhs—doubtless this bloody scene, and the recollection of the two thousand corpses, as they were taken out on the following morning, was ever dancing and flitting a horrible vision before their eyes, and fostered an unconquerable dread that, did they stand their ground on this occasion, a similar fate might befall them; and that as Sir Colin advanced against them on the one side, Sir James Outram, forcing the passage of one of the two regular bridges across the Goomtee, would take them in flank and rear, and that thus the tragedy of the 16th November[*] would be re-enacted; and to this dread, very probably, do we owe, in a great measure, their rapid desertion of their elaborate defences, and our comparatively easy capture of the city.

It will thus be evident that the army was now divided into two great divisions, the one under General Outram on the left bank, the other under Sir Colin Campbell on the right, both moving in the same direction, and parallel to one another, but the former always so far in advance of the latter as was requisite for the establishing of the batteries which were to drive away Pandy from his fortifications, by a deadly enfilade fire of shot and a dense shower of shell which night and day they poured incessantly into them. After they had accomplished this, Sir Colin would push forward his troops, capturing position after position in regular succession, General Outram the while moving forward, repeating the operation, bombarding and enfilading further defences, until they in their turns became untenable, and were captured.

And now, having as best I can, without plans or drawings, explained the principles of attack adopted, let me return to the force which I have kept waiting all this time in a very hot sun, impatient to advance.

We are in the middle of a plain. On our left lies Lucknow. We do not, however, continue parallel to the river, but make a wide sweep to the right, which occupies us for some time, and then again turning to the left, advance in our former direction at a rapid pace. It was now about eleven o'clock; the cavalry and horse artillery were far ahead, having trotted on, and we were, therefore, unable to see what they were doing; but reports began to be circulated that they were engaged, nor did these reports long want confirmation, for the sound of brisk firing became audible, and we shortly came upon some of their handiwork, and a sickening sight it was.

Some women were sitting weeping bitterly over a half-dozen gashed and mangled corpses, the bodies of a small picket of the enemy whom our cavalry had surprised. The poor women first looked up at us imploringly, with tearful eyes and clasped hands, as we passed, and then sadly down at the wretched, mutilated remains of perhaps all that was dear to them in this world. Some of them had covered the still warm bodies over with a cloth, as well they might, for many

* The day on which the Secunderabagh fell.

of the cuts were the most trenchant and ghastly I had ever seen; while others gazed, mute and horrified, on the disfigured features and severed skulls, and on the great red-gaping wounds, as idiots look upon a sight which fascinates while it terrifies them, and as though they sought in vain to realize the terrible and awful truth.

In the meantime where are the cavalry? They have swept onward, away past weeping women and dead men; away in hot pursuit of a flying rabble! A portion of the "Bays" and 9th Lancers are called upon to charge, and headlong they ride, dealing death around them with their long flashing swords, and cutting up a large number of the enemy. But, unfortunately, the "Bays," who were the leading regiment, advancing with that wild and reckless courage which the sight of blood stirs up, galloped on their work of destruction farther than necessity demanded or prudence prompted, till, in scattered groups of twos and threes, their ranks broken by the rugged nature of the ground, they reached the "race course," where the gallant Major Percy Smith with one or two privates (I believe) fell victims to their temerity.

Sir Hope Grant, seeing the disorderly nature of the charge, and fearing the results might be disastrous, had halted the 9th Lancers, and at last the "Bays" were checked in their mad career. But, in spite of the courageous self-devotion and strenuous efforts of Ensign Sneyd and Corporal Goad, they were unable to bring away Major Smith's body, which had to be left on the field to the mercy of a ruthless enemy, a circumstance which added greatly to the grief we all felt for this officer's loss; and sad were the faces of his regiment as they rode back exhausted and with breathless horses to join the rest of the column.

It is a sad moment that, when the excitement which hurried you on, and bore you unshrinking through the heat of battle, has died away, and you have nothing left but to count over the friends who are gone, and to familiarize yourself with the cruel thought that never again will that hand grasp yours, and that the dear eyes are closed for ever. A wretched waking it is on the morn which succeeds an action—a blank and joyless day that follows.

It is hard to seek in the glory you have won for the companions you have lost, and poorly does the success of yesterday fill up the gaps which shot and steel have made—the "old familiar faces" that you miss—the well-known footsteps that you hear no more—the kind voice, with its cheering accents of friendship and brotherhood—where are they now? Who among us soldiers has not in the course of his career had to ask this pitiful question? How few among us are there who, in the course of this wretched rebellion and its attendant war, have not felt that dreary blank and vacuum in their hearts as they mourned over some dear and well-loved comrade?

In the above skirmish the main body of the force had taken no part, but as we arrived on some rising ground we saw the horse artillery densely enveloped in self-created smoke, and firing away very fast in the direction of a large yellow bungalow (the *Chucker-wallah Khotee*, which I shall have occasion to mention again in the course of this narrative), situated on the "racecourse," and from which some guns were replying, and making the most unsatisfactory practice. I use the word "unsatisfactory" here in a selfish sense, for the shot which were, or ought to have been, intended for the Horse Artillery, would occasionally insist on plumping in among our poor selves, in by no means an agreeable manner.

We were halted, and had the supreme satisfaction of standing, or sitting quite still to be shot at for some few minutes—a period not wholly devoid of excitement, as thus: there was a cloud of smoke, then a distant report, then a few moments of comparative silence, then half a dozen cries of "Here comes another!" a small dark speck visible against the blue sky, a rapid hurtling through the air of the approaching missile, a *whish-sh-sh-sh* which became every moment louder—louder—louder, till it passes you with a sort of scream, and lodges in the ground behind. Hardly has it passed when another puff of smoke, and another distant report, announces the arrival of a fresh iron messenger. It was curious to hear the various speculations while the ball was still in flight, as to where it would fall.

"Here it comes, straight at us."

"No, it'll go over us."

"By G—d, it's into the Highlanders."

*Whish-sh-sh-sh-sh-sh-sh.*

"Just cleared them, by Jove!"

And a deep breath of relief is drawn as it falls harmless, tearing up turf, and stones, and dust, and ricocheting away in the distance, carrying dismay and causing confusion among the stragglers and spare horses.

However, our chief object, *viz.* that of making a reconnaissance of this portion of the enemy's position, and of establishing ourselves upon this side of the river, was effected; and General Outram ordered the troops to retire about two miles, and there to await the arrival of the baggage, which had been directed not to cross the Goomtee until we had sufficiently cleared the neighbourhood of the enemy to ensure its safety.

The position to which we retired was on the Chinhut road, and not far from the village of Chinhut itself—consequently on the site, or very nearly so, of the fight of the 30th June, 1857, the disastrous consequences of which (attributable mainly to the treachery of a portion of the hitherto seeming loyal native troops,) had probably hastened in a great measure the complete investment of the Residency of Lucknow.

Here, after watering our wearied nags, we sought shelter from the fierce rays of the sun in some friendly topes; and about one p.m., protected from Sepoy intrusion by the pickets which had been thrown out, thoroughly tired and exhausted, we lay down to take a "nap," after being some eleven hours in the saddle, six or seven of which, it must be remembered, were passed in the full glare and heat of an Indian sun.

Hungry though one may be, and hungry as we were, eating becomes but a secondary consideration on these occasions—every other feeling yields to the all-absorbing one of intense fatigue—alas! to return tenfold when one awakens, as I did in about two or three hours' time, only to find—like Dame Hubbard—that "the cupboard was bare," or comparatively so, for our united contributions amounted to a few potatoes—with a modicum of grease—which we fried, and contented ourselves withal. Such is campaigning.

When the heat of the day had in some degree subsided we issued from our tope, and amused ourselves by "laying out" our camp, and grooming the poor horses (who were thoroughly "done," all of them having been in harness for two whole days, and some of them for three,) for the baggage had not yet arrived, nor, indeed, did it all come up that night; so we even bivouacked, and made what beds we could in the soft, sandy soil, at the imminent risk of being stepped upon by a camel or an elephant, which animals bearing baggage, together with some horses who were wandering about all night in a state of semi-somnambulism, kept strolling through the camp from eve till morn.

How anyone ever found their own baggage, or the baggage its owners, it is hard to say, but the noise and confusion which continued all night was something past belief; long strings of camels with great piles of tables, portmanteaus, tents, and chairs, which looked in the gloom like houses, on their backs; and elephants bearing, apparently, whole cities, kept on passing continually, and treading alarmingly near one's face. Camp-followers and others shouted without intermission, and it seemed without ever drawing breath, for their *bhaies* (friends or brothers) the long night through; and there was an individual called Mattadeen, who seemed to be in the bonds of friendship and brotherhood with all the world, and to be *bhaie* in ordinary to humanity at large, judging from the constant cries of *"Ho, Mattadeen! Mattadeen, h-o-o-o-o-o-o!"* which echoed through the darkness; these, and various other little noises, tended to sour one's temper and disturb one's rest. But at last, in spite of baggage-animals, camp-followers, and Mattadeens, and of an undercurrent of snoring which was going on, I fell into a sound and delightful sleep.

********

On the following morning, March 7th, while preparing to go on outlying picket, and fortifying the inner man by laying in as good a breakfast as time would permit, we were astonished by a sharp fire, which commenced in our front.

At first we imagined that it was only the pickets disporting themselves, and getting up a small fight on their own accounts, as pickets are oft-times wont to do; but the sharp rattle of musketry becoming louder and nearer every moment, and then some shot coming whistling among our tents, warned us that something was really going on, and before many minutes were over an orderly came galloping down to tell us to "turn out immediately," and move up to the front, as the enemy were attacking the camp in force.

We got ready as soon as possible, and moved smartly up, but too late to take any part in this affair, in which our casualties were very few, but those of the enemy considerable.

It appeared that the enemy had made a systematic, and, as it seemed at one period, a formidable attack, advancing with cavalry, infantry, and artillery, in very good style until checked by our pickets. Doubtless they expected that, on seeing them approach, the little handful of men who composed these pickets would have immediately bolted, and that so our camp would have fallen a surprised and easy prey. What, then, must have been their astonishment (possibly tinged with horror) when they beheld the pickets, instead of fleeing, extend themselves in skirmishing order, and boldly advance to meet them! This gave time for reinforcements to come up, and for the artillery to open a brisk cannonade on them, the result of which was that the Sepoys were almost immediately driven back, and pursued by our troops for some distance, while we extended our position by advancing our outposts a distance of half a mile or so.

It was during this pursuit that Major Percy Smith's body was recovered. But even respect for the dead is unknown to our barbarous enemies, and the body was found, as we feared it would be, with the head and legs severed from it and the trunk otherwise horribly mutilated.

During that day there was not much done; a good deal of desultory firing was kept up by the pickets, but beyond this little or nothing. We occupied ourselves by taking long shots at Pandy whenever he gave us a chance; and as we soon found out that we received *our own shot back again,* instead of the lumps of hammered iron, to which he ordinarily treated us, we changed our tactics, and favoured himself thenceforth with shell instead of solid shot.

Of course that night on picket we had innumerable alarms, for as long as there are soldiers in the world, so long will they insist, while on sentry, on dark nights, in the presence of an enemy, in mistaking cows, stumps of trees, dark bits of shadow, and the rustling of the wind through the long grass, for advancing foes. And so surely as they do will there be heard either the sharp crack of the alarmed sentry's rifle, or a hurried whisper of "Stand to your arms!" to rouse one from one's slumbers, when one jumps up, peers into the darkness for about ten minutes, momentarily expecting to hear the whistling of bullets, and eventually discovering that the approaching enemy existed only in the sentry's fevered imagination, upon which one lies down again, mentally consigning said sentry to a place unmentionable.

On one occasion that night, however, we were much surprised by hearing some sharp firing going on *in our rear,* and by bullets *pinging* past us, or falling at our feet. What could it mean? Could the enemy have got round us? Oh, moment of horrible suspense! it was pitch dark, nothing could be distinguished, we stood to our arms, and brought one of our guns into action to the rear, in order that we might be ready for them, and then set to work to discover the interpretation of this mystery.

It transpired that our supporting picket, some seven or eight hundred yards behind us, were suffering from nightmare, bad dreams, indigestion, or something which had deluded them into the idea that it was their bounden duty to fire a volley or two into us, which they did accordingly. Matters were, however, soon set to rights, nobody was hurt, and with a polite request that, if it was all the same to them, they would abstain from repeating the performance, we once more lay down, and were not further disturbed that night.

On returning to camp on the morning of March 8, we found that some siege guns had arrived from the other side of the river, and that preparations were being made for getting some of them into position that evening.

In the afternoon, an order arrived for the greater part of the cavalry and horse artillery, and one field battery (Middleton's), to re-cross the river, to assist in the operations which were to take place on the morrow. In speaking of these operations, I can of course attempt only to describe those in which I personally took part, *viz.*, those on the left bank of the river, so that my readers will have to look elsewhere for a detailed description of the performances of the troops under Sir Colin, whose movements I shall only refer to from time to time, in a general way, and wherever I may find such reference necessary to make the successive steps leading to the fall of the city clearly understood.

At daybreak, on March 9, the force under General Outram assembled on the ground occupied by our advanced pickets, and when all was ready, the word was given, and away we go.

The Rifle Brigade throw out a cloud of skirmishers, the sharp crack of whose rifles ere long told us that our work had commenced; we were now advancing towards a thick wood, over some open, but broken ground, and a very pretty sight it was—the green-coated Riflemen running quickly forward, and springing actively over the rugged *nullahs* and streams which crossed our path, loading and firing as they go, and ever and anon completing with the bayonet the work which the bullet had left half-finished.

After advancing thus for some three-quarters of a mile, we find ourselves at the entrance of a dense jungle occupied by the enemy; the skirmishers are checked for a moment; we bring our guns into action, and *bang!* go half a dozen shells, whistling and crashing through the trees and long high grass, bursting inside with a loud report, and scouring the wood effectually; this precautionary measure enables us again to push on.

"Hark forward !" and away we go, the little Riflemen dashing into the high vegetation, followed by the rest of the column, and *pop! bang! crack! crack!* with now and again the *ping* of an inimical bullet, soon tell us that the enemy are about.

It is strange work this jungle fighting, where you know nothing of what is going on around you; where, for aught you know, sly gentlemen behind bushes may have their fingers upon the trigger which, once touched, would send you tumbling from your horse, a corpse; where foes and friends, Highlanders, Riflemen, and Sikhs, alike are lost to view among the trees, and of whose whereabouts you can only form an idea from the sharp and constant firing which is going on.

Hush! There is a breaking and rustling of the leaves; and look, a Sepoy in full flight dashes wildly across your path; but, even as he goes, the barrel of an Enfield is covering him—*bang!* a sharp, quick report—a whistling of a bullet—and now he is down, rolling a confused and bloody mass in the dust and dirt—a few convulsive struggles—a little clutching at the grass which is beneath him, and which his blood, as it wells forth, is fast dying a dark red—a low moan or two, perchance, and all is over.

Then, breaking through the bushes, follows a hot and excited Rifleman, his rifle still smoking, his lips black with powder, biting another cartridge as he comes, and scarcely glancing, as he passes, on the man whom he has done to death. *Ping! ping!* close to your ears!

Where are the enemy?—who can see them? There!—there, away to the right, see, lurking behind the mud walls of that village.

*Ping! Bang!*

"Halt! action right!"

In a moment the trail of a howitzer falls heavily upon the ground—*ping! ping! ping!* again close to your ear, and *crack! bang! bang!* from the responding rifles.

"Shrapnel-shell, my men—look sharp!"

*Boom!* Almost splitting the drum of your ear, and there burst from the muzzle a gritty volume of smoke, and as it clears away, and the startling noise rings echoing through the wood, see the faint puff, and hear the report of the bursting shell, the fragments of which fly whistling into hidden nooks and corners—and—

"Hurrah!—Now, riflemen, over with them!"—*crack!*—*bang!* in quick succession, as a shower of bullets rattle in among the disorganized rabble whom the shells have driven from the village, and who are fleeing for their lives, few of them turning to exchange shots with their assailants.

Hark! to that cheer—a wild *tally-ho.* What! is this, then, fox-hunting? No—but not unlike it, only more madly and terribly exciting even than that—it is man-hunting, my friend! and that cheer proclaims that we have "found."

Hark! to that quick volley which follows it, with death in its every note! See here and there a flying Sepoy, and here and there a dust-stained, still warm corpse—see, through the trees, the bright-glancing barrels of the deadly rifles as they are raised to deal the fatal blow; see the dark plumes of the Highlanders, and the grey turbans of the Sikhs, and the red coats of our men flitting to and fro—see that soldier fiercely plunging down his bayonet into some object at his feet—see, is it not red as he uplifts it for another blow?

Raise yourself in your stirrups and look down and behold that living thing, above which the steel is flashing so mercilessly: is it a dog, or some venomous and loathsome reptile? No—but a human being: it is a man who lies at that soldier's feet—a man disguised with wounds and dust and mortal agony, with blood gurgling from his lips, and with half-uttered curses upon his tongue, who is dying there; and the reeking bayonet is wiped hurriedly upon the grass, and the killer passes on, to drain, in the wild excitement of his triumph, every drop of that cup of blood which this day the God of War holds out to him, and which he sees foaming and brimming over before him.

Ugh! It is horrid work at the best; but that thought comes afterwards, and not now, when mad with excitement, your pulse beating quickly, and I fear me glad at the work of death, as the veriest butcher among them, you press forward, amid smoke, and noise, and *cracking* rifles, and burning houses and burning jungle, through an atmosphere thick with sulphurous smells, and choking dust, and heavy heat, while the scenes which I have just attempted to describe are going on, in all their licensed fury, on every side.

By this time, we have emerged from the wood into the open, and before us, at some eight hundred yards' distance, stands the yellow bungalow *(Chucker-wallah Khotee),* which I have before mentioned. Already a large body of the enemy were flying from it, but their retreat, though decidedly rapid, was a tolerably orderly one, and they seemed determined that, if they must run away, they would do it in as dignified a manner as possible; so, with heads erect, and even ranks, these Sepoys (six or seven hundred, I should think) passed away out of our sight. I must, however, do the leading files—*i.e.,* those who were furthest from danger—the justice to state that their bearing was much more philosophical and calm than that of the hindermost, among whom, I regret to say, there appeared tot be a *leetle* more pushing and indecent haste than there should have been.

The Bengal Fusiliers have been pushed forward, and advance at a "double" across the hot sand; but, arriving at the house breathless and exhausted, they are unable to take a steady aim, or do as much execution as might have been wished, and Pandy escapes comparatively scathless, though some few of them fall beneath the deadly Enfields to rise no more, and lie writhing in deadly agony among the mud cottages away there to the right.

The 23rd Royal Welsh Fusiliers, some Highlanders, Sikhs, and three guns have pushed on in the meantime yet farther to the right. From our position over the river we get a sight of the enemy (the body above mentioned) hurrying away below us, and we are enabled to bowl a few shot very pleasantly among them—a performance which accelerated their movements considerably; while the riflemen are keeping up a steady fire on the buildings on the opposite bank, among which stands conspicuous the celebrated Secunderabagh.

There is a splendid view of the city from this point, its domes and hundred temples, the vast courts of its palaces, the fine structures of the Shah Nujeef, Tara Khotee, Messhouse, Kaiserbagh, and Chutter Munzil, or old palace, by the water's edge, and many another begilt and gaudy building. There they all are, stretching, a glittering mass, beyond the little stream, and looking even more bright and beautiful than I had hitherto imagined them to be.

Yes! there lies the prize for which we are fighting, and for the possession of which so many lives will be laid down, and so much blood will flow—there it lies in all its glory before us, seeming proud of the high value which is set on it, and the price at which it is being won; little recks it whether Feringhee or——

"Look out, sir!" Ping past your ear, and "Bedad! But that fellow's a dangerous kyaracter," in rich Hibernian brogue, make you suddenly alive to the fact that there are moments when it is as well not to indulge in one's love of the picturesque too freely, and that even the contemplation of the beautiful is not always unattended with risk; and, moreover, that your services are required for the purpose of throwing some shell into those mud suburbs to expel several "dangerous kyaracters" therein assembled, who are keeping up a tolerably smart fire on our position, and whom it would be as well to silence.

This is done accordingly, and for about an hour is a quick

cannonade of round shot, shell, and rifle bullets directed upon the opposite bank. We could see but little of the enemy from the way in which they crept behind walls and houses, but we were cognisant of their presence from the continual dropping of bullets all around us, varied by an occasional round shot, the number of casualties on our side, however, being extremely small, owing to the excellent cover afforded to the men by some banks and mud walls.

********

At last we found that we could be of but little more use here, and our guns were withdrawn to make room for heavier metal, the siege guns having been brought down for the purpose of pouring a reverse fire on the enemy's entrenchments. We therefore retired, and stationed ourselves as spectators near the Yellow Bungalow, where a fierce combat on a small scale was still going on.

In the lower story of this house were some ten or twelve of the enemy, who had either not been aware of their comrades' departure at the time the bungalow was evacuated, or had purposely remained behind with the fanatical determination of dying in the defence of the place; but be the real reason what it might, there of a surety they were—a dozen or so of desperate men, for whom there was now no escape, and before whose eyes the bright-eyed *houris* of paradise were already waving their green scarves and beckoning to eternal bliss.

They occupied, as I have before said, the lower story of the house whereof we held the remainder, and many an attempt had been made to drive them out. There, however, in spite of every effort, they held their own, having already succeeded in killing some six or seven men, who had advanced with more, courage than caution into the dark rooms in which they were located, and where (from the fact of their entering from the out-door light and glare) they were comparatively blind, while the Sepoys' eyes being accustomed to the partial darkness, our soldiers had fallen an easy prey.

Shells with long fuses were thrown through holes cut in the floor of the upper story into the rooms they occupied, but with little or no result, as, by moving from room to room, they were easily able to avoid them. An attempt was made to burn them out, which partially succeeded, one man being burned to death, while some others, driven out by the fire, were shot as they fled; two or three more also had been killed, but still there were some remaining.

Captain St. George, 1st Bengal Fusiliers, accompanied, I believe, by another officer of the same regiment, then entered the house and shot two of the rebels with his revolver. Passing on, he found, as he imagined, the house empty, and concluded that the Sepoys were now all killed, but at last he came to a small and very dark room, which he entered, when two men—one on each side the doorway—fired, and a ball struck him in the lower part of the chest. He walked out, looking giddy and sick, with eyes glazed and heavy, and faintly assisted in unbuttoning his own coat, when it was found that the ball had passed completely through his body, from his chest to his back, whence it was afterwards cut out, being found buried very little below the surface. It was of course imagined that he was mortally wounded, no hopes whatever being entertained by the doctors of his recovery, but I am happy to say that he has since gone home, with every prospect of ultimate recovery.

A young officer of the Sikhs (Anderson, I think, by name,) was killed in this house while endeavouring to expel the desperate occupants, but his life, like that of several other brave men who were killed here, was laid down in vain, for still did the few who remained inside hold out.

At last, General Outram, seeing that it was death to anyone to attempt to enter, and thinking that enough lives had been sacrificed in the attempt, ordered some guns to be brought to bear on to the house; five accordingly came into action, and fired about twenty shells, in quick succession, at the windows and doorways of the building, and as the smoke of the last round cleared away, the Sikhs, who had been held in readiness for the purpose, received the signal, and dashing forward entered the house *en masse*.

It was most exciting to see them racing up to the place, where, when they reached it, there was for a moment a confused scrambling at the doorways, then a sharp report or two, then a sort of shout and scuffling, then again *bang! bang!* sharp and distinct, and finally there burst from the building, with loud yells, a crowd of Sikhs, bearing among them the sole survivor of this garrison, who had made such a gallant defence— for gallant it was, be the source whence the courage sprang, fanaticism, despair, or whatever you may choose to call it.

How many the Sikhs had killed inside I do not know—not more, I heard, than two or three—but this one, alas for him! they had dragged out alive. And now commenced one of the most frightful scenes I had ever witnessed.

Infuriated beyond measure by the death of their officer, the Sikhs (assisted, I regret to say, by some Englishmen) proceeded to take their revenge on this one wretched man. Seizing him by the two legs, *they attempted to tear him in two!* Failing in this, they dragged him along by the legs, stabbing him in the face with their bayonets as they went. I could see the poor wretch writhing as the blows fell upon him, and could hear his moans as his captors dug the sharp bayonets into his lacerated and trampled body, while his blood, trickling down, dyed the white sand over which he was being dragged. But the worst was yet to come: while still alive, though faint and feeble from his many wounds, he was deliberately placed upon a small fire of dry sticks, which had been improvised for the purpose, and there held down, in spite of his dying struggles, which, becoming weaker and more feeble every moment, were, from their very faintness and futile desperation, cruel to behold.

Once during this frightful operation, the wretched victim, maddened by pain, managed to break away from his tormentors, and, already horribly burnt, fled a short distance, but he was immediately brought back and placed upon the fire, and there held till life was extinct. It was his last despairing effort, and very sad to see; but I thought it sadder still that those hoarse, choking cries for mercy should have been disregarded as they were; his shrieks, his agonized convulsions, his bitter anguish alike unheeded; that those upturned eyes, searching for pity in the swarthy faces which gazed with savage pleasure on the frightful scene, should have searched in vain, and that so—with the horrible smell of his burning flesh as it cracked and blackened in the flames, rising up and poisoning the air—so in this nineteenth century, with its boasted civilization and humanity, a human being should lie roasting and consuming to death, while Englishmen and Sikhs, gathered in little knots around, looked calmly on. No one will deny, I think, that this man at least adequately expiated, by his frightful and cruel death, any crimes of which he may have been guilty.

Such was the state of excitement and rage that the Sikhs were in from the loss of their officer, that I firmly believe it would have been quite impossible to prevent this act of torture; and that many did make the attempt I have no doubt, but the whole business was done so quickly, and with such noise and confusion, that, to me who beheld it from a short distance (occupied as I then was on another duty), it seemed almost like a dream, till I rode up afterwards and saw the black trunk burned down to a stumpy, almost unrecognisable cinder.

The Yellow House was now ours—our heavy guns, from their position on the river's bank, were spinning shot into the enemy's entrenchments, and there was little more to be done, as far as we were concerned, beyond every now and then throwing some shells among and dispersing the enemy's sharpshooters, who, owing to the excellent cover they obtained in buildings and woods on the other side of the river, were still able to annoy us.

But all this time we have lost sight of the portion of our force which had earlier in the day parted from us, and pushed on to the right. Continuing their course parallel to the river for about a mile, through brushwood and jungle, burning villages and houses, and here and there getting flying shots at the Pandies as they flitted past them.

They had at last found themselves at the Badshah Bagh (king's garden)—a large walled enclosure containing a handsome palace for the use of its regal owners. All the elements of Oriental romance were here: dark passages and latticed windows to the *Zenanah*, suggestive of sparkling, love-glancing eyes, and "moonlight nights," and stolen interviews, erring Oriental Venuses, and amorous Hindus. Cool marble halls, too, there were, gilded and carved in a manner miraculous to behold, filled with mirrors, chandeliers, damasks, and furniture of the most startling and *outré* description; there too were pleasant wide-spreading trees, there were stone tanks and fountains, and marble baths (the sight alone of which refreshes one); and dark, secret hiding-places, where naughty *beebees* carried on their little witcheries, while a million summer insects were for ever *buzzing* noisily around; long shady walks, too, where the scent of citron and orange-blossoms hung heavy on the air, till the whole place was redolent (as some one graphically expressed it at the time) "of a strong odour of Arabian Nights."

Such was the place in which, after a sharp fight, our troops found themselves—not, however, to lounge indolently beneath the shady trees, or to indulge in a pleasant *dolce far niente* and dreamy reverie in the cool rooms of the palace, as the luxurious couches and chairs, with the generally indolent character of the place, would naturally prompt one to do, but to continue the work of death in which, since daybreak, they had been engaged, and to screen themselves by rough barricades, or as best they might, from the heavy fire to which they were exposed.

In fact, during the whole day, fighting, more or less, was kept up in and near the Badshah Bagh, from which place, however—once in our possession—the enemy found it impossible by even the most strenuous efforts to drive us. And so the day came to a close, and evening fell, and found us in possession of the whole of the villages, buildings, suburbs, detached houses, and walled gardens on the left of the Goomtee, from the point at which we had crossed up to the Badshah Bagh, while our heavy guns, placed in advantageous positions by these operations, were already at work demolishing, and rendering untenable, the defences on the right bank of the river.

Sir Colin quietly waited until the Martinière and the defences in front of it had been subjected to an efficient pounding, when he advanced, and, instead of having a severe fight, and losing several men, as would probably have been the case had said pounding not been administered, he captured these works *without opposition,* or, at least, with very little; for such of the enemy as had braved the destructive reverse and enfilade fire of our heavy guns, and made a show of holding out, became nervous at the first glimpse of the red coats and dark plumes of the Highlanders, and fairly ran when the glitter of the bayonets caught their eyes, firing only a few desultory shots as they went.

Thus, on the 9th March we had taken the first really decisive step in advance, and were now fairly settled down to our work; the Martinière and the somewhat formidable works in rear of it were ours; Outram's column occupied a strong position on the left bank of the river, and we were able to place our heavy guns so that from front and flank they could pour a destructive fire into the Begum Khotee, Shah Nujeef, Kaiserbagh, and other of the enemy's strongholds, and so pave the way for their capture. These great results had been attained with an almost miraculously small loss of life on our side, while it is probable that sustained by our opponents was considerable.

The night of March 9th was chiefly spent in getting guns into position on the ground we had captured, and with these on the following morning we opened fire.

There was some fighting here and there on both sides of the river, but nothing of any importance took place until the next day, March 11th, when we of General Outram's division again advanced. This time our force was divided into two columns, one of which, the left, moved from the Badshah Bagh in the direction of the Iron Bridge, the other through the woods and villages on its right, driving the enemy from any strongholds they might have there, while some cavalry and horse artillery were still further to the right, to cut off stragglers, cover our flank, and otherwise assist operations. It was my lot to accompany the second-named column, of whose doings I will therefore speak first.

We had not advanced very far before we found ourselves in a narrow road leading into a thick wood; here operations commenced, for, hidden in the jungle, or in the small cottages, which, snugly embosomed among the trees, formed excellent temporary fortresses, were parties of the enemy, who opened a smart fire on us as we advanced. Skirmishers were pushed forward, and two guns brought into action abreast, on the road, to riddle the woods with case-shot, and so drive out our hidden foes. Again were the scenes of the day but one preceding enacted—that sort of confused *banging* and *popping* on all sides which I have before endeavoured to describe, with the difference that this time the Pandies *did* stand for a while, secure in their invisibility, and popped at us in return.

What noise and wild confusion and excitement then prevailed, what a smell of gunpowder, and what hurrying about of skirmishers, and bursting of shells, and the like; and yet from this mass of chaos how clear and distinct do certain little incidents stand out in my memory: the flitting Pandies as they dodged about among the trees, their white garments making them visible for a brief moment, and then they were gone; the loud ear-splitting boom of the guns, as round after round of case-shot went tearing from the muzzles, crashing through the brushwood; the hot and dusty skirmishers leaning against trees in order to steady their aim; the constant *cracking* of their rifles, a sort of running accompaniment to the noisy guns; the whistling of bullets, which came thick and fast among us; the contorted form of the dead Sepoy lying out there on the road in front, ghastly enough; next a burly gunner, while in the act of sponging out a gun, with a sudden start, would turn white and giddy, and stagger, wounded, to the rear; then the short fragment of conversation which ensued:

"Man hit, sir."

"Badly?"

"No, sir; shot through leg."

"Put another man in his place, and blaze away."

*Ping! Ping! Bang!* right royally on all sides, while now and then a sharp cry would proclaim that a bullet had found its billet in some unfortunate, who would come bleeding past; a minute ago that man was the best runner, or the best jumper, or cricketer, it may be, in his regiment, and now he is a cripple for life. Quick work, is it not?

Some of the enemy had crept into a dry drain which ran underneath and across the road, and there, crouched in abject terror, mingled probably with the hope that we might pass them unseen, huddled up, one getting behind the other for shelter, they were discovered by our men, and a volley of bullets sent in among them.

It was horrible to see, through the semi-darkness, these poor wretches trying to screen themselves behind the corpses of their comrades, but trying in vain, for pitilessly did bullet after bullet whistle in among them, striking to death those in this doomed and dying mass of humanity who still lived; while their groans and shrieks seemed, reverberated as they were by the echoing, sonorous, arched roofs of their underground retreat, to acquire a strangely deep and awful tone. There was no escape, no pity; there, in their self-chosen grave, they all died, and there, for many a day after, they lay, a horrid heap of rottenness, and worm-eaten abomination.

[Majendie continued fighting in the battle to re-take Lucknow and the city finally returned to British control on 21st March, 1858.]

# Ways of Seeing

There is now a surfaced road which runs along the line of the Delhi Ridge where in 1857 the retaliating forces of the British gathered to lay siege to the Sepoys—and other insurgents within the city—who had, by then proclaimed the King of Delhi, the last of the Moghuls and then in his dotage—sovereign of India.

Where that undistinguished road runs toward New Delhi it is called Upper Ridge Road. Whilst this is appropriate for a highway that passes along a ridge, no one who knew India from the time of the Mutiny to the end of the Second World War would have had any doubt that this was not simply 'a ridge', but *the Ridge*—a Holy place of Empire. In the opposite direction this modern road passes close by the old city of Delhi. The walls of the old city enclose the Red Fort—another iconic building of those dreadful days—that is accessed *via* gates with famous and familiar names such as the Lahore Gate and that opposite the Grand Trunk Road—called the Kashmir Gate.

Today, the name of this road—sited on the centre of the British battle line of 1857—no longer refers to the ridge either geographically or commemoratively. It is called—tellingly—Rani Jhansi Road.

On this road, difficult to find and somewhat overgrown, is a memorial to the fallen built in the gothic style of the Victorian age. It is a British memorial. Its sides are inscribed with the names of heroes and for those with eyes that are prepared to see, there is something about those names which is immediately apparent. A number of them are not British names; many of them are as Indian as the ground upon which their monument stands.

Nearby is a plaque, more recent and less grandiose, but equally appropriately commemorating those who opposed the British to the death. These, the inscription reveals, are the heroes of the 'First War of Indian Independence'. Other such plaques appear at the sites of the conflict of 1857—58. Most notably, one appears on the preserved but battered walls of the Residency at Lucknow, inevitably another imperial Holy of Holies. This elevates the *mutineers* to respectability, but equally, by implication, damns the men commemorated on the British monument as all but traitors to both their nation and their own countrymen.

This is but one small indication of the complexity of emotion the Indian Mutiny evokes.

The Rani of Jhansi does not appear in detail within the pages of this book. The reader may be curious as to the significance of her name on the formerly named Ridge Road. One night on the banks of the Betwa River between Gwalior and Jhansi itself I listened to a local folk singer keening a song in which the words 'Rani Jhansi' featured prominently. Upon enquiry as to its lyrical content, the person to whom this book is dedicated replied that it was about the Rani of Jhansi and told of "all the good things she did for us".

It was clear that nearly 150 years after the event, irrespective of what the Rani of Jhansi actually did for the people of the countryside, she had become a folk hero of Joan of Arc—like stature. That the Rani became a larger than life figure is unsurprising. She was a strong woman in a world of men who could ride and fight expertly and who rose against the British and was among the last to fall. In the final battles of 1858 she remained defiant to the end.

All peoples are attracted to what they see as heroic figures they can claim as their own, and irrespective of how much closer scrutiny the reality of any such figure would bear before the myth became tarnished, the Rani was—and still is—an ideal candidate for ordinary Indians.

As with the best of legends, that of the Rani of Jhansi is one that has endured. From the time of its birth, through almost a century of absolute British rule and a further sixty years of nationhood for independent India, she has remained a national icon. This indicates the powerful sentiment she holds over the Indian psyche, something that should never be underestimated when the Indian Mutiny is reviewed—particularly by those of an Anglo-Saxon outlook.

It can therefore be appreciated why those who are still prepared to take sides on the subject of the Mutiny are prepared to dispute the matter as soon as the term 'Indian Mutiny' arises in conversation. These disputants will not be found in any number in the English shires however, but in India itself. In this 150th anniversary year of 2007, there are many young men on the Sub-Continent who will march under the sun to venerate the martyrs of 1857—their martyrs—with suffering of their own.

Why is this so?

Despite a history which can demonstrate civilisations stretching back into pre-history, India, as a nation, is one of the worlds youngest. Its people still appear to feel a need for a true sense of national identity, which is why it is easy to understand the view—widely held—of the Mutiny as a war of independence for India itself. This establishes, for the Indian people, the roots of the modern nation almost a century before its national flag was first legitimately raised over the administrative buildings of New Delhi. We should also recognise that there is much in a baptism of blood sacrifice that enhances a sense of nationhood in a way that a simple transference of power does not.

India persists in its love-hate relationship with the British. One can visit an Indian museum—housed in a building erected by the British—and find a history of the Sub-Continent, but whereas the Moghuls—also invaders—are embraced, the time of British rule is conspicuous by its absence, it has been excised, it is *unhistory*. Modern India has kept virtually every legacy of British rule—from the legal system to the railways—the list is a lengthy one. English words and expressions are unconsciously used in conversation, culture and education bear a strong British influence.

Most Indian people still seem to feel a special warmth towards the British, and yet there is a slight discomfort and unease as well. Is this because the British were the last of the conquerors of the Sub-Continent, that British rule is remembered by many still alive? If this is so, then it's easy to see why a conflict less than a century before true independence can still be highly significant, if not for the British then certainly for the Indian nation.

Are the commemorative plaques for the 'War of Independence' on Mutiny memorials to fallen British and loyal Indian forces excusable propaganda, or is their presence not only legitimate but essential to the Indian nation?

The Indian Mutiny has other titles even among British writers who were party to its events. It has been termed 'The Sepoy War' and the 'The Sepoy Revolt' or 'Rebellion'. None of these terms adequately describe what occurred in India in 1857, and if I attempted to apply a new definition, it would be rejected by vested interests on both sides, would be of no consequence to those who no longer care and would be meaningless to those who know anything of what took place. Too many of the endless pages of history have turned.

Although the confidence of the British in India was shaken by the events of 1857, those events were confined, in the main, to a region of north-eastern India called Oudh, which borders Nepal and through which flow the rivers Jumna, Ganges and Gumpta. Irrespective of the blood spilt, in an administrational sense—accounting for those parts of the Sub-Continent under British influence as well as under direct rule—the area that was problematic for the British was probably less than 10% of the whole.

Some might argue that the insurrection would have spread if it had not been suppressed, but there were no indications that this would be the case and nothing on such a scale happened again. These facts are beyond question. It may have been the wish of those with much at stake that the insurrection should spread, but that did not make it a movement of National independence or identity. Fact joins company with interpretation and supposition in the study of history—and this is as it should be—all that is required to read historical events is the ability to distinguish one from the other.

Today we recognise the homogeneity of India as a nation, and so it is easy for us to forget what the reality was in 1857.

Wars to bring the Sub-Continent under British rule had already been fought for over a century. Clive had made his reputation and fortune there and a young Duke of Wellington (before that title was conferred upon him) had fought what he always considered his hardest battle at Assaye. Enormous tracts were still to a degree under the control of Native rulers particularly the territories of the Nizam of Hyderabad. The Sikhs of the Punjab, arguably the mightiest and best organised army India had to offer had fought two wars with the British within more or less the previous decade. The last of them which resulted in their defeat had taken place at a distance from Delhi no further than the events of the Mutiny and had concluded just seven years previously.

The Sub-Continent is no more or less likely to have considered itself as a unified political and economic unit—a nation—than Europe would have done then or now. Add to this the enormous racial, cultural, and religious differences that existed and one has a fabulously rich and varied population but one with no national cohesion. Those who *were* inclined to view India as a cohesive whole—and they were mostly the British—had barely enough time to consider all they had gained as a *whole*. Those they ruled certainly did not consider the *whole*, since the plethora of royal ranks and interest groups held or lost their positions according to how well they worked with or against both the British and their neighbours.

The peoples of the Sub-Continent had no difficulty with their sense of identity. They were as they are today Jats, Sikhs, Marathas, Rajputs, and many more. Some had clashed with each other over centuries and some remained aloof in their own realms. If they were to be lumped together then that could only for the convenience of a foreign master. In 1857 the name 'India' was predominantly a geographical designation and if there was any indication of change, that a sense of nationhood was developing, then such ideas had barely impinged upon the minds of anyone other than those few who, at the time, saw advantage for themselves in such a development.

To understand this is to understand why there are so many Indian names upon the British memorial on Delhi Ridge. The Indian Mutiny was not a war of nations or peoples—it was a war of *sides*. The British had no choice as to theirs, but the Indians did and which one they chose was not—as some would have it—a matter of right or wrong, but was more concerned with ideologies, empathies, loyalties, religion, some vested interest and the no small matter of honour.

For some, loyalty was not to be put aside for any reason and could only end with death. Others, such as the Sikhs and the Ghurkhas, could combine their loyalty with an hereditary antipathy to those who now opposed the British, perhaps there was something of the 'settling of scores' here. Some knew the cause of the insurrectionists was a hopeless one from the outset. Some, from martial races, would not dignify themselves with treachery under any pretext. Some thought that whatever the trouble was—it was caused by someone else in a country far away from their own; if they were to be ordered to fight them, then so be it. Some fought because fighting was their profession and the enemy had always been another Indian.

There are, therefore, good reasons why the term 'mutiny' for the conflict of 1857 is appropriate, irrespective of the undeniably unpleasant implications for the integrity of those who instigated and took part in it.

Many of the regiments of the native Bengal Army did rise and slaughter their officers and families—that was both mutinous and criminal. The soldiers of those regiments were part of a volunteer army that had taken its oaths, drawn its pay and received its pensions after service. For native soldiers, unlike for British soldier at that time, membership of the military establishment bestowed a certain prestige. One of the memoirists in this book mentions dissatisfaction on the part of the native troops and suggests they would have remained loyal had arrears of pay been made up; but this is essentially an irrelevance. Arrears of pay were common, for both British and native troops, in the military of the time; in fact they were common in all armies, British, European, native and those of the native princes in India. As Kipling wrote authentically—'A shilling a day and lucky to get it'.

It has been suggested that these troops were of the wrong calibre and were poorly managed. This, however, is the 20/20 version of hindsight, for they had been good enough to fight and die on many a battlefied for the British. In fact, many of the officers of these native troops went to their deaths in the mutiny displaying total incredulity that their loyal soldiers could revolt in such a manner. It is also pointless to disparage them or their ability when we remember that they triumphed over the British on several occasions during the course of the mutiny.

Once troops of any army, of any period in history, had mutinied and murdered their superiors the consequences were prescribed, punitive and inevitable. The military is only legitimately the servant of the state that raised it and this action put the Sepoys in an irreconcilable position which would always be dealt with severely for the purposes of discipline and deterrent to others who might be of like mind.

Those who believe that mutiny in a common cause can be justified, should note that this was by no means the first mutiny within the Indian Army. There had been mutinies in 1806 and 1824 which had been ruthlessly suppressed. There had been another only thirteen years previously in 1844 within the memories of many who took part in the rising of 1857; perhaps fatally, on that occasion Lord Gough had reprieved most of those convicted.

If the Sepoys had constituted all the opposition the British had to contend with then the term 'mutiny' would serve; but although there could have been no rebellion without them, there was insurrection in other quarters also. Leading figures from the Indian community in the North Eastern region—particularly in the kingdom of Oudh—led the insurrection both politically and by force of arms. These landowners and aristocrats have been portrayed, by British writers with partisan motives as cruel, dissolute, treacherous, cowardly and greedy, and it has been asserted that reforms which disenfranchised them of land and income were their sole motivation for their part in the insurrection. It should be acknowledged that although these people had been receiving remuneration from the British, they had been given little choice in that arrangement either.

The fact is that the traditional privileges of the landowners had, for some, already been usurped by the British when the Hindu custom of accession was abolished by the 'Doctrine of Lapse' under which the Honourable East India Company absorbed states if there was no *natural* heir to succeed. Today we would probably regard this as theft—and that is exactly how those whose property was absorbed in this way regarded it. That their position was now to be worsened could not be expected to be met by their equanimity. British popular history would record the situation differently if this treatment were to be imposed on Englishmen in similar circumstances.

The British Empire required acquiescence from its sub-

ject peoples. That few may have objected is not an indication of the dispensation of justice, only of the quiet, effective
administration of power. It is useful to have those who did
object—particularly when they have gone so far as to rise in
rebellion—seen as the vilest of ingrates.

To achieve the aims of the rebellious native elite, manipu-
lation of the of the Sepoy army and whatever portions of
the civilian population could be brought onside as allies was
pre-requisite. This seemed reprehensible from the moral high
ground of British Imperial history, but in the now familiar
world of the 'real-politic' anyone in a similar position would
act in the same way. This does not excuse their actions, since
they were certainly, in some measure, exactly who and what
the British thought they were. Mostly they were an enemy
fighting a 'war to the knife' because they knew well there
could be no acceptable terms of settlement. When Spanish
guerillas fought a similar brutal war against the French during
the Napoleonic Wars, Britain abhorred its savagery, but fully
understood the motivation behind it—but perhaps this is because, at the time, the French were also *our* enemies.

None of the influence these people wielded would have
been possible without a spark of discontent which could
be fanned into a conflagration. Immediately prior to the
outbreaks of open rebellion British observers reported that
the people of the country, villages and towns became surly
instead—they noted with some surprise—of their usual
fawning servility, as though this was some bizarre departure from the natural order as they sensed a gradual decline
of British power. The British felt with some justification
that the country and its people were better served by them
rather than being subject to the whims of Indian autocrats
or the deprivations of brigands such as the Pindarees. In
this the British may have been correct, but there has always
been a perverse element in the human condition that pre-
fers the uncertainties of its own kind to the order imposed
by an invader.

Rome had discovered that, as Boudica laid waste to southeast England and burned Londinium to the ground, putting the population to the sword. The Romans, a developed civilisation and an expanding empire were an occupying force in a primitive land in their view occupied by savages given to barbarism. They had brought law, order and other benefits for those who obeyed the rules imposed upon them. Who could possibly have a problem with that? And who can fail to see the parallel with the British in India?

One of the main causes of the Indian Mutiny has been cited as the scandal of the new cartridge case grease allegedly offered to the Sepoy regiments. This is well known from school history lessons, and there is no reason to go into claim and counter-claim here, but, predictably, the British authorities denied the claim that caste polluting animal grease was being used as a way of attacking Hindus and their beliefs. An effective native army had existed for a century and whatever its shortcomings those in  charge had always appeared to respect the faiths of Islamic and Hindu soldiers. This respect and tolerance was often against the advice and irrespective of the demands of Christian clergymen and missionaries who themselves may share the blame for the mutiny because of fear of Christian conversion—which was both sanctioned and encouraged by the Charter Act of 1813.

It could be that the 'cartridge case' episode was a brilliant piece of what we now call 'spin'. If so, whoever started it, with incitement to rebellion in mind, did a fine job, for it 'hit the mark squarely'. It has mostly been claimed that this was nothing more than a malicious rumour—aimed at winning converts to the cause—that, like an urban legend, once started it spread like wildfire simply because it was something people very badly wanted to believe. If there is any truth in this episode, that it was a simple blunder founded in insensitivity or carelessness, would surely not be beyond possibility. It should be remembered that this was a time before mass production had properly arrived, there was no single factory churning out millions of identical cartridges. Even today, anyone who has ordered components of *identical* specification from two different sources may have had cause to regret it—things go wrong!

Were there any caste defiling cartridges? No-one has ever produced one *or* provided anything other than perpetual reassurance to prove that there were not. As we have learnt in our age of sophisticated communication, if a message is repeated often enough its veracity ceases to matter, it takes on a life of its own and becomes *the truth*. *The truth* is embraced all the more readily if it adds fuel to an already smouldering flame. In the case of the cartridges, those flames grew faster because irrespective of the original *truth* of the matter little sensitivity was shown to an issue that held deep meaning for the Indian troops. The British authorities changed the formulation of the cartridge grease in an effort to appease the sepoys, but the very act of doing so merely confirmed the suspicions of the mutinous troops that it must have been changed from something bad. This was obviously the wrong signal to send.

So it came to the spilling of blood. Whether that was avoidable or inevitable mattered not, the *reasons* were in place, the *causes* were established and the outcome would not necessarily favour those who were right, but those who had the power to prevail. To the ruin of those who opposed them, that was the British.

While it is clear that the Mutiny was not a war of national independence—or even the foundation of one—it is worth considering whether, almost a century later, it had any influence on the eventual birth of the Indian nation.

Certainly, less than four months after the last battle was fought, The Honourable East India Company was, on November 1, 1858, abolished by Royal proclamation and it was announced that henceforth the British Government would rule India in its entirety. It was an end to the time of the presidencies and the beginning of the 'Raj'—*the Rule*. There would be a single bureaucracy administrating one huge infrastructure. There would be one Indian Army, the regiments of which would be drawn from the traditional martial races— these were Rajputs, Dogras, Sikhs, Garhwalis, Ghurkhas and others—but never again would there be troops drawn from the population at large in Bengal.

What initiated this fundamental change in the management of India was a rationalisation of government to ensure that no regional variations, lapses or weaknesses would create the possibility for another insurrection. It also created the very *oneness* that a nation requires to function effectively. For the first time India was truly the whole that some Indians had envisioned—but it had not been brought into being by the Indians themselves, but by their rulers, in order to control them and administer the country the more efficiently.

Following the institution of new government, it was straightforward for Indian nationalists of future generations to work for a transference of power from a British to Indian oligarchy. Given the inherent effectiveness of the British government in India, by the time of independence all was in place to provide—theoretically—the necessary framework for a seamless transfer of power. This is not to suggest that there were no practical difficulties, but it would not have been possible a century before, irrespective of the local will to institute such measures, because factional interests would have prevented the introduction of a single, cohesive, 'national' solution. India was brought to independence by its own politicians, but it would only remain a whole by the will of its people. Only then would the reality of Indian 'nationality' be put to the test, for nothing remains whole that has no desire to be so.

Post-war history has provided many examples of countries created for political expedience being bloodily ripped apart by internal dissent and civil war; so, perhaps predictably, for the emergent Indian nation.

India achieved independence in August 1947 and it became clear—as many had realised would be the case for some time—that there could, given the cultural and religious divides created by the Hindu and Islamic faiths, now be no single harmonious nation. The time of the compulsion of conquerors had passed.

Partition created an India separated from both East and West Pakistan. As the nations and their populations tore themselves apart, hundreds of thousands of people died and there were thousands upon thousands of rapes and other acts of personal violence. During the mayhem caused by disenfranchisement of land and property which affected those who found themselves on the 'wrong' side of the line, between ten and twelve million people were displaced, many forcibly.

Mahatma Gandhi, the revered 'Father of the Nation' was assassinated in 1948, not by a Muslim but by a Hindu radical for whom the very spirit and philosophy of the great man was too much to tolerate when applied to the new enemy—Pakistan.

Even after partition there was no peace for the Sub-Continent. The final borders were never agreed upon and wars between the two new nations, that had been carved out of what had been British India, followed in 1947, 1965, 1971 and 1999. Kashmir continues to be a troubled and disputed territory to this day.

India's troubles were not confined to her north-eastern borders. Disaffected groups who felt that their place in the new India did not do justice to their own perceptions of their status, religion or caste rose up. In 1984, after President Indira Gandhi ordered troops into the Golden Temple at Amritsar— a holy place of the Sikhs, she was assassinated by two of her own bodyguards, Sikhs for whom ultimately no commission to protect the leader of the nation could take precedence over their sense of Sikh identity or loyalty.

In Delhi today there stands another monument—far more modern than the gothic spire built by the British on the Ridge. It depicts Mahatma Gandhi leading a group of Indians in file, ostensibly on a Salt March from the time of the movement for independence. Symbolically it is a noble and beautiful embodiment of Gandhi's teaching, since his followers represent all the peoples and castes of India joined together in common purpose—as singular as the one nation he strove to create. It is an idealistic work, because this was never an India that existed. As powerful as this monument is in form and sentiment, it does not represent an India that its people wanted; ultimately India rejected Gandhi's vision for India. It no more represents the truth than does the notion that the Indians whose names appear on the  monuments to the Mutiny on Delhi Ridge were all traitors or all patriots. They were, in the main, what they remain—which is true to themselves by whatever definition they chose to apply.

The truth is, perhaps, that in country as vast as the Sub-Continent, with all its ethnic, religious and cultural diversity, there always has been—and probably always will be—conflict. It did not take the British to start India's wars, nor their departure to solve its problems and end its bloodshed. India has seen invaders come and go and empires rise and fall. It took the British a century of wars to win the land and its rule lasted for less than a century from the time of total control to the time of independence. In India's long history of warfare, the Mutiny was simply one of many conflicts and a small one at that. If the Mutiny had happened 500 years earlier it might today—despite its horrors—already be a footnote in history.

Only the passage of time can ultimately determine what place the Mutiny will hold in the pages of history—whether it is to become a footnote or forever remain an essential part of the Indian nation's lore. Perhaps, in reality, it will be what each individual needs it to be—and that has nothing to do with history at all.

Now you have heard some of the Indian Mutiny's authentic voices. What has endured across time is their essential humanity; so perhaps, in the end our shared humanity—as is proper—will be the only truth that endures.

*James Humphries*
May, 2007

Printed in the United Kingdom
by Lightning Source UK Ltd.
123403UK00001B/53/A